HARDPRESS NET

ISBN: 9781314694642

Published by:
HardPress Publishing
8345 NW 66TH ST #2561
MIAMI FL 33166-2626

Email: info@hardpress.net
Web: http://www.hardpress.net

The Cambridge Psychological Library

AN INTRODUCTION TO THE STUDY OF COLOUR VISION

CAMBRIDGE UNIVERSITY PRESS
C. F. CLAY, MANAGER
London: FETTER LANE, E.C.
Edinburgh: 100, PRINCES STREET

London: H. K. LEWIS, 136 GOWER STREET, W.C.
Bombay and Calcutta: MACMILLAN AND CO., LTD.
Toronto: J. M. DENT AND SONS, LTD.
Tokyo: THE MARUZEN-KABUSHIKI-KAISHA

THE PRISMATIC SPECTRUM

Cambridge University Press

AN INTRODUCTION
TO THE STUDY OF
COLOUR VISION

BY

J. HERBERT PARSONS, D.Sc., F.R.C.S.,
OPHTHALMIC SURGEON, UNIVERSITY COLLEGE HOSPITAL;
SURGEON, ROYAL LONDON (MOORFIELDS) OPHTHALMIC HOSPITAL

Cambridge:
at the University Press
New York:
G. P. Putnam's Sons
1915

Cambridge:
PRINTED BY JOHN CLAY, M.A.
AT THE UNIVERSITY PRESS

PREFACE

THE vast literature on colour vision consists almost entirely of papers written in support of some particular theory. It is peculiarly difficult to obtain a general and unbiassed view of the subject. I have here endeavoured to separate the best established facts of colour vision from the theories, and have then discussed the chief theories in the light of these facts.

I wish to express my great indebtedness to Sir William Abney, K.C.B., F.R.S., Professor W. Watson, F.R.S., and Dr Myers for their invaluable assistance in a very difficult task, which demands a not inconsiderable knowledge of such diverse subjects as physics, physiology, and psychology. The chief references to the literature have been given in footnotes. The frequent references to "Abney" are to his *Researches in Colour Vision* (London, 1913), and to "v. Helmholtz" to his *Handbuch der physiologischen Optik*. In the latter case each of the three editions contains material which is absent from the others, and the exact reference is given in the footnote.

Note. Fig. 12, p. 47. The discrepancy in these curves has been found to be due to a technical defect in the apparatus. More recent observations show the identity of the curves obtained by the two methods, thus confirming Ives's results (Fig. 38).

J. H. P.

November, 1914

CONTENTS

PART I

THE CHIEF FACTS OF NORMAL COLOUR VISION

PART II

THE CHIEF FACTS OF COLOUR BLINDNESS

PART III

THE CHIEF THEORIES OF COLOUR VISION

The author wishes to make grateful acknowledgment for permission to reproduce the following illustrations:

to the Royal Society for Figs. 68—74; to the Royal Society and Messrs Longmans, Green & Co. for Figs. 11, 12, 14, 19—23, 28—33, 40, 41, 49, 61—65; to the Kaiserliche Akademie der Wissenschaft of Vienna for Figs. 5, 60, 66 and 67; to the proprietors of the *Journal of Physiology* for Figs. 2, 3 and 17, of the *British Journal of Psychology* for Figs. 34—37, 42 and 43, of the *Philosophical Magazine* for Figs. 38 and 39, of *Mind* for Fig. 75, and of the *Zeitschrift für Psychologie und Physiologie der Sinnesorgane* for Figs. 15, 16, 25—27, 45, 46 and 50—55; and to Messrs Vieweg und Sohn, Braunschweig, for Figs. 1, 6, 7, 13 and 57.

PART I

THE CHIEF FACTS OF NORMAL COLOUR VISION

SECTION I

THE BASES OF COLOUR VISION

CHAPTER I

THE PHYSICAL BASIS

What is generally understood by the term "light" is a composite congeries of allied manifestations of energy, comprising such apparently various phenomena as heat, light in the narrower sense of the word, and chemical action. Various as these phenomena are, they are physically identical in character, all consisting of radiant energy in the form of waves of identical character, differing only in the length and rapidity of the vibrations. Broadly speaking, the longest waves cause the sensation of heat, the shortest give rise to chemical action, whilst those of intermediate length cause the sensation of light.

If we take ordinary sunlight as the basis of our investigations, it is possible to split it up by appropriate means into its component "rays," differing from each other in wave-length. Of these certain are visible, and constitute light in the narrower sense of the word, but instead of giving rise to the sensation of white light, they, to the majority of people, show certain pure colours, viz. red, orange, yellow, green, blue, and violet, in order, the red having the longest and the violet the shortest wave-length. The visible spectrum extends from about 723 $\mu\mu$ at the red end to 397 $\mu\mu$ at the violet end. v. Helmholtz under the most favourable conditions was able to see as far as about 835 $\mu\mu$. The limitation of the spectrum at the violet end is less precise, because the rays in this neighbourhood are changed into rays of greater wave-length by the media of the eye, particularly the lens and retina. This "fluorescence" causes them to produce a lavender-hued sensation, which does not denote true visibility of the short wave-length rays. Beyond the red end are waves of greater length (extending to 60,000 $\mu\mu$), which when absorbed cause a rise in temperature; beyond the violet end are waves of smaller wave-length, which are capable of causing chemical action. So striking is the physiological phenomenon of the visibility of the intermediate series that the heat rays are commonly spoken of as "infra-red," and the actinic or chemical rays as "ultra-violet." This custom is unfortunate, since it tends to obscure the importance of the physical uniformity of the series. For example, not every normal individual is able to see all the rays from 723 $\mu\mu$ to 397 $\mu\mu$; for most people the range is less extensive, roughly from 700 $\mu\mu$ to 400 $\mu\mu$. Again, though the ultra-violet rays are particularly potent in inducing chemical action, the visible rays are also, but in less degree, actinic, and the same is true, in still less degree, of the infra-red rays. Further, all rays when absorbed cause a rise in temperature. The most convenient and striking method of demonstrating actinicity is by the photographic film, so that we have come to regard a photograph of the spectrum as a complete analysis of the light under observation, too often forgetting that the photographic effect varies with the specific sensitiveness of the film to particular groups of waves. Thus it is only by specially sensitized films, invented by Sir William Abney, that it is possible to demonstrate infra-red rays photographically.

It is further essential that the methods employed for analysis of the light be suitable for their purpose. For example, an ordinary spectroscope, with glass prisms and lenses, suffices to demonstrate the visible spectrum, but is almost useless for showing the ultra-violet rays, since these are absorbed by the glass. In order to demonstrate the full extent of the spectrum it is necessary to use a train of lenses and prisms made of quartz or Iceland spar, which allows a maximum of rays to pass unimpeded.

Probably more error has crept into the subject of colour vision from inexact description of experimental conditions and the nature of the stimuli employed than from any other cause. Two green lights may appear identical in colour to the eye, yet their physical characters may differ widely. Again, mixing a yellow and a blue pigment will produce a green pigment, yet the more general statement that green results from mixing yellow and blue is not accurate.

The complete range of simple colours can be obtained in a pure state by only two methods, dispersion and diffraction. When white light is passed through a glass prism, as in Sir Isaac Newton's original experiment, a spectrum is obtained. Only under certain, now well-defined conditions is such a spectrum pure, *i.e.* the colours do not overlap. It is commonly said that the white light is "split up" into its component parts, which are coloured. Lord Rayleigh has given sound reasons for the view that white light is not thus analysed into component parts, but that the periodicities characteristic of the several rays are in reality imposed by the prism and are not antecedently present in the white light. Be this as it may, dispersion of white light by prisms enables us to obtain coloured light in a pure state. By passing white light through a diffraction grating a pure spectrum can also be obtained. This method has the advantage that the deviation of the component rays varies within narrow limits directly with the wave-length, *i.e.* equal differences of wave-length are separated by equal distances in the spectrum. It suffers, however, from the disadvantage that the spectrum is less bright and less extended than the prismatic spectrum, and from the still greater objection that the interference spectrum is never free from scattered light. In the prismatic spectrum the dispersion increases as the wave-length diminishes, so that the violet end is much more extended than the red end and its intensity is diminished. Moreover the amount of dispersion depends upon the character of the prism or prisms employed. Hence it is necessary for accurate observations that each prismatic spectrum shall be calibrated. The Fraunhofer lines, being absolutely constant in situation, afford a series of fixed points from which the calibration curve of the given spectrum can be constructed[1]. The

		A. U.	
	A	= 7606	in extreme red.
	B	= 6869	in deep red.
Lithium		= 6707	in bright red.
Hydrogen	C	= 6564	in bright red.
Sodium	D_1	= 5897	in orange.
Sodium	D_2	= 5891	in orange.
Thallium		= 5351	in yellow green
	E	= 5271	in green.
Magnesium	b_1	= 5184	in green.
Magnesium	b_2	= 5174	in green.
Hydrogen	F	= 4862	in blue green.
Strontium		= 4609	in blue.
	G	= 4308	in violet.
Calcium	H	= 3969	in extreme violet.
Calcium	K	= 3934	in extreme violet.

[1] Burch, *Practical Exercises in Physiological Optics*, p. 102, Oxford, 1912.

table gives the principal lines in Ångström units (1 Å.U.—one ten millionth part of a millimetre = 0·1 $\mu\mu$).

The most convenient method of calibration, however, is by the mercury lines as given by the "mercury arc[1]."

In spite of the necessity for calibration the prismatic spectrum is more generally suited than the diffraction spectrum for physiological experiments on account of its greater brightness and relative freedom from scattered light.

Whatever spectrum be employed the source of light must be constant. Lights which we commonly regard as giving "white light," such as sunlight, the arc light, incandescent light, and so on, vary much in character and consequently in the constitution of their spectra. Sunlight varies so much that it is generally unsuitable for the purposes in view, the variations being not only in intensity but also in composition, owing to the unequal absorption of different rays by the atmosphere, and this absorption again varies greatly according to the amount and nature of the matter suspended in the air. The arc light is the most satisfactory, and after this probably the Nernst lamp, though the latter has not yet been sufficiently investigated[2]. Less satisfactory are gas light, petroleum and so on, but as many of the experiments of earlier observers have been made with such sources they have to be considered if these researches are to receive due appreciation. Some sources of illumination, especially used for investigation of the ultraviolet rays, such as the Schott uviol mercury vapour lamps, are wholly unsuited, since they do not give continuous spectra. For experiments on colour vision many such details which cannot be discussed here must be attended to[3].

Suffice it to say that by taking proper precautions it is possible to obtain a spectrum which is practically constant during the time necessary to take a series of observations and which can be reproduced from time to time with a minimum of variation.

If such a spectrum is viewed through the eyepiece of an ordinary spectroscope a *direct* spectrum is seen. This method has usually been adopted, as for example by Aubert, von Helmholtz, Clerk-Maxwell and others. By a slight change in the optical arrangements the spectrum

[1] Watson, *Practical Physics*, p. 309, 1906.

[2] Abney, *Researches in Colour Vision*, 1913, Chap. v.; Golant, *Ztsch. f. Sinnesphysiol.* XLIII. 70, 1908.

[3] *E.g.* Tigerstedt, *Handb. d. physiol. Methodik*, Bd. III. Abt. 2, *Sinnesphysiologie* II. Leipzig, 1909.

can be accurately focussed upon a screen. Such a *projected* spectrum can then be viewed by several observers at the same time, a very considerable advantage in testing colour vision. The use of a projected spectrum necessitates further care in detail, for the character of the spectrum will depend upon the optical properties of the screen[1]. A matt white surface must be used and that obtained with magnesium oxide is probably best.

In order to obtain the most accurate information from the experiments the observations must be as far as possible *quantitative* and not merely qualitative. In many physiological experiments this counsel of perfection cannot be complied with and we are reduced to the information which can be obtained from merely qualitative observations. When, however, it is possible to obtain quantitative results it is generally necessary to have a constant light for purposes of comparison. Now, photometry is admittedly one of the most faulty of physical measurements, chiefly, to use a paradox, because it is, in most cases, not really physical but physiological. One of the most important and unique features of Sir William Abney's apparatus is that the intensity of the comparison light bears a constant physical relationship to that of the spectrum used, since it is obtained by the reflection of a portion of the original beam of light from the surface of the first prism. Hence any variation in the original beam will cause similar and simultaneous variations in both the spectrum and the comparison light[2]. Measurable changes in the intensity of the light are best obtained by the use of rotating sectors, sometimes called the episcotister (Aubert), or by the annulus, a gelatine wedge impregnated with ivory black[3]. Reduction of intensity by means of Nicol prisms as in v. Helmholtz' spectrophotometer, may not be free from error, since quite an appreciable amount of polarisation of the light is produced by the prisms used to form the spectrum. Much of the German work has been done by this method, and care has by no means always been taken to calculate the corrections necessary owing to this cause.

Pure spectral colours rarely occur in nature, and much of the literature on colour vision is devoted to observations with pigments, coloured glasses and so on. It is necessary, therefore, to say a few words about these complex colours, chiefly with the object of putting the reader upon his guard. When white light passes through a red glass or transparent red fluid certain rays are absorbed. The red rays are transmitted

[1] Abney, p. 46. [2] *Ibid.* Chap. IV. [3] *Ibid.* Chap. VI.

in greatest quantity, so that the dominant colour of the light reaching the eye is red; but it is not pure red. Most blue substances, such as copper salts, allow the blue rays to pass, but also some of the green and violet, though few of the red and yellow. Yellow substances allow much red and green to pass as well as the yellow, but little blue and violet. The true composition of the transmitted light can only be determined with the spectroscope.

The case of pigments is similar. Each speck of powder is a small transparent body which absorbs certain rays of light. When light falls upon such a powder a small portion is reflected from the upper surface; this is white. The remainder passes deeper and is reflected from deeper layers. The deeper it passes the greater is the absorption and the more intense the colour. Hence a coarse powder appears more intensely coloured than one which is finely divided. Reflection varies with the number of surfaces, not with the thickness of the particles. The larger the latter the deeper the light must penetrate for the same number of surfaces to be met as when the particles are smaller. The absorption is therefore greater in a coarse than in a fine powder. The reflection at the surfaces is diminished when the intervals between the particles are filled with a fluid of refractive index nearer their own than that of air. Hence powders are generally whiter when dry than when mixed with water or oil.

The amount of absorption of light by a transparent body can be measured and expressed in the form of a coefficient. If a spectrum is viewed through an orange glass very little red, orange and yellow, but much green and all the blue are absorbed, as shown by dark bands in the regions of absorption. In this case the coefficient of absorption increases as the blue is approached. By knowing the coefficients of absorption of different media the effects of combining them in various ways can be calculated. By empirical experiments colour screens or filters can be made which transmit certain portions only of the spectrum, and in some cases approximately monochromatic light can be obtained in this manner. These filters are much used for photographic purposes. The characters of the absorption by Jena glass filters and by various fluid media are described in Tigerstedt's *Handbuch der physiologischen Methodik*[1], which also gives an excellent *résumé* of the methods which have been employed for the investigation of colour vision.

No pigments accurately represent spectral colours, for the reflected

[1] Bd. III. Abt. 2, *Sinnesphysiologie* II pp. 47 and 52.

light is always more or less impure. The nearest approach is given by the following list:

Red—vermilion (not scarlet vermilion) mixed with a small quantity of permanent violet.

Orange—orange cadmium.

Yellow—chrome yellow.

Green—Prussian blue mixed with aurelin.

Blue-green—viridian mixed with a small amount of cobalt blue.

Blue—ultramarine.

Violet—permanent violet mixed with a small amount of blue. (Abney.)

CHAPTER II

THE ANATOMICAL BASIS

I do not propose to discuss fully the anatomy and physiology of the eye and visual paths, but it is necessary to draw attention to certain features of special importance in colour vision. This course will doubtless emphasise the great complexity of the subject, which is too often wilfully ignored.

The eye resembles a photographic camera, in which the cornea and crystalline lens represent the lens-system, the iris the diaphragm, and the retina the sensitive plate. The size of the pupillary aperture is not under voluntary control, but varies with the intensity of light entering the eye and other causes. This fact has to be taken into consideration in some experiments. (The reader is recommended to read the earlier chapters in the author's *Manual of Diseases of the Eye*, 2nd edition, J. and A. Churchill, London, 1912.) The optical system of the normal eye at rest is focussed for distant objects, *i.e.* parallel rays are brought to a focus upon the retina. Focussing for near objects is brought about by automatically altering the " strength " of the crystalline lens (accommodation), not by altering the length of the eye as in the photographic camera. Some eyes are naturally too short or their optical system at rest is too weak, so that accommodation is required even for distant objects (hypermetropia). Others are too long or their optical system at rest is too strong so that it is impossible to focus distant objects without the aid of concave spectacles and near objects may be seen clearly without the aid of accommodation (myopia). Many eyes show slight differences in the radius of curvature of the cornea in meridians at right angles to each other and this is often associated with slight tilting of the lens (regular astigmatism). The lens always shows slight irregularities causing irregular astigmatism. For these and other reasons the retinal image of a luminous point is never accurately punctate[1].

Further, the optical system of the eye is not achromatic. This fact might be regarded as of extreme importance in the consideration of colour vision, but in general the effect is negligible. One would also expect diffraction at the edge of the pupil, and it can be demonstrated to occur, especially when the pupil is small; but this effect is also negligible under most conditions. There are, however, occasions when both these factors must be taken into account.

The crystalline lens normally possesses a slightly amber-yellow hue, which is inappreciable in youth, but increases as age advances. In elderly people the colour of the lens causes an appreciable absorption of the more refrangible rays (green, blue and violet). This fact must be borne in mind in estimating the visual sensations of such people.

The retina is a transparent membrane lining the back of the vitreous chamber. It is composed of several layers, the outer of which is a mosaic of *rods and cones*. The rods and cones are a neuro-epithelium, connected with bipolar cells which form the *outer nuclear layer*. A second set of cells forms the *inner nuclear layer*. The arborisations of these two sets of cells form an intermediate *outer reticular layer*. Arborisations from the inner nuclear layer and processes from the ganglion cell layer form the *inner reticular layer*. The *ganglion cell layer* is composed of larger cells which give rise to the axons of the optic nerve. These axons form a layer upon the inner surface of the ganglion cell layer, the *nerve fibre layer*.

The optic disc or head of the optic nerve is situated about 3 mm. to the inner or nasal side of the posterior pole of the eye. Light falling on this area causes no sensory impression (Mariotte's blind spot).

Outside the retina proper is the layer of retinal pigment epithelium. It consists of cells which are hexagonal in section and have processes passing forwards between the rods and cones. The cells contain minute needle-shaped crystals of pigment. This layer bears some resemblance to the "backing" of a photographic plate.

External to the retina is the choroid, a highly vascular membrane having the function of nourishing the outer layers of the retina. The inner layers of the retina are nourished by the retinal blood vessels, which spring from the disc and radiate over the surface of the nerve fibre layer. The walls of the retinal blood vessels are transparent, but

[1] Parsons, "The Perception of a Luminous Point," *Roy. Lond. Ophth. Hosp. Reports*, xviii. 239, 1912; xix. 104, 264, 274, 1913–4.

since the colouring matter of the blood is contained in highly refractile corpuscles the blood column is opaque.

The part of the retina to which most attention must be directed for the present purpose is that comprising the rods and cones and the pigment epithelium. It is shown conclusively by Purkinje's experiment, which depends upon the position of shadows thrown by the retinal vessels upon the percipient layer of the retina, that the primary seat of the visual impulses is in the layer of rods and cones. Here the most sharply defined image is formed by the optical system. As already stated it is not perfectly defined physically, but as will be seen later physiological and psychological compensation tends to counteract the physical defects.

The rods and cones, as their names imply, are minute cylindrical and conical structures. They project vertically—or more accurately radially—from the surface of the outer limiting membrane of the retina. Almost exactly at the posterior pole of the eye is situated a small area in which vision is most distinct. This area is impregnated with a yellow pigment and hence is called the *macula lutea* or yellow spot. In the centre of the yellow spot there is a conical pit, the *fovea centralis*, caused by thinning out of the retina. In this minute area the structures are reduced to little more than neuroepithelium and ganglion cells. Moreover the neuroepithelium in this region consists entirely of cones, though the cones are slender and elongated and are more rod-like here than elsewhere[1].

This change in structure of the cones may be evidence of some physiological combination of the functions of both rods and cones in this situation.

Passing peripherally in every direction from the central fovea it is found that rods gradually make their appearance between the cones, and soon the number of rods in a given area becomes greater than that of the cones, so that at the extreme periphery of the retina only a few scattered cones are to be found.

The following are some measurements of the diameter of the foveal cones: Max Schultze, 2·8 μ; H. Müller, not more than 3 μ; Merkel, 3 μ; Welcker, 3·1—3·5 μ; Wadsworth, 2·5 μ; Kuhnt, 2—2·5 μ; Kölliker, 4·5—5·4 μ; Koster, 4·4 μ; Greeff, 2·5 μ; Dimmer, 3—3·5 μ.

The foveal region is an elliptical area with the long axis horizontal. The long axis measures about 0·3 mm., the vertical 0·2 mm., and the total area is 0·5—0·6 sq. mm. Taking the diameter of the inner limbs

[1] Greeff, in Graefe-Saemisch *Handb. d. ges. Augenheilkunde*, Theil I. Bd. I. Cap. V. 1900.

of the foveal cones at 0·3 μ, there are about 300 in the long axis, and 60 in the short, 1300—1400 in 0·1 sq. mm. The diameter of the outer limbs is 0·6—0·75 μ. The cones are arranged in curved lines (Max Schultze) or spirals (Fritsch), and are not quite regular. There are small spaces between them, measuring from 0·05 to 0·27 of the transverse section of the inner limb. Greeff says that the cones are very closely packed in the fovea, and in a specimen of Heine's were hexagonal in transverse section.

Koster[1] examined three normal children's eyes and found that the part completely free from rods occupied a circular area 0·44—0·55 mm. in diameter, the part relatively free from rods 0·88 mm. In the eye of a youth aged 20, the rod-free area was 0·901 mm. He concludes that in the adult the rod-free area measures about 0·8 mm. in diameter, subtending a visual angle of 3° 3′. This is probably a maximum, and there is physiological evidence to show that the rod-free area varies in size in different individuals.

Three areas must be carefully distinguished :

Fovea Centralis, measuring 0·24—0·3 mm. in diameter, subtending 55′—70′ ;

Rod-free area, measuring 0·8 mm., subtending 3° 3′ ;

Macula, measuring 1—3 mm., subtending 4°—12°.

Dimmer[2] describes a fovea centralis, 1·5 mm. in diameter (the macula of Koster), containing in its centre a foveola (the fovea centralis of Koster).

Gullstrand[3] regards the yellow colouration of the macula lutea as a post-mortem change, a view which is scarcely consistent with its absorptive capacity for coloured lights during life.

Fritsch[4] describes the site of clearest vision as the area centralis, possessing a central depression, the fovea centralis, which may or may not contain a foveola.

Comparative Anatomy. The distribution of rods and cones in the retinae of lower animals is of great theoretical importance. Many erroneous statements have gained currency and have been used as arguments in favour of certain theories. The great variety in the forms of the neuroepithelial cells prevents any generalised classification.

Greeff[5] says that there are rods and cones in the retinae of most

[1] *Arch. f. Ophth.* XLI. 4, 1, 1895 ; *Arch. d'Opht.* XV 428, 1895

[2] *Arch. f. Ophth.* LXV. 486, 1907.

[3] *Arch. f. Ophth.* LXII. 1, 378, 1905 ; LXVI. 141, 1907.

[4] *Ueber Bau u. Bedeutung d. Area centralis des Menschen*, Berlin, 1908.

[5] Graefe-Saemisch *Handb. d ges. Augenheilkunde*, Theil I. Bd. I. Cap. V. 1900.

mammals, amphibia and fishes, the number of rods much exceeding that of cones. In birds, on the other hand, cones are much in excess of rods. In most reptiles (lizards, snakes, tortoises), only cones are found. There are vertebrates possessing only rods, *e.g.* amongst fishes, rays and dog-fish; amongst mammals, hedgehog, bat, mole and night-ape (*Nyctipithecus felinus*). There are also animals of nocturnal habits possessing only rods. Owls, mice, and rell-mice have only a few rudimentary cones; rats also possess a few cones.

Hess[1] found rods in fowls and pigeons, though they are few in the posterior and superior parts of the retina, which are most used in pecking. As regards nocturnal birds Schultze (1866), Krause (1894), Greeff (1900) and Piper (1905) give contradictory statements. Hess found a "not inconsiderable number" of yellow or brown oil globules in the retinae of the owl and hawk, and these are present only in cones. They are fairly uniformly distributed.

Coloured oil globules are found in the cones of birds and reptiles: similar colourless bodies are found in fishes and amphibia. The globules are more deeply coloured, yellow or brown, in night birds and in tortoises than in day birds. They are absent in the crocodile.

Research has shown that at any rate in lower animals stimulation of the retina by light is accompanied by structural, chemical, and electrical changes[2].

Structural Changes. The chief structural changes are the phototropic reaction of the pigment epithelium and the contraction of the cones. To these may be added changes in the Nissl granules of the ganglion cells[3].

When the frog's eye is exposed to light the pigment granules wander into the cell processes between the rods and cones. This light effect is complete after 5 to 10 minutes' exposure. The retreat of the granules to the complete dark position takes one to two hours. The light effect is limited to the area stimulated, so that an "epithelial optogram" can be produced (Kühne). The violet end of the spectrum is more strongly "retinomotor" than the red end (Angelucci[4], Engelmann[5]), and red light causes little reaction. Light on one eye causes wandering

[1] *Vergleichende Physiol. d. Gesichtsinnes*, Jena, 1912.

[2] Garten, in Graefe-Saemisch *Handb. d. ges. Augenheilkunde*. Theil I. Bd. III. Cap. xii. Anhang, 1907–8.

[3] Birch-Hirschfeld, *Arch. f. Ophth.* L. 166, 1900; LXIII. 1, 85, 1906.

[4] *Arch. f. Anat. u. Physiol.* 353, 1878.

[5] *Arch f. d. ges. Physiol.* XXXV. 498, 1885.

of the pigment in both (Engelmann). Light on the skin produces the effect in frogs; so too electrical stimulation of the optic nerve, probably through the centrifugal nerve fibres described by Ramón y Cajal[1]. The phototropic reaction of the pigment epithelium has not yet been proved to occur in mammals[2].

In the frog's eye in the state of rest (darkness) the cones are extended; on exposure to light they become contracted. This reaction occurs in all animals that have been examined, including man (van Genderen Stort[3]); but Garten (in Graefe-Saemisch, *loc. cit.*) found the reaction doubtful in monkeys. The reaction is slow, taking two or more minutes even with intense light. The violet end of the spectrum acts most strongly (Engelmann), but the reaction to the red end is greater than that of the pigment. Light on one eye causes reaction in both, as also light on the skin, so long as the brain is intact (Engelmann, Nahmacher[4]).

Chemical Changes. Light on the retina causes it to become acid (Angelucci, Lodato[5], Dittler[6]), and its staining reactions are said to alter.

The most important chemical change, however, has to do with the *visual purple* or rhodopsin. This remarkable substance was discovered in the rods of the frog's retina by H. Müller in 1851. Boll in 1876 discovered that it was bleached by exposure to light. Kühne in 1878 first studied it exhaustively. It occurs in all animals which possess rods, and is present in the rods only (Kühne). Hence it is absent from the fovea. This statement is denied by Edridge-Green and Devereux Marshall[7] for monkeys, but their observations have not been confirmed. Hering, however, points out that visual purple may possibly not be wholly absent from the cones, and the peculiar rod-like character of the human foveal cones makes it not improbable that they contain some of the substance. The question merits further investigation. Kühne investigated the chemical characteristics of rhodopsin, the most noteworthy facts being its solubility in bile acids and their salts, and its resistance to strong oxidising and reducing agents. It is not the cause of the fluorescence of the retina. It can only be seen ophthalmoscopically in fishes which possess a white tapetum (Abelsdorff[8]). Tait[9] and Boll

[1] *Die Retina der Wirbeltiere*, Wiesbaden, 1894.
[2] Hess, *Vergleichende Physiol. d. Gesichtsinnes*, Jena, 1912.
[3] *Arch. f. Ophth.* XXXIII. 3, 229, 1887. [4] *Arch. f. d. ges. Physiol.* LIII. 375, 1893.
[5] *Arch. di Ott.* IX. 267, 1902.
[6] *Arch. f. d. ges. Physiol.* CXX. 44, 1907.
[7] *Trans. Ophth. Soc.* XXII. 300, 1902.
[8] *Ztsch. f. Psychol. u. Physiol. d. Sinnesorg.* XIV. 77, 1897; *Sitz. d. Berliner Akad.* 1895.
[9] *Proc. R. S. of Edin.* VII. 605, 1869.

state that it can be seen entoptically on waking in the morning as a rose-red ring round the fixation point, projected against the white ceiling. Haab attributes this phenomenon, not to the visual purple, but to the pigment of the yellow spot. Edridge-Green[1] confirms Tait's and Boll's observations, and states that the purple can be seen to flow in waves from the periphery of the yellow spot towards the point of fixation.

The colour of the visual purple varies in different animals and under different circumstances[2], and gives different spectroscopic absorption bands (Kühne; Köttgen and Abelsdorff[3]). The maximum absorption in fishes is in the yellow (540 $\mu\mu$), in mammals in the blue-green (500 $\mu\mu$); hence it is reddish violet in fishes and purple in mammals. The occurrence of "visual yellow" as an intermediate stage in the bleaching of visual purple (Kühne) seems to have been conclusively disproved by Köttgen and Abelsdorff. They found that as the visual purple was bleached the relative absorption remained unchanged. The substance therefore becomes gradually less concentrated, without passing through a yellow stage.

The bleaching of visual purple is limited to the area exposed to light, so that an optogram or image of the luminous object, such as a window, can be obtained. Such an optogram can be partially preserved by alum solution, somewhat as a photographic negative is fixed, though the processes are entirely dissimilar. Two to seven minutes' exposure to light suffice to obtain a good optogram in the frog's retina. Light on one eye does not cause any bleaching of the visual purple of the other.

The bleaching of visual purple by monochromatic light has proved to be of great theoretical interest. Observations have been made by König[4], Köttgen and Abelsdorff, and Trendelenburg[5]. Trendelenburg took two specimens of frog's visual purple and exposed one to light of the sodium line (D, 589 $\mu\mu$) and the other to another light from the same dispersion spectrum, the diminution of absorption being measured by the spectrophotometer. The human achromatic scotopic luminosity

[1] *J. of Physiol.* XLI. 263, 1910; XLII 428, 1911; XLV. 70, 1913.

[2] Garten, in Graefe-Saemisch *Handb. d. ges. Augenheilkunde,* Teil I. Bd. III. Kap. xii, Plate VII, 1908.

[3] *Ztsch. f. Psychol. u. Physiol. d. Sinnesorg.* XII. 161, 1896.

[4] König, p. 388.

[5] *Centralbl. f. Physiol.* XVII. 1904; *Ztsch. f. Psychol. u. Physiol. d. Sinnesorg.* XXXVII. 1, 1904.

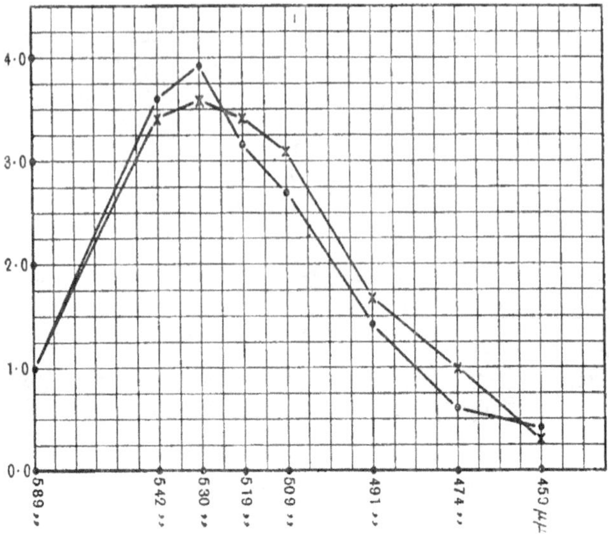

Fig. 1. ·—·—·— the bleaching values of spectral lights for frog's visual purple, and ×—×—× the human achromatic scotopic luminosity curve. Abscissae, wave-lengths of the prismatic spectrum of the Nernst light; ordinates, an arbitrary scale. (Trendelenburg.)

curve will be referred to later (pp. 53, 55). Actual readings are as follows:

Wave-length	589	542	530	519	509	491	474	459
Bleaching value	1	3·40	3·62	3·45	3·09	1·69	0·975	0·299
Scotopic luminosity	1	3·62	3·91	3·19	2·67	1·42	0·621	0·346

Visual purple is regenerated after bleaching in the living and "surviving" retina, but only on contact with the pigment epithelium. Regeneration commences in the frog after 29 minutes and is complete in one to two hours. The process is more rapid in the rabbit, commencing in seven minutes and being complete in 33 to 38 minutes. (It may be noted here for convenience that increase of sensibility in dark adaptation in man after good light adaptation commences in 7 to 8 minutes and reaches nearly the maximum in 40 to 45 minutes (Piper[1]).)

It has already been stated that the visual purple occurs in nearly if not all animals possessing rods from petromyzon to man. It is present in albinotic animals, *e.g.* rabbit, and has been found in the 9- and 7-months' human foetus (Kühne, Fuchs and Welponer[2]). Kühne said that it was absent in the bat (*Rhinolophus hipposiderus*), but this statement has been disproved by Trendelenburg. Kühne found no visual purple

[1] *Ztsch. f. Psychol. u. Physiol. d. Sinnesorg.* XXXI. 161, 1903.

[2] *Wiener med. Woch.* 221, 1877.

in fowls and pigeons, but Boll, Angelucci, and van Genderen Stort found it in pigeons. Hess dissolved out the oil globules with benzol, which does not affect the purple in frog's retina, and found traces of rhodopsin in both fowls and pigeons, but in far less amount than in man, ox, frog, etc. There was more present in the hawk, buzzard, goose and duck. Amongst reptiles the crocodile possesses many rods and is rich in visual purple.

Electrical Changes. The retina, connected through non-polarisable electrodes with a galvanometer or capillary electrometer, shows a "current of rest" (du Bois-Reymond). On exposure to light there is usually a short negative variation followed by a longer positive variation,

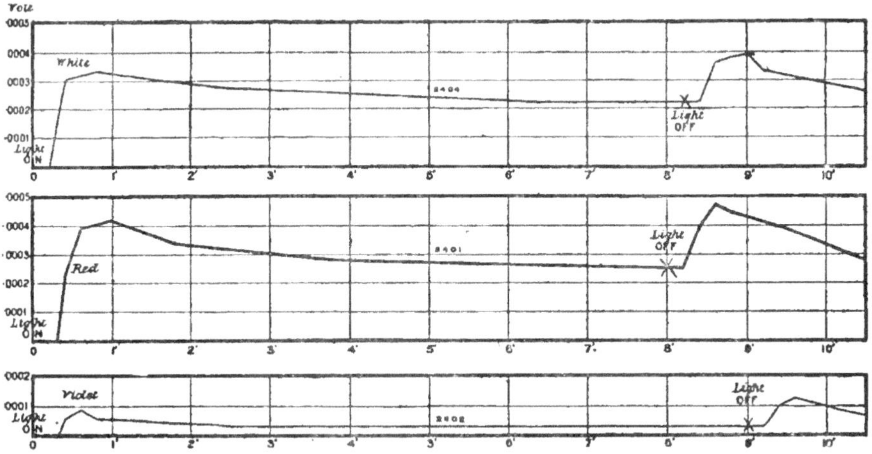

Fig. 2. Electrical changes in the frog's eye caused by light. Plotted curves from the analyses of three capillary electrometer records. The illumination in the case of the upper record was white light, in that of the middle red light, and in that of the lowest violet light. Abscissae, time after the commencement of the illumination in seconds; ordinates, the electromotive force in ten thousandths of a volt. (Gotch.)

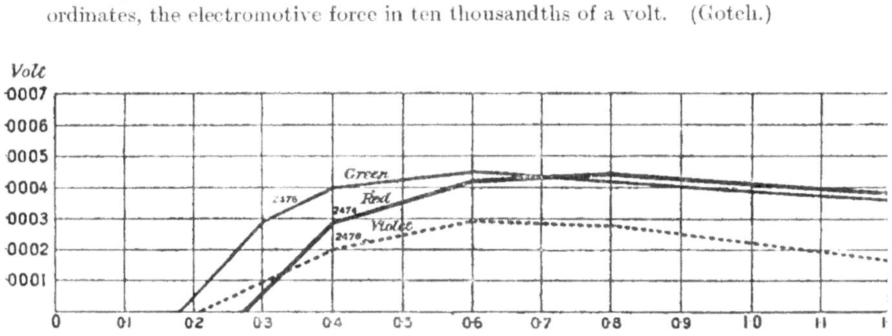

Fig. 3. Curves constructed from typical electrometer records of eyeball responses to the light from the red, green, and violet regions of the interference spectrum of the arc light. (Gotch.)

and cessation of the light stimulus causes a further positive variation (Holmgren), a fact of considerable theoretical interest. The electrical changes have been studied by Dewar and McKendrick[1], Kühne and Steiner[2], Fuchs[3], Waller[4], Himstedt and Nagel[5], and others, but Gotch's experiments with the capillary electrometer are the most conclusive[6]. He found that spectral red light gave a latent period of nearly $\frac{3}{10}$ second and a difference of potential of 0·0004 volt; green, $\frac{2}{10}''$ and 0·0005 volt; violet, $\frac{25}{100}''$ and 0·00024 volt. Himstedt and Nagel obtained a slight reaction with ultra-violet and Röntgen rays. They also found that in the dark-adapted eye the maximum effect was obtained at 544 $\mu\mu$, the site of maximum luminosity in dark adaptation in man (*vide infra*); in the light-adapted eye at about the D line (589 $\mu\mu$), the site of maximum luminosity in light adaptation; but though the light sensibility of the dark-adapted eye is more than a thousandfold that of the light-adapted for some colours, G. E. Müller[7] obtained no appreciable difference in the electrical reaction. Engelmann[8] found that stimulation of one eye caused a reaction in the other also, but the positive variation on removal of the stimulus was absent. The relation of intensity of stimulus to strength of response does not accurately follow the Weber-Fechner law (*vide infra*, p. 20), but Talbot's law (*v.* p. 92) is followed more accurately (de Haas[9]).

When an object is looked at directly a sharp image is formed on the fovea and the immediately surrounding area. An object therefore which subtends less than 3° at the nodal point of the eye will form its image entirely upon the rod-free area of the retina. Larger objects subtending 4°—12° will form their images on the macular region, in which only a few rods are present in the peripheral parts. Objects surrounding that fixated form images on the peripheral regions of the retina which are richly supplied with rods. The acuteness of form vision falls off rapidly in passing from the fovea to the periphery, but movements of objects having their images in the periphery are very readily observed.

Not only is form vision different according as the image is at the

[1] *Trans. R. S. Edin.* XXVII. 141, 1873.

[2] *Heidelb. Unters.* III. 327, 1880.

[3] *Arch. f. d. ges. Physiol.* LVI. 408, 1894.

[4] *Phil. Trans. Roy. Soc. Lond.* CXCIII. 123, 1900.

[5] *Ann. d. Physik*, IV. 1901; *Ber. d. Naturf. Ges.* Freiburg, 1901

[6] *J. of Physiol.* XXIX. 388, 1903; XXX. 10; XXXI. 1, 1904.

[7] *Ztsch. f. Psychol. u. Physiol. d. Sinnesorg.* XIV. 329, 1897.

[8] Helmholtz' *Festschrift*, 197, 1891.

[9] Inaug. Dissert., Leiden, 1903; ref. in Nagel's *Jahresbericht f. Ophth.*, 73. 1903.

fovea or peripheral, colour vision is also affected. *Foveal or central vision* must therefore be clearly distinguished from *peripheral or eccentric vision.*

Vision is profoundly affected by the condition of the retina at the moment of stimulation. The condition of the retina at any given part is determined by two factors, temporal and spatial. The temporal factor is the nature of the stimulation to which the retina has been previously submitted (temporal induction). If the eye has been exposed to bright light it is said to be light-adapted. I shall speak of vision under these circumstances as *photopia*, and the light-adapted eye as a photopic eye. If the eye has been kept completely free from light for a considerable period it is said to be dark-adapted. I shall speak of vision under these circumstances as *scotopia* (as an equivalent for the German *Dämmerungssehen*), and the dark-adapted eye as a scotopic eye.

The spatial factor in retinal sensibility is the reciprocal action of different areas upon each other. The excitability of a given area is affected by the condition of sensibility and stimulation of the surrounding areas (spatial induction).

CHAPTER III

THE PSYCHOLOGICAL BASIS

The physiology of the senses may be regarded as the intermediate link between the outer world and the consciousness of the individual. The physical stimuli come into contact with the sense organs and set up sensory neural physiological changes, which may be transformed into, or at all events accompanied by, mental processes leading to sensation, perception, and comparison. In this long and complicated path there are two points of contact, the physico-physiological and the physiologico-psychological. Of the former we know a little, and the elements of our knowledge have been discussed in the last chapter. Of the latter we know nothing, but of the final perfected perceptions we have some knowledge, the elements of which we must now discuss.

The awakened perceptions, their qualities and attributes, and their inter-relations belong to the domain of psychology. They depend in some occult manner upon the sensations aroused by the physiological processes which are set in activity by the physical stimuli. We have good reason to think that there are many gradients and junctions upon the physiological path, so that the resultant nervous activities set up in the higher centres of the brain are very different from those which started in the peripheral mechanism. Try as we may to dissociate the physiological from the attendant psychological phenomena we are unable to do so, for the act of analysis itself is a psychological process. We are practically limited to the consideration of the *relationships* which can be made out with greater or less certainty to exist between the stimuli and the resulting sensations.

With regard to these relationships there are certain generalisations which have been thought to hold good for all the so-called "senses." One of these generalisations, enunciated in 1785 by Bonnet and independently by Johannes Müller in 1826[1], is called Müller's Law of the Specific Energies of the Senses. It is to be noted that the word energy is not used here in its ordinary physical sense. Müller stated that we can experience no kinds of sensation through the intermediation of external causes which we cannot also experience through the sensation derived from the condition existing in the nervous organs without external agency. These internal causes call up different sensations in the different senses according to the nature of each sense. Further, *the same external stimuli arouse in the different sense mechanisms different sensations according to the particular sense;* and *different external or internal stimuli, acting upon the same sense mechanism, always arouse the same sensation.* The essential features of Müller's law are contained in the sentences in italics. He amplified the law by saying that a sensation is not the transference of a quality or condition of external bodies to the consciousness, but the transference of a quality or condition of a sensory mechanism to the consciousness, though that quality or condition is occasioned by external stimuli. These qualities or "energies" of the senses are specific to each sensory mechanism. Müller left it open as to the site of the specific energies, whether in the brain or elsewhere in the nervous paths, but he considered it certain that the central endings of the sensory nerve-paths in the brain were capable of arousing the specific sensations independently of the conducting paths. It is now generally held that the seat of the specific sensations is in the brain. If this assumption be true Müller's law relieves us of the necessity of predicating the conduction of different kinds of impulses by the peripheral nerve-paths.

It is customary to divide the stimuli which can arouse a specific

[1] *Zur vergleichenden Physiologie des Gesichtssinnes*, Leipzig, 1826; *Handb. d. Physiol. d. Menschen*, Coblenz, 1840.

sensation into adequate and inadequate. The former are those which arouse the sensation under ordinary circumstances, the latter are all other effectual stimuli. Thus light is an adequate stimulus for the eye, pressure on the eyeball an inadequate.

The next great step in the advance of our knowledge of the relationships subsisting between physical stimuli and sensations was made by E. H. Weber, the founder of modern psycho-physical methods. In general terms it may be stated that a stimulus must attain a certain intensity in order to excite a sensation and that stimuli of greater intensity excite stronger sensations. There is therefore a quantitative relationship between the stimulus and the sensation. The minimum effectual intensity of stimulus is called the *general threshold* or *the general liminal value*. A higher value may arouse a sensation differing in quality from the other; this value is called the *specific threshold* or the *specific liminal value*. Thus a coloured light of low intensity may excite a colourless sensation; when of a higher intensity it may excite a sensation of colour.

The intensity of the stimulus has to be increased by a definite amount before a difference in the amount of the sensation becomes appreciable. This amount may be called the *differential threshold* or the *liminal discrimination value*. Equal increases of physical intensity do not give equal increases of sensation. There are three chief psycho-physical methods whereby estimates can be obtained. (1) The method of least perceptible differences or the limiting method: one of two identical stimuli is regularly increased by small increments until a just perceptible difference between the constant and the variable stimulus is experienced. (2) The method of right and wrong answers or the constant method: the observer is asked which is the greater in the case of such pairs of stimuli (constant and variable), the variables here being fewer in number and presented with the constant in irregular order, and the average of a large number of such estimates being taken. (3) The method of mean error or the method of production: the observer picks out what he regards as just appreciably different stimuli; the sum of the differences from the standard divided by the number of trials gives a lower limit of the threshold value. These results are accurate only when submitted to strict statistical processes[1].

Weber stated his conclusions in the form of a law: *The just appreciable increase of stimulus bears a constant ratio to the original stimulus; i.e.* two stimuli in order to be discriminated must be in a constant ratio,

[1] See Myers, *Text-book of Exp Psychology*, Chaps. x. and xv. London, 1911.

which is independent of the absolute magnitudes of the stimuli. For white light Fechner could distinguish a difference of $\frac{1}{100}$, v. Helmholtz $\frac{1}{167}$, of the light intensity.

Fechner went further and attempted to express sensations in terms of quantitative units. His most important assumption was that all just noticeable differences of sensation contain an equal number of sensation-units.

Fechner's law states that *the sensation varies as the logarithm of the stimulus*; *i.e.* the sensation changes in arithmetical proportion as the stimulus increases in geometrical proportion.

Stated algebraically, if E is the measure of a sensation and δE the just appreciable difference, S the measure of the stimulus and δS a small increment, then

$$\delta E = C\frac{\delta S}{S} \text{ (Weber's Law)}$$

where C is a constant: therefore, on the questionable assumption that it is permissible to integrate small *finite* quantities (δE, etc.)

$$E = C\int\frac{\delta S}{S}$$

$$= C \log S + C' \text{ (Fechner's Law)}$$

where C' is another constant.

Weber's law does not hold good for very low or very high intensities of stimuli, and is only approximate at the best. An immense superstructure has been built up upon these psycho-physical foundations[1]. The bases are insecure on mathematical as well as on physiological grounds. So far as the latter are concerned we have no unit of sensation (cf. p. 61), and the variations, though quantitative, are only relative. The chief difficulty, however, is to be found in the ever-changing condition of the sensory apparatus. The deductions are not without value, for *some* quantitative relationship certainly exists, even if it be not so simple as Fechner's law implies.

The problem is still more complicated when we come to comparison of specific qualities in sensations. Thus we recognise brightness as a quality of coloured lights and we may say with some degree of certainty that a given red light has the same brightness or luminosity as a given blue light. We can thus estimate qualitatively equivalent stimuli and it is also true that we can attempt to estimate qualitatively equivalent

[1] Lipps, *Grundriss d. Psychophysik*, Leipzig, 1903; G. E. Müller, *Ergeb. d. Physiol.* II. 2. 267, 1903; v. Kries, in Nagel's *Handb. d. Physiol d. Menschen*, III. 16, 1904.

discrimination values. The question therefore arises whether sensations can be divided up into elementary qualitative parts. The simplest theory of such psychological analysis is that elaborated by Mach and others that each psychological element has a physiological counterpart, which is itself the expression of a physical counterpart. Each is indeed an accurate image of the other, or, to use Fechner's simile, the psychical and the physical are the concave and convex sides of the same curve. v. Kries, McDougall, and many others are of the opinion that this view is untenable. If two perceptions differ, yet possess a certain similar quality, that quality may be regarded either as made up of the sum of similar preformed parts in the various constituents of the two perceptions, or as a totally new psychological rearrangement of the underlying factors. Of these alternatives the latter is the more likely, and we must at present remain content to regard certain psychological similarities as not capable of analysis.

The psychological analysis of our sensations brings out other fundamental facts of importance. We not only see a light or a colour, but we see it at a definite time and in a definite place. Leaving aside the temporal element for the moment, we find that our orientation in space is largely dependent on vision. Hence it arises that our visual impressions are projected outwards to definite positions in the outer world. In this respect visual "sensations" differ from such sensations as pain, heat, cold, etc.[1] This unconscious projection of impressions is responsible for the fact that we associate our sensations with certain properties of external objects. We speak of objects as being round, bright, red, and so on,—an inaccuracy which is responsible for much confusion. A luminous object sets the ether in vibration; when these vibrations stimulate the retina they give rise to sensations, which we describe as bright, red, and so on. These qualities are therefore subjective and must be strictly dissociated from the physical stimuli which give rise to them.

This aspect of the subject has been lucidly treated by Hering[2]. As he says, "our visual world (*Sehwelt*) consists essentially of differently presented colours, and objects, as seen, that is visual objects (*Sehdinge*), are nothing but colours of different nature and form[3]." The whole of

[1] Cf. Hering, *Grundzüge der Lehre vom Lichtsinn*, in Graefe-Saemisch *Handb.* Th. I Bd. III. Kap. xii. 1905.

[2] *Loc. cit.*

[3] "The eye sees no form, inasmuch as light, shade, and colour together constitute that which to our vision distinguishes object from object, and the parts of an object from each other." Goethe (1810). "All vision is colour vision, for it is only by observing differences of colour that we distinguish the forms of objects." Clerk-Maxwell (1871).

the nervous apparatus of vision constitutes an "inner eye," which builds up a new visual world under the compulsion of the stimuli derived from the real objects of the outer world.

Things seen, visual objects, or colour forms must therefore be clearly distinguished from the real objects. The untutored regard the green of a leaf as an attribute of the leaf. The physicist, however, knows that colour depends upon the light reflected from the leaf and calls the reflected light green. The physiologist knows that the leaf, which appears green when looked at directly may appear yellow or grey when its image falls upon the peripheral part of the retina. He is therefore inclined to regard the colour as an attribute of the eye itself. Finally, to the psychologist the green is neither an attribute of the leaf, nor of the light, nor of the eye, but a psychical phenomenon, a definite qualitative entity in consciousness.

Colours therefore are visual qualities, and we are only justified in speaking of red or green objects, red or green rays, and so on in the broad sense that the objects or rays appear red or green respectively under the ordinary conditions of vision. Brightness and darkness, again, are not attributes of the objects or light rays, but of the colours as visual qualities. White, grey, and black must be included amongst the colours as visual qualities, but may be distinguished from the variegated or toned colours as untoned colours.

The common attribution of colours to the objects themselves, thus implying that the colours are properties of the objects, is largely a matter of memory. We say that snow is white, soot black, blood red, because under the ordinary conditions of life these objects appear to be of those hues. In this sense the colours may be well termed "memory colours" (*Gedächtnisfarben*, Hering[1]). The appearance of a given object at a given moment is by no means determined solely by the nature and intensity of the rays falling upon the eye and the condition of the nervous apparatus of vision at the time. These are but the primary and fundamental exciting factors. They awaken unconscious reproductions or memories of bygone experiences, which act as secondary but potent factors in the subconscious sphere, modifying and in many cases determining the ultimate conception. Thus it is that, though we are firmly convinced that snow is white and blood is red, the pink glow of a snow-clad mountain and the pallid hue of a face seen by the light of the mercury arc are regarded as accidental colours in no wise modifying our impressions of the actual colours of the objects. Every object with which we are

[1] Cf. Katz, *Centralbl. f. Physiol.*, xx. 1906.

familiar awakens a memory picture in our minds: "we see it through memory-coloured spectacles." Thus we often see it quite different from what it is, and our capacity to dissociate accidental colours from the so-called real colours of objects is very highly developed. Thus, the shadows on the surface of a body, which largely influence our perception of its shape, relief and distance, we instinctively regard as an epiphenomenon, and we think that we see the actual or real colours through the darkness of the shadows. A shadow on white paper appears quite different to us from a grey spot on the paper, even though both reflect exactly the same amount of light. Similarly a patch of cigarette ash on a black coat conveys a different impression from a patch of bright sunlight. Indeed, the difference manifests itself in words; the one we usually call white or grey or black, the other bright or dark.

Hering has devised some simple, but very instructive experiments to illustrate these facts. One example will suffice. In a room lighted by a window on one side, the opposite wall being white, standing with the back to the window and holding up a grey sheet of paper, the paper looks grey and the wall white. The wall however reflects only a portion of the light into the eye and "is" therefore grey. By looking through a tube it is possible to select a grey paper which exactly matches the greyness of the wall; yet directly the tube is removed the wall at once appears white, whilst the paper still remains grey. If, however, the edge of the paper is fixed with one eye only, the wall appears to be on the same plane and of the same tint as the paper. In this case different localisation produces different colour impressions, and the ultimate perceptions depend, not upon differences of physical light intensity, but upon other impressions which simultaneously enter into consciousness and modify judgment.

One does not generally pay special attention to the colours of objects, but uses them merely as indicators, specially associated with the objects; hence when the object is seen again the colour impression is immediately revived. Some dresses look blue by daylight, bluish-green by electric light, and the wearers often think it strange when in artificial light people say that they are bluish-green. Such people may even correct themselves and say that they are certainly blue, when they are told that they are blue.

Hering points out that these facts have nothing to do with simultaneous contrast (*v.* Section VI, Chap. II) as has sometimes been thought. They are indeed examples of the association of ideas or sympsychosis. They show, however, the necessity for eliminating as far as possible all subsidiary impressions, such as localisation, shape, dimensions, etc., when comparing colours. Further, it is easy to show that the apparent brightness and colour of objects can be altered within a wide range without disabusing our minds of the opinion that the colours are inherent properties of the objects. Thus, the paper of a book appears white and the print black, whether we read it in the morning or at mid-day or in the evening. Yet Hering has shown by accurate measurements that the print may actually reflect more light at mid-day than the paper did in the morning. Similarly the paper remains "white" and the print "black" whether the book be read by daylight or gas light or electric light or in the shadow of green trees. "The approximate constancy of the colours of visual objects in spite of gross quantitative and qualitative variations of the general illumination of the visual field is one of the most remarkable and weightiest facts in the domain of physiological optics" (Hering). We shall see that these gross variations are compensated for by processes of physiological adaptation of the visual nervous structures as a whole and that stimulation of retinal areas by light arouses reciprocal activities in neighbouring areas.

These complex processes should deter us from drawing too dogmatic conclusions from the psychological analysis of colour sensations. As McDougall[1] says, mental activity consists in the process of establishing in the mind relations between one thing and another. This process in its best-defined form is apperception, "the process by which a mental system appropriates a new element or otherwise receives a fresh determination[2]." Each mental system is gradually built up by a series of apperceptive processes, each such process consisting in the presentation of some one aspect or feature of the whole object through some sense-organ, and the bringing of this feature into mental relation with various other aspects and features previously apperceived and incorporated into the mental system. "In almost every moment of waking life an apperceptive process is taking place; whenever an object is attended to the presentation of it is apperceived[3]." Mental activity then consists essentially in the perpetual succession of apperceptive processes, and the essence of apperception is the appropriation of the relatively novel presentation by the mental system built up by previous apperceptions. At each apperception of any given presentation of an object the appropriation of it by the mental system is more ready and more complete, while the consciousness excited by

[1] *Brain*, xxiv. 605, 1901.
[2] Stout, *Analytic Psychology*, 1896.
[3] Stout, *loc. cit.* ii. p. 113.

this aspect of the object becomes less and less vivid, until finally, when the appropriation of it by the mental system becomes complete, it is implicitly apprehended, or, in terms of conation, the stimulus applied by this aspect of the object is responded to automatically, while some other aspect occupies the focus of consciousness.

If, however, bearing in mind the underlying complex factors, we attempt to make a psychological analysis of visual qualities it will be generally agreed that they can be divided into two groups of colour sensations, the untoned and the toned. The untoned or colourless form a continuous series from the blackest black through all gradations of grey to the whitest white. The toned or coloured include four, red, yellow, green and blue, together with all the gradations between them. So far as the insecure foundations of psychological analysis go red, yellow, green, and blue are simple or pure visual qualities. All other hues are psychologically mixtures of these qualities. Thus, orange obviously partakes of the nature of both red and yellow, purple of both red and blue, and so on. Yet that psychological analysis is necessary is shown by the acceptance of green as a simple colour sensation; for without analysis most people would say that green is a mixture of yellow and blue. That such is the case is doubtless due to familiarity with the behaviour of pigments, yet it may have a deeper significance, since the distinction between green and blue is vague amongst many primitive races and frequently amongst the uneducated classes.

Moreover, there are difficulties associated with black and white and two toned colours, brown and olive-green. "White" is particularly variable, chiefly owing to complexities arising from adaptation. Hering regards diffuse sunlight as distinctly yellow, and the "whites" of sunlight, arc light, incandescent gas light and so on, even when reflected from a surface of compressed magnesium oxide, show gross variations which are not submissible to psychological analysis. Opinion differs as to whether "black" is the negation of all sensation, as generally accepted by physicists, or an active sensation, as accepted by many psychologists. It is certain that there is a blacker blackness than that experienced when the eyes are carefully shaded from the light. Similarly the sensation of brown cannot be elicited by merely reducing the intensity of a yellowish-red or any other spectral light or mixture of spectral lights, and the same applies to olive-green. Under these circumstances the spectral colours approximate more and more nearly to black. In order that a brown sensation may be experienced the stimulus effect of the yellowish-red light must be "blackened" by simultaneous or successive contrast, or the appropriate pigment must be mixed with black.

We shall have to discuss these anomalies more fully in the sequel, but enough has been said to show that psychological analysis can afford no infallible criterion.

SECTION II

THE SPECTRUM AS SEEN BY THE LIGHT-ADAPTED (PHOTOPIC) EYE

CHAPTER I

THE SPECTRUM: HUE, LUMINOSITY, SATURATION

If a pure spectrum, *e.g.* that of the arc light, of moderate intensity is observed a band of colours is seen. Of these, four are clearly defined as separate and distinct from each other, viz. red, yellow, green and blue, the red region consisting of the least refracted rays, the blue of the most refracted. Between the red and yellow we distinguish a region which is called orange. The gradation from red to yellow is gradual and it will be generally admitted that orange partakes of the natures of both red and yellow psychologically, the red element diminishing as we pass from red to yellow and the yellow element correspondingly increasing. Between yellow and green a somewhat similar gradation occurs, the yellow gradually becoming more and more tinged with green until we fail to recognise any yellow at all and the colour gives the impression of pure green. Passing further towards the blue an intermediate green-blue region is met with, showing the same gradual transition until the blue no longer gives any impression of green. Passing beyond the blue we gradually come to a region in which the predominant sensation is still of the order "blue," but it is not pure blue. It is called violet. Now violet is a colour which occurs rarely in nature. There is, however, a colour in nature which is often called violet, but which is really purple. True purple does not occur in the spectrum, but it can be obtained by mixing pure red light with pure blue light, and we can pass from blue to red through violet and the mixtures of blue and red which are called purple and carmine.

We have thus travelled in a circle and returned to the original starting place, red. This is a very important fact, for it can be proved that with the help of the colours thus obtained, either pure or mixed with each other or with black in various proportions, all known colours and tints can be reproduced.

We can map out the spectrum into its separate colours, using the Fraunhofer lines as convenient fixed points, but as the colours pass gradually into each other the limits are more or less arbitrary. v. Helmholtz gives the following names to the different regions of the spectrum:

Line	Wave length in $\mu\mu$	Colour
A	760·40	Extreme red.
B	686·853	Red.
C	656·314	Junction of red and orange.
D	{589·625 589·024	Golden yellow.
E	526·990	Green.
F	486·164	Cyan blue.
G	430·825	Junction of indigo blue and violet.
H	396·879	Limit of violet.

Speaking generally then, change of wave-length causes a change in *colour*, or in the *hue* or *tone* of a colour. The tone changes most rapidly on both sides of the yellow, most slowly near the ends of the spectrum. For a certain distance at each end change of wave-length is no longer accompanied by change of tone, at the red end beyond 655 $\mu\mu$, at the violet end beyond 430 $\mu\mu$.

Apart from the change in colour the most striking feature of the spectrum is the difference in *brightness* or *luminosity* of different parts. The brightest part is in the yellow at about the *D* line, the luminosity diminishing continuously on both sides to the extreme ends. The brightness varies with the intensity of the light, but if the intensity is increased beyond a certain point the colours also change in tone. The colours on each side of about 500 $\mu\mu$ behave differently; the red, orange, yellow and green approximate to yellow, the blue-green, blue and violet approximate to blue.

Though the brightness of the colours increases with the intensity of the light it does not follow the curve of energy of the spectrum. Whereas the brightest part of the spectrum is in the yellow the curve of energy rises continuously from the violet to the red end[1].

[1] Nichols, *Phys. Rev.* XXI. 147, 1905; Krarup, *Physisch-ophthalmologische Grenzprobleme*. Leipzig, 1906, p. 4.

If now the pure spectral colours be successively mixed with gradually increasing quantities of white light they become paler until eventually no colour can be distinguished. They are said to become less *saturated.*

A given colour may therefore be defined by its hue, its luminosity, and its degree of saturation. In regard to the hue or tone the matter is relatively simple, so long as we adhere to the term hue or tone in this definite sense. The terms tint, nuance, shade and so on should be avoided.

With regard to luminosity and saturation the matter is by no means so simple. An unsaturated colour is also an impure colour in the physical sense of the word, for it no longer consists solely of rays from a single small region of the spectrum. But we are confronted with another fact, less easy of explanation, viz. that great increase of intensity of the light not only alters the hue, but also alters the saturation, so that eventually it produces only the sensation of white light. It would seem therefore that luminosity is in some recondite sense an inherent "whiteness" in the colour itself, differing in degree in different spectral colours and varying with the intensity of those colours. Clearly we are here, at the outset, face to face with a *physiological* fact of immense importance, and much of the difficulty of colour vision is concerned with this fact.

The terms hue or tone (*Farbenton*), brightness or luminosity (*Helligkeit*), and saturation or purity (*Sättigung*) are now generally used in the well-defined senses given above. One has to be careful, however, in reading the older and some modern works. Thus Aubert[1] uses *Farbenton* for Clerk-Maxwell's "hue" ("one may be more blue or more red than the other, that is, they may differ in hue"); *Farbennuance* for Helmholtz's "*Sättigungsgrad*" and Grassmann's *Intensität des beigemischten Weiss* and Clerk-Maxwell's "tint" ("one may be more or less decided in its colour; it may vary from purity on the one hand to neutrality on the other. This is sometimes expressed by saying that they may differ in tint"); *Farbenintensität* for Helmholtz's *Lichtstärke* and Clerk-Maxwell's "shade" ("one may be lighter or darker than the other; that is, the tints may differ in shade"). Edridge-Green uses the terms hue, luminosity and purity. Hue is employed in the usual sense. Of luminosity, however, he says: "No coloured object can have the luminosity of a white object reflecting practically the whole of the light impinging upon it. Therefore if we take absolute reflection as 100, a fraction of 100 will give the relative luminosity of any body."

[1] *Physiologie der Netzhaut*, Breslau, 1865.

Purity is "the freedom of the colour from admixture with white light," but he says "when I speak of a colour being mixed with white light, I have a different meaning from that which is signified by most writers on colour." His explanation should be read carefully[1], but he appears to use the term "white," which denotes a physiological sensation, in the sense of a physical property of the light.

CHAPTER II

THE DISCRIMINATION OF HUE IN THE SPECTRUM

Observations on the discrimination of hue in the spectrum have been made by Mandelstamm[2], Dobrowolski[3], Peirce[4], König and Dieterici[5], Uhthoff[6], Brodhun[7], F. Exner[8], Steindler[9], Edridge-Green[10] and others. Of these, the most accurate and complete are those of Steindler.

The maximum discrimination sensibility for hue, *i.e.* the smallest difference in wave-length ($\delta\lambda$) which gives rise to appreciable difference in colour-tone, occurs in the yellow and the blue-green. It has already been remarked (p. 28) that there are regions at each end of the spectrum in which differences of hue are no longer appreciated. Two neighbouring wave-lengths in these regions may appear to differ slightly in hue, but only owing to differences of intensity. When the intensities are suitably modified the differences disappear.

König and Dieterici found three maxima, I at 440 $\mu\mu$, II at 490 $\mu\mu$, and III at 570 $\mu\mu$ (Dieterici) or 590 $\mu\mu$ (König). Of these the greatest discrimination sensibility was II. The minima were at 450 $\mu\mu$ between I and II, and at 540 $\mu\mu$ between II and III. These results were obtained by the method of mean error (*v.* p. 19). (Fig. 4.)

[1] *Colour-blindness and Colour Perception*, 2nd ed. London, 1909, p. 60.

[2] *Arch. f. Ophth.* XIII. 2. 399, 1867.

[3] *Arch. f. Ophth.* XVIII. 1, 66, 1872.

[4] *Amer. J. of Sc.* XXVI. 299, 1883.

[5] *Ann. d. Physik*, XXII. 579, 1884; *Arch. f. Ophth.* XXX. 2, 158, 1884; König, *Ztsch. f. Psychol. u. Physiol. d. Sinnesorg.* VIII 375, 1895: in König, pp. 23, 105, 367.

[6] *Arch. f Ophth.* XXXIV. 4, 1, 1888.

[7] *Ztsch. f. Psychol. u. Physiol. d. Sinnesorg.* III. 89, 1892.

[8] *Sitz. d. Wiener Akad.* CXI. ii a, 857, 1902

[9] *Sitz. d. Wiener Akad.* CXV. ii a, 115, 1906.

[10] *Vide infra*, Part III

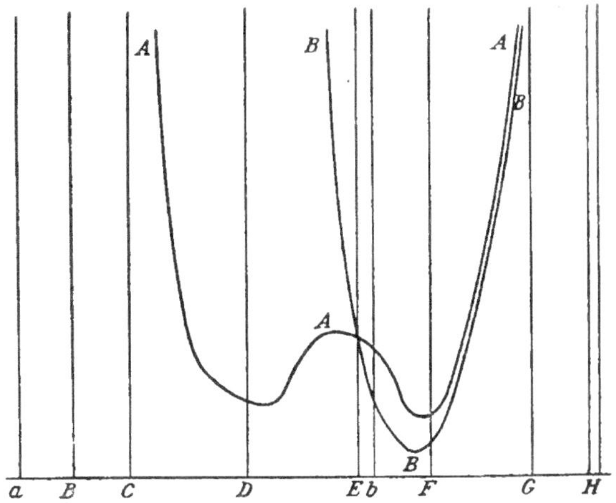

Fig. 4. Curves of discrimination sensibility for hues of the spectrum of gas light. *A, A, A*, for normal trichromat; *B, B, B*, for a deuteranope. Abscissae, wave-lengths. (König.)

Uhthoff used the method of least perceptible differences (*v.* p. 19), and obtained the following results.

λ	650	640	630	620	610	600	590	580	570	550	530	510
δλ	4·70	2·97	1·68	1·24	1·08	1·02	0·91	0·88	1·10	1·66	1·88	1·29
λ	490	480	470	460	450							
δλ	0·72	0·95	1·57	1·95	2·15							

His maxima are therefore II at 490 $\mu\mu$, and III at 580 $\mu\mu$.

v. Kries[1] points out that König's and Uhthoff's methods are not strictly comparable, since the former measures the general discrimination sensibility rather than the true specific or hue discrimination sensibility, which is measured by the latter.

Steindler used the interference spectrum of the arc-light, and examined twelve persons with normal colour vision. She obtained four maxima for her own right eye (Fig. 5): I at 435 $\mu\mu$; II at 497 $\mu\mu$; III at 585 $\mu\mu$; IV at 636 $\mu\mu$. The corresponding minima were between I and II at 454 $\mu\mu$; II and III, 535 $\mu\mu$; III and IV, 624 $\mu\mu$.

Comparing different individuals, II or III may show the greater discrimination sensibility. Thus her own III was greater than II whereas we have seen that König's and Dieterici's II was greater than III. The exact positions vary—for I, 15—20 $\mu\mu$; for II, 30 $\mu\mu$; for III, 15 $\mu\mu$; for IV, 15—20 $\mu\mu$. The average positions were—II, 492 $\mu\mu$;

[1] Nagel's *Handb. d. Physiol. d. Menschen*, III. p. 252.

III, 581 $\mu\mu$; IV, 635·5 $\mu\mu$: and of the corresponding minima—between I and II, 458 $\mu\mu$; II and III, 533 $\mu\mu$; III and IV, 627 $\mu\mu$.

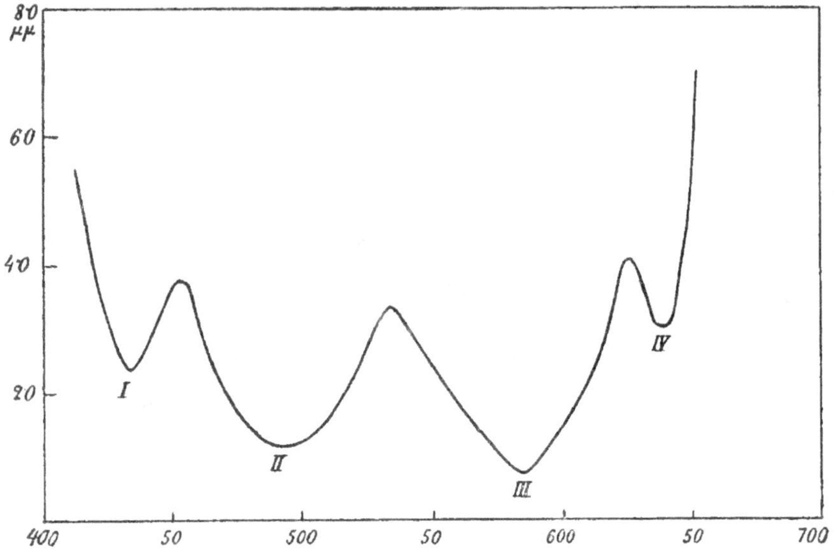

Fig. 5. Curve of discrimination sensibility for hues of the interference spectrum of the arc light. Abscissae, wave-lengths of the lights ; ordinates, differences of wave-length ($\delta\lambda$) capable of being discriminated. (Steindler.)

These results are of very considerable theoretical importance, and will be referred to again later.

The number of discriminable hues in the spectrum can be calculated from these data[1]. If λ and $\lambda + \delta\lambda$ are the wave-lengths of two just discriminable monochromatic lights, then $\delta\lambda$ varies with λ and may be regarded as a function of λ. The reciprocal value of $\delta\lambda$ therefore gives the number of hues which can be discriminated in an interval of the spectrum in which λ varies according to the same chosen unit. The total number of distinguishable spectral hues is therefore equal to the integral $\int \frac{1}{\delta\lambda} . d\lambda$ over the whole visible spectrum. Uhthoff's values for $\delta\lambda$ are given above. Since from 655 $\mu\mu$ to the red end and from 430 $\mu\mu$ to the violet end there are no changes in hue, $\frac{1}{\delta\lambda}$ is here = 0, and the integration can be performed graphically by drawing the curve and measuring the area enclosed between it and the axis of abscissae. From these calculations König concluded that Uhthoff could discriminate 165 hues in the spectrum.

[1] König, *Gesammelte Abhandlungen*, p. 367.

CHAPTER III

THE MIXTURE OF PURE-COLOUR STIMULI

Sir Isaac Newton (1704) first scientifically investigated the phenomena of colour mixtures. The fundamental laws were first enunciated by Grassmann (1853). They may be stated in the following form:

(1) Unlike lights mixed with like lights produce unlike mixtures: or, if in a mixture one component is continuously altered the appearance of the mixture will also continuously alter.

(2) Like lights mixed with like lights produce like mixtures: or, if two lights that look the same are each mixed with a third light the resultant mixtures will look alike.

Special Case: Proportional increase of intensity of each component does not destroy the match. This corollary will be found on further investigation to require some reservation.

(3) Every mixture of lights can be matched by a definite spectral light or a definite purple mixture which is mixed with a definite amount of white light: or, if we take any fixed homogeneous or composite light and mix it with the whole series of pure spectral lights, completed by purple, varying the proportions in the mixture from zero of one to zero of the other, we obtain every known variety of stimulus.

The importance of these laws is that matches of optical mixtures resemble algebraical equations and can be treated as such, the match holding good if any addition or subtraction is made to both optical mixtures.

Owing to the facts already stated on p. 27 it is clear that we can pass continuously from red to violet by two paths, one via the spectrum, the other via purple. This is represented graphically by a closed curve, and Newton naturally chose the circle as the simplest. It is not, however, the most comprehensive, as will be seen by the results of observing various colour mixtures. It is at once obvious, for instance, that the progress from red to violet via purple must be represented by a straight line, for experiment shows that purple can *only* be obtained by mixing red and violet, and therefore a given purple must be represented as a point on the chord joining the points which represent these colours.

The same applies to all hues of wave-length greater than $540\,\mu\mu$ (in the yellow-green). For example, any mixture of red light of $670\,\mu\mu$

and of yellow of 580 $\mu\mu$ causes a colour sensation which can be accurately matched with that derived from some spectral colour between those wave-lengths. The exact position, *i.e.* the wave-length, of this colour depends upon the relative amounts of the two colours in the mixture. If there is an excess of red the resultant mixture will match a colour nearer the red than the yellow-green. Moreover, the position of the colour will be accurately represented by the mass centre of the weights of the two components, *i.e.* by the centre of gravity, as Newton showed. v. Kries[1] gives the following matches of mixtures of 670·8 $\mu\mu$ and 552 $\mu\mu$ for the spectrum of gas light, the measurements being obtained with the Helmholtz-König spectrophotometer:

Amounts of red (670·8 $\mu\mu$) and green-yellow (552 $\mu\mu$) in the mixtures		Spectral match
670·8 $\mu\mu$	552 $\mu\mu$	$\mu\mu$
1·00	0	670·8
2·84	0·14	628
3·11	0·38	615
3·05	0·69	603
2·27	0·94	591
1·39	1·07	581
0·82	1·28	571
0·24	1·13	561
0	1·00	552

All the colour sensations in this region are therefore functions of a single variable and can be represented on a straight line, *AB*, where *A* represents about 800 $\mu\mu$ and *B* 540 $\mu\mu$. Each point on the line represents

Fig. 6. Representation of mixtures of lights of long wave-length on a straight line.

a colour sensation. If an amount, m_1, of light L_1, at *A* is mixed with an amount, m_2, of light L_2, at *B*, then the resultant sensation is a light, L_3, at *C* such that $CA : CB$ as $m_2 : m_1$. Similarly, if m_3 of L_3 at *C* be mixed with m_4 of L_2 at *B*, the resultant sensation is a light, L_4, at *D*, such that $DC : DB$ as $m_4 : m_3$, and so on. All mixtures therefore which give a sensation corresponding to a given point give rise to the same sensation or match accurately. Hence the range from 800 $\mu\mu$ to 540 $\mu\mu$ must, like the purple range, be represented in the colour diagram as a straight line.

[1] *Ztsch. f. Psychol. u. Physiol. d. Sinnesorg.* XIII. 281, 1896.

Complications arise when we pass beyond these limits. If a yellow is mixed with a blue-green the resultant mixture, though resembling a pure intermediate colour, does not match it perfectly. The match is made perfect by adding a certain proportion of white light to the pure spectral intermediate. In other words the mixture is paler, or less saturated, than the spectral match. As the distance between the mixing colours is increased the saturation becomes continuously less, until finally at one distance two colours are obtained which, when mixed, yield a sensation of white, free from all trace of colour sensation. Such colours are called *complementary colours*.

The following are v. Helmholtz's estimates of the wave-lengths for certain complementary colours:

Colour		Complementary Colour		Ratio of Wave-lengths
Red	656·2 $\mu\mu$	Green-blue	492·1 $\mu\mu$	1·334
Orange ..	607·7	Blue	489·7	1·340
Yellow	585·3	,,	485·4	1·240
,, ..	573·9	,,	482·1	1·190
,, ..	567 1	Indigo-blue	464·5	1·221
,, ...	564·4	,,	461·8	1·222
Green-yellow	563·6	Violet	433 and beyond	1 301

Observations have also been published by v. Frey and v. Kries[1], König and Dieterici[2], Angier and Trendelenburg[3] and others[4]. If these results are plotted as curves with wave-lengths from 400–500 $\mu\mu$ as abscissae and wave-lengths from 560–680 $\mu\mu$ as ordinates the curves nearly resemble hyperbolae, but differ slightly from each other. The differences have been attributed in part to macular pigmentation. Krarup[5] has re-investigated the subject and finds that the complementary colours change somewhat as the intensity of the illumination is altered. There is no change due to this cause from 460 to 480 $\mu\mu$, but a gradual increase from that point up to 512 $\mu\mu$. With a suitable, relatively low, illumination the curve is a rectangular hyperbola.

The ratio of the quantities of λ_1 to λ_2, where λ_1 and λ_2 are the wave-lengths of two complementary colours, is approximately constant and independent of the intensities of illumination. Glan[6] came to the conclusion that the energies of λ_1 and λ_2 at the percipient retinal structures

[1] *Arch. f. Anat. u. Physiol.* 336, 1881.
[2] *Wied. Ann.* XXXIII. 1887; in König, p. 261.
[3] *Ztsch. f. Psychol. u. Physiol. d. Sinnesorg.* XXXIX. 284, 1905.
[4] Helmholtz, 3rd ed., II. p. 107.
[5] *Physisch-ophthalmologische Grenzprobleme*, p. 100, Leipzig, 1906.
[6] *Arch. f. d. ges. Physiol.* XXIX. 53, 1886; *Wied. Ann.* XLVIII. 1893.

must be equal in order that white may be perceived. This law is not true, but Krarup points out that the ratio of the energies of λ_1 to λ_2 at the retina is independent of the intensities of illumination. The ratio is not constant, still less equal to unity, but if the energy ratios calculated from Angier and Trendelenburg's quantities (slit-widths) be plotted as ordinates, against wave-lengths as abscissae a symmetrical curve resembling a parabola and having its apex at about 608 $\mu\mu$ results.

Ebbinghaus[1] states that the brightness of the resultant white is equal to the sum of the brightnesses of the constituent complementary colours. Most observers have found that the white is brighter.

Complementary spectral colours have seldom the same luminosity, *i.e.* they do not look equally bright. The nearest approach to equal luminosity is orange, 607·7 $\mu\mu$, and blue, 489·7 $\mu\mu$. Colour mixing shows that the order of saturation of spectral colours diminishes from violet successively through indigo-blue, red and cyan-blue, orange and green, yellow (v. Helmholtz).

It will at once be observed that there is a range from about 560 to 492 $\mu\mu$, *i.e.* green, which possesses no spectral complementary. White can only be obtained from green by mixing it with both red and violet, *i.e.* purple.

There are hues with which we are familiar in pigments, etc., that do not at first sight fall into any of the categories mentioned. Of these the most striking is brown. Brown, olive green, and greys possessing some coloured hue are obtained by mixing black with a spectral colour or mixture of colours. Further evidence will accumulate in the course of our discussions in favour of the view that black is an actual and effective stimulus.

We can now return to the unfinished colour table or diagram, of which only two rectilinear portions have as yet been mapped out. It has been pointed out that the graph must be a closed figure in one plane and that the various points upon it follow the law of the centre of inertia of masses.

If three colours, neither of which can be obtained from a mixture of the other two, are represented by three points on a plane, then assigning to them values in terms of any unit, the situations and quantitative values of their mixtures can be ascertained. The problem is well stated by Greenwood[2]. "In order to establish the correctness of this method it is necessary to prove that, given the experimental

[1] *Ztsch. f. Psychol. u. Physiol. d. Sinnesorg* v. 176. 1893.

[2] *Physiology of the Special Senses*, London, 1910, p. 131.

laws of colour mixing, this construction is valid in all possible cases, *i.e.* that the situation of the mixed colour coincides with that of the mass centre of two equivalent masses (1) when the two constituents can be mixed from the three chosen colours ; (2) when one can and the other cannot so be mixed ; (3) when neither can be so mixed." v. Helmholtz[1] has supplied the mathematical proof.

The diagram will vary in form according to the source of light and according to the choice of units and fixed points. It is best represented in such a form as in Fig. 7.

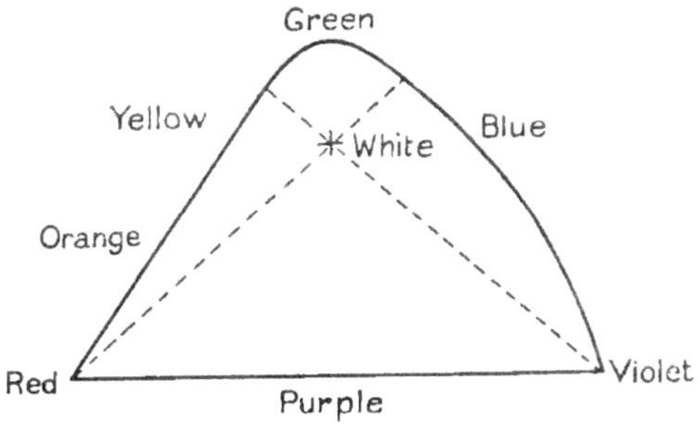

Fig. 7. Diagram of a colour table.

The position of the pure white sensation is obtained by dividing the line joining any two complementary colours according to the relative amounts of those colours required to produce white when mixed together. The deviation of the curve from a straight line beyond 540 $\mu\mu$ indicates the unsaturated nature of the mixtures.

Since, for example, mixtures of green and violet are less saturated than spectral cyan-blue, the curve must deviate further from the white point than the straight line joining green and violet. From experimental results it is found that the curvature is sharpest in the green.

These facts are quite independent of any theory of colour vision whatever, and their importance is absolutely fundamental. "The colour table merely expresses in systematic manner directly observed physiological equivalents of objectively different lights" (v. Kries). The facts show that the totality of physiological activities comprises far fewer elements than the objective stimuli. The varieties of stimuli of all possible mixtures derived from a source of constant intensity can be reproduced on a co-ordinate system as points in a plane.

If we introduce variations of intensity the law can be stated in general terms: "*The entire physiological valency of every conceivable light and*

[1] Helmholtz, 3rd ed., II. p. 112.

light mixture can be comprehensively represented as the function of three variables" (v. Kries). Hence a colour diagram representing varying intensities of colours and colour mixtures must be in three dimensions, as in Lambert's colour pyramid[1] or Runge's sphere[2].

Within a certain range, which includes all ordinary conditions of colour vision except those mentioned on p. 36, this law shows that every conceivable light or light mixture gives rise to a sensation which can be accurately matched by the sensation produced by a suitable mixture of only three lights. In other words, from the point of view of stimuli *normal colour vision is trichromatic.*

It is to be noted carefully that the colour table does not express the change in physiological valency which corresponds to variation in absolute intensity. The unit of intensity is fixed for the given table, as is also the choice of the three variables. Theoretically the choice of unit intensity of the three variables is arbitrary. The choice of variables merely involves a change in the co-ordinate axes. If the variables are selected too close together the table involves negative stimuli and the stimulus values cannot be reproduced experimentally. This is, however, of no theoretical importance.

We have here the basis of *colour equations.* For example, if spectral green-blue (Bg) is mixed with red (R) in certain proportions it matches a mixture of green (Gr) and violet (V), which may be expressed thus :

$$\alpha Bg + \beta R = \gamma Gr + \epsilon V.$$

Hence we can obtain a value for Bg

$$\alpha Bg = \gamma Gr + \epsilon V - \beta R,$$

which is strictly accurate though incapable of objective interpretation. As Greenwood well puts it[3] in colour equations "addition is uniform, the same result being always obtained when the same quantities are summed; it is commutative, the order of operations does not affect the result; it is associative and homogeneous....If we define subtraction, *in terms of arithmetical quantity* as uniform, non-commutative and non-associative, similar analogies can be observed; but this is of little importance, since a justification of the use of the symbol of addition will suffice for our purposes."

[1] *Beschreibung einer mit dem Calau'schen Wachse ausgemahlten Farbenpyramide*, Berlin, 1772.

[2] *Die Farbenkugel.* Hamburg, 1810. Cf. Chevreul, *Exposé d'un moyen de définir et de nommer les couleurs*, Paris, 1861; Höfler, *Ztsch. f. Psychol. u. Physiol. d. Sinnesorg.* LVIII. 356, 1911.

[3] *Loc. cit.* p. 133.

From the experimental point of view a constant spectrum is chosen and three colours are selected, *e.g.* a red, a green and a blue. Each part of the spectrum is then matched by mixing different quantities of the three together. This process is called "gauging the spectrum" (*Aichung des Spektrums*, v. Kries). There are many technical difficulties and the results are not wholly free from objection. The best published results are those of König and Dieterici[1] and Abney and Watson. The colour tables deduced from these results are seen in Figs. 8 and 9.

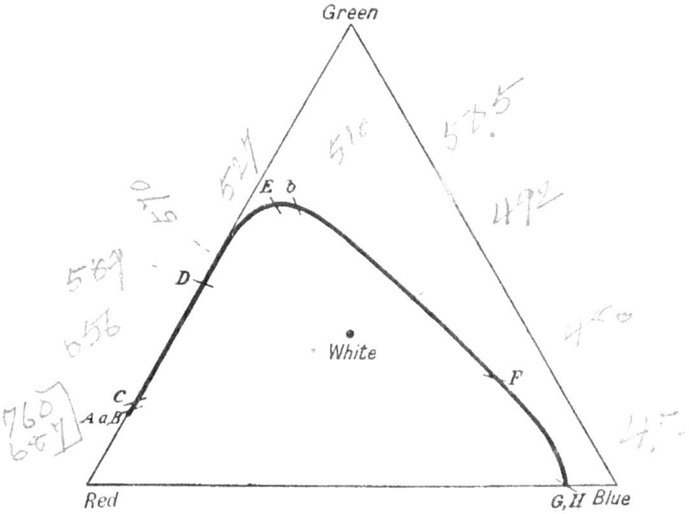

Fig. 8. Colour triangle. *A*, *B*, *C*, etc., Fraunhofer lines. (König.)

In König's curve the sudden bend at the extreme end of the violet is probably due to fluorescence.

As already mentioned colour mixtures often produce unsaturated colour sensations. Consequently the match has then to be made by a suitable addition of white light to the comparison spectral colour.

No three spectral colours can be chosen which when mixed will accurately match in hue and *saturation all* spectral colours. There is good physiological evidence of colour-sensations of much greater saturation than the spectral colours (*vide infra*, Section V, Chap. II). Such colours, being less mixed with white, must lie outside the colour table, in some such positions as shown at the angles of the circumscribed triangles in Figs. 8 and 9.

[1] *Ztsch. f. Psychol. u. Physiol. d. Sinnesorg.* IV. 241, 1893.

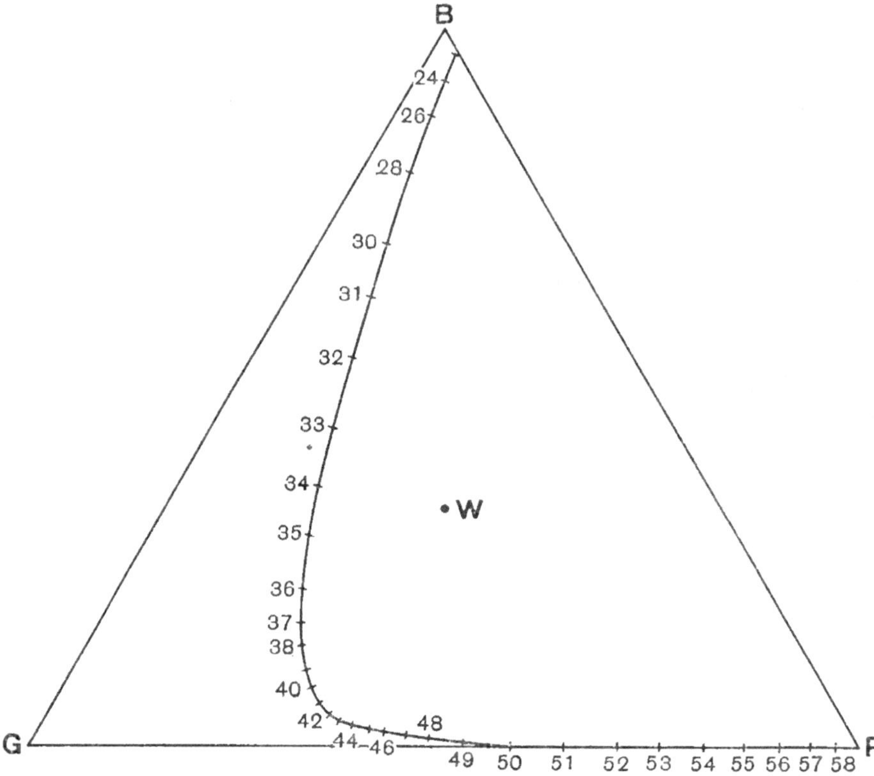

Fig. 9. Colour triangle. *W*, white ; *R*, red ; *G*, green ; *B*, blue. The numbers are those of an arbitrary scale of the spectrum of the arc light. (Abney and Watson.)

The Influence of Macular Pigmentation. The macula lutea, as its name implies, is permeated with a yellow pigment, and therefore absorbs certain spectral rays more than others. The variations in colour matches and in the estimation of complementary colours by various normal-sighted individuals were attributed by Maxwell[1] to this cause. Glan[2] and Sachs[3] examined the absorption of the yellow pigment from the macula of human eyes. Sachs found that absorption is inappreciable in the red and orange, commences in the yellow-green and gradually increases towards the violet end. Moreover, the amount of pigment varies considerably in different individuals. Sachs examined nine specimens: the mean coefficients of transmission of monochromatic lights of these cases are as follows (Krarup)[4]:

[1] *Phil. Trans. Roy. Soc. Lond.* CL. 57, 1860.

[2] *Arch. f. d. ges. Physiol.* XXXIX. 53, 1886.

[3] *Ibid.* L 574, 1891.

[4] *Loc. cit.* p. 18.

λ = 670—590	580	575	570	560	555	550	540	535	530
1	0·991	0·986	0·981	0·971	0·966	0·962	0·951	0·946	0·941
λ = 520	510	505	500	490	480	474	470	464	454—420
0·905	0·800	0·770	0·740	0·700	0·680	0·677	0·675	0·672	0·670

Owing to this absorption one would expect variations in colour mixtures, and it is indeed found that, for example, in matching a homogeneous yellow with a mixture of red and green, some people require slightly more green than others, so that a given match appears too green to some, too red to others. If such people make the match eccentrically, so that the images fall just outside the macula, where there is no yellow pigment, their matches agree[1]. v. Frey and v. Kries[2] exhaustively investigated the matches of numerous normal-sighted individuals (students) and found that the deviations were such as would be expected from pigmentary absorption. This variation in individuals is therefore purely *physical*, and must not be confounded with allied variations which are due to physiological abnormalities. (See Part II, Chap. III.) Since the physiological abnormalities very rarely affect the blue end of the spectrum, a ready method of distinguishing the effects of macular pigmentation from them is by measuring their match between spectral blue-green and a mixture of blue and green. v. Kries[3] found that reduction of blue by minimum and maximum macular pigmentation was in the ratio 1 : 0·31, the corresponding ratio for green (517 $\mu\mu$) being 1 : 0·5. (See also Section IV, Chap. II.)

The Influence of Lenticular Pigmentation. With advancing years the crystalline lens becomes tinged with a yellow pigment. The effect is similar to that of macular pigmentation, but does not manifest itself until late adult life. König[4] estimated the coefficients of transmission of monochromatic lights by the lens of a man, *aet.* 55.

[1] Cf. Hering, *Arch. f. d. ges. Physiol.* LIV. 277, 1893; Breuer, *Ztsch. f. Psychol. u. Physiol. d. Sinnesorg.* XIII. 464, 1897.

[2] *Arch. f. Anat. u. Physiol.* 336, 1881.

[3] *Ztsch. f. Psychol. u. Physiol. d. Sinnesorg.* XIII. 284, 1896.

[4] König, p. 346.

CHAPTER IV

THE LUMINOSITY OF THE SPECTRUM

"It is to be noted that the most luminous of the prismatic colours are the yellow and orange. These affect the senses more strongly than all the rest together; and next to these in strength are the red and green. The blue compared to these is a faint and dark colour, and the indigo and violet are much darker and fainter, so that these compared with the stronger colours are little to be regarded[1]."

Fraunhofer[2] first published in 1817 measurements of the brightness of the various parts of the spectrum. Vierordt[3] published a very similar curve of the "strengths of coloured light" of the sun's spectrum. He measured the amounts of the white light which must be added to various parts of the spectrum in order to produce a just appreciable diminution in saturation. Fraunhofer's and Vierordt's curves agree well except towards the violet end, a fact which is of considerable theoretical importance[4]. Draper[5] however found all parts of the diffraction spectrum equal by this method, and the red brightest in the prismatic spectrum. Accurate investigations of more importance for our purpose date from those of Abney and Festing[6] and König and Ritter[7], but before entering upon these and other researches we must attack the difficult problem of realising what exactly is being measured. It may be stated at once that we shall be unable to give a completely satisfactory solution to the problem at this stage, but as we proceed in our discussion the profound importance and significance of luminosity in colour vision will become more apparent.

Two white lights of different intensity impress the senses with stimuli which are interpreted as differing in brightness or luminosity. The measurement of differences of luminosity is the function of photometry.

Weber's and Fechner's laws (p. 20) suffice to show that even with white light the relationship of the sensations to the stimuli is by no means simple. When lights of different colours are compared the difficulties

[1] Sir Isaac Newton, *Optics*, Bk. I. Part I, Prop. vii. Theor. VI. 1704.
[2] *Gesammelte Schriften*, p. 1, München, 1888.
[3] *Pogg. Ann.* CXXXVII. 200, 1869.
[4] Cf. Helmholtz, *Ztsch. f. Psychol. u. Physiol. d. Sinnesorg.* II. I, 1891.
[5] Lond., Edin. and Dublin *Philos. Mag.* VIII. 75, 1879.
[6] *Phil. Trans. Roy. Soc. Lond.* 1886, 1888, 1892, 1899, etc.
[7] 1891, in König, p. 144.

are greatly increased. The comparison of brightness or luminosity of coloured lights is known as "heterochromic photometry" (Brücke).

In conformity with Newton's remarks, quoted at the beginning of this chapter, and with the general consensus of opinion, brightness must be regarded as a quantitative conception. When one colour is added to another on the same field we are conscious that the brightness of the field is greater than with either colour separately. An exact match between two colour mixtures means that they have the same hue and the same luminosity, and v. Helmholtz draws the conclusion that Grassmann's second law (p. 33) can be extended to include brightness[1]. He does not admit, however, that "equally bright lights added give equally bright mixtures," and there is no doubt that this statement is incorrect under certain circumstances (Purkinje's phenomenon, *v.* p. 57). Apparently this is not the only exception v. Helmholtz would admit, for as he says "equally bright red or blue doubled give the red brighter than the blue." Brückner[2] also holds that the brightness of a mixture is not always equal to the sum of the luminosities of its components, blue and yellow especially giving a brighter mixture.

v. Helmholtz indeed expresses quite candidly his doubts as to the accuracy of direct comparison of the luminosities of different coloured areas. "I scarcely trust my judgement upon the equivalence of the heterochromic brightnesses, at any rate upon greater and smaller in extreme cases. I admit, however, that one can gradually so darken one of two coloured fields that no doubt remains as to the other being now the brighter."..."As far as my own senses are concerned I have the impression that in heterochromic luminosity equations it is not a question of the comparison of one magnitude, but of the combination of two, brightness and colour-glow (*Farbenglüth*), for which I do not know how to form any simple sum, and which too I cannot further define in scientific terms."

v. Kries[3] says that "it must not be considered as an obvious fact that *e.g.* a given blue and a given red sensation are necessarily in the strictest sense equally bright. For we could only state this definitely if we were certain that the equality of the luminosity impression corresponded with a particular physiological condition so that we could substitute a well defined physiological entity for the subjective conception of brightness; but this is by no means the case."

[1] Helmholtz, 2nd ed., p. 440. [2] *Arch. f. d. ges. Physiol.* XCVIII. 90. 1904.
[3] Nagel's *Handb. d. Physiol. d. Menschen*, III. 259.

Whether or not we agree with these words, that a high degree of accuracy in such estimations can be attained is shown by Abney's results, notably the following[1]:

"To test the illuminating value of colour mixtures, three slits were placed in the spectrum, in the red, green and violet. The luminosities of the rays coming through each were measured—(1) separately; (2) in pairs; (3) the whole combined.

R	203
$(R+G)$	242
G	38·5
$(G+V)$	45
V	8·5
$(R+V)$	214
$(R+G+V)$	250

Combining these together we get:

$$R+G+V=250$$
$$(R+G)+V=250{\cdot}5$$
$$(R+V)+G=252{\cdot}5$$
$$(G+V)+R=248$$
$$(R+G+V)=250$$
$$=250{\cdot}25 \text{ by least squares.}$$

Within the limits of error of observation the luminosity of the combined spectrum measured as white is equal to the luminosity of spectrum colours measured separately."

The very fairly coordinated results of different observers and different methods show that in these luminosity measurements there is *something* measured which appeals to their senses as of the same order. Most will agree that it is a complex "something" which is expressed by v. Helmholtz as a combination of "brightness and colour glow," and which we shall see later is an integral part of Hering's theory and is expressed as the "white valency" of the colours. Further analysis of this "something" must be left till a later stage. In the meantime we will designate it "luminosity."

Direct comparison or "equality of brightness[2]" is not the only method of measuring the luminosity of spectral colours and mixtures. So early as 1735 Celsius employed the visual acuity to determine the relative brightness of various regions of the spectrum, and this method was also employed by Buffon and Sir Wm. Herschel[3]. The same principle has been applied to white light in the discrimination photometers of Houston

[1] Abney. p. 105. [2] This is the term usually applied to this method by physicists.
[3] Parsons. *Roy. Lond. Ophth. Hosp. Rep.* XIX. 277, 1914.

and Kennelly, Fleming and others[1]. This method, however, is too inaccurate for the purpose in view, though Crova's curves[2] are interesting[3].

Charpentier[4] and Haycraft[5] used the method of finding the distance at which small areas of different colours become invisible. Another method, based on the fact that the size of the pupil depends, *inter alia*, upon the intensity of the light, has been advocated by Gorham[6], and has also given good results with coloured papers. Rivers[7], Martius[8], and Brückner[9] have suggested other methods.

Heterochromic photometry has become of importance technically since about 1880 on the introduction of the arc light for commercial purposes. Hence a considerable amount of attention has been devoted to it[10]. Apart from the equality of brightness method adopted by Abney and Festing, and König and Ritter, the method which provides most accurate data for physiological purposes is flicker photometry, suggested by Talbot (1834), but first used by Schafhäutl (1855), and subsequently by Rood[11], Polimanti[12] and others. When before two lights of different luminosities an episcotister (a metal disc containing alternate closed and open sectors) is rapidly rotated, an unpleasant flickering of each light is seen at certain rates of rotation. Now it is found that the flickering ceases at the same speed of rotation of the episcotister for the two lights when their luminosities are the same. The causes of flicker are complex and will require further attention later (Section V, Chap. I). The results obtained are not free from criticism, but if due precautions are taken they agree well with those yielded by the equality of brightness method.

König's luminosity curves for the gas spectrum with different light intensities are given in Fig. 10. They were obtained by the equality of brightness method.

We are concerned here only with the higher intensities (F, G, H). The curves have the same ordinate at $535\,\mu\mu$, because that ordinate was taken as unity. It will be noted, however, that they all cross and reverse their relative positions. This is due to the Purkinje

[1] Trotter, *Illumination*, London, 1911.
[2] *Ann. de Chim. et de Phys.* VI. 528, 1885; *La Lumière élec.* XVIII. 549, 1885.
[3] Trotter's *Illumination*, p. 171.
[4] *La Lumière et les Couleurs*, Paris, 1888.
[5] *J. of Physiol.* XXI. 126, 1897.
[6] *Proc. Roy. Soc. Lond.* XXXVII 425, 1884.
[7] *J. of Physiol.* XXII. 137, 1897.
[8] *Beiträge zur Psychol. u. Philos.* I. 95, 1896.
[9] *Arch. f. d. ges. Physiol.* XCVIII. 90, 1904.
[10] Trotter, *loc. cit.* 161.
[11] *Amer. J. of Sc.* XLVI. 173, 1893; *Science*, VII. 757; VIII. 11, 1898.
[12] *Ztsch. f. Psychol. u. Physiol. d. Sinnesorg.* XIX. 263, 1899.

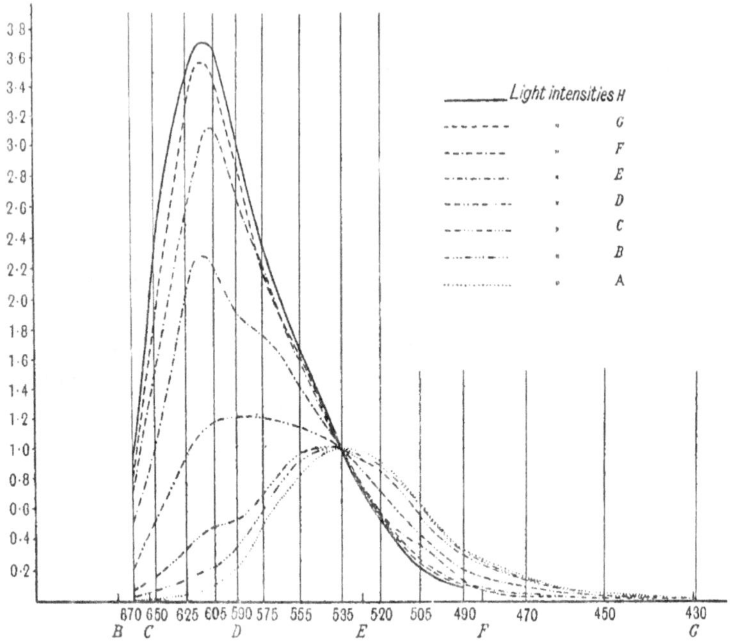

Fig. 10. Normal trichromat's luminosity curves for different intensities of light (*A*, *B*, *C*, etc.; *A* being the lowest, and *H* the highest intensity). Abscissae, wave-lengths of the prismatic spectrum of gas light; ordinates, an arbitrary scale. (König.)

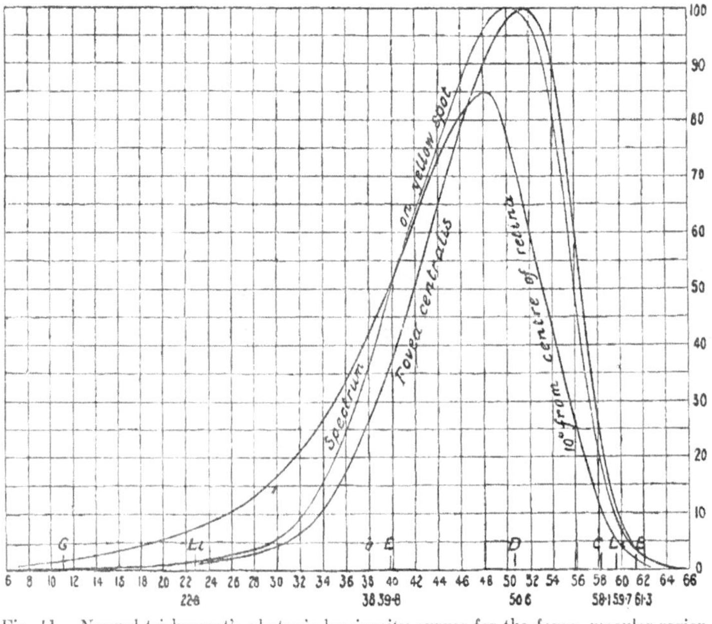

Fig. 11. Normal trichromat's photopic luminosity curves for the fovea, macular region, and 10° from the fovea. Abscissae, arbitrary scale of the prismatic spectrum of the arc light, the Fraunhofer lines and some important wave-lengths being indicated; ordinates, arbitrary scale, the maximum luminosity being 100. (Abney.)

phenomenon (p. 57). Maximum luminosity is at about 610 $\mu\mu$ with these intensities. Krarup[1] has calculated the curves from König's results in terms of the energy values of the spectrum, making allowance for absorption by the macular pigment, so that the results are independent of the particular source of light.

Abney's luminosity curves for the spectrum of the arc light with inclined carbons are shown in Fig. 11. They were also obtained by the equality of brightness method.

The following are the macular luminosities for the chief Fraunhofer lines, the source of light being the crater of the positive pole of the electric arc, with sloping carbons :

Line	λ	Luminosity
B	686·6 $\mu\mu$	4
Li (red)	670·5	8
C	656·2	17
D	589·2	99·5
E	526·9	48
b (Mg)	518·3	36
F	486·0	6
Li (blue)	460·3	2
G	430·7	0·6

The difference between the luminosity curve by the equality of brightness method and the flicker luminosity curve is shown in Fig. 12.

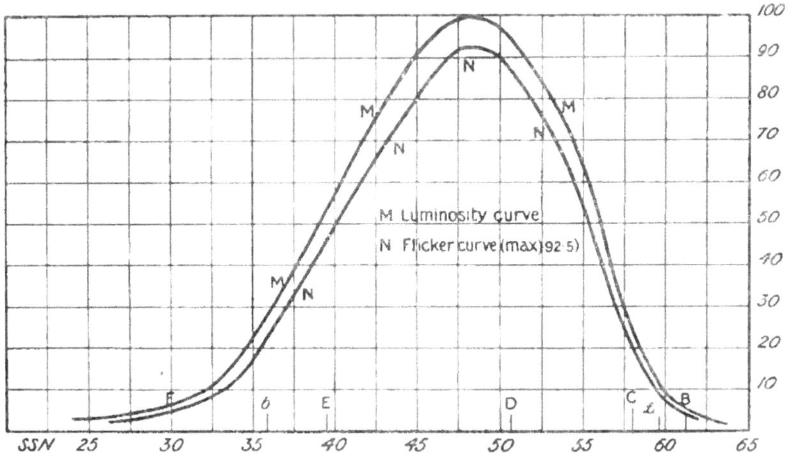

Fig. 12. Normal trichromat's photopic luminosity curves with the equality of brightness and the flicker methods. Abscissae, arbitrary scale of the prismatic spectrum of the arc light ; ordinates, arbitrary scale, the maximum luminosity by the equality of brightness method being 100. (Abney.) (Cf. Fig. 38.)

[1] *Loc. cit.* p. 46.

The flicker curve was taken with Prof. W. Watson's flicker apparatus used in conjunction with Sir Wm. Abney's apparatus. The conditions were—arc light with positive carbon horizontal, current 18 amps., *D* line = 1 metre candle, patch 1 sq. inch observed at a distance of 3 ft. It will be noticed that the flicker maximum is less than the equality of brightness maximum, and in the proportion 92·5 : 100, but Ives's results (*v.* p. 96, Figs. 38, 39) show almost complete coincidence.

The most striking confirmation of the general accuracy of these methods is that the luminosity values thus found agree with their periphery values. We shall see later (p. 67) that at the periphery of the retina colours of moderate intensity cease to convey the impression of colour and appear white, so that the periphery values are not complicated by the intrusion of the colour factor. Polimanti[1] confirmed this fact for the flicker method.

[1] *Loc. cit.*

SECTION III

THE SPECTRUM AS SEEN BY THE DARK-ADAPTED (SCOTOPIC) EYE

CHAPTER I

ADAPTATION OR TEMPORAL INDUCTION

When we pass suddenly from bright sunlight into a dimly lighted room we can see nothing for a time until we become "accustomed to the darkness." When we pass from the dark into bright light vision is also difficult and may be painful. We therefore infer that the sensibility of the retina becomes increased at low illuminations. This automatic process of levelling the sensibility of the retina to the requirements of the moment is called dark or light "adaptation" (Aubert) or "temporal induction."

Dark adaptation is a relatively slow process. It is characterised by a rise in the sensitiveness of the retina to light, which is slow during the first ten minutes of exclusion of light from the eyes, rapid during the following twenty or thirty minutes, and again slow or almost negligible after that period. The general character of the curve of retinal sensibility is the same in all cases, but there are marked individual variations in the rapidity and amount of the rise, thus explaining the fact that some people see very much better in a dull light than others, though variations in the size of the pupils and other factors (*vide infra*) are not without importance in this respect. In night-blind people there may be only a very slow rise, the ultimate sensibility after an hour being near the normal limit. In severe cases there is very little rise even after several hours.

Such adaptation is normal in the colour-blind, even the totally colour-blind[1]. Strychnin and brucin cause increase in the amount and rapidity

[1] Tschermak, *Ergebnisse d. Physiol.* I. 1, 700, 1902.

of the rise of sensibility: santonin has no effect. Mydriatics have an indirect effect; the first slow rise is prolonged from ten to twenty minutes but is followed by the normal rapid rise to the normal height.

Very short exposure to bright light, *e.g.* striking a match, causes a very temporary fall without materially altering the course of the curve. The increase in sensibility after very prolonged dark adaptation is more transient than the increase during the first hour, *i.e.* it is more quickly and completely abolished by exposure to light. Dark adaptation of one eye has no effect upon the other[1].

Besides this temporal variation in the sensitiveness of the retina there is a well-marked regional variation. In the condition of light adaptation the fovea is the most sensitive part of the retina, though little attention has been paid to the degree of adaptation in the researches published on this subject. (The light sensitiveness of the various parts of the retina must be carefully distinguished from their visual acuity for form.) The regional sensibility for colours of the retina of the light-adapted eye has been worked out by Vaughan and Boltunow[2], v. Kries[3], and Guillery[4]. Vaughan and Boltunow found the sensitiveness at 10° from the fovea to be $\frac{1}{4}$, at 20° to be $\frac{1}{10}$, and at 35° to be $\frac{1}{40}$ of that of the fovea itself. In dark adaptation the fovea is the least sensitive part of the retina[5]. In other words the fovea is a region of physiological night-blindness (v. Kries).

The relative central scotoma in dark adaptation was long ago recognised by astronomers, who noticed that stars of small magnitude were seen better if viewed somewhat eccentrically. "Pour apercevoir un objet très peu lumineux, il faut ne pas le regarder" (Arago). It is strikingly illustrated in viewing the Pleiades: by direct fixation four or at most five stars are seen; by indirect fixation a number of weaker stars become visible. Different observers use different parafoveal[6] spots for clearest vision in dark adaptation[7] and the spots vary with the degree of dark adaptation. The nearer the intensity of the stimulus is to the threshold of the dark-adapted fovea the nearer is the spot to the fovea: the feebler the light the more eccentric is fixation. With a given sub-minimal foveal stimulus Simon found that he fixed 2° from

[1] Charpentier, *La Lumière et les Couleurs*, p. 175. Paris, 1888.

[2] *Ztsch. f. Sinnesphysiol.* XLII. 1, 1907.

[3] *Ztsch. f. Psychol. u. Physiol. d. Sinnesorg.* IX. 81, 1896.

[4] *Ibid.* XII. 261, 1896; XIII. 189, 1897.

[5] Donders, *Brit. Med. J.* 1880.

[6] *I.e.* in the region near the fovea.

[7] Christine Ladd-Franklin, in König, p. 353; Simon, *Ztsch. f. Psychol. u. Physiol. d. Sinnesorg.* XXXVI. 186, 1904.

the fovea after ten minutes dark adaptation, $1\frac{1}{2}°$ after twenty minutes, and 1° after an hour. The direction is constant for the same eye and varies with different eyes; it depends upon muscular balance and refraction rather than upon the specific sensibility of the parts of the parafoveal region (Simon).

Although the fovea is night-blind relatively to the periphery it is capable of a slight degree of dark adaptation[1], but the small rise in sensitiveness of the fovea is only appreciable after previous very strong light adaptation, such as looking at the open sky.

Breuer and Pertz[2] showed that the peripheral rise in retinal sensibility in dark adaptation is rapid from 1° to 4° around the fovea, then slower to a maximum between 10° and 20° beyond which it falls. This is seen graphically in Fig. 13, where the sensibility of the fovea and the

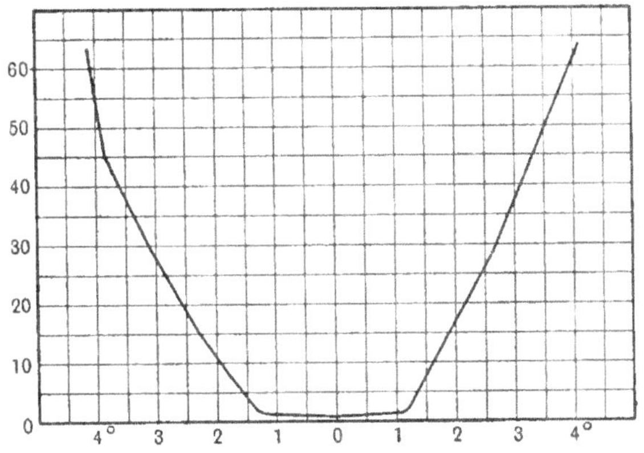

Fig. 13. Sensibility of the fovea and parafoveal region for mixed bluish-white light. Abscissae, to the left of zero degrees to the temporal, to the right, degrees to the nasal side of the fovea (0): abscissae, arbitrary scale. (Breuer and Pertz.)

parafoveal region to bluish-white light are shown. The abscissae to the left represent the temporal side, to the right the nasal. Pertz's experiments show that the scotopic fovea is more sensitive to red light than the periphery, though the difference is slight. Blue light gives a curve resembling that in Fig. 13. Yellow shows a slight rise in the paracentral area.

The alterations in sensibility differ according to the size of the area

[1] Charpentier, *Arch. d'Opht.* IV. 291, 1884; XVI. 87, 1896; Fick, *Arch. f. d. ges. Physiol* XLIII. 481, 1888; Treitel, *Arch. f. Ophth.* XXXV. 1, 50, 1889; v. Kries, *Arch. f. Ophth.* XLII. 3, 95, 1896; Tschermak, *Arch. f. d. ges. Physiol.* LXX. 320, 1898; Bloom and Garten, *ibid.* LXXII. 1898.

[2] v. Kries, *Ztsch. f. Psychol. u. Physiol. d. Sinnesorg.* XV. 327, 1897.

stimulated, and the relations between sensibility and the area stimulated are different in the light- and dark-adapted eye, and also in the foveal region and the periphery. For foveal vision the sensibility is proportional to the area stimulated (Riccò, Loeser[1]). In the dark-adapted periphery the sensibility is proportional to the square root of the area stimulated[2], but only for composite-white light and objects subtending a visual angle of 1° to 10°. Above 10° the sensibility rises more slowly. The rise is still less even for smaller angles with red light. The rise of the curve of sensibility in dark adaptation therefore varies with the size of the area of retina stimulated and with the nature of the light. In the light-adapted eye there is no definite relationship between the rise of sensibility and the size of the visual angle.

In dark-adapted eyes binocular summation of stimuli occurs, so that the sensibility is about twice as great with both eyes as with only one (Piper), though individual variations occur. In light-adapted eyes no such binocular summation occurs (Fechner[3]), but care must be taken that there is good light adaptation, and one eye must be covered for only a very short period, otherwise partial dark adaptation occurs. In this respect there is a noteworthy analogy to the effects of the size of the area of the retina stimulated: with complete light adaptation the stimuli to different parts of the retina are not summated, given that the visual angle exceeds a certain (small) size, nor are the stimuli to the two eyes summated, whereas in the condition of dark adaptation both summations occur.

CHAPTER II

SCOTOPIA OR TWILIGHT VISION

It will be readily appreciated that complete dark adaptation rarely occurs under normal conditions of life. Scotopia is the condition of vision in which there is a relatively high degree of dark adaptation. It will be best to consider the conditions of vision after prolonged stay in a feebly lighted room. If now coloured objects are viewed under feeble illumination the colours cannot be distinguished, but all appear to be of various shades of grey. The eye is totally colour-blind.

[1] Parsons, *Roy. Lond. Ophth. Hosp. Rep.* XIX. 114, 1913.
[2] Piper, *Ztsch. f. Psychol. u. Physiol. d. Sinnesorg.* XXXII. 98, 1904.
[3] v. Helmholtz, 3rd ed. II. 287.

A spectrum of low intensity appears as a colourless bright streak, varying, however, in brightness in different parts. Consequently accurate matches can be made between any two parts of the spectrum by merely modifying the intensity of one light.

If the intensity of the spectrum is slightly raised the colours become evident in a definite order and the relative brightness of the different parts becomes altered. As the intensity is still further raised the eye becomes light adapted and the spectrum shows all its hues with the relative brightnesses described in Section II. Scotopic vision at very low intensities is therefore achromatic; with slightly raised intensities of light it becomes chromatic. We may distinguish the two conditions as *achromatic* and *chromatic scotopia* respectively.

The achromatic scotopic values of different parts of the spectrum were first investigated by Hering and Hillebrand[1] for the dispersion spectrum of daylight. Abney and Festing's curve[2] is shown in Fig. 14.

The striking feature is that the brightest part, instead of being in the neighbourhood of the *D* line (yellow), is moved further towards the violet end, and is at about 530 $\mu\mu$ instead of at about 580 $\mu\mu$. The luminosity curve falls slowly towards the violet end, and sharply towards the red; the red end is shortened. It may be stated at once that *all* types of colour blind give almost identical achromatic scotopic curves[3]. Hence we can consider here results obtained both by normal observers and by colour-blind observers like Nagel[4] (a deuteranope). Very accurate observations were made by Schaternikoff[5] in v. Kries's laboratory. Fig. 15 shows the similarity between Nagel's (deuteranopic) and Schaternikoff's (normal) curves.

Fig. 16 shows the sunlight, Nernst light, and gas light curves[6].

The summits of the gas light curve (537·2 $\mu\mu$) and the sunlight curve (529·3 $\mu\mu$) differ slightly, and light from cloudless sky gives a rather higher value in the green-blue and blue than direct sunlight. An Auer lamp, which is rich in green rays, will give a slightly different curve from a carbon filament electric lamp, which is rich in red rays. The curve will depend upon the energy distribution in the given spectrum, and of course the diffraction or interference spectrum curve

[1] *Sitzungsber. d. Wiener Akad., math.-naturw. Kl.* XCVIII. 70, 1889.

[2] *Phil. Trans. Roy. Soc. Lond.* CLXXXIII. A, 531, 1892.

[3] Raehlmann, *Ztsch. f. Augenhlk.* II. 315, 403, 1899, for a possible exception; also Tschermak, *Ergeb. d. Physiol.* I. 2, 703, 747, 1902.

[4] v. Kries and Nagel, *Ztsch. f. Psychol. u. Physiol. d. Sinnesorg.* XII. i, 1896.

[5] *Ibid.* XXIX. 255, 1902.

[6] Trendelenburg, *Ztsch. f. Psychol. u. Physiol. d. Sinnesorg.* XXXVII. 1, 1904

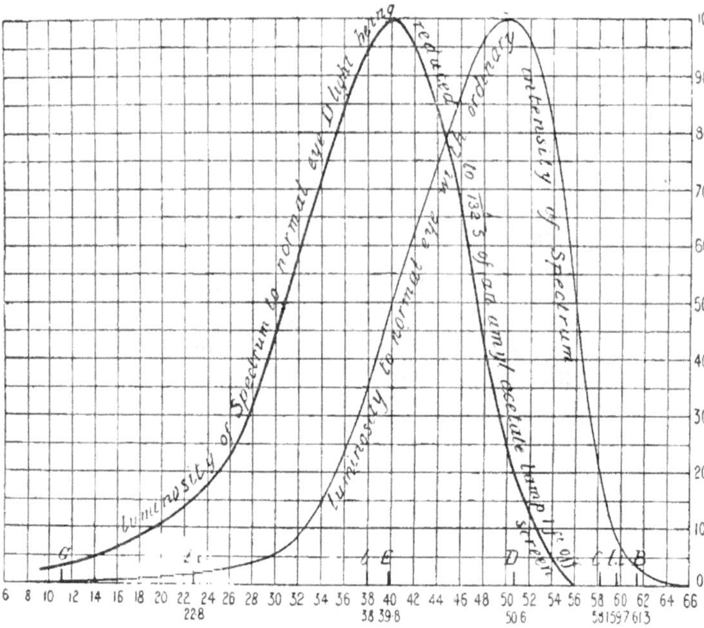

Fig. 14. Normal trichromat's photopic and scotopic luminosity curves. (One amyl acetate or Hefner unit is equal to 0·9 international candle power.) Abscissae, arbitrary scale of the prismatic spectrum of the arc light; ordinates, arbitrary scale, the maximum of luminosity being in each case 100. (Abney and Festing.)

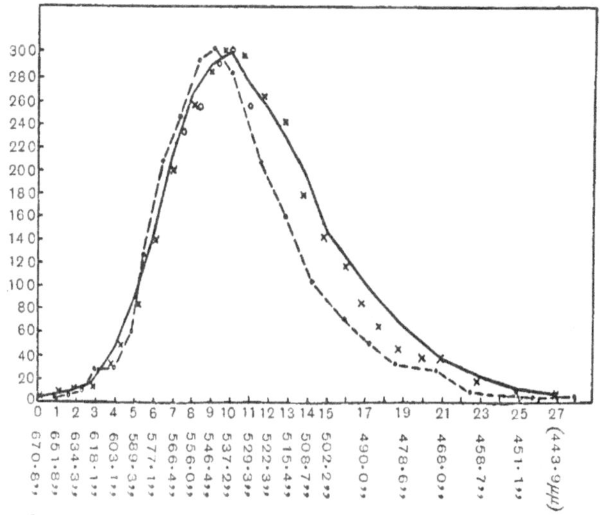

Fig. 15. Scotopic luminosity curves. ———— Schaternikoff's curve (normal trichromat). – – – – Nagel's curve (deuteranope). × × × × × and o o o o o, other observations by Nagel. Abscissae, wave-lengths of the prismatic spectrum of gas light; ordinates, arbitrary scale. (Schaternikoff.)

will differ from the prismatic curve. Krarup[1], using the energy values for the Hefner light calculated by Ångström, and allowing for absorption by the macular pigment on the basis of Sachs's researches, has calculated the achromatic scotopic luminosity curve from König's results. This curve is independent of the source of light employed and shows a remarkable agreement with (1) the curve of absorption of visual purple; (2) the luminosity curve of the totally colour-blind (*vide infra*); and (3) the similarly corrected achromatic scotopic luminosity curve of a protanope investigated by König.

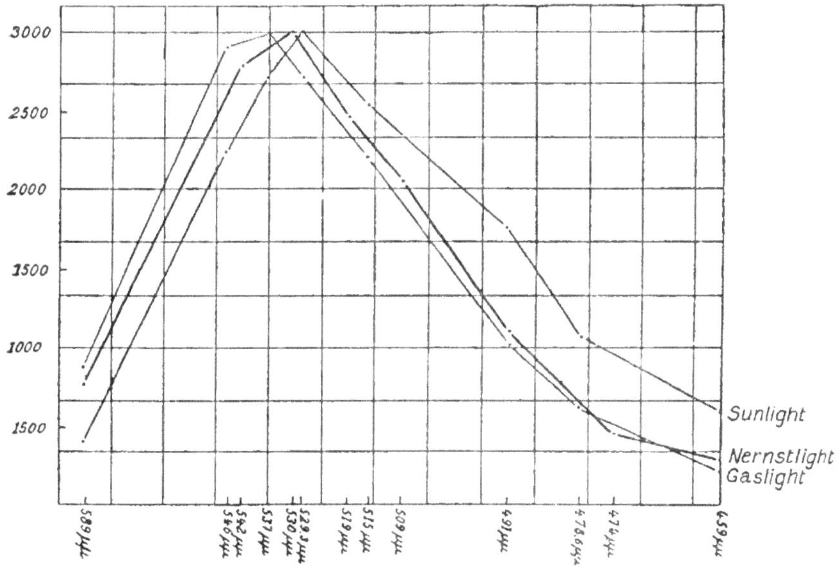

Fig. 16. Scotopic luminosity curves for direct sunlight (Schaternikoff), gas light (Schaternikoff), and Nernst light (Trendelenburg), reflected from a magnesium oxide-coated surface. Abscissae, wave-lengths of the prismatic spectrum; ordinates, arbitrary scale, the maximum of luminosity being in each case 3000. (Trendelenburg.)

The flicker method gives concordant results. Fig. 17 shows Haycraft's[2] results for colour-discs with three intensities. The ordinates show the number of revolutions of a semi-disc per second which were found necessary to abolish flicker: the abscissae are wave-lengths.

The extraordinary similarity between the scotopic luminosity curve and the curve of values of different monochromatic lights for bleaching frog's visual purple (Trendelenburg) (Fig. 1), seems to point to some underlying physiological fact of great significance. We shall return to this point later.

[1] *Loc. cit.* p. 21. [2] *J. of Physiol.* XXI. 126. 1897.

As may be easily imagined there are many practical difficulties about the observations. Before examining these and other such experiments more in detail it will be well to consider briefly some of the outstanding peculiarities of scotopia or twilight vision as compared with photopia or daylight vision.

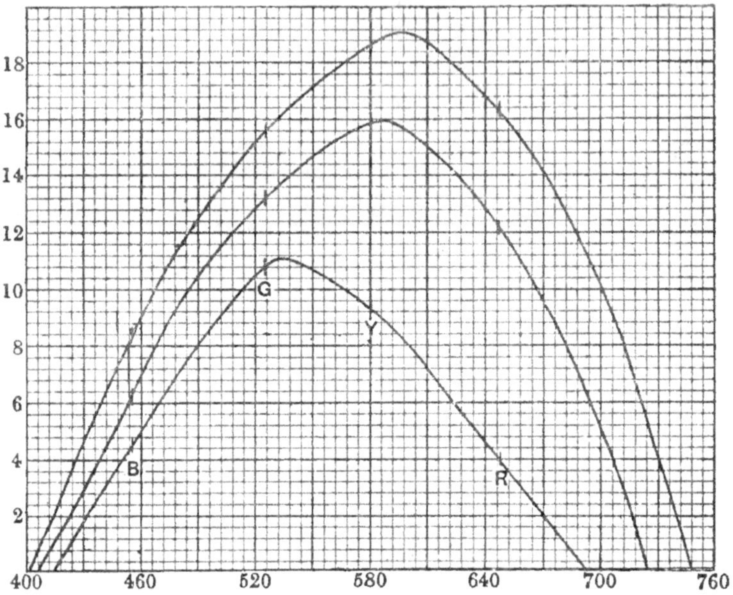

Fig. 17. Luminosity curves determined by the flicker method (critical frequency readings). The upper curve represents a bright spectrum, the lower a dark spectrum, and the middle curve one of intermediate intensity. (Haycraft.)

"At nightfall in the summer the order of disappearance of colour may often be seen; orange flowers may be plainly visible, yet a red geranium may appear black as night; the green grass will be grey when the colour of the yellow flowers may yet be just visible. An early morning start in the autumn before daybreak will give an ample opportunity of satisfying oneself as to the order in which colours gradually reappear as daybreak approaches. Red flowers will be at the outset black, whilst other colours will be visible as grey. As more light comes from the sky the pale yellow and blue flowers will next be distinguished, though the grass may still be a nondescript grey. Then, as the light still increases, every colour will burst out, if not in their full brilliance, yet into their own undoubted hue[1]." It is instructive with good dark adaptation in a dull light, to arrange different coloured cards, about

[1] Abney, Colour Vision (Tyndall Lectures), p. 107, 1895.

the size of a postcard, according to their apparent brightness. Red and green will occupy the dark and light ends of the series and orange will match a dark blue. Similar experiments can be made to give quantitative estimates with the colour top.

The explanation of these facts is found in the scotopic luminosity curves. In the bright prismatic spectrum of gas light the red (670 $\mu\mu$) appears about ten times as bright as the blue (480 $\mu\mu$). On the other hand the achromatic scotopic value of the red is less than one-sixteenth that of the blue. Hence with failing light the brightness of different coloured objects alters, the colours towards the red end of the spectrum becoming relatively darker, those towards the violet end brighter, so that finally the reds appear almost black and the blues bright. This fact was first investigated by Purkinje (1825) and is known as *Purkinje's phenomenon*. Hering[1] drew attention to the fact that the brightness of the blues increases much more rapidly than that of the reds diminishes. This depends upon the condition of dark adaptation of the retina. König[2] (*v.* p. 45) paid more attention to variations in the intensity of the light. The differences of these two authors on the subject of Purkinje's phenomenon depend upon the fact that *two* factors have to be considered—*dark adaptation and stimulus-intensity* (*vide infra*).

It is to be noted that in every-day experience we are not dealing with complete dark adaptation. The scotopic luminosity curves given above apply only to very thorough dark adaptation. In such experiments as König's (Fig. 10) the adaptation was certainly changing, though there must have been a fair degree of dark adaptation, and the main alteration in the form of the curves is rightly attributed to intensity of stimulus. It will be seen from these and other such curves that the shift in sensation intensity with diminished stimulus intensity is gradual. I wish to avoid as far as possible introducing theoretical considerations into this part of my book, but it will simplify comprehension of the subject if it is pointed out at once that the easiest explanation of the gradual shift of the curves is the simultaneous action of two processes, one especially related to vision with relatively high stimulus values and light adaptation, the other to vision with low stimulus values and dark adaptation. Upon this explanation scotopic vision is a relative condition, its nature depending upon low stimulus values and a *comparatively* high degree of dark adaptation. Whether the processes are subserved by independent physiological mechanisms is a question to be

[1] *Arch. f. d. ges. Physiol.* LX. 516, 1895. [2] König, p. 114.

deferred, though what has been said in the last sentence is hardly intelligible on any other assumption.

Complete dark adaptation is only reached after prolonged exclusion of light. Hence a moderate degree of scotopia is generally present in every-day life, sufficient indeed to elicit the Purkinje phenomenon merely by sudden diminution of the intensity of the stimulus. If after remaining for a considerable time in a moderately lighted room the illumination is suddenly diminished reds at once appear much darker and blues much brighter[1].

The relative rôles played by dark adaptation and by intensity of stimulus may be stated somewhat as follows. *Dark adaptation* determines the degree of scotopia. This is shown by the fact that the colour threshold or threshold value of photopic vision (*Schwellenwert des Tagessehens*, v. Kries) remains constant whilst the general threshold becomes lowered. Hence with good dark adaptation scotopic luminosity values are high. As light adaptation increases the photopic values increase and ultimately preponderate: hence Purkinje's phenomenon. With still stronger light adaptation intensities of stimuli below the photopic values are sub-liminal.

As regards *intensity of stimulus*, as soon as it reaches the chromatic threshold the luminosity values increase throughout the spectrum, but the increase in the red is very slight as compared with that in the blue.

The older authors (Dove, Grailich, Helmholtz) directed their attention almost entirely to the intensity, so that König lays stress upon the alteration in colour matches as "deviations from Newton's law of colour mixtures[2]." Hering[3] and his pupil Tschermak[4], on the other hand, regard adaptation as the sole cause. Hering[5] used two rooms separated by a partition which had round holes in it filled with coloured glass. Alteration in the illumination in one room varied the adaptation and in that of the other the intensity of the light observed. He found that with continued light adaptation, diminution of intensity of red and blue caused equal change in the luminosity of the two colours. Red, however, retained its colour slightly longer and appeared slightly brighter. With dark adaptation the blue became whiter and brighter

[1] Hering, *loc. cit.*

[2] König, pp. 108, 416; cf. Tonn, *Ztsch. f. Psychol. u. Physiol. d. Sinnesorg.* VII. 279, 1894.

[3] Lotos, VI. 1885; VII. 1886.

[4] *Arch. f. d. ges. Physiol.* LXX. 297, 1898.

[5] *Arch. f d. ges. Physiol.* LX. 519, 1895.

than the red without bringing about any change in intensity. Even momentary adaptation on lowering the illumination elicits the Purkinje phenomenon. These experiments cannot be regarded as conclusive, partly on account of the different amounts of white light transmitted by the coloured glasses, but undoubtedly adaptation plays the preponderant rôle[1].

As might be expected from our previous experiences of luminosity phenomena the scotopic relative increase in brightness is associated with a diminution in saturation. Those red rays which have little (620—670 $\mu\mu$) or no (beyond 670 $\mu\mu$) scotopic stimulus value, show no change.

The effect of Purkinje's phenomenon is seen graphically in Fig. 18, where the abscissae represent intensities of red lights (670 $\mu\mu$) and the ordinates those of blue light (450 $\mu\mu$); points on the curve represent equivalent luminosities[2]. The deviation from a straight line at low intensities shows the relative increase in brightness of the blue light.

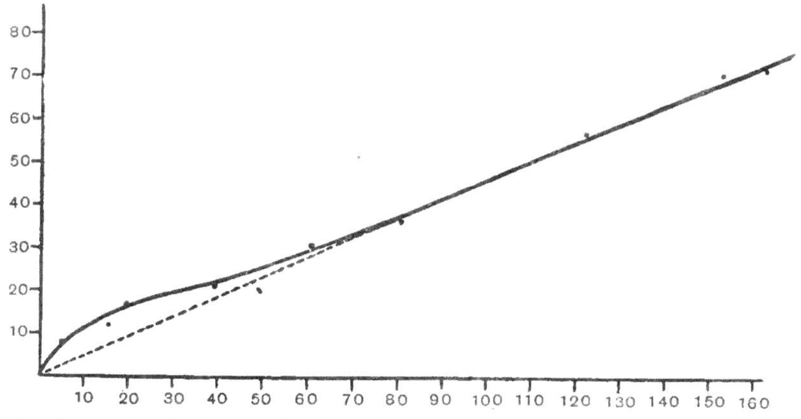

Fig. 18. Curve of equivalent luminosities of red (670 $\mu\mu$) and blue (450 $\mu\mu$) lights at different intensities (slit-widths). (König.)

Although different colours alter their appearance on diminution of their intensity it might be thought that accurate photopic matches would remain valid for the scotopic eye. This, however, is not the case. Albert[3] noticed that spectral yellow when matched with a suitable mixture of red and green ceased to match on diminishing the intensity, the mixture becoming brighter and less saturated than the homogeneous

[1] Cf. Feilchenfeld, *Ztsch. f. Sinnesphysiol.* XLIV. 51, 1909.
[2] König and Brodhun, in König, p. 144.
[3] *Wiedemann's Ann.* XVI. 129, 1882.

colour. Ebbinghaus[1] and Christine Ladd-Franklin[2] almost simultaneously drew attention to the significance of the facts. They showed that three whites made by mixture of red and blue-green, yellow and blue, and green-yellow and violet darken unequally with proportionally diminishing intensity, the first least, the second more, and the third most. König's experiments[3] with complementary colours are confirmatory. Still more so are observations on the colour-blind.

On the other hand as soon as dark adaptation is sufficiently great to abolish the sensations of colour any alteration of the intensity of the light which does not exceed the colour threshold fails to alter the various matches. It is true that Stegmann[4] found slight differences, but they were too slight to be of much importance, and such as they were were in a direction opposite to that taken in the Purkinje phenomenon.

As Lummer[5] pointed out, the peculiarities of scotopic vision explain an observation of Williams[6], H. F. Weber[7], and Aubert[8] that a body heated to redness in the dark first shows a *grey* glow. This occurs at 400° C. (H. F. Weber ; 379° C., Gray[9]) ; as the temperature rises the yellow-green rays increase and cause a yellowish-grey glow. At about 525° C. (Draper) the red glow commences, but the temperature varies with the conditions of the experiment. If the observer is light-adapted these preliminary stages are invisible. Abney[10] had previously recognised the explanation of these facts.

From what has already been said we see that there are two thresholds of vision—a *general threshold*, the minimal stimulus producing the sensation of light ; and a *specific or colour threshold*, the minimal stimulus producing the sensation of colour. The interval between them is known as the *colourless* or *photochromatic interval*. It depends upon the scotopic visibility of the given light below the threshold of photopic vision, and varies with the condition of adaptation and the nature of the light stimulus[11]. The colourless interval increases with increasing dark adaptation, and this is due to lowering of the general

[1] *Ztsch. f. Psychol. u. Physiol. d. Sinnesorg.* v. 145, 1893.

[2] *Nature*, XLVIII. 517, 1893.

[3] König, p. 373.

[4] *Ztsch. f. Psychol. u. Physiol. d. Sinnesorg.* XXV. 226, 1901.

[5] *Wiedemann's Ann.* LXII. 14, 1897.

[6] *Pogg. Ann.* XXXVI. 494, 1835.

[7] *Wied. Ann.* XXXII. 256, 1887.

[8] *Physiologie der Netzhaut*, p. 41, 1865.

[9] *Proc. Phys. Soc.* XIII. 122, 1894.

[10] Colour Vision, Tyndall Lectures, p. 35, 1895

[11] Nagel and Schäfer, *Ztsch. f. Psychol. u. Physiol. d. Sinnesorg.* XXXIV. 271, 1904; Loeser, *Ibid.* XXXVI. 1, 1904.

threshold, the specific threshold remaining almost or quite constant. As regards the nature of the light stimulus the colourless interval is greatest for light of short wave-length and least for light of long wave-length. In the orange it is small even with good dark adaptation. In the red beyond 670 $\mu\mu$ it is almost completely abolished. In fact even with very good dark adaptation such a red light excites the sensation of red[1], and the only evidence of a colourless interval is the alteration in the character of the sensation as dark adaptation becomes more complete, the red disappearing or becoming paler and brighter according to whether its wave-length is greater or less than about 670 $\mu\mu$. A minimal colourless interval can, however, be elicited under suitable conditions—degree of dark adaptation, size of field, paracentral or peripheral stimulation (Charpentier)[2] (*v.* p. 81).

The general light-threshold has been held to meet the requirements of a physiological unit of luminosity, for it has been accepted as an axiom that at their achromatic scotopic thresholds all lights are of equal brightness. "The light which can just be perceived has always the same brightness, no matter what be the light which acts as the stimulus" (König[3]).

Abney and Festing[4] early recognised the importance of investigating what are here called the chromatic and general thresholds for different parts of the spectrum. Light from a monochromatic beam was matched with that from a white beam, both being altered in intensity by the use of rotating sectors (episcotister), or in Abney's later experiments by the annulus (p. 5). Accurate photometric observations of the comparison light were made and the experimental variations were calculated from the aperture of the sectors or the scale of the annulus. The "extinction of colour" was measured thus. The light from the *D* line was taken as a standard and was arranged so that the illumination on the screen was 1 foot-candle. The intensity of the monochromatic light was then reduced by the annulus or episcotister until it appeared colourless and matched the comparison "white." The amounts of reduction necessary for various monochromatic lights throughout the spectrum were thus obtained. From these results the amounts of

[1] Parinaud, *Compt. rend. de l'Acad. fr.*, 286, 1881; König, p. 144; v. Kries, *Ztsch. f. Psychol. u. Physiol. d. Sinnesorg.* IX. 86, 1896.

[2] *Arch. de Physiol.* 1877; *Arch. d'Opht.* XVI. 337, 1896; Hering, *Arch. f. d. ges. Physiol.* LX. 535, 1895; Koster, *Arch. f. Ophth.* XLI. 4. 13, 1895; Tschermak, *Arch. f. d. ges. Physiol.* LXX. 320, 1898; v. Kries and Nagel, *Ztsch. f. Psychol. u. Physiol. d. Sinnesorg.* XII. 15, 1896.

[3] König, p. 190.

[4] *Phil. Trans. Roy. Soc. Lond.* CLXXXIII. 537, 1892.

reduction necessary when the illumination on the screen by each monochromatic light was 1 foot-candle were calculated. These results give the actual illumination at the point of extinction of colour in terms of foot-candles. Thus, when the illumination with *SSN*[1] 50 (558 $\mu\mu$) was 0·0016 foot-candle at the screen the colour just disappeared, and so on. Fig. 19 shows one of the curves obtained.

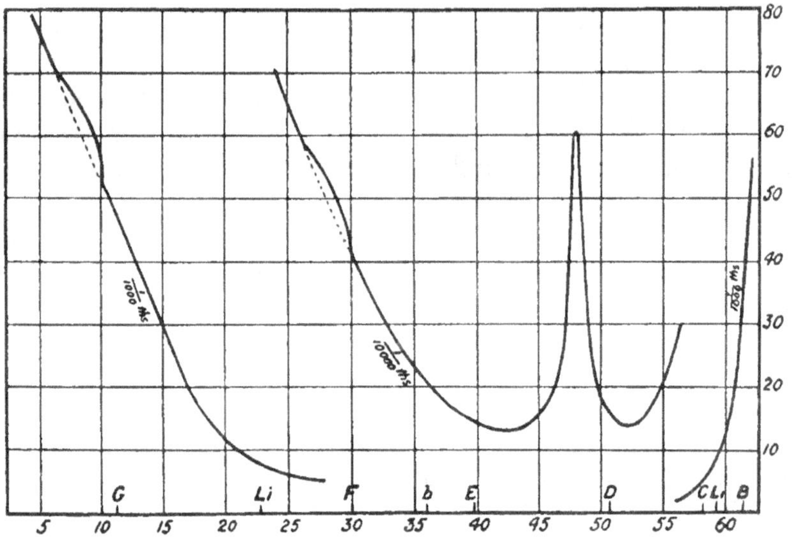

Fig 19. "Extinction of colour" curve. Abscissae, wave-lengths of the prismatic spectrum; ordinates, intensity of the illumination in candle-feet on the screen when the colour just vanishes. (Abney.)

In the "extinction of light" a curve was plotted showing what was the fraction of the beam from each part of the spectrum which was just invisible. The absolute luminosity of each part of the spectrum was determined, and from these values a second curve was plotted with ordinates representing the absolute luminosities at the points of extinction. The second curve shows the illumination in fractions of a foot-candle at the screen by each monochromatic light which would be just invisible. The branching of the curves (Fig. 20) beyond the green towards the violet end is due to macular pigmentation, the "whole eye" curve showing the intensities when the eye was allowed to wander. If a curve is plotted from the reciprocals of the extinctions the "persistency curve" (Abney and Festing) is obtained.. This is obviously the luminosity curve of the spectrum at the points of extinction. It is

[1] *SSN* is the scale-number on Abney's arbitrary scale of the spectrum.

identical with the luminosity curve of a feeble spectrum when the maxima are made equal. Fig. 21 shows such a curve.

Such are the conditions of the chromatic and general thresholds in the dark-adapted eye. What are the conditions of extinction of colour and light in the photopic eye? This difficult problem has been

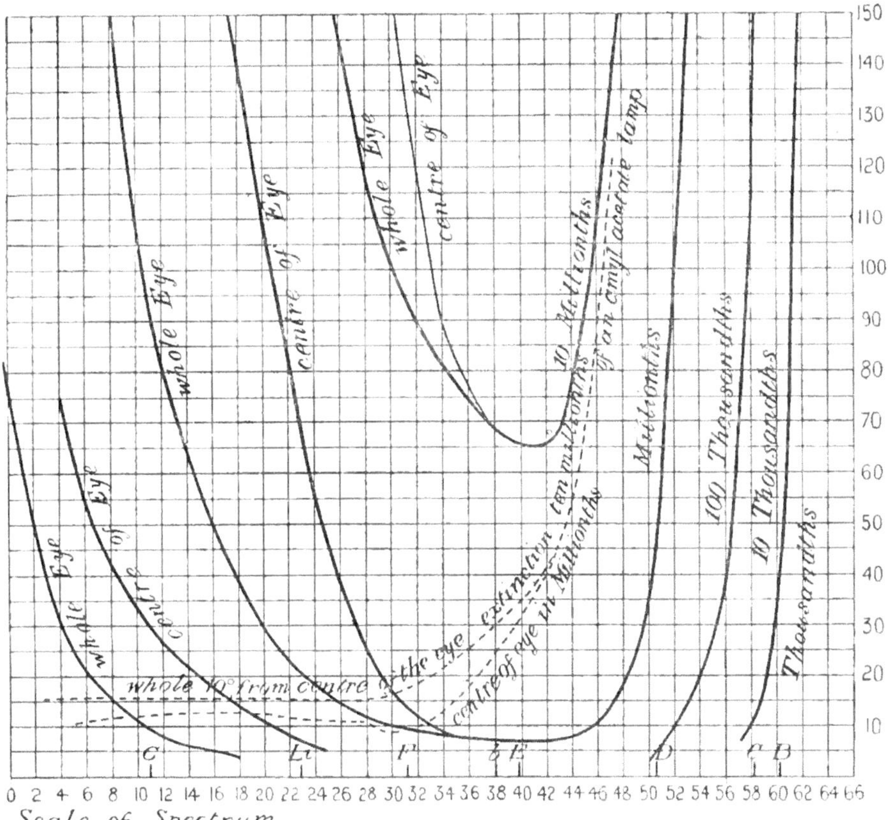

Fig. 20. "Extinction of light" curve. Abscissae, wave-lengths of the prismatic spectrum: ordinates, the fractions of the beams which are just invisible, the unreduced illumination of the *D* light at the screen being one Hefner-foot (0·9 candle-foot). The dotted lines show the proportion on the assumption that each beam has the same intensity as that of the *D* light.

attacked for the general threshold by Abney[1] in the following manner. A disc of matt white paper, 4 inches in diameter, was illuminated by white light. Through a hole in the centre, $\frac{1}{2}$ inch in diameter, a coloured light was viewed. The fovea was thus stimulated with monochromatic,

[1] *Proc. Roy. Soc. Lond.* A, LXXXVII. 1912.

and the parafoveal zone with white light, of known intensities. A small spot of shadow was thrown upon the white disc from which the parafoveal zone was illuminated. The blackness of this shadow is the same, irrespective of the intensity of the white light, though it appears to be different according to that intensity. The monochromatic light was then reduced until the spot illuminated by it matched the shadow spot in blackness.

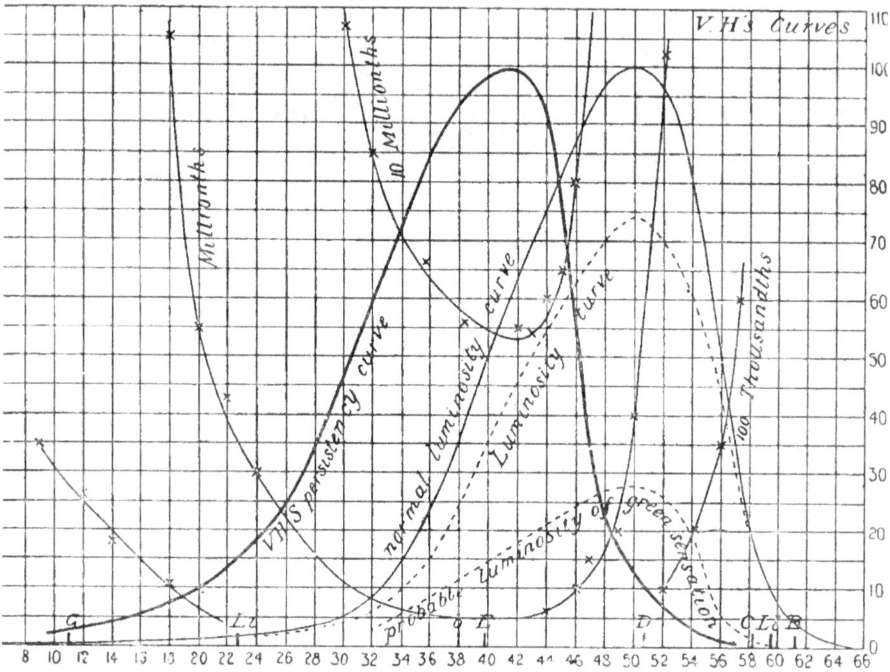

Fig. 21. "Persistency curve" of a deuteranope. The values are the reciprocals of the "extinction of light" values, which are also shown. The "normal luminosity curve" is the curve for higher intensities of light (the photopic luminosity curve). The persistency curve is the achromatic scotopic luminosity curve (compare Fig. 14). (Abney and Festing.)

The illumination of the white area was modified by the annulus so that intensities from 0·2 to 0·00078 foot-candle were obtained. Fig. 22 shows the logarithms of the intensities of the light for different wave-lengths for extinction with different strengths of illumination of the parafoveal zone with white light.

Fig. 23 shows the corresponding persistency curves. These, as before pointed out, give the luminosity curves of the spectrum at the points of extinction, and we see that they correspond with König's and other luminosity curves. With 0·2 foot-candle of parafoveal illumination the curve is the luminosity curve of the photopic eye.

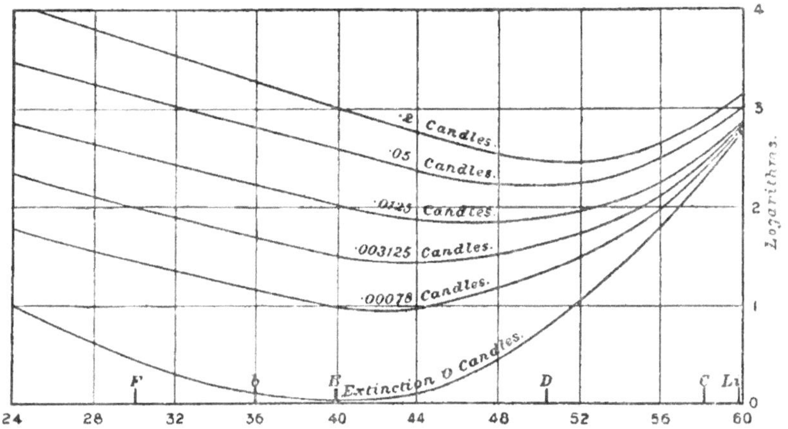

Fig. 22. "Extinction of light" curves for different degrees of light adaptation. Abscissae, wave-lengths; ordinates, logarithms of the intensities of the light. (Abney.)

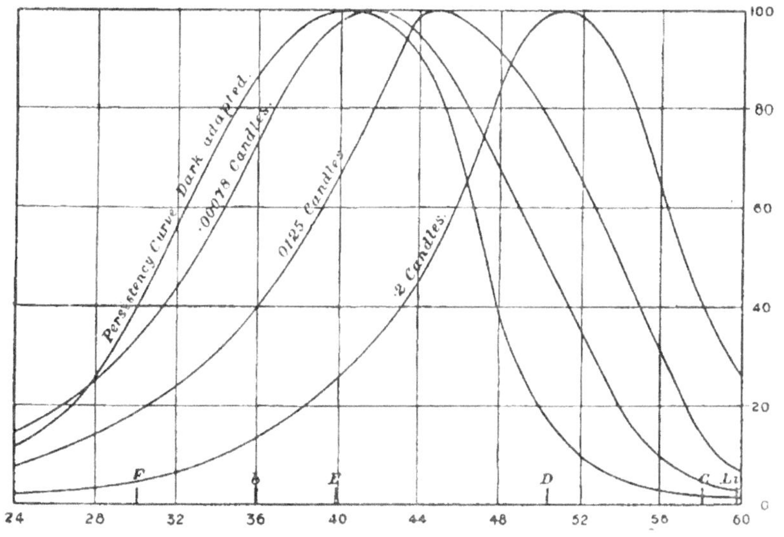

Fig. 23. "Persistency of light" curves corresponding to the "extinction of light" curves for different degrees of light adaptation. Abscissae, wave-lengths; ordinates, reciprocals of extinction values. (Abney.)

As the parafoveal illumination diminishes the curve shifts towards the violet end, so that the scotopic curve for complete dark adaptation is finally reached.

It has been found in experiments on the colour threshold that if the colour is just extinguished very slight illumination of the retina with white light will cause it to reappear without making any alteration in the intensity of the coloured light. Boswell[1], working under Nagel's direction, showed that the same phenomenon occurred on the addition of any light of considerable scotopic value, such as green. Since the eye is dark adapted the summation of the colourless scotopic values of the coloured lights throws the value of the stronger above the chromatic threshold. It is not a question of contrast, as is shown by the action of white light, nor of complementary colours. The same fact is borne out by Abney's experiments, where the extinction intensity for retinal illumination of 0·2 foot-candle is 2·6 times that of illumination of 0·00078 foot-candle.

[1] *Ztsch. f Sinnesphysiol* XLI 364, 1907.

SECTION IV

REGIONAL EFFECTS

CHAPTER I

THE FIELD OF VISION FOR COLOURS

When we look at or fixate a particular object we are conscious of the presence and movement of other objects situated around the object fixated. The image of the object fixated is formed at the fovea, those of surrounding objects at various points in the peripheral parts of the retina. The area over which such outlying objects can be perceived is called the *field of vision*, which is therefore the projection outwards of all the points upon the retina which can initiate visual sensations. Its limits are usually plotted upon a chart by means of a perimeter[1].

The normal photopic field of vision for a well-illuminated white object, 10 mm. square at a distance of 45 cm., is a horizontally oval area extending upwards about 50°, outwards 90°, downwards 70°, and inwards 60°. It varies with the illumination, the size of the test object, the contrast of the test object with the background, and the state of adaptation of the eye[2].

The fields for colours are smaller (Purkinje): by the ordinary clinical methods those for blue and yellow pigmented objects are about 10° smaller than that for white; those for red and green 20° smaller, the red field being usually smaller than the green, and violet smallest of all.

[1] See Parsons, *Diseases of the Eye*, p. 166, 2nd ed. 1912.

[2] See Landolt, in *Graefe-Saemisch Hand. d. ges. Augenheilkunde*, IV. 1, 548, 1904 (with Bibliography).

Charpentier[1] obtained the following results with coloured paper of 20 sq. mm.

	Violet	Blue-green	Yellow-green	Red	Orange	Yellow	Blue
Inwards	35	38	45	55	60	67	70
Downwards	33	43	49	58	59	62	60
Outwards	45	52	60	65	70	78	78
Upwards	34	39	44	53	58	59	59

Hess's field for invariable red and green (*vide infra*, p. 70) with an object subtending 3° was 21° inwards, 43° outwards, 17° upwards, and 14° downwards.

The fields for colours are approximately concentric with that for white. The colours change in appearance in passing from the point of fixation towards the periphery. Those at the red end of the spectrum pass through yellow to grey; those at the violet end through blue to grey. Blue-green becomes green, then yellow-green, then yellowish white (Hering).

Baird[2], who has paid particular attention to this point, finds that the changes in colour in passing from the periphery towards the centre are as follow. Red first appeared yellowish, then passed through yellow, orange and orange-red before it finally appeared red. Orange first appeared yellow, becoming more and more orange. Yellow appeared yellowish and gradually increased in saturation. Green appeared yellowish at first, gradually increased in saturation, assuming a greenish and finally a green tint. Blue became more and more saturated. Violet appeared bluish, then blue, and finally violet. Purple gave the longest and richest series of transitions: beginning with yellowish, its tone gradually moved down the spectrum, passing through orange-yellow, orange, red, and purplish red, before the pure tone finally appeared.

Aubert[3] found the limits of the coloured fields determined by the intensity of the light, and this result was confirmed by Landolt, Charpentier and others. The periphery is therefore dyschromatopic rather than achromatopic (Charpentier). The diminution in intensity, as measured by the distance of visibility of coloured spots, is given in Fig. 24. The sudden curve in the blue at the macula is due to macular pigmentation and also probably to dark adaptation.

[1] *La Lumière et les Couleurs*, p. 193.

[2] *The Color Sensitivity of the Peripheral Retina*. Washington, 1905.

[3] *Physiologie der Netzhaut*, p. 116, 1865.

The limits of the colour fields vary not only with the intensity of the light, but also with the saturation of the colour, and, above all, the size of the object. If these are sufficiently great colours may be recognised, almost, if not quite, at the extreme periphery (Donders, Landolt).

As already mentioned only the foveal region gives the unadulterated photopic reactions, unless the eye is very completely adapted to light, so that all traces of scotopia are eliminated from the peripheral field.

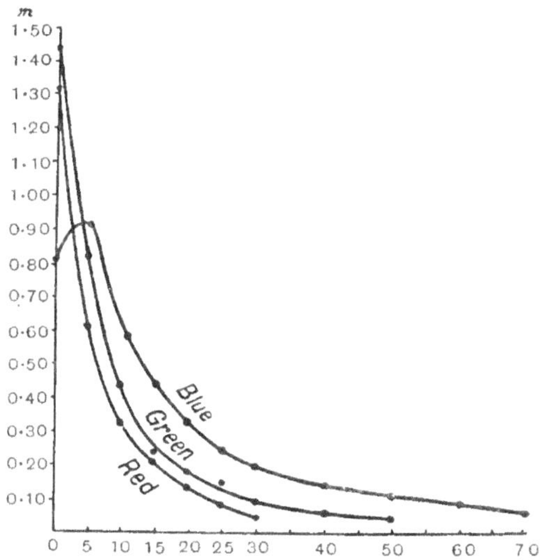

Fig. 24. Perception of colours in different parts of the field of vision. Abscissae, degrees to the nasal side of the fovea (*O*); ordinates, maximum distance at which the colour is perceptible in a coloured paper 2 mm. square. (Charpentier.)

Ordinary observations with the perimeter do not afford accurate details for comparison. If light adaptation is rendered as complete as possible by exposure to bright sunlight many points of interest are elicited. Under these circumstances it appears—within the limits of experimental error—that colour matches, spectral or composite, which hold good for the fovea remain good when viewed eccentrically, but though the matches remain matches the values alter, the colours changing in the mid-peripheral region, and becoming colourless in the extreme periphery. It may therefore be concluded that *in the photopic eye* peripheral vision differs from central vision only in the direction of a diminution in sensibility, and not in the direction of a change in character of sensation.

Further, all colour mixtures which appear colourless by central vision remain colourless by peripheral vision. Allowance must, however be made for macular pigmentation (*vide infra*, p. 124). The deduction is therefore more accurate if paracentral and peripheral regions are compared[1]. Care must be taken that light adaptation is complete and has been induced by colourless light, and that long exposure to coloured lights is avoided.

Ole Bull[2] was the first to employ stimuli the saturations and luminosities of which were equalised and to discover colours which do not change in hue in peripheral vision. His "physiologically pure" colours were a purplish red, a bluish green, a yellow, and a blue. He found that the limits of the purple-red zone coincide with those of the blue-green zone, and that those of the yellow and blue approximately coincide. The yellow-blue zone is considerably wider than the red-green zone. He employed colour papers.

Hess[3], also using coloured papers, similarly showed that with light adaptation colour pairs of fixed size, intensity, and saturation can be selected which lose their colour simultaneously and form a grey match when viewed peripherally, viz. green (495 $\mu\mu$) and red mixed with a small amount of blue; and yellow (574·5 $\mu\mu$) and blue (471 $\mu\mu$). These colours are complementary. All colours of greater wave-length than 549 $\mu\mu$ approximate yellow, all of less wave-length blue, in passing from central to peripheral vision. Thus orange and green-yellow become yellow; blue-green, violet and purple become blue. Hence there are only four colours which gradually become paler without altering their colour tone, ultimately becoming colourless, as one passes from central to peripheral vision. Hess calls these colours "invariable" red, yellow, green and blue. The limits of the zones at which the colours become colourless vary with conditions already mentioned, but the limits for invariable red and green are the same, as also for invariable yellow and blue.

Hegg[4], Baird, and Dreher[5] confirmed Hess's results. Baird found the "stable" or invariable colours to be a purplish-red, a yellow (about 570 $\mu\mu$), a bluish-green (about 490 $\mu\mu$), and a blue (about 460 $\mu\mu$). Dreher's values for the three last were 568 $\mu\mu$, 483 $\mu\mu$, and 461 $\mu\mu$. Baird found that the coincidence of the zones of each pair of stable colours holds good for the dark-adapted as well as for the light-adapted

[1] Hess, *Arch. f. Ophth.* XXXV. 4, 1, 1889; v Kries, *Ztsch. f. Psychol. u. Physiol. d. Sinnesorg.* XV. 263, 1897.

[2] *Arch. f. Ophth.* XXVII. 1, 54, 1881; XXIX. 3, 71, 1883.

[3] *Ibid.* XXXV. 4, 1, 1889.

[4] *Ibid.* XXXVIII. 3, 145, 1892; *Ann. d'ocul.* CIX. 321, 1893; CXI. 122, 1894.

[5] *Ztsch. f. Sinnesphysiol.* XLVI. 1, 1911.

eye. He used gelatine filters which transmitted approximately monochromatic lights.

The yellow-blue zone is "dichromatic." Beyond this zone there is an extreme peripheral zone which is "monochromatic" or totally colour-blind. It is best demonstrated in the nasal and upper and lower portions of the field, but only with very small test objects in the peripheral portion. If the luminosity curve for different colours is worked out for this zone it is found to be quite different from the achromatic scotopic luminosity curve. v. Kries[1] determined the peripheral luminosity values and compared them with Nagel's corresponding values for the achromatic scotopic luminosity curve:

Wave lengths	680	651	629	608	589	573	558	530	512
Periphery values	9·6	37·5	77·5	101	100	79·6	52·2	28·5	14·6
Scotopic values	?	3·4	14·0	35·5	100	256	351	321	198

The curves are shown in Fig. 25.

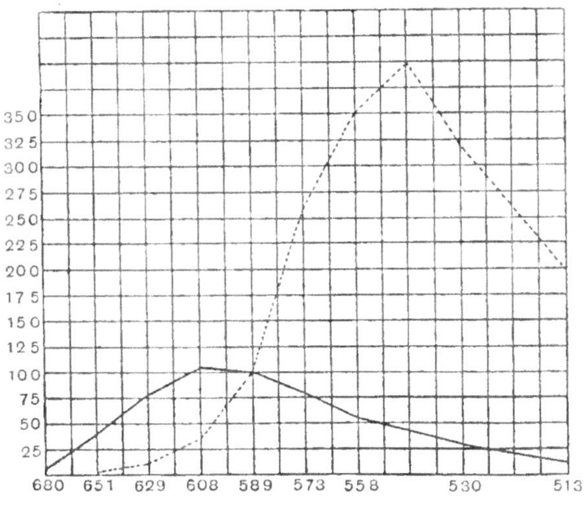

Fig. 25. ———— Photopic luminosity curve for the totally colour-blind peripheral zone of the retina. .... Scotopic luminosity curve. Abscissae, wave-lengths of the prismatic spectrum of gas light; ordinates, arbitrary scale. (v. Kries.)

The peripheral luminosity curve is highest at about 608 $\mu\mu$ instead of 544 $\mu\mu$, thus nearly approximating the luminosity curve for the fovea. We have here a further proof that peripheral vision is to be regarded as central vision diminished in sensibility, whereas scotopia is a different form of vision; the former is a quantitative variation, the latter qualitative.

[1] *Ztsch. f. Psychol. u. Physiol. d. Sinnesorg.* xv. 247, 1897.

The dissimilarity of the peripheral and achromatic scotopic luminosity curves shows that Hess's experiments do not prove all that he attributed to them, for he chose colours of equivalent "white value" and stated that they remained good matches both in peripheral photopic and in scotopic vision. The matches are valid only for peripheral photopic *or* scotopic vision.

On comparison of the peripheral photopic luminosity curve with König's and Abney's luminosity curves, making allowance for the fact that the two former are with gas light, the latter with arc light, we see that they agree, so that the statement on p. 71 is correct. Polimanti[1] has confirmed the statement on the same individuals using the same apparatus and source of light with the flicker method (Fig. 26).

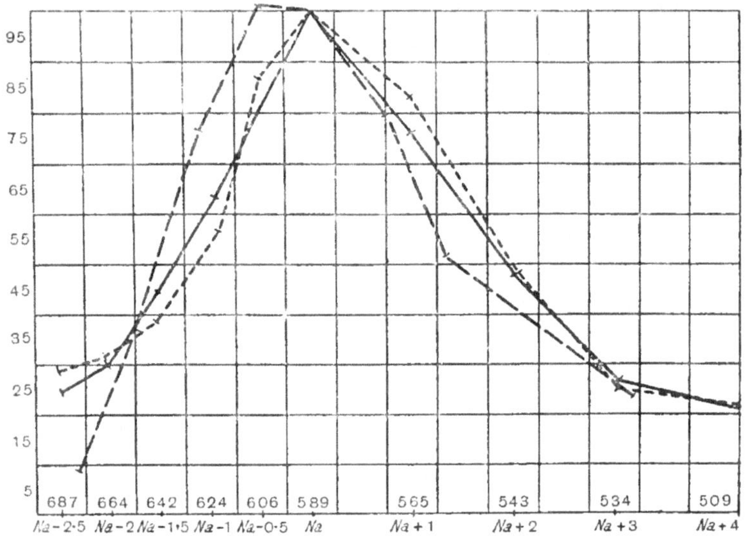

Fig. 26. ——— Photopic periphery luminosity curve (flicker method). - - - - - - - Photopic central luminosity curve (flicker method). — — — — Photopic periphery luminosity curve (equality of brightness method). Abscissae, arbitrary scale of wave-lengths of prismatic spectrum of gas light, measured from the *D* line (*Na*), with certain absolute wave-lengths indicated; ordinates, arbitrary scale. (Polimanti.)

Siebeck[2], using minimal fields, has adduced further confirmation. He found that with spectral lights of moderate intensity it was impossible with accurate foveal fixation to abolish the sensation of colour without that of light by reduction of the field, but that this was readily effected 1°·5 from the centre. He compared the luminosities of the lights under

[1] *Ztsch. f. Psychol. u. Physiol. d. Sinnesorg.* XIX. 272, 1899. [2] *Ibid.* XLI. 89. 1907.

these circumstances and found that these "minimal field luminosities" agree with both the ordinary and the peripheral photopic luminosity curves, and therefore disagree with the achromatic scotopic luminosity curve. He found the maximum luminosity by this method at 601·3 $\mu\mu$:

Wave-lengths	642·4	620·8	607·8	601·3	595·3	589·3	584·2
Minimal-field luminosities	66·6	91·5	112·8	128	110·9	100	90
Wave-lengths	579·1	574·1	564·8	551·4			
Minimal-field luminosities	81·6	79·5	68·6	52			

The minimal-field and luminosity curves are shown in Fig. 27.

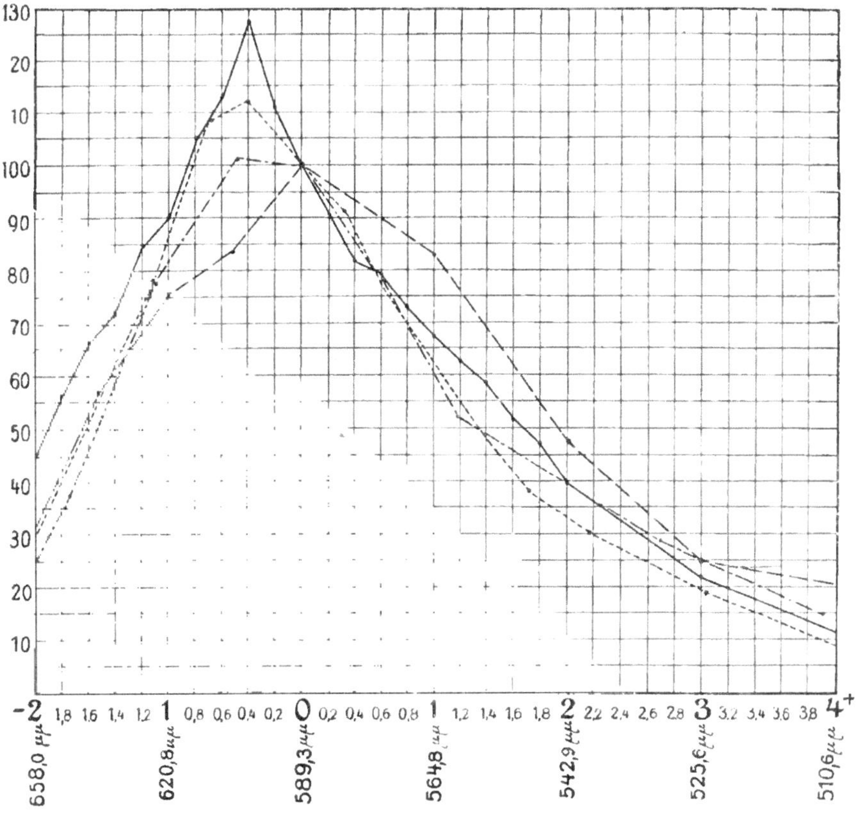

Fig. 27. ———— "Minimal-field luminosity curve." —·—·—·— Photopic periphery luminosity curve. — — — — Photopic central luminosity curve (flicker method). .... "W-curve" of a deuteranope (see Fig. 45). (Siebeck.)

Zahn[1] has investigated the "minimal-time luminosities." In these experiments the coloured light is exposed momentarily, when it appears colourless, and is compared in brightness with a surrounding white surface. The minimal-time luminosities completely confirm the results obtained by minimal fields and periphery values, as is shown by the following values:

Wave-lengths	659	621	601	589	564	542	523	506
Minimal-time luminosities	22·5	79·0	105·0	100	76·6	59·4	38·0	15·2
Minimal-field luminosities	24·4	70·2	104·8	100	74·4	58·3	37·5	20·2
Periphery values	21·6	73·9	99·6	100	79·9	54·7	36·7	15·2

Hess[2], Hering[3], and Tschermak[4] have examined the relative luminosity of different lights in different regions of the retina. Hess found that red and green pigments on a grey background, when viewed by dull daylight with moderate dark adaptation, became darker and brighter respectively in peripheral as compared with central vision. Hering confirmed this result with spectral lights. Tschermak used Hering's "double room" (*v.* p. 58) with spectral lights from Auer-gas or arc light against a daylit background. He found a relative increase in luminosity from 516 to 466 $\mu\mu$, a relative decrease from 693 to 525 $\mu\mu$, and no change from 525 to 516 $\mu\mu$, on indirect fixation. In the dark-adapted eye there is similarly a change in relative luminosity, and it occurs in the same sense as the Purkinje phenomenon. Hering[5] has shown that for the dark-adapted eye, even on momentary dark adaptation, lights of equal brightness by direct fixation appear very unlike in luminosity on indirect fixation. He describes these alterations in luminosity as Purkinje's phenomenon produced by change of position in the visual field without change of light intensity.

The limits of the colour fields of the partially dark-adapted eye for spectral colours have been worked out very thoroughly by Abney[6].

[1] *Ztsch. f. Sinnesphysiol.* XLVI. 287, 1911. [2] *Arch. f. Ophth.* XXV. 4, 1. 1889.
[3] *Arch. f. d. ges. Physiol.* XLVII. 417, 1890.
[4] *Ibid.* LXXXII. 559, 1900. [5] *Ibid.* LX. 519. 1895
[6] Abney, p. 190; *Phil. Trans. Roy. Soc.* CXC. 155, 1897.

Fig. 28 shows the fields with

red	670·5 $\mu\mu$	0·27	foot-candle
yellow ..	589·2 ,,	3·95	,,
green ..	508·5 ,,	1·89	,,
blue	460·3 ,,	0·36	,,

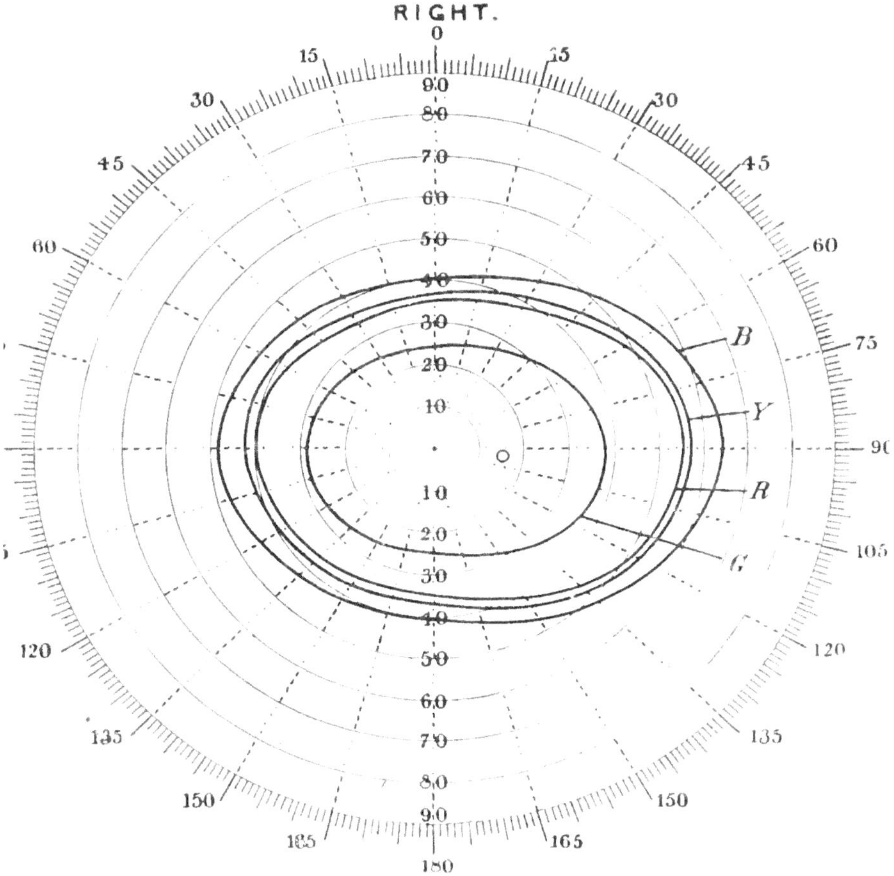

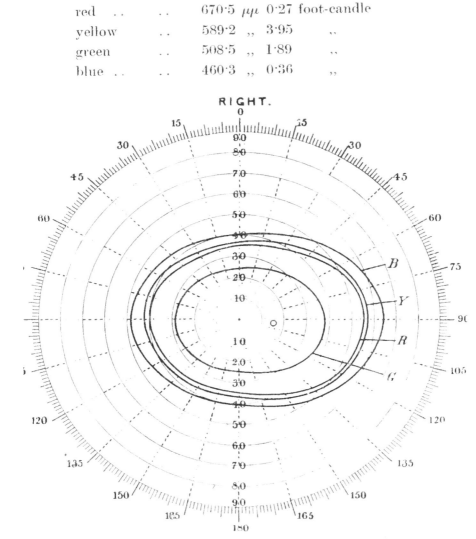

Fig. 28. The fields of vision for spectral colours with moderate illumination (D light = 3·95 foot-candles at the screen). (Abney.)

Fig. 29 shows the fields with

red ..	..	670·5 $\mu\mu$	
yellow	..	589·2 ,,	0·21 foot-candle
green	..	530 ,,	
blue ..	..	460·3 ,,	

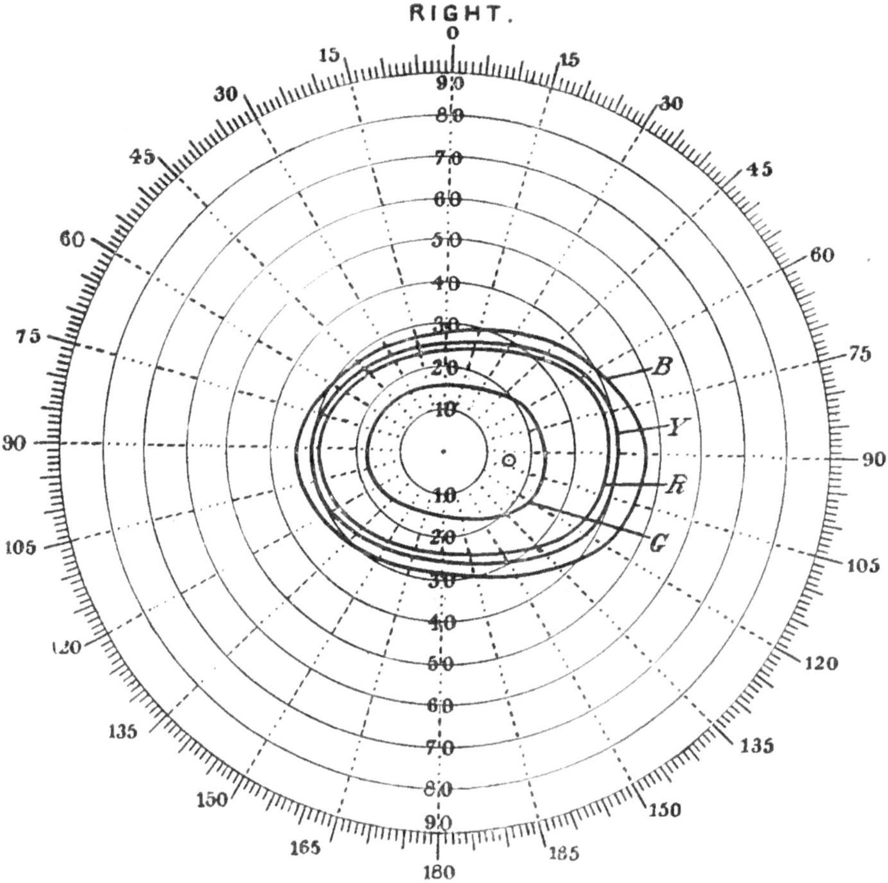

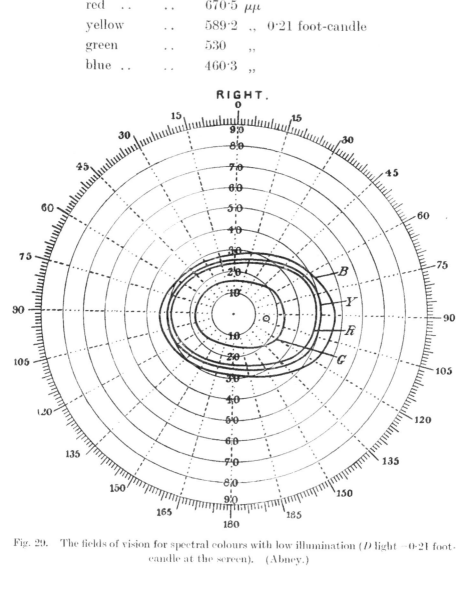

Fig. 29. The fields of vision for spectral colours with low illumination (D light = 0·21 foot-candle at the screen). (Abney.)

Fig. 30 shows the fields with complementary colours :

red	650·0 $\mu\mu$
green.. ..	500·2 ,,
yellow-green..	561·4 ,,
blue	460·3 ,,

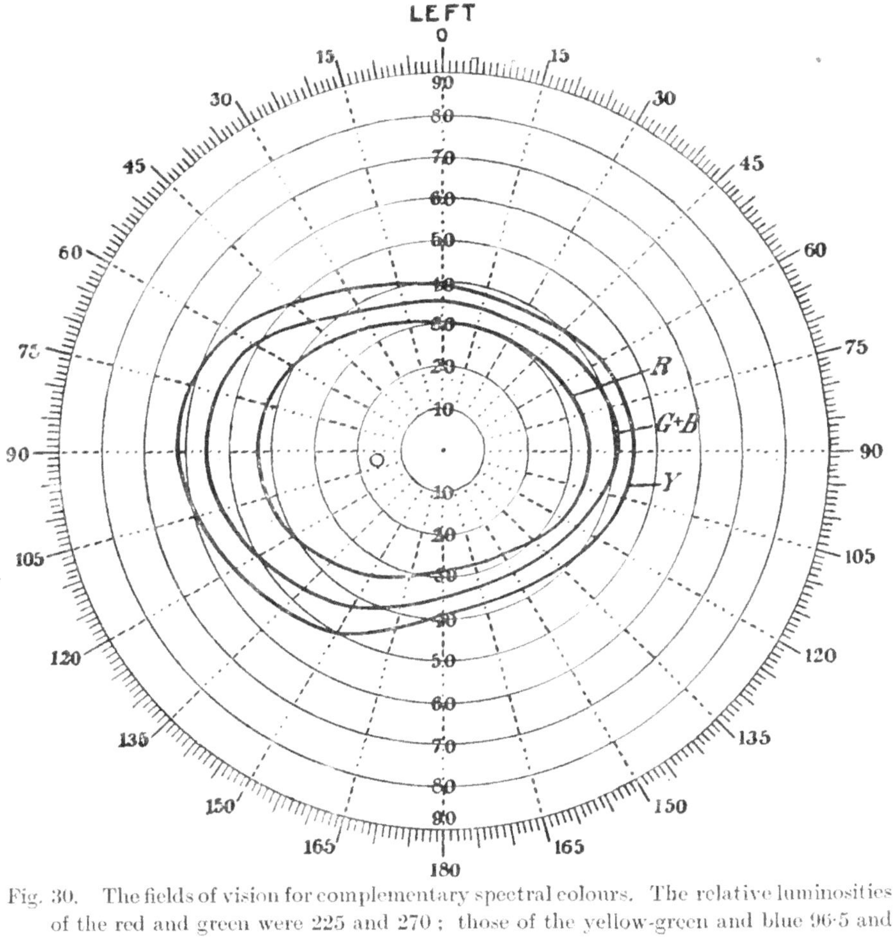

Fig. 30. The fields of vision for complementary spectral colours. The relative luminosities of the red and green were 225 and 270 ; those of the yellow-green and blue 96·5 and 21·5. (Abney.)

If a red and a green light are mixed to match the *D* light (589·2 $\mu\mu$) in hue and luminosity the *D* field is considerably larger than that of the mixture, as are also the fields of the red and green separately.

Colours of pigments do not give the same fields as the spectrum colours with which they approximately match, since they are impure colours (Abney[1]).

Fig. 31 gives the data for the fields for the whole range of the spectrum with three different intensities, the luminosities of the *D* line being 3·95, 0·99, and 0·45 foot-candle respectively. (In the first two the aperture was 0·525 inch at 1 ft., in the last 0·086 inch at 1 ft.) The abscissae are scale numbers (wave-lengths), the ordinates degrees of field.

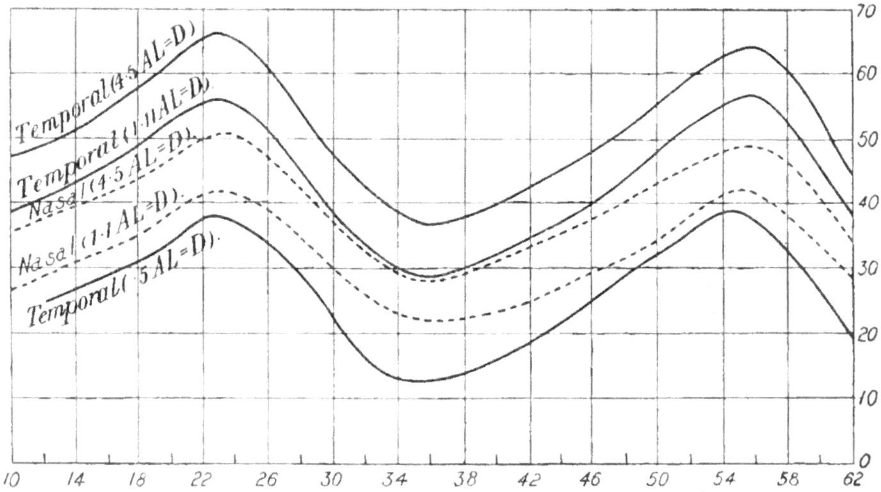

Fig. 31. The temporal and nasal limits of the fields of vision for spectral colours at three different intensities of illumination. (Abney.)

It will be seen that when the temporal field reads 40° the nasal reads 30°, and that as the field increases $7\frac{1}{2}$° on the temporal side it increases nearly 6° on the nasal, *irrespective of the particular colour.*

The curves for variations in intensity of the light are particularly interesting. They were taken in the horizontal directions only (Fig. 32).

The rays used were blue 430·3 $\mu\mu$, yellow 589·2 $\mu\mu$, red 670·5 $\mu\mu$, green *SSN* 41·7 (about 530 $\mu\mu$). Unit intensity was yellow = 3·95 foot-candles, red = 0·45 ft.-c., green = 2·8 ft.-c., blue = 0·27 ft.-c. The abscissae are intensities of light, the ordinates degrees of field.

[1] Abney, p. 203.

Since the curves are straight lines it follows that *as the intensity diminishes in geometrical progression the angle of field diminishes in arithmetical progression.*

The effect of the area of the retina stimulated upon the size of the field may be most conveniently considered here. Charpentier[1] found that for white the size was immaterial so long as it exceeded a diameter of about 0·17 mm. If it were smaller the field remained the same when the brightness was increased in inverse proportion to the size.

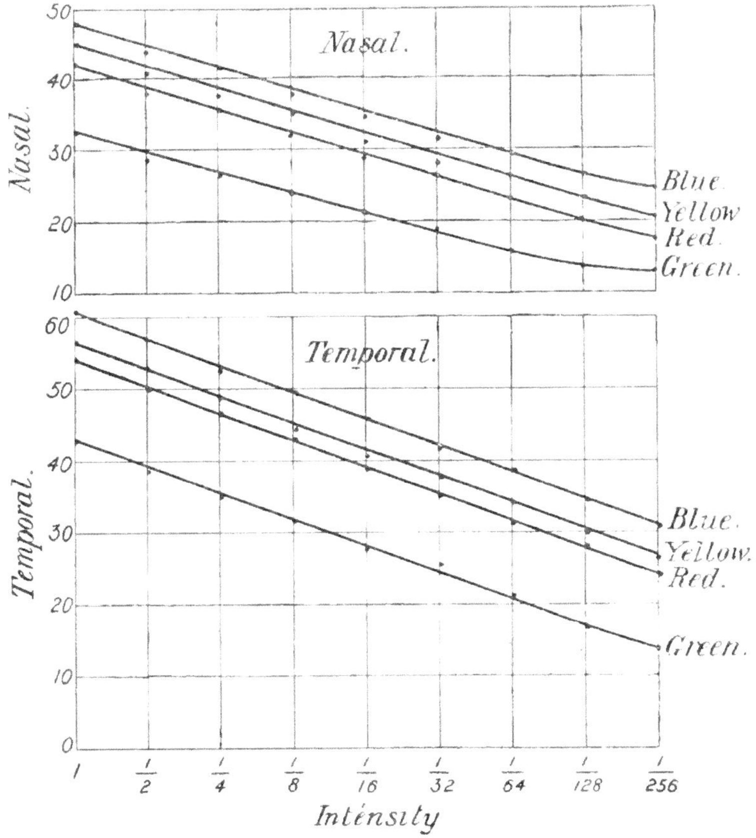

Fig. 32. The temporal and nasal limits of the fields of vision for four spectral colours at different intensities of illumination. (Abney.)

For colours Abney[2] found that between apertures subtending 4° 28′ and 10′ the fields decrease in extent in such a manner that for each diminution in aperture to half the diameter the diminution in field is 5° on the temporal and 4° on the nasal side.

[1] *Arch. d'Opht.* VII. 13, 1887

[2] Abney, p. 208.

This is the same ratio, 5 : 4, as for diminution of intensity of light by quarters (p. 79). *The diminution by each quarter of the area is thus equivalent to a quarter of the intensity of light. Any aperture subtending more than 5° will give the same field.*

Guillery[1] confirmed Hess's results by using the size of the area stimulated as a guide to the size of the colour fields. For each colour a gradual increase is necessary in passing towards the periphery. The increase for yellow and blue and for red and green agree respectively, but of course the red-green increase differs from the yellow-blue increase.

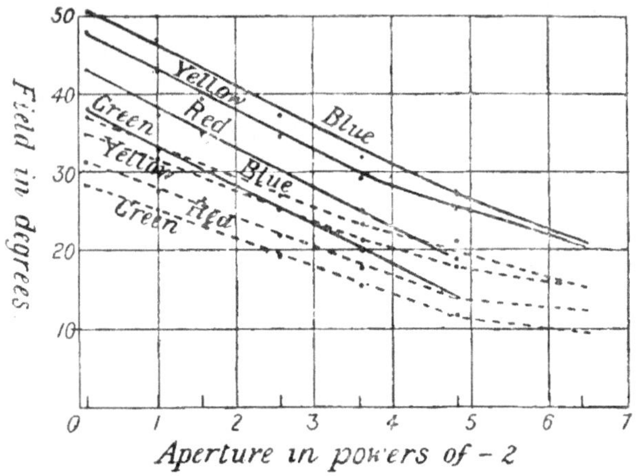

Fig. 33. The temporal (————) and nasal (- - - - - - - - -) limits of the fields of vision for four spectral colours for different areas of stimulation. (Abney.)

The general threshold of light at the periphery is difficult to measure. Abney used a small spot of luminous paint for fixation. At 10° from the fovea he found that the extinction of all light from red light takes place when the light is about one-third brighter than is required for the fovea. With white paraffin light it is somewhat less. With green light at about the *E* line and with blue at the Lithium line the necessary reduction of the light is greater than for the centre of the eye. The photochromatic interval is greater for the peripheral than for the central part of the retina.

[1] *Ztsch. f. Psychol. u. Physiol. d. Sinnesorg.* XII. 267, 1896

CHAPTER II

THE MACULA LUTEA AND FOVEA CENTRALIS

The Macula Lutea. The chief feature of macular vision is the unequal absorption of different rays by the pigment of the yellow spot. It has been necessary to refer to this disturbing feature at an earlier stage (pp. 40, 70).

The Fovea Centralis. The photopic luminosity curve for the fovea is shown in Fig. 11, and calculations show that it is about one-sixth more sensitive to the *D* light than the macula (Abney). To the green and blue it appears to be less sensitive, and König[1] even says it is blue-blind. This observation is certainly untrue and is probably due to the low scotopic luminosity value of the fovea combined with the absorption by the pigment which probably extends to this region.

We have already referred incidentally to many features in which foveal vision differs from paracentral and peripheral vision. With its exceedingly high sensibility for form we have little to do here, but it should be borne in mind. More important for the present purpose are its high photopic chromatic sensibility, and its very low scotopic sensibility.

It has already been mentioned that for white light achromatic scotopic sensibility is proportional to the area stimulated (p. 52; see also Section VI, Chap. I). For the fovea, in order to produce a luminous sensation, the total quantity of light, *i.e.*, the product of the area and the illumination, must attain a certain value, and this value is constant for a given condition of adaptation.

Since the colourless interval increases in dark adaptation owing to lowering of the general threshold, the chromatic threshold remaining almost or quite constant (*v.* p. 60), and since dark adaptation increases the foveal sensibility little or not at all, one might expect a very great diminution or even absence of the photochromatic interval at the fovea. Charpentier[2] demonstrated a photochromatic interval for colours at the fovea, and Koster[3] and Tschermak[4] confirmed the results, thus differing from A. E. Fick[5], Parinaud[6], and König and v. Kries. If it exists for

[1] König, p. 353. [2] *Arch. d'Opht.* XVI. 337, 1896; *La Lumière et les Couleurs*, p. 206.
[3] *Arch. f. Ophth.* XLI. 4, 13, 1895.
[4] *Arch. f. d. ges. Physiol.* LXX. 320, 1898. [5] *Ibid.* XLIII., 481, 1888.
[6] *Ann. d'ocul.* CXII. 228, 1894; *Arch. d'Opht.* XVI. 87, 1896.

the fovea it is much less than for the periphery. The point is one having a very practical bearing and some experiments made by Gotch[1] may be quoted.

"If the eye is fixed in the dark room on one small spot of light (A) and a second small coloured light (B) is flashed out at some little distance, then the sensation produced by A varies with the position and hue of B.

"If B is spectral green or blue, and is some degrees away from A (A being fixed by the visual gaze and thus in the centre of the field of vision), B gives rise to a sensation of rather dazzling white. This is especially the case when the light itself is of very small angular area. The sensation continues when B is moved nearer to A, and tends to mask any recognition of green or blue colour. In my own case such colour recognition may not occur with the Board of Trade light green light until this is focussed on the retina within $1\frac{1}{2}°$ to 2° from the centre when the dazzle disappears and the colour becomes quite plain.

"If B is red, then neither the colour nor the light itself is recognised when it is so situated as to be focussed on the retina over 8° or 10° outside A. In my own case with a dim Board of Trade light red, the limit of failure of colour recognition was a little under $6\frac{1}{2}°$. Beyond such recognition limiting distance there was no sensation of white dazzle, but a barely perceptible dull grey spot was sometimes seen instead of the red light. Further out this light became quite invisible. When brought as near as 6° it always showed as a distinct red spot, and continued so however close it was brought. There was no simultaneous white dazzle to mask the hue; thus the light, if visible was easily recognised.

"A number of experiments on individuals ascertained to possess normal colour vision support the view that, in the dark-adapted eye red light is recognised as red over an area whose radius is three or four times that observed with green light; yet the red light is not seen at all outside this larger area. On the other hand green (or blue) light, whilst it is only recognisable as green over the much more restricted central area, is seen as a bright light of a dazzling white type over a very extensive area.

"As illustrations of such visual phenomena in connection with what is termed 'dark adaptation perimetry,' I append a few experimental results obtained from ten different observers, all with normal colour vision.

[1] Report of Departmental Committee on Sight Tests, Appendix 3, 152, 1912.

Number of Observer	Angular Distances from Centre within which the Colour of a Spectral Light 30″ Diameter was recognised	
	Red Light (λ 6563)	Green Light (λ 5169)
1	Within 6° or 7°	Within 1½° or 2°
2	,, 7½° ,, 8½°	,, 1½° ,, 2½°
3	,, 9° ,, 10°	,, 2½° ,, 3½°
4	,, 6° ,, 7°	,, 2° ,, 2½°
5	,, 7° ,, 8°	,, 2° ,, 3°
6	,, 8° ,, 9°	,, 2° ,, 2½°
7	,, 8° ,, 9°	,, 2½° ,, 3°
8	,, 8½° ,, 9½°	,, 2½° ,, 3°
9	,, 6° ,, 7½°	,, 2° ,, 2½°
10	,, 8° ,, 9°	,, 2° ,, 2½°

"It may be added that with the red spot of light any recognition of light immediately beyond the sensitive limit given above was very doubtful or non-existent, although with practice a dull grey spot can be perceived for a short distance. On the other hand, with the green spot of light there was, from 3° outwards, most definite recognition of light over a very large area, the appearance being a white or bright dazzle. This was also present with blue light, but the hue was unrecognisable as regards both blue and green. Yellow light also gave the same bright dazzle; it was often blended with a reddish sensation if it lay from the centre about 3° or 4°.

"The recognition of small areas of red or green by the dark-adapted eye is, as regards colour, thus only possible when these are focussed near the fovea, *i.e.*, lie near or at the centre of the field of vision. This is particularly the case with the peripheral vision of green; presumably these rays, by exciting rods, evoke a sensation of white, which has a dazzling effect and masks the true colour. Such white dazzling sensation is still present, but to a less degree, as the green light approaches the centre of the field of vision, but it ceases when this light is 1° to 2° from the centre. According to v. Kries the explanation is the differential stimulation of both rods and cones, that of the rods giving rise to the dazzling white sensation in addition to the colour sensation produced by the stimulation of the cones."

Although the fovea is night-blind compared with the periphery it is capable of some degree of dark adaptation. It is necessary to have very strong preliminary light adaptation, as from looking at the clear sky, in order to demonstrate it (Nagel and Schäfer[1]). Tschermak[2] also obtained foveal dark adaptation and thought that it was slower

[1] *Ztsch. f. Psychol. u. Physiol. d. Sinnesorg.* XXXIV. 271, 1904.

[2] *Arch. f. d. ges. Physiol.* LXX. 297, 1898.

than peripheral, but he used too large test objects and thus exceeded the foveal limits (Nagel). More recently a slight increase in the foveal sensibility on dark adaptation has been proved by Wolfflin[1] and by Dittler and Koike[2]. In the experiments of the latter one eye only was dark-adapted and the luminosities of the binocular double images of the illuminated object were compared. The adaptation at the fovea is so slight that one would not expect to obtain Purkinje's phenomenon there under ordinary circumstances. The demonstration of its absence is beset with difficulties—accurate foveal fixation, comparison of brightness of very small areas, etc.—and opinions are therefore divided. Tschermak[3], Koster[4] and Sherman[5] are in favour of its presence, but their methods were less satisfactory than those of König[6], Lummer[7] and Nagel and v. Kries[8]. v. Kries and Nagel have proved fairly conclusively that Purkinje's phenomenon is absent over a central field not greater than 2°, *i.e.*, not exceeding the rod-free area. The longer the dark adaptation the better was the delimitation of the area. If a red and a blue spot are fixed with this area, the red being brighter than the blue, then on diminishing the intensity of the light the relative luminosity remains the same. On the slightest deviation of the eyes, however, the blue at once appears the brighter and less saturated. Hering[9] found that small fields of red and green, equally bright when fixed centrally, become of different brightness when fixed eccentrically ("Purkinje's phenomenon by change of position in the visual field without change of the intensity of the light"), and he also stated[10] that the deviations from Newton's law "become less marked the smaller the area of the retina stimulated, and are absent when the field is made sufficiently small."

[1] *Arch. f. Ophth.* LXXVI. 464, 1910.
[2] *Ztsch. f. Sinnesphysiol.* XLVI. 166, 1912.
[3] *Arch. f. d. ges. Physiol.* LXX. 297, 1898.
[4] *Arch. f. Ophth.* XLI. 4, 1, 1895.
[5] Wundt's *Philos. Stud.* XIII. 1898.
[6] König, p. 338.
[7] *Verhandl. d. Deutschen physik. Gesellschft.* VI. 2, 1904.
[8] *Ztsch. f. Psychol. u. Physiol. d. Sinnesorg.* XXIII. 167, 1900; v. Kries, *loc. cit.* IX. 81, 1896; *Arch. f. Ophth.* XLII. 3, 95, 1896; *Centralbl. f. Physiol.* 1896.
[9] *Arch. f. d. ges. Physiol.* LX. 533, 1895.
[10] *Ibid.* LIV. 277, 1893.

SECTION V

TEMPORAL EFFECTS

CHAPTER I

RECURRENT VISION; THE TALBOT-PLATEAU LAW; THE FLICKER PHENOMENON

We have already had evidence (p. 57) from stimulation of the dark-adapted retina by light of low intensity that two mechanisms are involved. One, which may be called the "scotopic mechanism," in the condition of maximum dark adaptation, responds to light of low intensity by a colourless light sensation, no matter what the nature of the light stimulus so long as it be an "adequate" stimulus (*v.* p. 19). The other, which may be called the "photopic mechanism," responds to light of higher intensity (which in itself induces a relatively high degree of light adaptation) by a light sensation of greater intensity and greater complexity, the sensation being that of white or colour according to the nature of the stimulus. It may at once be admitted that theoretical conceptions of definite mechanisms subserving these diverse though allied functions are here introduced. They will be allowed to intrude as little as possible in the description of the facts, but the comprehension of the description is facilitated by permitting their use.

The sensational response to a single short-lived stimulus is not a single, equally short-lived light sensation. Except in the case of a very feeble stimulus it is "a series of pulses of sensation of diminishing intensity rapidly succeeding one another[1]." Attention was early called to these recurring responses by C. A. Young in 1872[2]. He found that when a discharge from a powerful electric machine momentarily illuminates a room the objects may be seen, not once only, but two, three or four times in rapid succession, although the spark is single. He called

[1] McDougall, *Brit. Jl. of Psychology*, I. 78, 1904.

[2] *Nature*, V. 512, 1872; *Philos. Mag.* XLIII. 343; *Sill. Jl.* III. 262.

the phenomenon "recurrent vision," and the observation was confirmed by Shelford Bidwell[1]. An allied phenomenon was described by Purkinje[2], rediscovered by A. S. Davis[3], and is commonly called "Bidwell's ghost"; Hamaker[4] called it the "satellite", v. Kries "the following image." The ghost is seen in typical form when a light of moderate brightness is moved across a dark field of view at a moderate speed while the eye remains at rest, appearing as a second dimmer image following the primary image after a short interval, usually about $\frac{1}{5}$ sec., of darkness. The subject has been specially studied by Bosscha[5], Charpentier[6], Hess[7], v. Kries[8], Samojloff[9], Munk[10], Exner[11], and McDougall[12].

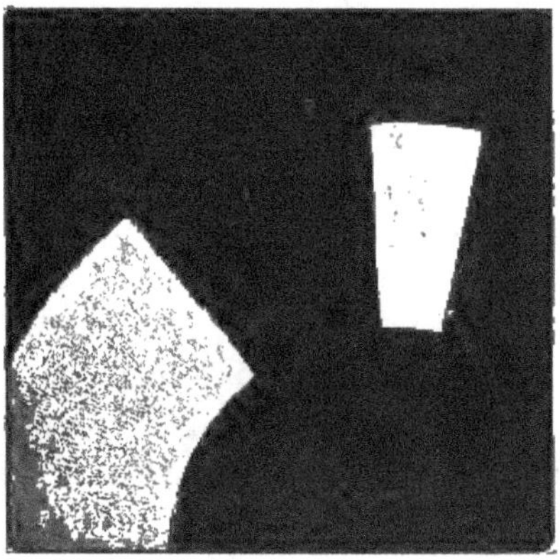

Fig. 34.

Fig. 35.

Fig. 34. Appearance of a radial slit 2° in width and 7 cm. in length, with its mid-point 15 cm. from the centre of the disc, rotating at the rate of one revolution per 3″ before a glass illuminated by four acetylene-gas jets. (McDougall.)

Fig. 35. Appearance with slightly increased speed of revolution—"Charpentier's bands." (McDougall.)

[1] *Proc. Roy. Soc. Lond.* LVI. 132, 1894; *Curiosities of Light and Sight*, London. 1899.

[2] *Beobachtungen zur Physiol. d. Sinne*, II. 110, 1825.

[3] *Lond. and Edin. Philosoph. Mag.* XLIV. 526, 1872.

[4] *Ztsch. f. Psychol. u. Physiol. d. Sinnesorg.* XXI. 1, 1899.

[5] *Arch. f. Ophth.* XL. 2, 22, 1894.

[6] *Arch. de Physiol.* IV. 541 1892; VI. 677, 1896.

[7] *Arch. f. d. ges. Physiol.* XLIX. 190, 1891; *Arch. f. Ophth.* XL. 2, 259, 1894; XLIV. 3, 445, 1897; LI. 2, 225, 1900; *Arch. f. d. ges. Physiol.* CI. 226, 1904; CVII. 290, 1905.

[8] *Ztsch. f. Psychol. u. Physiol. d. Sinnesorg.* XII. 81, 1896; *Arch. f. Ophth.* XLII. 3, 1896; *Ztsch. f. Psychol. u. Physiol. d. Sinnesorg.* XXV. 239, 1901; XXIX. 81, 1902; *Arch. f. d. ges. Physiol.* CIII. 167, 1904.

[9] *Ztsch. f. Psychol. u. Physiol. d. Sinnesorg.* XX. 118, 1899.

[10] *Ibid.* XXIII. 66, 1900.

[11] *Arch. f. d. ges. Physiol.* CIII. 1905.

[12] *Loc. cit.*

The Primary Image. With momentary stimulation by a stationary light McDougall found that a brief stimulus of low intensity provokes a single brief pulse of sensation, and that a stimulus of higher intensity provokes two, three, four or more pulses according to its intensity, and that the extrafoveal region, being more sensitive under dark adaptation than the fovea responds to a stimulus of any given low intensity with a rather longer series of pulses than is provoked by the same stimulus when applied to the fovea. If the stimulus is given by a radial slit in a rotating disc the image is spread out into a sector, varying in width according to the rapidity of rotation. This is due to the persistency of the sensation beyond the time of stimulation. The sector is not of uniform brightness, but is marked with alternate light and dark bands which vary in intensity and width according to speed of rotation and so on. These fan-like bands are commonly known as "Charpentier's bands[1]," though they had been previously described by Bidwell (1894).

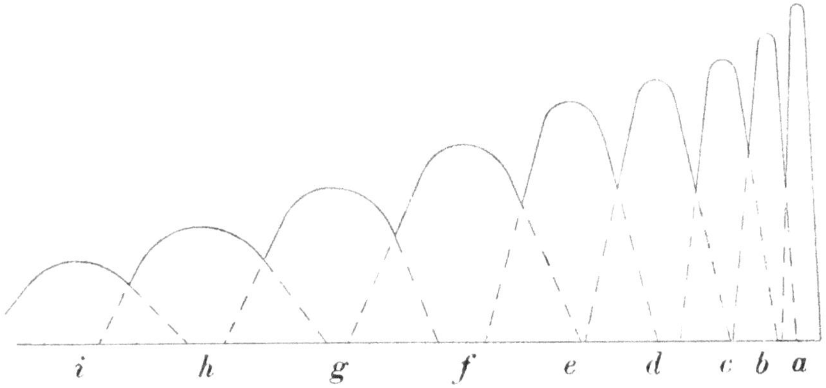

Fig. 36. Diagram illustrating the primary response to a single momentary stimulus. The series of pulses of sensation commences at *a* and lasts through a period of about ⅔ sec., represented by *a*—*i*. The height to which each curve rises represents the intensity of the pulse of sensation. The effects of a momentary stimulus of less intensity are represented by a part of the series of curves, *e.g.*, *e*—*i*. The overlapping of the curves represents the fact that the intervals between the pulses of sensation are not quite dark. (McDougall.)

The Secondary Image. The above is not the only response. In the case of momentary stimulation by a stationary light a secondary image of much less luminosity seems to appear at a great distance at the moment in which the pulsating image comes to an end, and rushing up towards the eye to stop suddenly, filling the position of the primary

[1] *Arch. de Physiol.* IV. 541, 1892; VIII. 677, 1896

image. The secondary image fades gradually and slowly. In the case of the travelling object the secondary image appears abruptly at a brief interval after the last bands of the primary image, and fills a part or the whole of the track of the image. If the object light is coloured and of high intensity the secondary image is in both cases tinged with the same colour; but if the object light is coloured and of low intensity the secondary image is grey in the case of blue and green light, but is absent in the case of pure red light. The secondary image is the ordinary positive after-image (*vide infra*).

The interval between the primary and the secondary images is not always completely dark. As the rate of movement of a travelling object light is increased dim grey bands appear in the interval. They are dimmer and broader than the leading bands and differ markedly in quality, the leading bands being yellowish-white, these others a neutral grey. The interval-bands show the following peculiarities: (1) they are brightest when the object light is green, absent when it is red; (2) they are absent where they cross the fovea, even with a green object light; (3) they have the neutral ghostly quality, inclining towards blue, characteristic of the scotopic spectrum; (4) they are absent when the eye is light-adapted.

It is probable therefore that the primary response is a response of the photopic mechanism, any response of the scotopic mechanism being obscured by the preponderant photopic effect. On the cessation of the photopic response the scotopic response becomes manifest under favourable circumstances. There is reason to believe that the latent period of the photopic reaction is shorter than that of the scotopic by about $\frac{1}{18}$ sec.

The secondary image is similarly complex. With an object light of low intensity it is a pure scotopic reaction, as shown by its grey quality and its absence with a pure red object light. With a brighter object light it is a combined photopic and scotopic reaction, the photopic preponderating with strong lights, as shown by the colour and saturation of the secondary image.

McDougall has further shown that the bright initial reactions which constitute the primary image exert an inhibitory effect upon the immediately succeeding reactions. *Bidwell's ghost* is the last of the series of pulses of sensation, the intermediate members being thus inhibited. In its typical form it is a pure scotopic reaction, but that it is not necessarily so is shown by the fact that it can be obtained by a pure red object light of high intensity and does not then jump the fovea.

I have hitherto followed McDougall's excellent paper. It will be readily appreciated that since the response differs in the number and character of the pulses of sensation according to the intensity and nature of the light stimulus, and since the stimulus acts upon two mechanisms of different intensity-response and different latent period, the nature of the phases of the response vary greatly according to the conditions of the experiment.

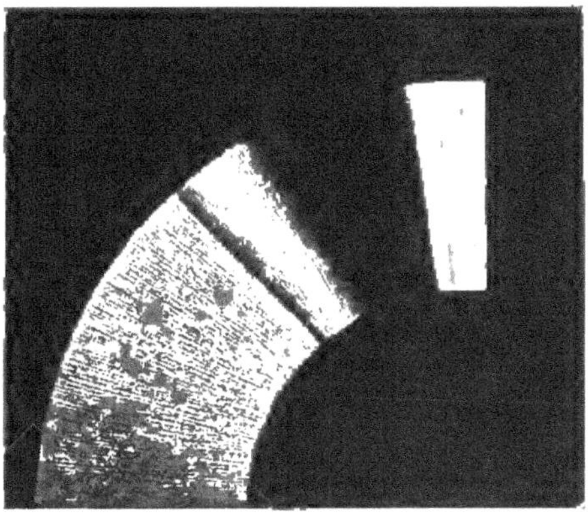

Fig. 37. Appearance of a narrow slit, 2° to 5° in width, in a large disc, rotating at one revolution per 3″, before a milk-glass illuminated with *one* acetylene-gas burner, as seen by the light-adapted eye which has been kept covered for about three minutes and then fixed upon any point in or near the path of the moving slit—"Bidwell's ghost." (McDougall.)

It is not surprising, then, that under appropriate conditions v. Kries found the following series of events: (1) a primary image; (2) a short dark interval; (3) a secondary image, complementary in colour to the primary (the satellite or ghost); (4) a second dark interval; (5) a tertiary image (Snellen, Bosscha), faintly tinged with the colour of the primary; (6) a third dark interval. The secondary image in this series follows the primary by $\frac{1}{4}$—$\frac{1}{6}$ sec. It is absent with foveal fixation. It increases in brightness and extent in the early stages of dark adaptation, but is absent after prolonged dark adaptation. It is also absent with red light and its brightness corresponds to the scotopic value of the exciting light (v. Kries). Much discussion has arisen around the colour of the secondary image. According to Charpentier it is violet with low, and colourless with high intensity. Hess describes it as faintly tinged with the same colour as the primary[1]. With regard to

[1] Cf. v. Kries, *Ztsch. f. Psychol. u. Physiol. d. Sinnesorg.* XII. 81, 1896; Hess, *Arch. f.*

the tertiary image its hue is best appreciated when red is chosen as the stimulus. With increasing dark adaptation the tertiary gains in brightness but loses in chromatic value. There is some difference of opinion as to whether the tertiary image can be seen at the fovea.

Hamaker described the secondary image as coloured with the complementary colour and lasting $\frac{1}{3}$ sec., the tertiary as homochromatic and lasting several seconds. Dark adaptation had little influence. The secondary image was the better seen for all colours; the tertiary better for red and yellow than green and blue. With stationary light he found the following phases: (1) the primary image; (2) a dark interval, often absent; (3) the secondary image; (4) a dark interval ($\frac{1}{2}$ sec.); (5) the tertiary image; (6) a dark interval, often absent; (7) with stimulus of 1 to 4 secs. a quaternary image, accompanied by shortening of the tertiary. The quaternary is a true negative after-image, of complementary colour and surrounded by a bright halo. With moving light he found the following phases: (1) the primary image (*e.g.*, 3°), passing into (2) a short homochromatic or white tail (6°); (3) a dark interval (10°—15°); (4) the complementary, coloured or colourless secondary image (satellite, 3°, absent with red light); (5) a dark interval (50°); (6) the tertiary, faintly coloured homochromatic image (about 360°). As regards the region of retina stimulated, with stationary light, red and green gave a very marked complementary secondary foveal image, which was absent for yellow and blue; the tertiary image was absent with foveal stimulation. With moving light the fovea gave no secondary and apparently also no tertiary image.

The "action-time" of a light stimulus (McDougall), *i.e.*, the least time during which a light of given intensity must act upon the retina in order to excite the most intense sensation it is capable of exciting, has been studied by Swan[1], Exner[2], Kunkel[3], Charpentier[4], Martius[5], and McDougall[6]. It is a necessary preliminary to the proper understanding of flicker phenomena.

It may be accepted that the sensation curve rises rapidly to a maximum and falls gradually. The rapidity of the rise varies with

Ophth. XLIV. 3, 445, 1897; Samojloff, *Ztsch. f. Psychol. u. Physiol. d. Sinnesorg.* XX. 118, 1899; Hamaker, *loc. cit.* XXI. 1, 1899; P. Müller, *Arch. f. d. ges. Psychol.* XIV. 358, 1909; Kinoshita, *Ztsch. f. Sinnesphysiol.* XLIII. 420, 434, 1909; Hering, *Arch. f. d. ges. Physiol.* CXXVI. 604, 1909; Dittler and Eisenmeier, *ibid.* CXXVI. 610, 1909.

[1] *Trans. R. S. Edin.* II. 230, 1849; XXII. 33, 1861.

[2] *Sitz. d. Wiener Akad.* LVIII. 2, 601, 1868.

[3] *Arch. f. d. ges. Physiol.* IX. 197, 1874.

[4] *C. r. soc. de biol.* IV. 1887.

[5] *Beitr. z. Psychol. u. Philos.* I. 2, 1902.

[6] *Brit. Jl. of Psychol.* I. 151, 1904.

the intensity of the stimulus, and the rate of diminution of the action-time with increase of intensity of the light diminishes as the intensity increases, so that with light of ordinary, fairly high, intensity it is very small. It has been pointed out above that when the duration of stimulation is very short the response is a series of pulses of sensation. If the stimulus be other than very brief the sensation shows no such pulses. McDougall has shown that with a light whose action-time is 61^{σ} ($\frac{61}{1000}$ sec.) the multiple character of the response persists until the duration of its action exceeds its action-time by about 16^{σ}, and ceases altogether when the duration of the action of the light exceeds its action-time by about 40^{σ}. As regards the variation of the intensity of the sensation with the duration of the stimulus when that duration is less than the action-time McDougall concludes that it follows the "photographic law," *i.e.*, for such duration *the intensity of the sensation varies directly with the duration of the action of the light.* In mathematical terms the law may be stated thus: $S \propto I \,.\, \delta t$, where S is the intensity of the sensation, I the intensity of the stimulus, and δt a small increment of time. This law is a corollary of the Talbot-Plateau law (*vide infra*), and was assumed by Talbot. With very dim lights of scotopic value the action-time is probably slightly greater than 200^{σ} or $\frac{1}{5}$ sec. The practical conclusion—that the dimmest light visible to the peripheral retina of the dark-adapted eye, *i.e.*, the dimmest light perceptible under the most favourable conditions, must be allowed to act for a period of not less than 200^{σ} or $\frac{1}{5}$ sec. in order to be perceptible—is of great importance in the construction of lighthouse flash-lights and so on. Its practical importance is increased, as well as the theoretical significance, by McDougall's observations which show that the action-times of red, green and blue lights are the same for lights of equal intensities, *i.e.*, intensities which excite sensations of equal luminosities.

Brückner and Kirsch[1] have investigated the chromatic action-time or the minimum time during which a coloured light must stimulate the retina in order that the colour may be discriminated (*Farbenzeitschwelle* or *specifische Zeitschwelle*). They found that the time varies with the intensity of the white light acting upon the retina both before and after stimulation with the coloured light and is nearly proportional to the brightness of this "grey" sensation. The chromatic action-time follows Weber's law, at any rate within certain limits. It varies inversely as the width of the pupil and the size of the retinal area stimulated, but not proportionally. The intensity of the following

[1] *Ztsch. f. Sinnesphysiol.* XLVI. 229, 1911.

white stimulation appears to have a greater effect than that of the preceding white stimulation, though the authors can give no explanation of the fact. If a colour stimulation follows instead of white, the effect on the action-time depends largely upon the similarity or dissimilarity between this light and that which is being tested.

THE TALBOT-PLATEAU LAW.

When periodic excitations follow each other with sufficient rapidity the resulting sensation is one of continuous light of uniform brightness. Talbot[1] and Plateau[2] investigated the relationship of the brightness of the individual periodic stimuli and of the resultant sensation. Their conclusions are usually known as the *Talbot-Plateau Law*, which states that *the resultant impression is the mean of the periodic impressions*, *i.e.*, the resultant brightness is that which would have arisen if the amount of light intermittently reaching the retina had been uniformly distributed over the whole period of stimulation. v. Helmholtz confirmed the law for ordinary physical intensities of light. Fick[3] found some deviations, low intensities giving a continuous sensation brighter than the intermittent. O. Grünbaum[4] also found deviations for high intensities, the intermittent light being brighter than the continuous.

The accuracy or otherwise of the Talbot-Plateau Law is of considerable importance in the investigation of colour vision, for the principle of the episcotister depends upon its accuracy. Abney finds that the adjustable sectors, *i.e.*, those which can be altered during rotation, are only available for accurate measurement when the angles of aperture lie between 180° and 10°, chiefly owing to the errors in reading being proportional to the angles of aperture. With fixed sectors angles of 2° or even 1° can be used. It is not certain, however, that the method is reliable for very low intensities of light, and for these the annulus (*v.* p. 5) is to be preferred. The experiments of Abney, Lummer and Brodhun[5], Hyde[6] and others show that the law applies accurately over a wide range of physical intensities. Hyde's experiments were very carefully conducted, the probable errors of measurement being under 0·1 per cent. The average deviation of the observations for any given angular aperture of the sectors was in no case as large as 0·2 per cent.

[1] *Lond., Edin. and Dublin Phil. Mag.* v. 327, 1834.

[2] *Ann. d. Phys. u. Chem.* XXXV. 457, 1835.

[3] *Arch. f. Anat. Physiol. u. wiss. Med.* 754, 1863.

[4] *J. of Physiol.* XXII. 433, 1898.

[5] *Ztsch. f. Instrumentenkunde*, XVI. 299 1896.

[6] *Bull. of the Bureau of Standards*, Washington, II. 1, 1906.

It has been seen that McDougall arrived at the conclusion that the relationship $S \propto I . \delta t$ is *probably* correct. Viewed from the purely physical standpoint this relationship and hence the Talbot-Plateau law are such as might be anticipated[1]. From the physiological standpoint one might rather have anticipated that the resultant sensation from intermittent stimuli would follow the analogy of muscle tetanus, *i.e.*, that the application of new stimuli in the course of the curve of sensation produced by the primary stimulus would suffice to prolong the sensation curve at or near the maximum of the primary curve. It appears therefore that the superposition of fresh stimuli during the progress of the sensation curve of the primary stimulus produces positive or inhibitory effects of such a nature that the resultant sensation curve shows rapid oscillations about a mean sensation intensity. If the oscillations are sufficiently rapid a continuous mean sensation results, in accordance with the Talbot-Plateau law. If the oscillations are less rapid the sensation of flicker is felt. The analogy to muscle tetanus is therefore not one to be pressed, but physiologists will have no difficulty in finding analogies in the domain of neurology to the inhibitory effect of superposed stimuli. One may direct attention particularly to Sherrington's work[2].

THE FLICKER PHENOMENON.

If the oscillations produced by intermittent stimulation are not sufficiently rapid to cause complete fusion, a sensation of flickering is felt. If black and white sectors are rotated with gradually increasing velocity there is first separate vision of the individual sectors. This is followed by a peculiarly unpleasant coarse flickering, which passes into a fine tremulous appearance, after which complete fusion occurs. Careful observation reveals further interesting, though complicating details. At a certain stage there is a peculiar glittering, the brightness being greater than that of the continuous sensation after complete fusion. Brücke[3] found the maximum with 17·6 stimuli per second. It may be explained by an absence of those inhibitory effects referred to above, or by reinforcement of each white stimulus by the recurrent image of the preceding sector (Brücke), or by temporal induction (*vide infra*), or by a combination of such causes. v. Helmholtz noticed that at one

[1] Cf. v. Kries, in Nagel's *Handb. d. Physiol. d. Menschen*, p. 231.

[2] *The Integrative Action of the Nervous System*, London, 1906; cf. also McDougall, *Brain*, XXVI. 153. 1903.

[3] *Sitz. d. k. Akad. d. Wissensch.*, Wien, XLIX. 2. 128, 1864.

stage the forward edge of the white sectors appears reddish, the backward edge bluish. Fechner[1], by a suitable arrangement of black and white sectors obtained a pattern of yellow and blue. Subsequent observers have succeeded in eliciting all gradations of colour. This phenomenon is most easily seen in Benham's top[2]. It is probable that successive induction (Section V, Chap. II) plays a prominent part in these phenomena, and they are clearly of great importance in the theory of colour vision. Exner[3], Burch[4] and others have made important observations on this subject, using coloured lights.

More important for our present purpose is the relationship between flicker and the conditions of stimulation—intensity and nature of stimulus, rapidity of stimulation, adaptation of the retina, and region and area of the retina stimulated. Various methods of producing intermittent stimulation other than by the usual rotating pigment-coloured discs, have been devised by Rood[5], Whitman[6], v. Kries[7], Simmance and Abady[8], Kruss[9], Wild[10], Ives[11], and Watson[12], and the subject has been investigated not only by them but by others, notably by Ferry[13], Sherrington[14], Haycraft[15], O. Grünbaum[16], Polimanti[17], T. C. Porter[18], Allen[19], Kennelly and Whiting[20], Dow[21], Tufts[22], Millar[23], and Morris Airey[24].

As regards the intensity of the stimulus, more rapid stimulation is required for complete fusion with increased intensity. Up to a certain point with alternate darkness and light as the intensity is

[1] *Ann. d. Phys. u. Chem.* XLV. 227, 1838.

[2] Bidwell, *Proc. Roy. Soc.* LX. 368, 1896; LXI. 268, 1897; Percival, *Trans. Ophth. Soc.* XXIX. 119, 1909.

[3] *Arch. f. d. ges. Physiol.* I. 375, 1868.

[4] *J. of Physiol.* XXI. 431, 1897.

[5] *Amer. J. of Sc.* (3) XLVI. 173, 1893; (4) VIII. 194, 1899; *Science*, VII. 757; VIII. 11, 1898.

[6] *Phys. Rev.* III. 241, 1895.

[7] In Polimanti, *Ztsch. f. Psychol. u. Physiol. d. Sinnesorg.* XIX. 263, 1899.

[8] *Proc. Phys. Soc.* XIX. 39.

[9] *Phys. Zeitung*, III. 65; *Jl. f. Gas u. Wass.* XLVII. 129, 1904.

[10] *London Electrician*, 1909; *The Illuminating Engineer*, I. 825, 1908.

[11] *Philos. Mag.* 1912.

[12] In Abney, p. 107.

[13] *Amer. J. of Sc.* (3) XLIV. 193, 1892.

[14] *J. of Physiol.* XXI. 33, 1897.

[15] *Ibid.* XXI. 126, 1897.

[16] *Ibid.* XXII. 433, 1898.

[17] *Loc. cit.*

[18] *Proc. Roy. Soc. Lond.* LXIII. 347, 1898; LXX. 313, 1902.

[19] *Phys. Rev.* XI. 257, 1900; XV. 1902; XXVIII. 45, 1908.

[20] *The Illuminating Engineer*, New York, II. 347, 1907.

[21] *Proc. Phys. Soc.* XX. 644, 1907; XXII. 58, 1910; *Philos. Mag.* 120, 1906; 58, 1910; *The Electrician*, LVIII, 609, 1907.

[22] *Phys. Rev.* XXV. 433, 1907.

[23] *The Illuminating Engineer*, New York, IV. 769, 1909.

[24] *J. Inst. Elec. Engs.* XLIV. 177, 1910.

increased in geometrical proportion the rapidity of stimulation increases in arithmetical proportion. Grünbaum found that with high intensities the law fails, just as he found the Talbot-Plateau law to fail. If light alternates with less light the point of fusion is lowered by the diminution of the differences of intensity.

Filehne[1], Schenck[2] and others found that with rotating discs the number of sectors influences the result. The more numerous the sectors the greater the number of rotations necessary per second for fusion. The difference is less marked when the disc is viewed through a slit (Schenck)[3]. Grünbaum worked out the relations and found the explanation in successive contrast (*vide infra*). Sherrington with coloured discs found the results markedly affected by simultaneous contrast (*vide infra*). We may therefore conclude that "the point of fusion of intermittent stimuli, so as to produce a continuous sensation, depends, not on the physical intensities of the stimuli, but on their *physiological* intensities, as determined by the condition and nature of the stimulated retina" (Rivers)[4].

This fact is further borne out by the areal and regional differences. Exner[5] found that the duration of the sensory process decreased in arithmetical proportion as the size of the retinal image increased in geometrical proportion; and Charpentier[6] similarly found that increase in the size of the area of retina stimulated raised the point of fusion. Exner found that the fusion frequency was less for the fovea than for a region 1·33 mm. outside it, and all agree that flicker persists longer in the peripheral than in the central areas of the retina. Bellarminoff[7] found differences between the nasal and temporal areas.

T. C. Porter's researches have increased the knowledge of flicker phenomenon materially. Using black and white sectors illuminated by pure spectral lights from the interference spectrum of lime-light, he found that the speed at which flicker was abolished for yellow was nearly double that for violet; green and the last distinctly visible red occupying the mid-position. Having regard to the increase in speed with increasing intensity of the light, he concluded that as the retinal stimulus increases in intensity the sensation produced retains its maximum for a shorter and shorter time. With constant illumination, altering the relative sizes of the white and black sectors, he found

[1] *Arch. f. Ophth.* XXI. 2, 20, 1885. [2] *Arch. f. d. ges. Physiol.* CXII. 1, 1906.
[3] *Ibid.* LXIV. 165, 1896. [4] In Schäfer's *Text Book of Physiology*, II. 1072, 1900.
[5] *Sitz. d. k. Akad. d. Wissensch.* Wien, LVIII. 2, 601, 1868.
[6] *Arch. d'Opht.* X. 340, 1890. [7] *Arch. f. Ophth.* XXXV. 1, 25, 1889.

that at the point of fusion the effective stimulus at any point of the retina is to the maximum stimulus as the angle of the bright sector to 360°. The fact that the colour stimulus requires a finite time to produce its maximum effect was confirmed by this method. The period during which the sensation remains undiminished appears to decrease as the time of stimulation increases, though within narrow limits of variation one of these quantities is nearly inversely proportional to the other. He found that the relation between the intensity of illumination (I) and the number of revolutions (n) per minute at which a disc half white and half black must be run in order that the flicker may just disappear, the distance of the eye remaining constant, is

$$n = k \,.\, \log I + k'$$

k and k' being constants. He therefore proved the geometrical-arithmetical relationship between intensity and rapidity of stimulation. The relation was found rigidly true for illuminations from 0·25 metre candle to 12,800 times this value. For intensities below 0·25 metre candle the constant k suddenly changed its value to practically half its former value. We have here further evidence of the duplex mechanism involved, the higher value of k applying to the photopic, the lower to the scotopic mechanism. T. C. Porter also proved that *the duration of the undiminished sensation produced by different spectral hues depends solely on the luminosity of the colours and not on their wave frequency.*

Ives's researches have elicited several highly important results and are specially valuable owing to the great care taken to secure accuracy in his methods. The flicker method can be applied in two ways. In one, that used by Haycraft, Ferry and Allen, the critical frequency of alternation of the lights is measured, *i.e.*, two lights are regarded as being of the same luminosity when the flicker produced by rapid alternation of each with black disappears at the same speed of alternation. The other method is that employed by T. C. Porter and generally used in flicker photometry. By it two lights are regarded as being of the same brightness when no flicker results on alternating one with the other, the speed of alternation being such that the slightest change of intensity of either light causes flicker. Ives found that the second or ordinary method is more sensitive than the equality of brightness method used by Abney and others (*v.* p. 44). The results are reproduced with much greater constancy, since in the latter method psychological factors influence the judgment in arriving at the results. On decreasing the illumination the maximum shifts towards the blue (Purkinje's phenomenon) by the equality of brightness method; by the flicker method it shifts towards the red. On the other hand, decrease of the area stimulated at low intensities shifts the maximum of luminosity towards the red by the equality of brightness method, towards the blue by the flicker method. Ives found the relative positions of the two kinds of spectral luminosity curves generally different. They differ most in position at low illuminations with large areas; least at high illuminations with small areas. The mean curves of several observers show close agreement in the position of the maxima and the shape of the two curves at high intensities, but the areas of the curves are not equal. At low illuminations all observers agree in showing the Purkinje and the reversed Purkinje effects.

Haycraft, by the critical frequency method, obtained a pronounced Purkinje shift at low intensities. Ives obtained the reverse effect, except at very low intensities (0·5 metre-candle), when he confirmed Haycraft's result. Ives sought an explanation in Porter's change in the logarithmic rates at which critical frequency varies with the illumination. In Porter's equation

$$n = k \, . \log I + k'$$

k has a different value above and below 0·25 metre-candle. If the critical frequencies are plotted against the logarithms of the illumination for white light two straight lines of different slope, which meet at about 0·25 metre-candle, are obtained. The reversed Purkinje effect occurs above, the true Purkinje effect below this point.

When separate colours are investigated and plotted in the same manner, a set of straight lines of differing slope results. The most remarkable curves are those for red (650 $\mu\mu$) and blue (480 $\mu\mu$). The former maintains its direction unchanged; the latter suddenly changes from a diagonal to a horizontal, *i.e.*, the critical frequency becomes a constant, independent of the (low) illumination. The curves for other colours take an intermediate course. Hence Porter's law for white light holds good for different colours if the values of the constants are changed.

$$F = K_\lambda \, . \log S_\lambda + K_\lambda',$$

where F is the critical frequency, S_λ is the slit-width, K_λ is a constant involving the relationship between critical frequency and intensity of radiation for the individual eye for the colour in question and for the size of the area stimulated, and K_λ' is a constant involving the quantity of energy emitted by the source, the dispersion, etc. of the instrument, and the sensibility of the observer's eye to flicker for different colours at a given speed. The Purkinje effect, and its reversal above 0·25 metre-candle, follow at once from these facts.

In the flicker phenomenon with colours two causes of flicker are at work, the colour element and the luminosity element[1]. Of these colour-flicker ceases first. Hence the total flicker effect may be the resultant of the two flicker sensations. Ives has shown that the flicker photometer is largely influenced by the critical frequency phenomenon, but that it does not obey the simple law which would follow were it a mere dovetailing of two pure flickers.

Allen and others[2] found that the peripheral retina is more sensitive than the fovea to flicker, as might be expected from its high sensitiveness to movements. Ives, however, found that this result is only true for momentary observation. Adaptation or fatigue sets in very rapidly and then the periphery becomes less sensitive. The fovea is more sensitive to red flicker, the periphery to blue, and this difference is more striking at low intensities (Dow, Ives).

If the comparison light is coloured or the stimulating area is surrounded by white instead of black the equality of brightness method produces irregular and unsystematic shifts and distortions of the spectral luminosity curves, possibly owing to the increase in distracting psychological factors. Such changes produce no alteration in the luminosity curves by the flicker method. A curve almost identical with the flicker curve can be obtained by the equality of brightness method if it is built up of small steps of slight hue-difference and with small areas. By this so-called "cascade" method the differences in hue are made so small that they do not disturb the judgment of brightness.

When the areas of the luminosity curves by different methods are compared it is found that the visual acuity method (*v.* p. 44) gives a curve many (about five) times as great as the equality of brightness, the flicker and the critical frequency curves, which agree much more nearly. The enormous area of the visual acuity curve is due to the chromatic aberration of the eye. It has been shown by Bell[3] and Luckiesh[4] that the resolving power of the eye is much greater for monochromatic than for complex light of the same hue. For a method of measurement to be accurate it should conform to two axioms: things equal to the same thing are equal to one another; and the whole is

[1] Cf. Liebermann, *Ztsch. f. Sinnesphysiol.* XLV. 117, 1911.

[2] Cf. Lohmann, *Arch. f. Ophth.* LXVIII. 395, 1908.

[3] *Elec. World*, LVII. 1163, 1911.

[4] *Ibid.* LVIII. 450, 1911.

equal to the sum of its parts. Most physical measurements conform to these axioms, but it cannot be assumed that the same agreement holds good for measurements involving qualitative differences, such as those of colour. The reliability of a method of heterochromatic photometry must be judged according to the following criteria. First, the shape of the luminosity curve must not be altered by change in the reference standard. Second, the sum of the measurements of the brightness of the parts of the spectrum must be equal to the brightness of the recombined spectrum.

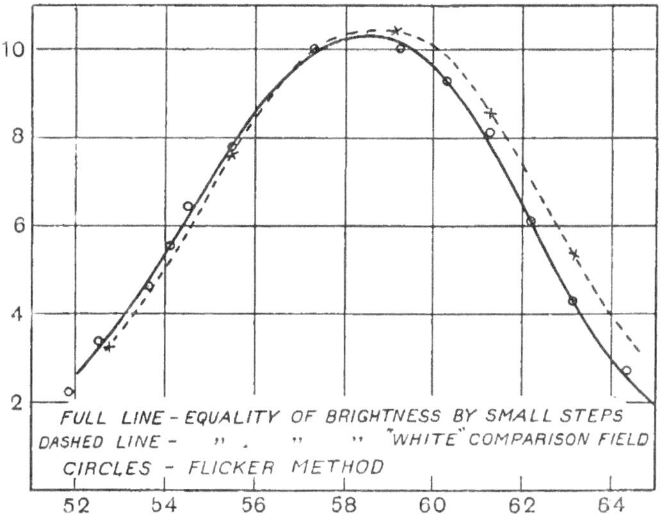

Fig. 38. Photopic luminosity curves taken by the flicker and equality of brightness methods. Abscissae, wave-lengths from 520 $\mu\mu$ to 640 $\mu\mu$; ordinates, arbitrary scale. (Ives.)

So far as the position of maxima and the general form of the curves are concerned all the methods agree fairly well. Comparison of the different methods shows that the areas of their curves differ most for the visual acuity method as compared with the other three. These latter do not agree well. Of them, the equality of brightness method gives greatest variations, the critical frequency method smaller, and the flicker method least. The crucial test has been applied to the flicker method by Whitman[1], Tufts[2] and Ives. Of these the last named is by far the most accurate. The method consists essentially in measuring the luminosities of the parts of the spectrum against a standard which

[1] *Phys. Rev.* III. 241, 1896.

[2] *Ibid.* XXV. 433, 1907.

is identical with the source of light of the spectrum. Ives obtained a remarkable confirmation of the accuracy of the flicker method, and arrived at the conclusion that it surpasses all other photometric methods in sensitiveness and accuracy.

Finally, Ives measured the luminosity curves of eighteen observers with normal colour vision at 25 metre-candles illumination of a magnesium oxide surface. The average curve deduced from these experiments is shown in Fig. 39 and is compared with König's curve as reduced by Nutting[1] and with Thürmel's curve[2].

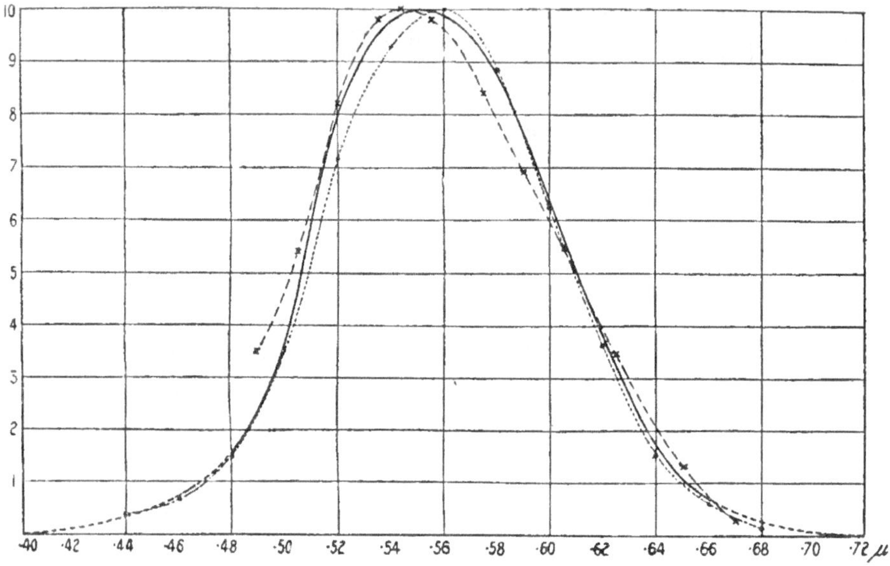

Fig. 39. ———————. Average photopic luminosity curve of 18 observers.
— — — — —. König's photopic luminosity curve (equality of brightness method).
.... Thürmel's photopic luminosity curve (flicker method). (Ives.)

In conclusion it may be stated that in the case of colours it is generally agreed that the fusion frequency depends solely on the luminosities of the alternating fields, and the coincidence of the equality of brightness curve with the flicker luminosity curve (Figs. 38, 39) bears out the assumption. We may at any rate assume with confidence that both the methods measure the "something" (p. 44) which we call brightness or luminosity.

[1] *Bull. of the Bureau of Standards*, VII. 2, 235.
[2] *Ann. d. Physik.* XXXIII. 1154, 1910.

CHAPTER II

SUCCESSIVE INDUCTION OR AFTER-IMAGES

After the stimulation of an area of the retina with light, the withdrawal of the stimulus does not result in the obliteration of all visual sensation. The succeeding sensations vary according to the nature and intensity of the primary stimulus, the condition of adaptation of the retina, the region of the retina stimulated, etc. If a second stimulus is applied to the same area of the retina during the course of the after-effects of the primary stimulus the resulting sensation is modified by these after-effects. The effect produced by the secondary stimulus can be measured by comparing it with that obtained from a retinal area not previously exposed to the primary stimulus. The stimulus applied to such a resting area is called the comparison light[1].

The sensations obtained from the persistence of the physiological processes set up by a primary stimulus, whether altered by the effects of succeeding stimuli, or unadulterated, *i.e.*, observed under the condition of complete exclusion of fresh stimuli, are commonly called "after-images." After looking for from 20 to 40 seconds at a white spot of light and then directing the gaze upon a white surface a black spot surrounded by a bright halo is seen. This is the "negative after-image." If the spot or light is coloured the after-image is seen to be tinged with the complementary colour. This is the "complementary after-image."

If care be exercised a different phenomenon will be observed. Direct the eyes towards a bright spot or light, but keep them carefully covered with the hand for a minute or so. Remove the hand rapidly but without any sudden or violent action and quickly replace it, so that the object is momentarily seen. If the experiment is properly carried out the spot will be seen as a persistent after-image in its original brightness and detail. This is the "positive after-image." If the object is coloured it is seen tinged with the same colour; this is the "homochromatic after-image."

Although in ordinary circumstances negative after-images are more easily obtained than positive McDougall[2] has shown that under suitable

[1] In Germany the effect of the primary stimulus is called "tuning" the retina (Hering). The primary stimulus is called the "retuning light" (*das umstimmende Licht*); the secondary stimulus the "reacting light" (*das reagirende Licht*).

[2] *Mind*, x. N.S. 74 sqq., 1901.

conditions the reverse is the case. If the primary stimulus is an area of white light which is sharply defined and surrounded by a dark background the negative after-image, bordered by a halo as described, is observed. If however the transition from the illuminated area to the background is made gradual a positive after-image is almost invariably obtained. McDougall used a ground glass disc, 12 cm. in diameter, illuminated from behind. On the far side about a dozen sheets of white paper were pasted, each with a circular hole in it concentric with the edge of the disc. Of these holes the smallest was 2 cm. in diameter, and each of the others was about 1 cm. larger in diameter than the preceding one. Such a "shaded disc," when illuminated, showed a central evenly lighted circle, 2 cm. in diameter, surrounded by a zone, 5 cm. in breadth, in which the brightness diminished regularly to the periphery, where it became negligible. The shaded disc gives with white light a positive after-image without any halo. On the other hand with colours, though the after-image is often homochromatic in the first one or two seconds, with most intensities of light it is approximately complementary through almost the whole of its course. In the case of red and green especially it is very constantly the rule that red predominates in the after-image of green, and *vice versa*. Sufficient attention does not appear to have been paid hitherto to this fundamental difference between the relation of black to white and that of green to red and blue to yellow in such after-images from "shaded" lights.

Though positive and negative after-images are opposed there is no discontinuity between them. If the positive after-image is developed and the eyes are then uncovered and directed towards a uniform moderately illuminated field the negative after-image at once appears. If the illumination of the field is suitably chosen no after-image is seen. The nature of the after-image depends therefore upon the nature and intensity of the primary stimulus and upon the nature and intensity of the secondary stimulus. Great diversity of after-images may therefore be obtained. The after-image of a white spot may be coloured[1]; that of a coloured spot may not be accurately the complementary of the primary stimulus. Anomalous colouration may be due to light passing through the sclerotic and the iris, or to abnormal conditions of the retina (Hilbert[2]). Moreover, Burch[3] has brought

[1] Aristotle; Goethe, *Farbenlehre* (1810), Eastlake's trans. p. 16, 1840.

[2] *Ztsch. f. Psychol. u. Physiol. d. Sinnesorg.* IV. 74, 1893.

[3] *Proc. Roy. Soc. Lond.* B. LXXVI. 212, 1905.

forward evidence to show that the after-effects of a primary stimulus are much more prolonged than has been generally recognised, and these later after-effects may materially alter the character of the after-image. So complex indeed are the effects that the greatest care should be exercised in making theoretical deductions from after-images.

With primary stimuli of considerable intensity a very short exposure is necessary to induce the after-image, which may be so strongly developed as to nullify successive stimuli to the same part of the retina for a considerable time ("positive scotoma"). W. Tschermak stated that primary stimuli with coloured lights of such low intensity as to be below the chromatic threshold were followed by coloured after-images, but it was not found to be so by Titchener and Pyle[1].

Analogy with other physiological processes would lead us to the conclusion that the positive after-image results from a persistence of those processes which have been set in action by the primary stimulus, and that the negative after-image is the expression of a diminished excitability of the stimulated area to fresh stimuli (Fechner, v. Helmholtz). The fact that a stimulus usually gives rise to a rhythmical response, as has already been shown (p. 87), makes the periodical variations in the after-image, which were first described by Plateau, intelligible. Under suitable conditions, with the eyes motionless, the negative image disappears and reappears at intervals of three or four seconds, sometimes alternating with positive images. Sudden movements of the eyes, distraction of the attention, and other like influences abolish the after-image; hence they are seldom noticed in every-day life.

Moreover with prolonged or strong stimuli the condition of altered sensibility of the affected part of the retina may persist materially longer than the apparent after-effect as shown by the negative after-image. When the latter seems to have quite disappeared if the eye is thoroughly darkened the affected portion of retina gives rise to a sensation of blackness which is more intense than that derived from the surrounding areas.

It might seem that the effect of a single isolated stimulus, without any secondary stimulus, was a simple matter. This is, however, by no means the case. The negative after-image of a white object appears as a black spot in the midst of a less black field. There is therefore a sensation of blackness which is blacker than that obtained from the eye when all external light is excluded. The entopic sensation when the eyes have long been completely excluded from light is variously

[1] *Proc. Amer. Philos. Soc.* XL. 366, 1908.

described by different people, but all agree that it is not an impenetrable darkness. There are waves or points of light, and the general sensation is one of very dark greyness. So far as negative after-images are concerned this "light chaos" or "light dust" acts as a grey surface on which the black image is projected. Many explanations of this "intrinsic light" have been suggested. That endogenous stimuli are the cause can scarcely be doubted, but whether these are primarily retinal or of central nervous origin remains uncertain[1], though it is now generally agreed that they are central. The question is of theoretical importance and will receive further treatment in Part III.

McDougall[2] found certain features which, he claims, are quite constant in the after-images of coloured lights. They are as follow: (1) The after-images show in nearly every case a play or succession of colours, in which each of the three simple colours, red, green, and blue, makes itself felt in some phase. (2) The brighter the coloured light fixated, the brighter are the colours of the after-image, and the more keen is the antagonism between the three simple colours, so that these colours fuse less than in the after-images of duller colours. When the primary stimuli are very bright the three simple colours tend to appear pure and saturated in turn in a recurring scale, the unchanging phases of pure colour being separated by periods of struggle between the fading and the succeeding colour, just as is the case in the after-image of bright white light. (3) In the case of fixation of one of the three simple colours, red, green, and blue, the lower intensities are followed by after-images in which the other two colours predominate, more or less fused, *i.e.*, the after-image is predominantly complementary; while when the colour fixated is very bright the first phase of the after-image is usually homochromatic and of considerable duration. The like holds good for the compound colours, but in their case the phases of the after-image tend to be rather more varied. (4) The order of occurrence and the duration of the different phases vary readily with slight variations in the conditions. (5) With any given light, the vividness and duration of the after-image, observed in the dark, increase with increase of duration of fixation of the light from about 10 secs. to 90—100 secs., but with further increase of the period of fixation, the duration and vividness of the after-image diminish, so that after very prolonged fixation the after-image is either dull or of short duration or is not seen at all.

As with white light, a sharply bounded patch of coloured light,

[1] See v. Helmholtz, 3rd ed. p. 12 sqq.

[2] *Mind*, x, N. S. 1901.

fixated for more than a few seconds, gives rise to an after-image surrounded by a halo. If the coloured light is not very bright, and the fixation not very prolonged, the halo is of the same colour. The longer fixation is continued, the brighter and the less saturated is the colour of the halo, until after prolonged fixation it becomes white or even tinged with the complementary colour, and is so much brighter than the after-image itself as to inhibit it partially or wholly. The colours of the after-image and its halo tend to be complementary to one another, for during the observation of an after-image in the dark the conditions are very favourable to contrast effects (See Section VI).

The effects of a secondary stimulus on a previously stimulated area are of great importance in considering the facts of colour vision. We have seen that the primary stimulus alters the excitability of the retina so that it is lowered for a succeeding stimulus of the same nature. So far at any rate as colours are concerned we may carry the matter further and say that it is raised for a secondary stimulus of the complementary colour. If a complementary after-image of any spectral colour be obtained and the secondary stimulus be this complementary itself, a sensation of this complementary colour is produced which far exceeds in purity and saturation any such colour which is found in nature or in the spectrum. If for instance a complementary after-image of green obtained from a suitable purple field be compared with a patch of the corresponding spectral green, it will appear of extraordinary brilliancy and saturation.

The question therefore arises whether these after-effects seriously complicate the equations of colour matches. It may be said at once that so far as the peripheral retina is concerned they do, because we have already seen that the periphery values are not the same as the foveal values and they are far more susceptible to variations in adaptation. *With regard to the fovea*, however, it is found that *all colour matches still remain valid, no matter what kind of light may have previously stimulated the retina*. Thus a match of monochromatic yellow with a mixture of red and green remains a match after previous illumination with yellow and blue. If yellow has been used, both become paler; if blue, both become more saturated yellow; but they still match. This law has been systematically investigated by Bühler[1] under v. Kries' direction[2]. It may be stated

[1] *Diss.* Freiburg, 1903.

[2] See also v. Kries, *Arch. f. Anat.* 503, 1878; and Dittler and Orbeli, *Arch. f. d. ges. Physiol.* CXXXII. 338, 1910.

at once that it also holds good for the ordinary types of colour blind (dichromats)[1].

The law has, however, been denied by Hering[2] and Tschermak[3], and Watson[4] has shown that it is at best an incomplete statement of the facts. He confirmed the fact that colour matches remain valid after previous stimulation with another light. He obtained the following results:

Character of match	Width of "green" slit — Resting retina	Width of "green" slit — Previously stimulated retina
Correct	22·7	23·5
Too little green	20·5	11·0
Too much green	25·0	27·2

In each case white was matched by a mixture of spectral red, green and violet lights by altering the width of the slits through which the coloured light proceeded. When the match was correct for the resting eye it was found to be also correct for the eye which had been previously stimulated with a colour, *e.g.*, red. If now the slits through which the red and violet lights passed were kept constant, while the green slit was altered, being reduced until the deficiency of green was just observable and opened until the excess of green was just perceptible, it was found that the range through which the green slit could be altered while still preserving a correct match with the white light was much greater for the eye previously exposed to red light than for the eye not thus previously stimulated. As shown above, the range between a perceptible excess and a perceptible deficiency of green was 4·5 for the resting eye and 16·2 for the previously stimulated eye.

These experiments therefore show that the statement that "all colour matches still remain valid," though true, is not the whole truth, and is indeed misleading. After previous stimulation the range of intensities which give a valid match is much wider than for the resting eye.

If we accept the law of the validity of optical equations irrespective of previous stimulation, we can obtain a relation between the changes in appearance of various lights caused by previous stimulation. If R is the measure of the stimulus, the sensation will be αR, where α is the measure of the retinal excitability for the particular stimulus R.

[1] v. Kries and Nagel. *Ztsch. f. Psychol. u. Physiol. d. Sinnesorg.* XII. 1, 1896; XXIII. 161, 1900.

[2] *Arch. f. d. ges. Physiol.* LIV. 309, 1893.

[3] *Ibid.* LXX. 297, 1898.

[4] Abney and Watson, *Proc. Roy. Soc. Lond.* A. LXXXIX. 1913.

Further, if L_1 at one retinal point gives rise to the same sensation as L_2 at another, previously stimulated by a different light, and M_1 at the first point gives rise to the same sensation as M_2 at the second, then $L_1 + M_1$ will have the same action at the first as $L_2 + M_2$ at the second. As a special example, *proportional* alteration of intensity of two stimuli acting on retinal areas which have been previously exposed to different excitations will produce the same alteration in sensation. This is the "Law of Coefficients" (v. Kries[1]), adumbrated by Wirth[2] as the Fechner-Helmholtz law. From the law it follows that if the change from normal produced by stimulation with three different lights or light mixtures is known the change produced in any other light mixture can be deduced.

The law applies only to the photopic condition. It is therefore least subject to deviation for foveal values. For peripheral values, which are so subject to scotopic variations, and for stimuli of low intensity, which so readily induce the scotopic condition, it ceases to be valid. Moreover, with feeble stimuli the endogenous stimulus of the intrinsic light becomes measurable relatively to the exogenous stimuli.

When the primary and secondary lights are identical the result is a gradual diminution of luminosity (local adaptation, Hering). Such a diminution in differences of brightness occurs when two similar coloured fields of unequal luminosity are fixed for a considerable time. Besides the alteration in brightness there is also a diminution in saturation with coloured lights, and further, though it is scarcely noticeable without a comparison light, there is also a change in hue. Voeste[3] found that a yellow of wave-length 560 $\mu\mu$, a green of 500 $\mu\mu$, and a blue of 460 $\mu\mu$, show no appreciable change of hue. Hues between 500 and 560 $\mu\mu$ change towards 560 $\mu\mu$, those between 500 $\mu\mu$ and 460 $\mu\mu$ towards 460 $\mu\mu$ on prolonged fixation. These facts are of importance in the equality of brightness method of estimating luminosity matches. In Abney's[4] method "the angles of the sectors are *rapidly* altered from "too light" to "too dark" and back again, and the range of angle is gradually diminished until the observer sees both to be equally bright." The change in brightness on prolonged fixation constitutes one of the difficulties of this method with unintelligent examinees, and is an argument in favour of the flicker method.

If the primary stimulus is white and the secondary stimulus coloured

[1] Nagel, p. 211. [2] Wundt's *Philos. Stud.* XVI. 4; XVII. 3; XVIII. 4.

[3] *Ztsch. f. Psychol. u. Physiol. d. Sinnesorg.* XVIII. 257, 1898.

[4] Abney, p. 88.

the exposure to white changes the chromatic stimulus values. Thus, using a comparison light, and experimenting with rotating discs v. Kries[1] found that if the coloured sectors were made the same both for the stimulated and the comparison area there was never even an approximate match; and if, keeping the same coloured sectors, the white sectors were chosen such that the luminosities were equal, the colours seen by the stimulated area were of far too low saturation. In order to produce a match it was necessary for the amounts of coloured light in the secondary and comparison to be about 3 : 1 (blue sectors 270° : 97°; red, 270° : 84°; yellow, 270° : 97°). These experiments have been adversely criticised by Hering[2] and diverse results have been obtained by Dittler and Richter[3].

Dittler and Richter arranged that two contiguous areas of the retina were stimulated with homogeneous blue lights so that an exact match was obtained. The stimulus was then cut off from one area and the other was stimulated with a binary white light obtained by mixing the blue with its complementary colour. The previous blue matches were then replaced and it was now found that the blue of the stimulated area was much more saturated than that of the resting area. Increase of intensity of the blue of the stimulated area failed to re-establish a match, but addition of white light effected a much better match.

If the primary stimulus is coloured and the secondary stimulus white the chromatic excitation causes the white to be coloured with the complementary colour. This is the ordinary complementary after-image, a red, yellow, green, or blue object giving a blue-green, blue, purple, or yellow after-image respectively when a white or grey field is fixed. If the sensation is matched with a comparison light on a neighbouring retinal area it can be shown that it is nearly if not quite as saturated as the spectral colour, even if the exciting light is of moderate intensity and has acted for only 30 to 40 seconds. Exact coincidence with the complementary colour of the exciting light is not generally found[4].

The colour of the resultant sensation is not a mixture of the colour which would be observed with the darkened eye without any secondary

[1] *Berichte d. Freiburger Naturf. Gesellschaft*, 1894.

[2] *Arch. f. d. ges. Physiol.* XCIV. 533, 1903.

[3] *Ztsch. f. Sinnesphysiol.* XLV. 1, 1910; Dittler and Orbeli, *Arch. f. d. ges. Physiol.* CXXXII. 338, 1910.

[4] Cf. Tschermak, *Ergeb. d. Physiol.* II. 2, 763, 1903.

stimulus plus the white light of the white or grey surface. If it were, after stimulation with blue, for example, the yellow of the after-image would always be compensated by mixing the same amount of blue with the secondary light, so that a white after-image would result. By the coefficient law, with increasing intensity of the white light the amount of blue added should increase proportionately, and this is found to be the case (v. Kries). The complementary after-image is therefore not the result of a mere additive process, but is a genuine qualitative change in the white light, though it may also involve a change of intensity.

If the primary stimulus is coloured and the secondary stimulus also coloured various coloured after-images are obtained. It has already been mentioned that if the secondary stimulus is the complementary colour of the primary the resulting sensation is that of the extremely saturated complementary colour. This is specially true of the red-yellow end of the spectrum and for secondary lights of high intensity. It may indeed be far more saturated than any spectral colour, so that it is impossible to obtain a comparison light which will match it. This is a fact of profound theoretical significance, since it shows that we are capable of experiencing visual sensations which cannot be elicited by the application of any known physical stimulus to the resting eye.

If the secondary stimulus differs from both the primary and its complementary the most diverse results may be obtained, but as a rule the complementary colour of the primary stimulus predominates. After green yellow appears reddish orange, blue purple, and so on. After red, yellow (589 $\mu\mu$) matched greenish-yellow (556 $\mu\mu$); after green, 517 $\mu\mu$ matched 565 $\mu\mu$ (Hess[1]).

Attempts have been made by v. Kries[2] for white, and by Schön[3] for coloured lights, to obtain the time relations of after-images. The sensation derived from the secondary light is matched at rapid intervals with a comparison light. The results are of little value owing to rapidly changing adaptation and the difficulty of avoiding parafoveal stimulation. v. Kries[4] also studied the time relations of recovery from the primary stimulus. It is unknown whether the effect passes off as a smooth curve (Fechner, v. Helmholtz, v. Kries) or in rhythmical waves

[1] *Arch. f. Ophth.* XXXIX. 2, 45, 1893. Cf. A. W. Porter and Edridge-Green, *Proc. Roy. Soc. Lond.* B. LXXXV. 434, 1912; Edridge-Green, *loc. cit.* LXXXVI. 110, 1913.

[2] *Arch. f. Ophth.* XXIII. 2, 1, 1877.

[3] *Ibid.* XX. 2, 273, 1874.

[4] *loc. cit.*

(Plateau, Hess[1]). From analogy the latter is the more probable, but the question requires further elucidation[2].

The fading of after-images. The observations recorded above deal with successive induction resulting from short exposures. There are a number of careful observations by some of the older authors, notably Plateau[3], Fechner[4], Séguin[5] and v. Helmholtz[6], which are of importance in the theory of colour vision. They deal with the subjective impressions which occur during the fading of the after-images of a light stimulus.

If the primary stimulus be of sufficient intensity the passage of the positive into the negative or complementary after-image is accompanied by a series of colour sensations. Of particular interest for our present purpose is *the subjective development of colour sensations from stimulation with white light.* The series varies according to the intensity and duration of the primary stimulus. Momentary excitation of white light produces an after-image which "passes rapidly through greenish blue (green, Séguin) into beautiful indigo blue, later into violet or rose-red. These colours are bright and clear. Then follows a dirty or grey orange, during which the positive after-image generally changes to a negative, and in the negative image this orange often becomes a dirty yellow-green[7]." When the negative after-image has developed it appears dark against the background of the "intrinsic light" (*v.* p. 104). If white light of low intensity is now admitted the after-image passes on into the later coloured phases, and retreats again if the white light is again diminished. Thus, if the image when the eye is covered is blue the introduction of dim light causes it to pass through rose-red to a negative yellow. If the eye is again quickly covered the blue reappears. If the image in darkness is rose-red, a weak white light turns it yellowish-red, and so on. If the positive image has completely disappeared from the darkened eye a dim white light develops a grey or green-grey negative after-image surrounded by a rose-red halo.

If the primary stimulus is more intense or acts for a longer time colouration may commence before obscuring the eye (Fechner). It is first yellow, then blue-grey or blue, without passing through green,

[1] *Arch. f. d. ges. Physiol.* CI. 226, 1904.

[2] Cf. Fick and Gürber, *Arch. f. Ophth.* XXXVI. 2, 245, 1890; Fick, *loc. cit.* XXXVIII. 1, 118, 1892; Hering, *loc. cit.* XXXVIII. 2, 252, 1892; Fick, *loc. cit.* XXXVIII. 3, 300, 1892.

[3] *Essai d'une Théorie gén. etc.* Bruxelles, 1834.

[4] *Ann. d. Physik*, L. 220, 1840.

[5] *Ann. de Chimie*, 3rd series, XLI. 415, 1850.

[6] 3rd ed. II. p. 208.

[7] v. Helmholtz, *loc. cit.* II. p. 208.

then red-violet or red. The yellow phase is shortest. After longer and stronger stimulation by white light the after-image in the darkened eye passes through white, blue, green, red, blue, and on exposure to dim white light blue-green and yellow. Different authors give different phases with stronger excitation, but blue always starts the series. The after-images from direct exposure to sunlight are still more complicated[1].

The fading phases of after-images have been more recently investigated by Miss Washburn[2] and McDougall[3]. The latter has shown that it is unnecessary to use stimuli of excessive strength. He found that after excitation with white light a very constant feature was the tendency of the three simple colours to follow one another in a recurring cycle of the order green, red, blue, green, red, blue. If the white light be only moderately bright, red is usually the first colour to appear and is then succeeded by green, which persists to the end. After brighter light green comes first, and is succeeded by red, then blue, and then green again. If the light is still a little brighter, McDougall describes the green as being "usually mixed with red from the first, *i.e.*, it appears yellow with a red edge." If the light be very bright then the first phase of the after-image is white or bright blue of very low saturation; the blue soon passes through blue-green to green, which is then followed by the cycle of pure colours.

According to McDougall "an important feature of the after-images of bright white light is that, after a first short period in which two colours fuse to give yellow, or, as is the case after the brightest lights, all three fuse to give white, the colours that in turn occupy the area of the after-image, alone and unchanging for considerable periods, are red, green, and blue only, and these are in every case of exactly the same colour-tone although varying in brightness in different cases and in different stages of one after-image. The red is a rich crimson red, decidedly less orange than the red of the solar spectrum, the blue is a rich ultra-marine, and the green a pure green having no inclination towards blue or yellow[4]." McDougall states that "they are the purest, richest, most saturated colours that I have ever experienced, and I believe that in this way, and this way only, one may experience absolutely simple, *i.e.*, unmixed and fully saturated colour-sensations."

The fading phases of the after-images from coloured lights are also not limited to the homochromatic positive and the complementary

[1] v. Helmholtz, *loc. cit.* II. 211.
[2] *Psychol. Rev.* VII. 1900.
[3] *Mind*, X. N. S. 235, 1901.
[4] Cf. Part III.

after-images. As the former passes into the latter in the case of a strong primary stimulus the image does not simply become paler, but unsaturated hues appear. The homochromatic hue of the positive image first disappears and the image resembles that of the after-image of a white object in which the rose-red phase predominates. "Then the complementary colour of the negative after-image gradually developes, but it may be already visible before the positive image has become negative; it may therefore appear brighter than the dark background. I think that the appearance of the complementary colour may be attributed to the fact that the positive image, which at this phase has become feeble and white, is superposed upon the negative and complementary images induced in the intrinsic light chaos by the fatigue of the eye. It is clear that by such a superposition after exposure to red the positive white and the negative blue-green can together give a greenish white positive image. These positive complementary images are mentioned by several observers (Purkinje[1], Fechner[2], Brücke[3])[4]." It is an instructive experiment to view the spectrum momentarily and then to observe the phases of the after-images.

Burch[5] has adduced strong evidence to show that the duration of after-image effects is much longer than has been commonly supposed. He has observed changes occurring in the subjective sensations for as long as two hours. As with all subjective observations of this kind generalisations from them are to be accepted with caution.

It is unnecessary to pursue this complicated problem further. The older experiments, especially Fechner's with coloured stimuli, were mostly made with impure lights. The matter requires further investigation with homogeneous lights and due regard for adaptation, etc.

CHAPTER III

THE EFFECTS OF "FATIGUE"

The term "fatigue" has been avoided in the previous consideration of the effects of retinal stimulation. With our increased knowledge of adaptation it has become difficult to estimate the importance of fatigue and further discussion must be postponed until we deal with the theory

[1] *Zur Physiol. d. Sinne*, II. 110. 1819.
[2] *Ann. d. Physik*, L. 213, 1840.
[3] *Wiener Denkschr.* III. 12, 1850.
[4] v. Helmholtz, *loc. cit.* II. 213.
[5] *Proc. Roy. Soc. Lond.* B, LXXVI. 212, 1905.

of colour vision. Earlier authors, including v. Helmholtz, and most physicists make free use of the conception of fatigue to account for successive induction, but the facts, and especially those of simultaneous contrast (*vide infra*), negative so simple an explanation. There is, however, a group of phenomena associated with prolonged or intense stimulation to which the term may be fittingly applied, though even in this case it should be done "without prejudice." These phenomena have been studied particularly by Burch[1]. By flooding the eye with bright sunlight which had passed through a lens of 2 inch focus and a suitable colour screen or by a similar process with a spectrum of wide dispersion Burch was able to study the after-effects of fatigue for the various colours.

After fatigue for *red*, scarlet geraniums appear black, calceolarias and sunflowers various shades of green, and marigolds green shaded with black in the parts that are orange to the normal eye. Purple flowers, such as candytuft and clematis look violet, and pink roses bright sky-blue. Short exposures—a few seconds to two or three minutes—suffice, and the effect is transient, passing off in about ten minutes.

After fatigue for *violet*, violet wools look black, purple flowers crimson, some blues greenish, green a richer hue. A noticeable effect is the tinging of all objects which do not reflect violet with that colour, and the same applies to "dazzling" with other colours.

Fatiguing with *green* makes the landscape look like a picture painted with vermilion, ultramarine and flake-white, variously blended. The foliage is reddish-grey or bluish-grey, blue flowers are dirty blue, red flowers are impure red, and every colour but green is tinged with green.

Fatiguing with *purple* (*i.e.* red and blue) makes everything look monochromatic green. All red, purple or blue flowers look black, and green looks a quite unnaturally brilliant green. The red fatigue passes off first, the observer then being in a condition of violet fatigue, which passes off in 15—60 minutes.

Fatigue of one eye with purple and of the other with green produced a very weird and exaggerated stereoscopic effect.

In fatiguing the eye with the colours of the spectrum comparatively simple changes, differing in degree but not in kind, occur with four regions, viz. the regions which give the sensations of pure red,

[1] *Phil. Trans. Roy. Soc. Lond.* B, CXCI. 1, 1898; *Proc. Roy. Soc. Lond.* LXVI. 216, 1900.

unmixed green, unmixed blue, and pure violet. The changes are as follow :

(1) All direct sensation of the fatiguing colour is abolished, not merely from the corresponding part of the spectrum, but also from those regions in which it overlaps other colours. It is rather the sensation of the particular colour that is weakened than the sensitiveness of the eye to a particular part of the spectrum. Thus, in red fatigue, the red end is shortened, but the green appears with full intensity at the *D* line and reaches almost as far as the *C* line. In green fatigue the green is replaced by red and blue, which not only meet but overlap.

(2) The fatiguing colour produces a homochromatic after-effect like a luminous fog, by which the hue of all the other colours is modified if they are relatively weak, but which is unnoticed if they are bright. "A strong light not only fatigues the eye, but dazzles it ; that is to say, the sensation of light persists after the source of light has been withdrawn" (Burch). Each "dazzle-tint" has its own rate of development and of subsidence, and each is independent of the rest. Red passes off first, then green, then blue, and last violet. The positive after-effect of light between the *C* and *D* lines is at first red, but it comprises two dazzle-tints—red and green, of which red soon vanishes, leaving green. The dazzle-tint becomes unnoticeable long before the colour sensation is fully restored.

(3) Fatigue with one colour has no effect upon the intensity of the remaining colour sensations.

Fatigue with intermediate portions of the spectrum produces intermediate effects. Thus fatigue with orange or yellow affects not only the appearance of the orange or yellow, but that of the red and green also ; similarly with the blue-greens and the indigo.

By fatiguing with red for 30 seconds and then finding pure yellow, fatiguing with *E* for 30 seconds and then finding the beginning of blue, fatiguing with *F* for 30 seconds, and then finding the beginning of violet, and again working backwards on the same plan, it has been possible to map out the range of the colour sensations. The averages of 70 people with normal colour vision give the extent of

red	= 760·6	to 551	$\mu\mu$.
green	= 593	to 484	,,
blue	= 517	to 443	,,
violet	= 454	to 397·5	,,

"In reality each colour sensation extends so much further that red and blue overlap, and so do green and violet, the only colours which I have not proved to do so being red and violet" (Burch).

From the data in Clerk-Maxwell's papers and from his own observations Burch estimates the transition point between

Maxwell, red and green, 583·7; Burch (average of 70 persons) 573;
,, green and blue, 500·3; Burch (average of 70 persons) 500·3;
,, blue-indigo = 449·8;
Burch, blue and violet = 448.

Pure colours—
Maxwell—red = 630·9; green = 529·7; blue = 457·4.
Burch (average of 70 persons)—red = 625; green = 525; blue = 471; violet = 415.

Burch therefore thinks there are usually four colour sensations—red, green, blue, and violet. He is unable to detect the existence of a separate yellow by this method.

It should be pointed out that these are facts independent of any theory of colour vision, but it must be remembered that the fatiguing lights were of great intensity and might well produce changes which are quasi-pathological.

Edridge-Green and Marshall[1] controvert some of Burch's statements, especially those relating to fatigue for the *D* line. Their experiments differ from his in that the intensity of the fatiguing light was much less. They find that after exposure of the eye to the sodium flame for from three to fifteen minutes and then looking at the spectrum the yellow is entirely obliterated and only a faint band of orange separates the red and green. If the eye is still further fatigued this also is obliterated, the red and green meeting. The red looked rather more purple, the green bluish. The blue and violet appeared diminished in intensity. There was no shortening of the red end of the spectrum.

It should be noted in this connection that Burch does not deny the existence of a yellow sensation in some people, but states that he finds no evidence of it himself. On the other hand Edridge-Green and Marshall's experiments do not produce nearly so complete a fatigue of the sensations—whether true yellow (according to them) or red and green (according to Burch)—as in Burch's experiments.

A. W. Porter and Edridge-Green[2] have also investigated the effects of fatigue with spectral lights. The eyes were fatigued for about 20 secs. with monochromatic light and then fixed a spectrum of weaker intensity

[1] *Trans. Ophth. Soc.* XXIX. 211, 1909.
[2] *Proc. Roy. Soc. Lond.* B. LXXXV. 434, 1912.

so that the after-image formed a band across the middle of the spectrum. After fatigue with 654—675 $\mu\mu$ the extreme red was slightly diminished, there was no change in the orange, yellow, or green, and the blue and violet became darker and bluer. If only red and orange were viewed the red disappeared and the orange remained. The sodium flame appeared unchanged (Porter), slightly greener (Edridge-Green). After fatigue with orange, 619—631 $\mu\mu$, the dark blue after-image was seen right across the spectrum except in the region of the orange, which appeared unaffected. If only red and orange were viewed the red was replaced by the green-blue after-image, whilst the orange appeared unaffected. After fatigue with orange-yellow, 585—595 $\mu\mu$, the purple after-image appeared as if painted over the spectrum, the red being affected most. Fatigue with yellow-green, 545—550 $\mu\mu$, gave a similar result, with least effect in the orange. Fatigue with blue-green, 496—500 $\mu\mu$, gave the same effect,a purple (not red) after-image, with orange least affected : the sodium flame appeared unchanged (Porter), slightly redder (Edridge-Green). After fatigue with blue, 478—480 $\mu\mu$, there was no change in the red and orange, and the reddish purple after-image was seen over the rest of the spectrum. With blue, 445—455 $\mu\mu$, the after-image was yellow-green (Porter), orange (Edridge-Green) ; the violet and blue were cut off, red and green became yellower ; if only green and red were viewed the former was obliterated, the latter unaffected. With violet, 425—436 $\mu\mu$, the after-image was green ; the red and orange were unchanged, the green became yellow-green, and the violet and blue appeared green.

The authors found that " the stability of the after-image was remarkable ; it did not change colour, and was not influenced by subsequent light falling on the retina when this was not of too great intensity." Thus, if after viewing the reacting spectrum the eyes were turned to the dark screen the after-image appeared as a uniform dark band, darker than the screen. In contradiction to previous observers the authors found that " the complementary to the exciting light is never strengthened in the spectrum on the screen by the after-image." They also found no change in colour of the after-image as it fades.

Wanach[1] found that the eye fatigues more quickly for some spectral colours than for others, and least for the more refrangible. Macular fatigue lasts longer than peripheral.

The consideration of Abney's researches on colour fatigue will be postponed (Part III).

[1] *Ztsch. f. Sinnesphysiol.* XLIII. 443, 1908.

SECTION VI

AREAL EFFECTS

CHAPTER I

THE LOCAL QUANTITATIVE EFFECT

Some effects of the *size of the area stimulated* have already been touched upon (*v*. pp. 51, 79, 95). They are of considerable importance and demand more detailed consideration.

With regard to *foveal* vision it may be said that given a sufficiently intense illumination for a given condition of adaptation a mathematical point of light will be visible. Its image on the retina is always a diffusion area, the central parts of which afford at least a minimal effective stimulus if they anywhere impinge upon a retinal cone. If the effective area is so small as to occupy an interconal space a slight movement of the eye must be predicated in order that the point may be visible. It is probable that for a given condition of retinal adaptation a subminimal stimulus for a single cone may become a minimal or effective stimulus if spread over several cones.

Riccò[1] conducted a very careful series of experiments bearing upon this point. The experiments were carried out in six different ways[2]. He found that at the threshold of sensibility the quantity of light entering the eye is constant, or, in other words, the light intensity and the area of the retinal image are reciprocal functions, or the product of the area into the light intensity is constant. In terms of the visual angle, the law is that the minimum visual angle varies inversely as the square root of the light intensity, or the product of the minimum visual angle and the square root of the light intensity is constant. The limit of the law is determined by the size of the foveal region; it ceases to be accurate for visual angles above 40′ to 50′.

[1] *Ann. di Ottal.* VI. 1877.

[2] Parsons, *Roy. Lond. Ophth. Hosp. Rep.* XIX. 1, 114, 1913.

Charpentier[1] published a series of experiments which confirm and extend those of Riccò. He used small bright squares up to 12 mm., viewed at 20 cm. distance. Below 2 mm. the smaller the surface the greater the minimum illumination necessary for perception. Two millimetres at this distance correspond to about 0·17 mm. on the retina, *i.e.*, about the size of the fovea. For larger areas the area has no effect. It follows, therefore, that in order to produce a luminous sensation at the fovea the total quantity of light, *i.e.*, the product of the area and the illumination, must attain a certain value, and that that value is constant for a given condition of adaptation. "The fovea centralis forms a sort of autonomous territory, in which the luminous excitation diffuses itself, and which always requires a certain quantity of light to be set in activity." Charpentier showed, in answer to criticisms by Leroy, that the diffusion could not be accounted for by irradiation due to dioptric aberrations.

Asher[2] found that for the range of light intensities used by him up to a visual angle of 2′ to 3′ the apparent size depends entirely upon the quantity of the light. According to him, therefore, vision of objects subtending angles up to this size is a function purely of the light sense and not of the form sense. The earliest observations bearing upon this aspect of the subject were by Volkmann (1863) and Aubert (1865). Aubert used lines 2 mm. wide and 50 mm. long, and determined the distance the lines had to be apart in order that the interspace might look the same as the breadth of the lines. He found that when the breadth of the lines was varied by Volkmann's macroscope so that they subtended visual angles of from 10″ to 45″ the angular distance apart of the lines varied from 104″ to 112″ for black lines on a white background, and from 140″ to 153″ for white lines on a black background. Asher used small black, white, and grey squares and rectangles of paper and determined the distance at which a difference of size could be detected, the light intensities of the papers being calculated by the colour top and by Hering's polarisation photometer. He found that visual angles between 23″ and 78″ might be increased by 25″ to 100″ (average 58″) under the given differences of light intensity (from 360 to 6) before a difference in size could be detected. At a great distance from the different sized objects they appear either of equal size and brightness, or, if the objective brightness of the smaller is much greater than that of the larger, of equal size but unequal brightness, the smaller being the

[1] *Compt. rend.* XCI. 1880 : *Arch. d'Opht.* II. 234, 487, 1882.
[2] *Ztsch. f. Biol.* XXXV. 394, 1897.

brighter. Sometimes the smaller appeared the larger. On approaching the objects the difference in apparent brightness increased whilst the sizes remained equal. Then followed a stage in which the difference in apparent brightness diminished, the sizes remaining equal ; both might even appear of the same brightness. On still further approximation the difference in brightness again became manifest, and simultaneously or shortly afterwards the larger object showed indefiniteness of the edges and greater apparent size. In many cases the size and brightness remained the same until the difference in size became distinguishable.

Asher's explanation is as follows : So long as the objects subtend so small a visual angle that they cover a single sensibility area[1] they appear equal, since the same quantity of light acts upon the sensibility area. With increase of the visual angle the influence of aberration becomes manifest. The larger object has a larger light area which is larger than a sensibility area, but the periphery of the light area has so low an intensity that the effective light area is not larger than a sensibility area. The smaller object, on the other hand, has a smaller light area, the effective part of which, however, is as large as a sensibility area. The ordinates corresponding to an effective brightness may extend farther from the centre for the smaller than for the larger object, so that the smaller may appear the brighter. So long as the relationship of the objects is such that the sensibility areas of both cover one or an equal number of sensibility areas they must appear of equal size, though the aberration areas may be very different. The conditions of light and contrast may easily be such that the smaller sensibility area may belong to the larger aberration area.

Asher denies that any proof has yet been given that it is possible to produce a retinal image so small as to stimulate only one cone.

Schoute[2] does not agree with Asher that it is impossible to stimulate a single cone, and he holds that for single cone images the impression of size is dependent solely upon the product of the area into the light intensity. If only one cone is stimulated the object always appears

[1] Mach (1866) first distinguished between the physical distribution of light over the area of a retinal image and the physiological distribution of brightness over the same area. If the retina be imagined flattened out and ordinates erected upon it, the lengths of which correspond with the intensities of light at the given spots, the area obtained by joining the summits of the ordinates will give an area representing the light intensity, or more briefly a "light area." If the ordinates represent the apparent brightness of the light at the spots as seen by the observer, the area will represent the sensibility and is briefly termed a "sensibility area."

[2] *Ztsch. f. Psychol. u. Physiol. d. Sinnesorg.* XIX. 252, 1899 ; *Ztsch. f. Augenhlk.* VIII. 419, 1902.

round, but differences in size are still appreciable. If the objects are of equal size the brighter appears the larger, *i.e.*, the apparent size varies with the light intensity. Schoute, like v. Helmholtz, attributes this to psychological causes, *i.e.*, to an error of judgment.

Loeser[1] has entirely confirmed Riccò's law for foveal vision. The law is stated in one form thus: The product of the minimum visual angle and the square root of the light intensity is constant. Loeser's results are shown in the following table:

Distance of object, E m.	Diameter of object, D mm.	Visual angle, D/E	Sq. rt. of light intensity, J	Product. DJ/E
8	20·0	2·5	0·87	2·18
,,	14·0	1·75	1·27	2·22
,,	8·5	1·06	2·4	2·5
,,	5·0	0·63	3·45	2·26

The photochromatic interval (*v.* p. 60) can be demonstrated by altering the area of the retina stimulated. Thus Donders[2] found that in full daylight the hue of intensely coloured papers on a dark background could be distinguished when they subtended a visual angle of 0·7 minute (1 sq. mm. at 5 metres distance).

The dependence of the discrimination of hue on visual angle is readily demonstrated with relatively unsaturated colours. Coloured objects on a white background appear dark or grey under the smallest angles at which they are visible. It is possible to select a grey background of such a luminosity that the colourless interval is abolished, *i.e.*, as the visual angle is increased the colour of the object is recognised as soon as the object becomes visible.

Charpentier[3] determined the absolute and the chromatic thresholds from the area stimulated for the fovea of the dark-adapted eye. Since there is little adaptation at the fovea, this factor is of relatively slight importance. He obtained the following results, the measurements being the diameters of the diaphragm of the photometer.

Colour (sunlight spectrum)	Absolute Threshold	Chromatic Threshold	Ratio
Extreme red	0·5 mm.	1 mm.	4.
Orange	0·9 ,,	2·1 ,,	5·5
Yellow	1 ,,	3·1 ,,	9·6
Green	0·3 ,,	4·2 ,,	196
Blue	0·3 ,,	7·5 ,,	625

[1] Hirschberg's *Festschrift*, 1905; Feilchenfeld and Loeser, *Arch. f. Ophth.* LX. 97, 1905
[2] *Ann. d'ocul.* LXXIX. 1878.
[3] *La Lumière et les Couleurs*, pp. 213, 238.

Conversely, diminution of the area stimulated causes the colour to lose in apparent intensity—red less than green, green less than blue. The law associating area stimulated and intensity is therefore not so simple as that for white light.

Abney[1] in his experiments on the extinction of colour and light, *i.e.*, on the point in the diminution of the intensity of light which just causes, first the colour, and then the light to become invisible, made a series of investigations on the influence of the area stimulated. He found, as was to be expected from the results of previous observers, that *the smaller the disc the less reduction in intensity of the ray was required to extinguish it and the same ratio existed between the extinction of the different colours.* Plotting curves with aperture diameters in powers of 2 as abscissae and logarithms of light intensities as ordinates, with apertures less than $1\frac{1}{2}$ inches diameter the curves become straight lines, all of which are parallel. Hence "from that point the intensity of a light which will be just extinguished with a certain diameter of aperture may be increased 10 times and yet be invisible when an aperture with one quarter of that diameter is employed; if the intensity of the light be increased 100 times, we have only to diminish the diameter of the aperture to $\frac{1}{16}$ and it will again disappear, or if to $\frac{1}{64}$, the light may be increased 1000 times." *When the angular aperture exceeds 4° apparently the upper limit is reached, all extinctions being the same beyond it.*

With regard to the point of extinction, Abney[2] says: "The light from a square, or a disc, or an oblong, just before extinction, is a fuzzy patch of grey, and appears finally to depart almost as a point. This can scarcely account for the smallest width of an illuminated surface determining the intensity of the light just not visible; but it tells us that the light is still exercising some kind of stimulus on the visual apparatus, even when all sensation of light is gone from the outer portions. The fact that the disappearance of the image takes place in the same manner whether viewed centrally or excentrically tells us that this has nothing to do with the yellow spot, or fovea, but is probably due to a radiation of sensation (if it may be so called) in every direction on the retinal surface. Supposing some part of the stimulus impressed on one retinal element did radiate in all directions over the surface of the retina, the effect would be greatest in the immediate neighbourhood, and would be inappreciable at a small distance, but the influence exerted upon an adjacent element might depend not only on its distance, but also upon whether it was or was not itself excited independently.

[1] Abney, pp. 169, 174. [2] *Ibid.* p. 177.

Following the matter out further we should eventually arrive at the centre of an area as the part which was the recipient of the greatest amount of the radiated stimuli, and consequently that would be the last to disappear. With a slit aperture the slit is visible till extinction is very nearly executed, but it finally merges into a fuzzy spot at the moment before it finally fails to make any impression of light."

Fig. 40 shows that there is an angular aperture or size of retinal area stimulated at which any ray will be extinguished both for colour and light at the same time. The aperture is largest for red.

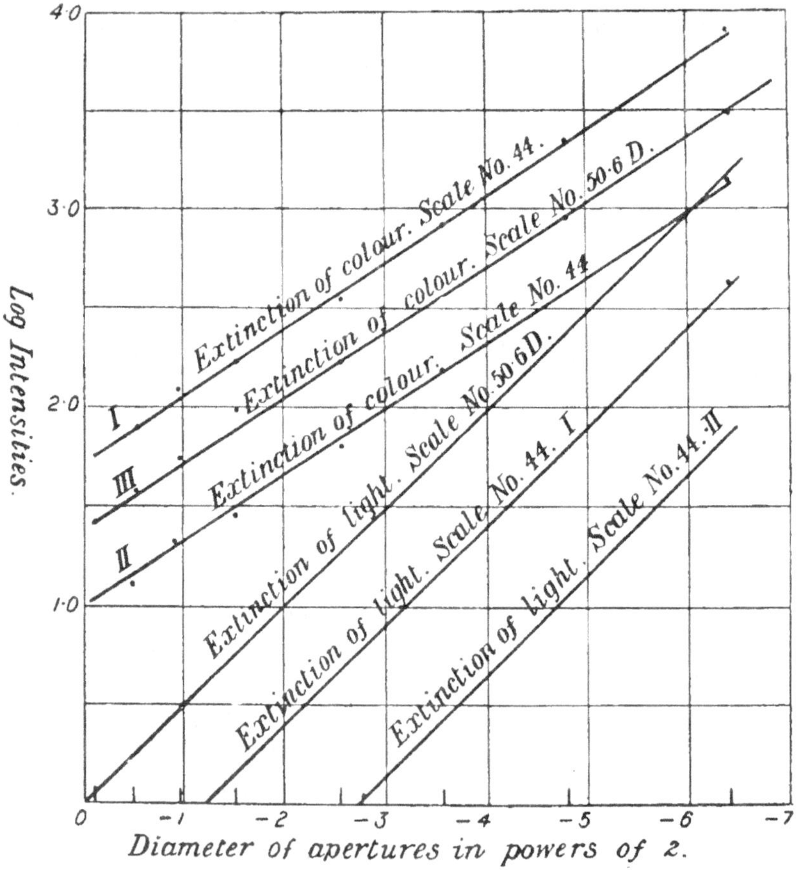

Fig. 40. Extinction of colour and light curves with different areas of stimulation. *SSN* 44 = 548·1 $\mu\mu$; *SSN* 50·6 = *D* line: I and II, different observers and different intensities. (Abney.)

Abney has also compared the luminosity of the spectral light from apertures of different size. Fig. 41 shows the curves for scale numbers

27·3 and 50·6 (yellow *D* line, 589 $\mu\mu$), the logarithms of the annulus values of the two apertures being plotted as abscissae and ordinates. For points on the curve the luminosity of the large aperture is equal to that of the small, equality being obtained by means of the annulus. If the luminosity of the spots of light were always equal, irrespective of size, the inclination of the curves would be 45°.

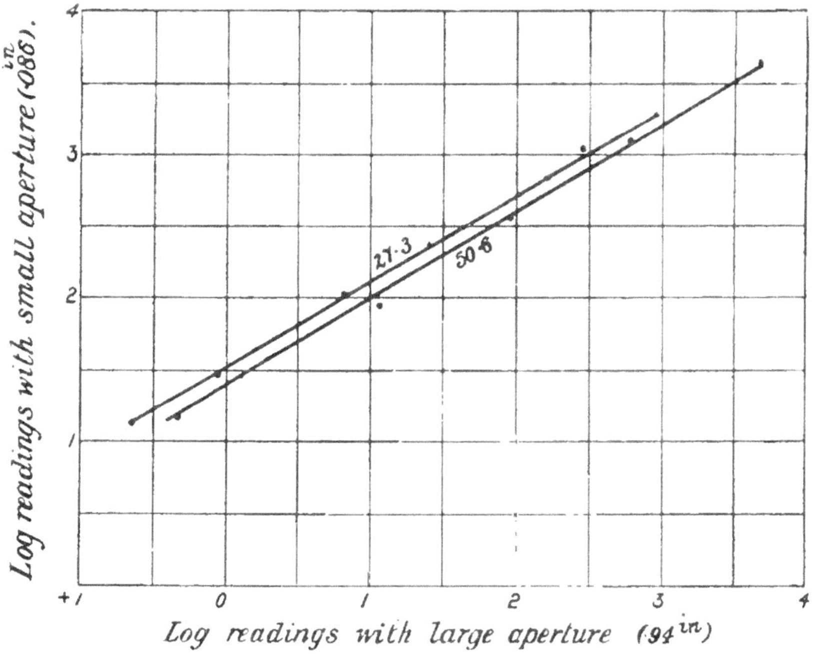

Fig. 41. Equality of brightness curves for different sized apertures. *SSN* 27·3 = 575 $\mu\mu$; *SSN* 50·6 = *D* line. (Abney.)

The relation of area stimulated to intensity for the *periphery* of the retina has been studied by Piper[1], Loeser[2], Henius[3], and Fujita[4]. Piper gives the following table for the dark-adapted periphery:

Area	$\sqrt{\text{Area}}$ or Angular size	Threshold value	Relative stimulation value	Product of angular size and threshold value
1	1	10·0	1	10·0
10	3·15	2·94	3·4	9·3
25	5	1·96	5·1	9·8
100	10	1·02	9·8	10·2

[1] *Ztsch. f. Psychol. u. Physiol. d. Sinnesorg.* XXXII. 98, 1904.
[2] Hirschberg's *Festschrift*, 1905; Feilchenfeld and Loeser. *Arch. f. Ophth.* LX. 97, 1905.
[3] *Ztsch. f. Sinnesphysiol.* XLIII. 99, 1908.
[4] *Ibid.* XLIII. 243, 1908.

There is therefore obviously not the same relationship between area and threshold intensity that appertains to the fovea. There is, however, a relationship between the square root of the area (which is equivalent to the visual angle subtended by circular objects) and the threshold intensity. Piper states the law thus: For the dark-adapted periphery the stimulation value of a luminous surface is proportional to the square root of the area of the retinal image; or in other words, the product of the threshold value and the square root of the area of the retinal image is constant. Henius and Fujita showed that the law is valid only for mixed white light and objects subtending a visual angle up to 10°. Above 10° the sensitiveness of the retina increases much more slowly than the visual angle increases, and still more slowly for red light. Fujita showed too that the law is not valid below 1°.

For the light-adapted periphery Fujita showed that there was no simple relationship between area and threshold intensity. For small objects, however, subtending less than 2° the threshold value diminishes with the visual angle, but not so quickly as for the fovea.

Owing therefore to the great difference between the photopic and scotopic periphery threshold values, especially for relatively large luminous areas, the condition of adaptation is of great importance, especially as it itself changes with the actual stimulation.

The relationship of the region of the retina and the size of the area stimulated respectively to the sensations derived from colourless mixtures and equations have been studied by v. Helmholtz[1], v. Frey and v. Kries[2], and Hering[3]. Hering observed colourless mixtures of complementary monochromatic lights of a given area and studied the effects of altering the size or shifting the fixation point. A mixture of red and blue-green became redder and darker on diminution, greener and brighter on augmentation of the area. The foveal colourless mixture became greener and brighter on direct fixation; the peripheral colourless mixture became redder and darker on central fixation. A colourless mixture of yellow-green and violet became yellow-green on diminishing the area, rose-red on increasing the area or observation by indirect fixation, but the effects were much less than in the first case.

Hering found that colourless equations with spectral lights become invalid, both with light and dark adaptation, if the area is increased or fixation changed from direct to indirect (contrast p. 69). So too in a match between a mixture of spectral red and blue-green (A) and yellow

[1] 1st ed. p. 301. [2] *Arch. f. Physiol.* 336, 1881.
[3] *Arch. f. d. ges. Physiol.* LIV. 277, 1893.

and blue (B), A becomes green and brighter, B lilac and darker. These changes are probably due to macular absorption. Tschermak[1], for example, was unable to distinguish definite variations in parafoveal matches on increasing the eccentricity of fixation, thus confirming earlier results by Hess and v. Kries. Under such conditions, however, he found slight changes on increasing the size of the area stimulated, and these were of the same kind as those found by Hering.

The effect of the size of the area stimulated on the photochromatic interval at the periphery and on the size of the field of vision has already been discussed (p. 79).

CHAPTER II

SIMULTANEOUS CONTRAST OR SPATIAL INDUCTION

We have seen (Section V, Chap. II) that stimulation of a retinal area is followed at a certain interval by sensations, potential or kinetic, of an opposite nature, a phenomenon known as "succedaneous" or "successive contrast." There are numerous facts which tend to show that the sensation resulting from stimulation of a retinal area is modified by the condition of the surrounding areas, and *per contra* that stimulation of a retinal area itself causes a change in the condition of excitability of the surrounding area. This reciprocal interaction of retinal areas, or, in terms less open to criticism, of contiguous or nearly contiguous areas in the field of visual sensations is called "simultaneous contrast." The term contrast (Chevreul) in each case indicates opponent activities. Less open to objection is the term "induction" (Brücke), though this term has unfortunately been used in a more restricted sense by Hering. He uses "simultaneous induction" to connote change during fixation, "successive induction," change occurring after removal of stimulation. We shall use "induction" in the broadest sense, temporal induction being any change in a visual area due directly to stimulation (and therefore including adaptation), and spatial induction being any change in other areas resulting from the primary stimulation. To avoid circumlocution we shall speak of "retinal" areas, without prejudice as to the exact site at which the change manifests itself.

Spatial induction manifests itself by changes both in luminosity (or brightness) and hue. A patch of grey paper on a white background

[1] *Arch. f. d. ges. Physiol.* LXXXII. 559, 1900.

looks darker than a patch of the same paper on a black background (Goethe). Innumerable experiments have been devised to demonstrate luminosity (or brightness) contrast. Especially instructive are those with Hering's double-room or double-screen method, in which an aperture in a screen is variously illuminated from behind, whilst the illumination on the front of the screen can also be varied independently at will.

It has been recognised since the time of Leonardo da Vinci that coloured surfaces are altered in hue by their surroundings, and *vice versa*. Brücke called a coloured surface surrounded by white the inducing colour. It must, however, be well borne in mind that the phenomenon is reciprocal, no matter what the luminosity or hue of the two fields may be. Tschermak[1], who has written an excellent résumé of our knowledge of contrast, enumerates five methods of demonstrating colour contrast.

(1) The background method was early studied by Chevreul[2]. In its simplest form white, grey, black, or coloured patches or strips are laid on coloured backgrounds. The contrast is accentuated by placing tissue-paper over both[3]. Maxwell's top can also be used (Dove, v. Helmholtz, H. Meyer, Hering[4], and others), or a projection apparatus (Rollet).

(2) The mirror method, used by Goethe, is familiar in Ragona Scina's well-known experiment, which has been modified and improved by Hering[5].

(3) The method of coloured shadows dates from Goethe, and has been much used, notably in recent years by Hering[6] and Abney for the detection of colour-blindness.

(4) The double-image method was introduced by v. Helmholtz[7] and modified by Hering[8].

(5) Negative after-images have also been used by Hering[9].

Chevreul, Fechner, and Wundt[10] showed that actual contiguity of the reacting surfaces was not essential. Aubert[11] showed that weak and localised stimulation altered the excitability of the whole retina. The

[1] *Ergebnisse d. Physiol.* II. 2, 726–798, 1903.
[2] *De la Loi du Contraste simultané des Couleurs*, Strassburg, 1839; new ed. Paris, 1890.
[3] Joh. Müller, *Handb. d. Physiol.* II. 1837; H. Meyer, *Ann. d. Physik.* XCV. 170. 1855.
[4] *Arch. f. d. ges. Physiol.* XLI. 1, 1887.
[5] *Ibid.* XLI. 358, 1887.
[6] *Ibid.* XLII. 119, 1888.
[7] 1st ed. p. 406; 2nd ed. p. 559.
[8] *Arch. f. d. ges. Physiol.* XLVII. 236, 1890
[9] *Sitz. d. Wiener Akad.* 1872–4.
[10] *Philos. Stud.* IV. 112. 1887.
[11] *Physiol. d. Netzhaut*, 1865.

extent of the background, as well as its luminosity and colour, modifies the luminosity and saturation of the contrast colour.

The contrast effect is not uniform over the whole surface, but is most marked at the edges. A distinction is therefore sometimes made between "surface-contrast" (*Flächenkontrast*) and "border-contrast" (*Randkontrast*). The disparity diminishes on prolonged fixation ("simultaneous induction," Hering). Border contrast is easily demonstrated with black and white, or coloured sectors on a rotating disc (Mach[1], Aubert, v. Helmholtz), or by the shadow method (Goethe, A. Fick[2]). It is visible by momentary stimulation and is reversed in the negative after-image (Mach): in the latter case it may be more obvious than in the primary image. With colour-contrast the saturation is greater at the borders than in the middle.

Contrast effects are diminished by separation of the contrasting fields, and are therefore seen better with small than large fields. A narrow black line between the fields diminishes contrast markedly (v. Helmholtz), and the effects are greatest at contiguous contours (Mach).

Jurin (1783) and Brandes (1827) attempted to explain simultaneous contrast by successive contrast, due to slight movements of the eyes. Though this factor is a frequent complication and requires special heed to its elimination it is not the cause (Fechner[3], Hering). With the greatest care in controlling the movements of the eyes and keeping accurate fixation, simultaneous contrast manifests itself immediately. Moreover it occurs with colours of such weak saturation that no coloured after-image is induced. Aubert, Mach, Meyer[4] and Rollet[5] have shown that it occurs on momentary stimulation.

Attempts have been made to obtain quantitative measurements of simultaneous contrast by means of a comparison field by Lehmann[6], Ebbinghaus[7], Hess and Pretori[8] and others.

For black and white or pure luminosity (brightness) contrast Ebbinghaus found that the increase in brightness of a patch on a darker background is proportional to the difference of the two light intensities, irrespective of their absolute values. Hess and Pretori found that the apparent luminosity of a small bright surface on a dark background

[1] *Sitz. d. Wiener Akad.* LII. 2, 303, 1865.

[2] Hermann's *Handb. d. Physiol.* III. 1, 3, 1879.

[3] *Ann. d. Physik* XLIV. 513, 1838; L. 193, 427, 1840.

[4] *Amer. J. of Sc.* XLVI. 1, 1893.

[5] *Sitz. d. Wiener Akad.* LV. 424, 1867.

[6] Wundt's *Philos. Stud.* III. 497, 1886.

[7] *Sitz. d. Akad. d. Wiss.* Berlin, 994, 1887.

[8] *Arch. f. Ophth.* XL. 4, 1, 1894.

remains constant when the increase of illumination of the surface bears a constant ratio to the increase of illumination of the background. The contrast effect therefore varies directly with the inducing stimulus and is independent of its absolute value. Ebbinghaus and Hess and Pretori agree therefore as to increase of brightness by contrast or contrast-brightening. Hess and Pretori find that the law also applies to contrast-darkening, therein differing from Ebbinghaus, but the results of the latter are probably due to error in technique. Kirschmann[1] found that the amount of contrast varies as the square root of the area of the inducing field, *i.e.*, the relationship between the area and the intensity of the inducing light is reciprocal.

For colour-contrast Fechner showed that the brightness of a grey background must be appropriately chosen. Under optimum conditions an inducing colour of very slight saturation suffices to induce marked contrast. The statement, however, that simultaneous contrast is most evident with slight differences of colour between the reacting fields (v. Helmholtz) is not true (Fechner, Rollet). Hering[2] showed that with optimum black-white background conditions contrast increases with the saturation of the coloured inducing field, an observation confirmed by Pretori and Sachs[3]. Kirschmann (1892) had previously arrived at the same result, but found that the increase was not proportional, but probably a logarithmic function. Colour-contrast, as might be expected, is accompanied by change in luminosity, and this subject has been exhaustively studied by Pretori and Sachs under Hering's guidance. Their results will be considered in Part III.

The most important element in colour-contrast from our present point of view is the opponent or complementary effect, early noticed by Brücke[4]. Under ordinary circumstances the induced colour is not the precise complementary of the inducing, as was known to Goethe, and has been fully investigated by Hering[5]. Various physical factors conduce to the effect, such as the variable nature of "white" light and "grey" surfaces, macular pigmentation (Hering, Sachs), the pigment of the lens (Hering), the brown pigment of the retinal epithelium (Tschermak), and the reddening by the blood of the light which passes through the sclerotic (Hering, Hess). These do not suffice to explain all the facts. There are other, physiological, factors, such as the

[1] Wundt's *Philos. Stud.* VI. 417, 1890; VII. 362, 1891; *Amer. J. of Psychol.* IV. 4, 74, 542, 1892.

[2] *Arch. f. d. ges. Physiol.* XLI. 1, 1887; XLII. 117, 1888.

[3] *Ibid.* LX. 71, 1895.

[4] *Ann. d. Physik,* LXXXIV. 418, 1851.

[5] *Zur Lehre vom Lichtsinne,* 1876.

previous stimulation of the eye (Hering, Hess[1], Tschermak) and fatigue (Tschermak and Krause). The discrepancy between the induced and the complementary colour is said to be absent when the eye is dark-adapted (Mayer, Kuhnt[2]). There are also psychological factors, which form at any rate the most probable explanation of simultaneous contrast over colour-scotomatous areas (Tschermak[3]) and over the blind spot. The entoptic visibility of the blind spot[4] is itself evidence of contrast, as are also the effects of stimulation of the optic nerve by the constant current (G. E. Müller[5]).

Simultaneous contrast is under ordinary conditions limited to the eye stimulated (Hering[6]), but binocular contrast can also be proved to occur[7].

[1] *Arch. f. Ophth.* xxxv. 4, 1, 1889; xxxvi. 1, 1, 1890.

[2] *Loc. cit.* xxvii. 3, 1, 1881.

[3] *Arch. f. d. ges. Physiol.* lxxxii. 559, 1900.

[4] Brewster; Purkinje; Aubert; v. Helmholtz; Charpentier, *Compt. rend.* cxxvi. 1634, 1898.

[5] *Ztsch. f. Psychol. u. Physiol. d. Sinnesorg.* xiv. 329, 1897.

[6] *Loc. cit.* i. 18, 1890.

[7] Fechner; H. Meyer; v. Helmholtz; Hering, in Hermann's *Handb. d. Physiol.* iii. i. 600, 1879; Ebbinghaus, *Arch. f. d. ges. Physiol.* xlvi. 498, 1894; Chauveau, *Compt. rend.* cxiii. 1891; D. Axenfeld, *Arch. ital. de Biol.* xii. 28, 1889; xxvii. 103, 1897; Burch, *Jl. of Physiol.* xxv. 1900.

SECTION VII

THE EVOLUTION OF COLOUR VISION

CHAPTER I

INTRODUCTION

A priori we should expect some light to be thrown upon the fully developed colour sense of man by a knowledge of the stages through which that colour sense has evolved. The sources of our information on the evolution of colour vision are few and the methods of investigation difficult and arduous. Only recently have the researches been carried out in a scientific manner and yielded valuable results.

Positive evidence is derived from three chief sources. In the first place we naturally appeal to the visual sensations of lower animals. These are extremely difficult to investigate since we are almost wholly dependent upon observation of motor responses which the animals make to various light-stimuli, though some deductions can be made from the structure of the visual organs. In the invertebrata little can be done beyond recording the phototropism of the animal, *i.e.*, its attraction or repulsion by lights of different wave-length and intensity, as exhibited by its movements towards (positive phototropism) or away from (negative phototropism) the light[1]. As we ascend the animal scale the increase in complexity of the nervous system and of the visual organs is accompanied by a corresponding increase in complexity of the motor responses, associated with a greater difficulty in their interpretation. On the other hand, as we descend the animal scale from man there is an unwarranted tendency to interpret the apparently purposeful responses of the animal in an anthropomorphic manner which is not necessarily justified on neurological and psychological grounds. For example, we have little knowledge of the psychology

[1] Mast, *Light and the Behavior of Organisms*, New York, 1911.

of the lower mammal, with its less highly developed nervous system. The temptation to interpret such an animal's actions in terms appropriate only to the human mind has proved very great and has undoubtedly given rise to error in the past. Our deductions must of necessity be anthropomorphic, since such terms as visual sensation, attraction, repulsion, pleasure, pain, and so on, have no meaning for us except in so far as these processes form a part of the contents of our own minds[1]. Yet it should be a guarded anthropomorphism, neither exaggerating the psychological elements nor flying to the impossible antithesis of imagining that the anthropomorphism can be eliminated by a new terminology.

In the second place a study of the colour vision of primitive races may throw some light on the evolution of visual sensations. It may be that some primitive races are in a condition of arrested development—of vision, as of other faculties. We have only just crossed the threshold of this part of the investigation and it is to be hoped that no time will be lost in carrying it forward, lest the material for the research be obliterated by the march of civilisation.

The third source of information is the development of visual sensations in the infant. It is generally admitted that "ontogeny is a compressed phylogeny,"—that each individual passes rapidly through the same stages of development which have marked the upgrowth of the race. Here again, little progress has been made, and the investigation is arduous and full of pitfalls.

Besides these main sources there are others of less security. We are familiar with congenital defects of vision, and it may be that some of them are atavistic, that development has become arrested at a stage which corresponds with an earlier stage in the development of the race. Some arguments too may be derived from the careful study of normal colour vision, but the evidence derived from both these sources is too uncertain to be of much value.

CHAPTER II

THE COMPARATIVE PSYCHOLOGY OF COLOUR VISION

I shall briefly review the comparative psychology of vision in vertebrates only, laying particular stress upon points of theoretical interest.

[1] Cf. Washburn, *The Animal Mind*, New York, 1908.

The most recent and most exhaustive experiments have been made by Hess[1].

Mammals. Graber[2] experimented on nine dogs by his "preference method." A poodle and a fox terrier showed definite preferences. When black and white were presented white was chosen 56 times, black 4: when light red and blue, blue 53 times, red 7; when the same and a much darker blue, blue 32 times, red 28. The results may have been due to preference for the brighter colour. Lubbock[3] experimented with a poodle. Three pairs of cards coloured blue, yellow, and orange, were used. One card from each pair was placed on the floor and the remaining card of one of the pairs shown to the dog in the hope that she would learn to select from the three cards before her the one that was of the same colour as that held up. Training for ten weeks proved entirely without success. Lubbock himself remarks that negative results prove nothing as to the colour vision of the animal. Himstedt and Nagel[4] taught a poodle to fetch coloured balls. On being ordered to fetch "red" it brought first scarlet or bright red, then orange, but only the latter when there were no more conspicuous red balls left. Balls coloured with Bismarck brown were a cause of difficulty to it. "Blue and grey were obviously quite different to it from red, even in all degrees of brightness of each."

Elmer Gates[5] experimented with dogs and food receptacles of various colours, including grey: only receptacles of one particular colour actually contained food. In some experiments coloured metal plates were laid on a passage, certain colours being connected with a battery, so that if the dog stepped upon them it received a shock. Gates concluded from his researches that dogs could distinguish not only colours but relatively fine differences of hue. The description is so meagre that it is impossible to determine whether due precautions were observed.

Samojloff and Pheophilaktowa[6] tested whether a dog could be taught by much training to distinguish between different colours as well as between different brightnesses. Three boxes were placed in a row;

[1] *Vergleichende Physiologie des Gesichtsinnes*, Jena, 1912 (Bibliography): "Birds"—*Arch. f. Augenhlk.* LVII. 4, 298, 317, 1907; LIX. 2, 142, 1908: "Fishes"—*loc. cit.* LXIV. Ergänzungsheft, 1, 1909; *Arch. f. d. ges. Physiol.* CXXXIV. 1910: CXLII. 1911; *Zool. Jahrb.* 1912; "Reptiles and Amphibia"—*Arch. f. d. ges. Physiol.* CXXXII. 255, 1910.

[2] *Grundlinien zur Erforschung des Helligkeits- u. Farbensinnes der Thiere*, Prag, 1884.

[3] *On the Senses, Instincts, and Intelligence of Animals*, p. 280, London, 1888.

[4] *Festschrift d. Univ. Freiburg*, 1902.

[5] *The Monist*, p. 574, 1895.

[6] *Centralbl. f. Physiol.* XXI. 133, 1907.

each had a disc in front, 25 cm. in diameter, of which two held grey papers and one a saturated green. The "green" box contained a biscuit. After training it was found that out of fifty papers, ranging from black to white there was no grey which, when presented to the subject for discrimination from the standard green, yielded a percentage of errors greater than 31. Later tests showed that such discrimination only occurred under certain conditions. If the grey was presented as a square and the green as a circle, green was chosen: but if the green was a triangle or square, the grey square was invariably chosen. Hence the discrimination of a colour from a series of greys is only possible when the conditions have been thoroughly learnt.

Nicolai[1], did not succeed in teaching his two dogs to distinguish between red and green bowls. Colvin and Burford[2] experimented in the same manner with three dogs, a cat, and a squirrel, food being placed in red receptacles amongst similar empty receptacles of other colours. The colour was distinguished in 87·3 per cent. of trials, the squirrel responding best. Kinnaman[3] attempted in a series of similar feeding experiments to eliminate the ambiguity of discrimination of brightness and colour-differences. Monkeys were tested with glass tumblers covered with papers of different colours, and when it had been shown that they were able to identify a vessel of a particular colour as associated with food, the power of distinguishing the colour from greys of the same brightness was tested. Kinnaman came to the conclusion that the capacity to distinguish colours as such in monkeys was undoubted.

J. B. Watson[4], criticising Kinnaman's results, says that the use of coloured papers can never give a satisfactory test of colour vision in animals. He himself used a spectrometer apparatus which illuminated a screen with two monochromatic red and green patches. Food boxes were placed beneath the patches, one being empty, the other containing a grape. If the red box were opened the grape was obtained; if the green, the monkey was pulled back. In early tests with red and green the animals failed to react to red. Blue-yellow discrimination arose more rapidly than red-green in all cases (three monkeys). The experiments were early vitiated by the onset of position habits.

Yerkes[5] made very exhaustive experiments on the Japanese dancing

[1] *Jl. f. Psychol. u. Neurol.* x. 1907.

[2] *Psychol. Rev., Psychol. Monographs*, XI. 1, 1909.

[3] *Amer. J. of Psychol.* XIII. 98, 173, 1902.

[4] *J. of Comp. Neur. and Psychol.* XIX. 1, 1909.

[5] *The Dancing Mouse*, New York, 1902.

mouse. The method consisted in teaching the animals to associate one of two differently illuminated compartments with a disagreeable electric shock. Light blue and orange, green and red, violet and red, were distinguished even when their luminosities were considerably varied. The possibility that these discriminations were made from brightness rather than colour was not wholly eliminated. Yerkes concluded, however, that the mice have a certain degree of ability to distinguish red, green, and violet as colours. No ability to discriminate green and blue was shown unless there was a great difference in brightness. There is evidence that the red end of the spectrum is much darker to the mouse's than to the human eye. Waugh[1] on the other hand found that his mice could only distinguish red from white and light greys with great difficulty.

Davis and Cole[2] experimented on racoons by the feeding method and found that while discrimination of black from white, yellow, red, blue or green appeared easy, that of blue from yellow and red from green was difficult. Davis thought it probable that the animals were colour-blind, but Hess does not agree with this conclusion.

Washburn and Abbott[3] made attempts to discover the brightness value of red for the light-adapted eye of the rabbit. They arrived at the conclusion that this animal can discriminate between a saturated red and a grey paper, and that the discrimination is based upon luminosity rather than colour. Red has a low stimulus value for the rabbit. The experiments furnish no evidence that it sees red as a colour, but do not prove that it does not do so.

An elaborate series of researches has been carried out in Pawlow's laboratory[4] with a view to establishing "conditional reflexes." The salivary secretion was used as the indicator. An indifferent stimulus, *e.g.*, a strong electrical stimulus to the skin, is at first applied simultaneously with the placing of food or acid in the mouth. After a short time the salivary secretion is called forth by the application of the indifferent stimulus alone. Orbéli[5] studied the effects of coloured optical stimuli. After exposure of a red square on a white screen reflex salivary secretion was obtained. The same recurred when other colours were exhibited. If red and grey squares were exhibited successively and the dog fed only after exhibition of the red square the

[1] *J. of Comp. Neur. and Psychol.* xv. 549, 1905.

[2] Cole, *loc. cit.* xvii. 211, 1907.

[3] *J. of Animal Behavior*, ii. 145.

[4] Pawlow, *Brit. Med. Jl.* ii. 473, 1913.

[5] *Comptes rend de la Soc. méd. russe*, St Petersburg, 1907; *Arch. des Sc. biol.* xiv. 1908.

salivary reflex eventually followed the red stimulus only. It was found, however, that the reflex in dogs was conditioned by the change in intensity of the light, not by variations in the wave-length. The experiments are not of a nature to demonstrate colour-blindness in the dogs.

Kalischer[1] has published interesting experiments on dogs. His animals were placed in a dark chamber which could be illuminated by means of light from a lamp, transmitted through coloured glass. On the appearance of red light the dog was given food, which was, however, withheld during the period when light was excluded. When a perfect reaction habit had been formed, the experiment was varied sometimes by transmitting the light through blue, instead of through red glass, though the subject was still only fed when a red light was exposed. In order to render the comparison of brightness between the different lights more difficult, their successive exposure was always followed by a dark interval. At first the subjects reacted in a similar manner to either coloured light, but after some further training the difference was duly learnt, and eventually discrimination became so perfect that no matter how the brightness of the red or the blue light might be changed the reaction was almost invariably correct.

Observations were also made with green, yellow and red-violet lights, but discrimination was found to be the most definite when red and blue were used ; red and yellow proving very difficult to learn, and red with red-violet almost impossible. Colvin and Burford likewise found that when their subjects were required to discriminate between red and violet, only a relatively low percentage of right choices was obtained.

In later experiments Kalischer left his subjects untested for two or three days, and then presented a blue or a green light previous to the exposure of the food-colour, red. Though these experiments were repeated many times and under varied conditions, the animals never failed to react correctly to the food-colour when it appeared.

It is of importance to note that not only did the animals learn to discriminate, during the course of the experiments, between different colours irrespective of the degree of their luminosity, but that in addition the behaviour shown on the appearance of each colour was characteristic, *e.g.*, on the exposure of a blue light the subject would appear frightened and quickly withdraw his head from the food ; whereas when a green or a yellow light was exposed great hesitation was shown, the head was allowed to fall gradually nearer and nearer towards the meat as though to seize it, and was then suddenly jerked away.

[1] *Arch. f. Anat.* p. 316, 1909.

The conclusions which Kalischer draws from his experiments are as follow:

(*a*) That there is no doubt of the ability of dogs to perceive differences of hue as well as differences of brightness.

(*b*) That whereas such colour discrimination is cortical, brightness discrimination is to some extent sub-cortical, reactions to changes of illumination being found to occur even after extirpation of the visual cortex.

(*c*) That there exist considerable individual differences in the sensibility of dogs to colours.

By far the most exhaustive experiments on dogs have been carried out by Miss E. M. Smith[1]. The apparatus used is shown in Figs. 42 and

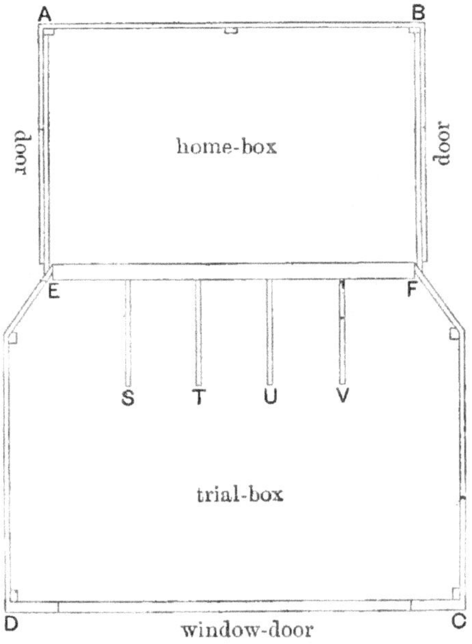

Fig. 42. Ground plan of experimental dog box. (E. M. Smith.)

43. It will be noticed that the "home box" is separated from the "trial box" by a partition in which there are five glass screens S_{1-5}. Cards of various colours could be introduced into these screens. The dog was placed in the home box and let into the trial box through S_1, which was then closed. The preliminary "general training" consisted first in teaching the dog to pass through the screens. These

[1] *Brit. Jl. of Psychol.* v. 119, 1912.

were left transparent and a biscuit was placed within view in the home box. Next, cards of medium grey were placed in S_2, S_3, S_4, and S_5. Finally, only one shutter contained a grey card. The dogs were thus taught always to go to the opaque screen in order to get through into the home box and receive the reward.

The various test series were then commenced. (1) "Colour preference series." Maximum blue, red, yellow and green cards were put in four screens and the frequency with which each was selected was noted in 70 tests. For one dog the numbers were red 32, blue 26, yellow 8, green 4. The red and blue were much darker to the human eye than the yellow and green. (2) "Approximate brightness value series."

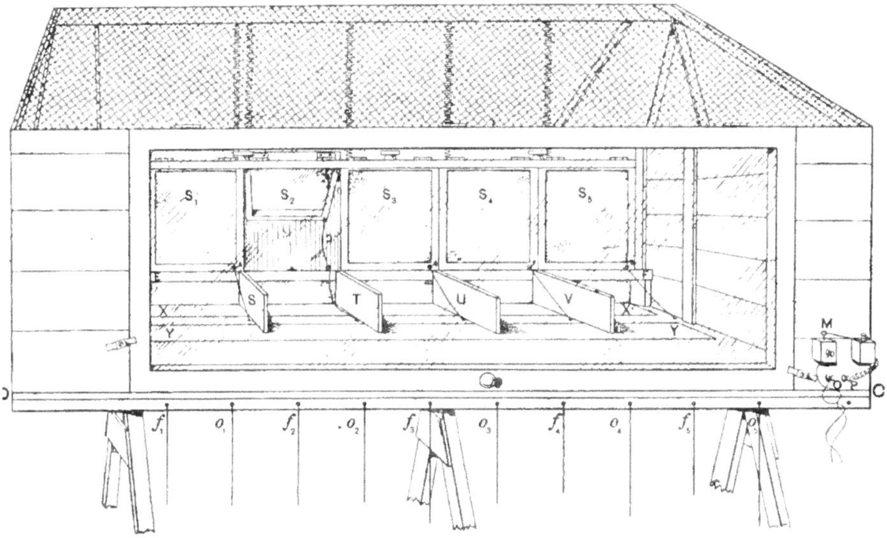

Fig. 43. Elevation of experimental dog box. (E. M. Smith.)

Red, blue, yellow, green, and 14 shades of grey were used. First, the particular colour was presented simultaneously with the grey which was most remote from it in brightness. When the animal had given proof of its ability to discriminate between these two the next grey, differing only slightly less in brightness, was substituted. Second, all the greys, in the same order as before, were presented on the same day for discrimination from the standard colour, each grey being exposed 5 times in succession. Next, the colour and the greys were presented in irregular order. It was found that in the case of the most intelligent dog the average percentage of right reactions was much higher for green and yellow than for blue and red: further the first colour tested, blue, had the smallest, and the last, green, the largest percentage of right cases. To test if this were due to general improvement from increased practice rather than specific qualitative differences the "repeat brightness value series" was given. In this series all four colours were re-tested with additional precautions. (3) "Hue discrimination series." (*a*) Coloured cards and equivalent greys were exhibited in pairs: and (*b*) two coloured cards were shown simultaneously, such that (α) the pairs were equal in brightness and saturation; (β) the standard colour was slightly or obviously darker than the other; (γ) the standard colour was slightly or obviously lighter than the other. (4) "Grey difference threshold series." (5) "Colour threshold series."

Enough has been described to show that the tests were exhaustive, and elaborate efforts were made to determine the nature of the discrimination evinced. Perhaps the most serious objection which can be brought against the experiments is their extreme elaboration. Anyone who has had experience of testing the colour vision of untrained human observers knows the frequency with which luminosity and colour matches are confused. How much more this source of error is likely to be present in dogs needs only to be mentioned. It was allowed for to a certain extent by a graduated method of marking. As Miss Smith says, "In view of their relative difficulty, sensory discrimination tests on the higher vertebrates might aptly be compared to complicated intellectual tests on man, in which the subject, unable to grasp completely the point at issue, has to rely on a series of sporadic gleams."

Only a summary of the chief results can be given here, the reader being referred for details to the admirably thought out original paper. In favour of the view that dogs are only able to perceive differences of brightness are (1) the result of the "colour preference series"; (2) the greater the difference in brightness between a standard colour and grey, the more definite is the discrimination; (3) the length of time required to establish a successful discrimination habit between blue and red; (4) the fact that whereas change of colour frequently appeared to pass unnoticed, a marked change of brightness often caused confusion; (5) the fact that green and yellow were not at all, or only with the greatest difficulty, discriminated from white; (6) the fact that during a prolonged series increased confusion and uncertainty in discrimination were shown from day to day.

In favour of the view that dogs possess rudimentary colour discrimination are (1) the decreased time for training required by each new colour in the "approximate brightness value series"; (2) the unique physiological effects produced by the different colours even when of approximately the same brightness (greater affective value of red compared with blue, etc.); (3) the evidence afforded by the "approximate brightness value series" that on the whole no grey was found that was indistinguishable from the standard colours employed, training being still imperfect; (4) the difficulty and confusion of the "grey difference threshold series" as compared with the parallel "approximate brightness value series"; (5) the results obtained from the "hue discrimination series"; (6) the difference in the approximate thresholds of the four colours and grey as determined by the "colour threshold series."

Whereas the facts recorded in the first group of items of evidence are not incompatible with the assumption that dogs possess some sort of colour vision, those in the second group are quite irreconcilable with the view that the subjects are limited to brightness vision.

Miss Smith draws the following conclusions: (1) That while evidence has been obtained to show that some dogs possess a rudimentary power of colour discrimination, such discrimination is highly unstable and cannot be supposed to play any part in the animal's normal existence.

(2) That the colour sense is, as shown by the high colour threshold, very weak.

(3) That colour discrimination, even where clearly established, may be readily inhibited by differences of luminosity or position.

Piper[1] investigated the electrical reactions of dogs, cats and rabbits. In dogs and cats he found the reactions in both light- and dark-adapted eyes to correspond with the achromatic scotopic values for man. In rabbits the strongest photopic value was 570 $\mu\mu$, scotopic 540 $\mu\mu$.

Hess tested a monkey in the following manner. Grain was scattered over a black surface, upon part of which a spectrum was thrown. The monkey gathered all the grains from the extreme red to the extreme violet, leaving those unilluminated. When the animal was dark-adapted and the intensity of the light diminished until the grains were visible to the dark-adapted experimenter only in the yellow and green, only these grains were gathered. Hess concluded that the extent of the visible spectrum is the same for the monkey as for man, and that it is brightest for the dark-adapted monkey in the region where it is also brightest for the dark-adapted man.

Hess also studied the effects of different spectral lights and the lights transmitted by coloured glasses on the pupil reactions of cats and rabbits.

[1] *Arch. f. Anat.*, Suppl. 1905.

It was shown by Sachs[1] that in man the extent of the pupil reaction varies with the subjective luminosity of the light. Similarly Abelsdorff[2] showed that the maximal pupillomotor effect for the light-adapted eye was at 600 $\mu\mu$, for the dark-adapted eye at 540 $\mu\mu$. Hess found the photopic and scotopic values for cats and rabbits about the same as for man.

It appears therefore that mammals have the same spectral limits as man; that they have a similar capacity for dark adaptation; and that their luminosity curves are similar.

Birds. Lloyd Morgan[3] experimented with chickens. A chicken which picked out bits of yolk of hard-boiled egg from the white was given pieces of orange peel, which it found distasteful. Afterwards for some time it was suspicious of yolk. On the other hand after having learned to avoid bad-tasting black and yellow caterpillars, it did not object to wasps, but probably points of difference other than colour were apparent to it.

J. P. Porter[4] investigated the colour vision of the English sparrow and other birds by feeding experiments. A number of glasses of like size and shape were covered inside and out with coloured papers, including dark and light grey. The glasses were placed in a row on a board, and food was always put in the same coloured glass, the position of which was changed. The sparrow and cowbird learned to pick out the right vessel. Rouse[5] investigated pigeons by Graber's method of allowing a choice between compartments illuminated by different coloured glasses. The pigeons showed a preference for green and blue. A greater rapidity of breathing was recorded under green and blue lights than under others.

Hess experimented with birds of diurnal habits (chickens, pigeons) and nocturnal habits (owls) in the same manner as for mammals.

For *diurnal* birds corn or rice grains were scattered over a matt black surface, part of which was illuminated by a spectrum. They usually pecked at the grains in the orange and red first, then those in the green and yellow, and some in the blue-green. Those in the green-blue, blue and violet were left untouched. Dark-adapted chickens

[1] *Arch. f. d. ges. Physiol.* LII. 79, 1892; *Arch. f. Ophth.* XXXIX. 3, 1893; *Ztsch. f. Psychol. u. Physiol. d. Sinnesorg.* XXII. 388, 1900.

[2] *Ztsch. f. Psychol. u. Physiol. d. Sinnesorg.* XXI. 451. 1900; *Arch. f. Augenhlk.* XLI. 155, 1900; *Arch. f. Anat. u. Physiol.* 561. 1900.

[3] *Habit and Instinct*, London. 1896.

[4] *Amer. J. of Psychol.* XV. 313, 1904; XVII. 248. 1906.

[5] *Harvard Psych. Studies*, II. 580, 1906

generally pecked somewhat farther towards the blue, but seldom in the blue and violet. When the spectrum was reduced until it was almost colourless for the dark-adapted human eye they pecked chiefly or solely in a region corresponding to the yellow and orange-yellow, *i.e.*, rather red-wards of the human scotopic maximum luminosity. Chickens 48 hours after hatching behaved in the same way as older birds. Hawks (*Falco tinnunculus*), fed with pieces of meat, showed the same shortening of the violet end of the spectrum. All the birds first pecked in the region which is brightest for man, and then sought regions of less luminosity. If half the field were illuminated with light transmitted through a red glass and the other half with blue light, light- or partially dark-adapted birds pecked first in the red half, turning to the blue half only when the red was cleared of grains. By suitable alterations of the strengths of the lights, the blue half was left untouched, even though the red grains appeared to the human eye very dark red and scarcely visible whilst the blue were clearly seen. Blue grains, however, were as eagerly pecked as red if the light were made sufficiently strong. Dark adaptation increases the sensitiveness of birds' vision very markedly. The "pecking-limit" is for them only slightly, if at all, higher than the extrafoveal threshold visibility of the grains for a 1—2 hours' dark-adapted human eye. Adaptation appears to be slower in hawks and buzzards than in the human eye.

Nocturnal birds were investigated in the same manner. If an owl, which has perched for several hours in sunlight, is examined with a moderately bright spectrum illuminating white pieces of meat, these are snapped up first in the red, yellow, green, or blue-green. The spectrum extends further violet-wards for nocturnal than for diurnal birds, but is still much shortened at this end. When thoroughly dark-adapted owls snap at meat in the blue and violet; they snap first in that part of the achromatic spectrum which is brightest for man, or slightly farther towards the violet. Dark adaptation causes a rapid rise of sensibility during the first half-hour and the maximum sensibility appears to be much greater than for man.

The pupil reactions of birds are somewhat complicated. The maximum constriction for diurnal birds (fowl and pigeon) is in the region of the orange and yellow, diminishing gradually towards both ends of the spectrum, more rapidly towards the violet the less the dark adaptation. For the dark-adapted eyes of nocturnal birds the maximum is in the yellow-green and green, falling slowly towards the violet end.

It appears therefore that diurnal birds see the spectrum shortened towards the violet end, much as it would be seen by the human eye through a reddish yellow glass. The shortening is similar but rather less for nocturnal birds. Both types possess a power of dark adaptation the same as or very similar to that of man.

Reptiles. Hess investigated several varieties of tortoise, and found that their vision nearly resembles that of birds. They have the same shortening of the spectrum towards the violet end. More remarkable is the fact that they possess a high degree of dark adaptation, the increase in sensibility being seemingly the same as that of the human eye looking through a suitable orange-tinged glass. It may be mentioned here that these animals are generally admitted to possess no rods or visual purple in their retinae.

Hess noticed that the only animals which he examined and found to possess a shortened spectrum towards the violet end were such as possess coloured oil globules in their cones. At the same time he points out the difficulties in accepting this fact as a complete and satisfactory explanation.

Amphibia. Yerkes[1] caused a green frog to go through a simple labyrinth leading to a tank of water. At the point where the first choice between two paths occurred a red card was placed on one side and a white on the other. When the frog had learned to take the correct path the cards were exchanged and the confusion of the animals showed that they discriminated between the cards, though it may have been a luminosity- rather than a colour-discrimination. Loeb[2] found that frogs showed negative phototropism, and preferred red to blue light. Torelle[3] found that two species of frog showed positive phototropism, associated with a tendency to prefer blue to red light. The phototropism persists when the animal is blinded, although in the normal animal the eyes are involved in the reaction since it occurs when the skin is covered and the eyes left intact[4]. Cole[5] found that the phototropism of *Rana clamata* differs according to the surrounding temperature. Pearse[6] found some amphibia positively, and others negatively heliotropic.

[1] *Harvard Psych. Studies*, I. 579, 1903.

[2] *Der Heliotropismus der Tiere*, Würzburg, 1890.

[3] *Amer. J. of Physiol.* IX. 466, 1903.

[4] Koranyi, *Centralbl. f. Physiol.* VI. 6. 1892; G. H. Parker, *Amer. J. of Physiol.* X. 28, 1903.

[5] *J. of Comp. Neur. and Psychol.* XVII. 193, 1907.

[6] *Proc. of the Amer. Acad. of Arts and Sc.* XLV. 161, 1910.

Hess examined an American salamander (*Diemictylus viridescens*), the ordinary toad (*Bufo vulgaris*), and the African spurred frog (*Xenopus Mülleri*). He found that the spectrum does not appear shortened to them. He also found that their range of adaptation appeared to be the same as for the human eye.

Fish. Graber[1] tested two species of fish, but no convincing proof of their powers of colour discrimination were obtained. Bateson[2] placed food on coloured tiles and found that fish picked it off most readily from white and pale blue, and least readily from dark red and dark blue, a fact which can be explained by luminosity differences. Zolotnitzki[3] fixed dark red *Cheironomus* larvae and white, green, yellow, and red pieces of wool of the same size and shape as the larvae to the wall of the fish tank. The fish showed decided preference for the red, swam past the white and green, while some of them paused at the yellow. Washburn and Bentley[4] investigated the chub (*Semotilus atromaculatus*). Two dissecting forceps were used, alike except that to the legs of one were fastened, with rubber bands, small sticks painted red, while to those of the other similar green sticks were attached. The forceps were fastened to a wooden bar projecting from a wooden screen, which divided the circular tank into two compartments, and hung down into the water. Food was always placed in the red pair of forceps, which were made frequently to change places with the green; and the fish was caused to enter the compartment half of the time on one side, and half of the time on the other. This was to prevent identification of the food fork by its position or the direction in which the fish had to turn. The animal quickly learned to single out the red fork as the one important to its welfare, and in forty experiments, mingled with others so that the association might not be weakened, where there was no food in either fork, and where the forceps and rubber bands were changed so that no odour of food could linger, it never failed to bite first at the red. Moreover, the probability that its discrimination was based upon brightness was greatly lessened by using, when experimenting without food, a different red much lighter than that in the food tests. The fish successfully discriminated red from blue paints in the same way, and it was

[1] *Grundlinien zur Erforschung des Helligkeits- u. Farbensinnes der Thiere*, Prag and Leipzig, 1884.

[2] *Jl. of the Marine Biol. Assoc. U. K.* I. 225, 1887.

[3] *Arch. de Zool. expér.* IX. 1901.

[4] *J. of Comp. Neur. and Psychol.* XVI. 113, 1906; Washburn, *The Animal Mind*, New York, 1908.

afterwards trained by putting food in the green fork, to break the earlier association and bite first at the green.

Reighard[1] fed grey snappers (*Lutianus griseus*) with small *Atherinae* which were artificially coloured with seven hues. On simultaneous presentation of white and blue the white was generally seized first, with blue and light or dark red or yellow the blue first; no difference was apparent between blue and green. If *Cassiopea* tentacles were fastened to the *Atherinae* the snappers soon learnt to avoid them. After they had learnt to avoid red *Atherinae* with tentacles it was found that they also rejected red ones without tentacles, but that they still took those stained any other colour.

The researches of Zolotnitzki, Washburn and Bentley, and Reighard are consistent with the view that the fish are totally colour-blind.

Hess examined a number of species of fish and found that they appeared to behave exactly as if they had the visual perceptions of a totally colour-blind man (see Part II). In the light of the spectrum young *Atherinae* rapidly congregated in the yellow-green and green, *i.e.*, the brightest part of the human achromatic scotopic spectrum. Far fewer were found in the yellow and scarcely any in the red; there were rather more in the blue. If the spectrum were displaced the fish rapidly rearranged themselves in the same fashion. By moving a card along the spectrum so as to intercept certain rays the fish could be driven up to the blue or violet ends. If the red-yellow and green-blue regions were intercepted the fish spread in both directions towards the ends. If only the red and yellow-red and the blue and violet were exposed many more fish collected at the violet than at the red end though to the human photopic eye the red is much brighter. Just as to the human achromatic scotopic eye, the red end was shortened so that the extreme red produced no more effect on the fish than complete darkness. By lighting one half of the basin with homogeneous light and the other with equivalent mixed light which could be varied in intensity it was possible to get the fish to arrange themselves evenly in the two halves. In this manner the luminosity values of different parts of the spectrum were worked out and it was found that the luminosity curve agreed very well with that of the achromatic scotopic or totally colour-blind human eye. Hess was also able to measure the effects of dark adaptation. He found that after 15—20 minutes in the dark the sensibility of the fish for light was many hundred times as great as immediately after transference from light to dark. By using red and blue

[1] Carnegie Inst., Washington, II. 257, 1908.

lights of suitable intensity he was able to prove that the Purkinje phenomenon is not shown by fishes.

Owing to the forward movement of the pigment in the pigment epithelium of fishes when exposed to light they possess a certain amount of physical adaptation. Owing to the absorption by the pigment they are in the photopic condition less sensitive to the violet end of the spectrum.

Hess used various coloured imitation baits against different backgrounds, and showed that their visibility to the fish depended upon their luminosity and not upon their colour. If the brightness of the grey background corresponded to the achromatic scotopic brightness of the bait it was not seen.

Hess's results have been criticised by Bauer[1], v. Frisch[2] and Franz[3], without, however, seriously shaking his position.

Amphioxus. The response of amphioxus by movements to light show that the curve of stimulus values of different homogeneous lights agrees nearly, if not completely, with the luminosity curve for fishes and for the totally colour-blind man, and that the adaptative changes of sensibility to light in amphioxus with its primitive visual organs, nearly resemble those of higher vertebrates.

CHAPTER III

THE COLOUR VISION OF PRIMITIVE RACES

Attention was first drawn to the colour vision of primitive people by Gladstone, in 1858. In his *Studies on Homer and the Homeric Age* he drew attention to the vagueness of the colour terminology of Homer, and concluded that the ideas of colour at that time must have been different from our own. Ten years later Geiger[4] came to the conclusion that the colour sense of the ancients must have been defective. Not only in Greek literature, but also in the Indian Vedic hymns, in the Zendavesta, in the Norse Eddas, and in ancient Chinese and Semitic writings there is evidence of the paucity of colour terms, especially in

[1] *Centralbl. f. Physiol.* XXIII. 1909; *Arch. f. d. ges. Physiol.* CXXXIII. 7, 1910; CXXXVII. 1911.

[2] *Verhandl. d. Deutsch. Zool. Gesellsch.* 220, 1911.

[3] *Internat. Rev. d. ges. Hydrobiol. u. Hydrogr.* 1910.

[4] *Contributions to the History of the Development of the Human Race*, p. 48, 1880.

the case of names for green and blue. Geiger advanced the view that the sensation of red had been evolved first, then yellow and green, and finally blue. Magnus[1] came to the same conclusions from still more extensive researches, and Gladstone[2] returned to the subject in the same year.

These views were strongly criticised by Grant Allen[3]. It was shown that modern poems showed similar peculiarities, red occurring much more often than blue in Swinburne's *Poems and Ballads* and in Tennyson's *Princess*. La Fontaine used an epithet for blue once only in all his poems (Javal[4]).

Philological evidence on matters of this kind is notoriously open to doubt, but it is probable that the opposition to the views of Gladstone, Geiger, and Magnus was carried too far. The examination of two parties of Nubians, who were travelling in Germany in 1877, by Virchow and others did much to bring about this result. It was found that they used the same word for blue as for black and other dark colours, yet they sorted coloured papers and wools correctly.

The use of pigments by the Egyptians, Assyrians, Greeks and others has also been brought forward in opposition to Geiger's views. Green and blue pigments were used by the Egyptians long before the time of Homer, and green and blue beads are found in the prehistoric Egyptian tombs. Bénzaky[5] has collected the evidence from ancient monuments and considers that it conclusively disproves any colour defect in the Egyptians and Greeks. As Rivers points out, however, the colour sense of the Egyptians—and they appear to have had two names for green and one for blue—has no direct bearing on that of the Greeks, who may have remained in a state of arrested development. Moreover, even in Egypt human statues with blue hair have been found, and in the Acropolis there may be seen a blue bull, a blue horse, and a man with blue hair and beard, all dating from later than the time of Homer[6].

Magnus[7] pointed out that the same defect of terminology for green and blue which characterises ancient writings still exists among many primitive races.

1 *Die geschichtliche Entwickelung des Farbensinnes*, Leipzig, 1877.

2 *Nineteenth Century*, II. 366, 1877.

3 *The Colour Sense*, London, 1879.

4 *Bull. de la Soc. d'Anthropologie de Paris*, XII. 480, 1877.

5 *Du Sens chromatique dans l'antiquité*, Paris, 1897.

6 Cf. E. A. Gardner, *Handbook of Greek Sculpture*, p. 28, 1902.

7 *Untersuchungen u. d. Farbensinn d. Naturvölker*. Jena, 1880; *Ueber ethnol. Untersuch. d. Farbensinnes*, Breslau, 1883.

By far the most important contributions on the subject are those of Rivers[1].

In the Torres Straits expedition Rivers examined the colour vision of two tribes of Papuans, of natives of the island of Kiwai, and of members of several Australian tribes. The languages of these people showed different stages in the evolution of colour terminology, which correspond in a striking manner with the course of evolution derived from ancient writings by Geiger. Some Australian natives from the district of Seven Rivers used only three colour epithets; one for red, purple, and orange; another for white, yellow and green; and a third for black, blue, indigo and violet. In Kiwai there was a very definite name for red, and a less definite for yellow; greens were called by the same names as white and black or light and dark; blue, violet, and black had the same name; other Kiwaians had a name for green which was also applied to blue and violet. The natives of Murray Island and of the Island of Mabuiag showed two further stages in the evolution of colour language.

In these four stages the lowest possesses only a definite term for red apart from white and black. In the next stage there are definite terms for red and yellow, and an indefinite term for green. In the third stage there are definite terms for red, yellow, and green, and a term for blue has been borrowed from another language; while in the highest stage there are terms for both green and blue, but these tend to be confused with one another. The series corresponds with the order of the natives in general intellectual and cultural development.

The absence of a definite term for blue is very common. In some the word for blue and black is the same, *e.g.*, Kiwaians, Hovas, Bushmen, and many Australian and Melanesian tribes. In many others the word for blue and green is the same, *e.g.*, in African and South American races and in Jamaica. The absence of a term for brown is also common in Australian and Melanesian languages, as well as in Tamil, Singhalese, Eskimo, Welsh, etc., a brown object being called red, yellow, or dark.

Rivers tested 150 natives of Murray Island with Holmgren's wools and failed to find any who confused red and green, but blue and green and blue and violet were constantly confused. Examination with Lovibond's tintometer showed a relatively greater sensibility to red and less to blue than in the European.

[1] *Pop. Sci. Mo.* LIX. 44, 1901; *Jl. of the Anthropological Ins.* XXXI. 229, 1901; *Rep. of the Cambridge Expedition to Torres Straits*, II. 1, 1901; "Observations on the Senses of the Todas," *Brit. Jl. of Psychol.* I. 321, 1905; *The Todas of the Nilgiri Hills*, Cambridge, 1906.

Rivers suggests that the insensitiveness to blue may be due to greater macular pigmentation. The natives were able to recognise blue readily on the peripheral retina.

Rivers tested 50 natives of Upper Egypt with Holmgren's wools, Nagel's cards, and Lovibond's tintometer. He found much confusion in their colour names, but general agreement with the characteristics of primitive colour nomenclature in other parts of the world. There was a very definite word, *aḥmar*, in use for red, but it was also applied to colours containing a red element, such as orange, purple, violet and brown. A somewhat less definite term, *aṣfar*, was employed for yellow, also for orange and brown and occasionally for green and faint red. The word for green, *akhḍar*, was still less definite, being very often applied to blue, violet, grey and brown. There was no definite word for blue. The word *azraq*, usually regarded as the Arabic equivalent of blue, was never used by these people for light blue, and was applied by them more frequently to black than to an indigo blue. The nearest approach to a word for blue was *läbänî*, milk colour, which was, however, often used also for green, grey, and brown. *Azraq* and *iswid* (black) were used indiscriminately for black, blue, and violet, and also for dark brown. The Arabic term for brown, *asmar*, was never once used for this colour though occasionally applied to blue and grey. Over twenty different names were used for brown papers and wools, but generally *aḥmar* or *aṣfar*.

Of 80 natives of Upper Egypt tested by Randall-MacIver and Rivers four were certainly colour-blind (" red-green blind "), making the characteristic mistakes with Holmgren's wools (see Part II). Others made the same kind of matches as the Torres Straits' natives, *i.e.*, they behaved normally with the red, pink, and yellow test wools, but compared green with blue, and blue with violet. Two distinct tendencies were also noted, viz., to match according to saturation rather than according to colour tone, and to put together wools which would be called by them the same name. The colour thresholds for red and yellow were low, that for blue much above the European average.

Amongst the Todas there was a definite word for red which also meant blood. Orange was often called " blood " or " earth." Yellow was called *ârsena*, probably a borrowed word. Green had many names—" leaf," " moss," including the Tamil name and *nîl*, blue, and *kâg*, dark or black. Blue and indigo were generally called *nîl*, a word used by all the Dravidian races of Southern India, but sometimes *kâg* or *kâthiti*, black. The nomenclature for violet and brown was very indefinite. There was a definite name for white, and greys were called white or black, or occasionally "ashes," a common term for this colour in Southern India.

Rivers tested 503 Todas with Holmgren's wools: 43 were found to be definitely colour-blind. The normal individuals matched the wools well, but most confused red and pink, green and blue, violet and blue, and there was a general tendency to confuse faintly coloured wools. One confused blue with grey and brown, and two blue with brown. The defects of this kind were less marked than among the Uralis and Sholagas examined in India[1] and the Egyptians. All showed a tendency to discriminate greens, blues, and violets less definitely than reds and yellows, indicating that the deficiencies in nomenclature for the former group of colours were accompanied by a certain degree of deficiency in their discrimination.

Quantitative observations on the colour thresholds were made with Lovibond's tintometer. The table gives the results obtained by Rivers in five different communities.

	No. examined.	Red	M.V.	σ	C.V.	Yellow	M.V.	σ	C.V.	Blue	M.V.	σ	C.V.
Todas ..	47	32·1	18·1	24·3	75·5	29·2	15 6	21·3	73·1	53·3	20·7	23·4	44·0
Uralis and Sholagas ..	14	31·1	13·5	16·6	53·4	26·4	7·9	8·7	33·1	66·4	15·5	17·6	26·4
Egyptians	26	28·7	14·2	15·8	55·3	26·0	10·5	12·3	47·5	85·4	34·3	43·4	50·9
Murray Islanders	17	17·6	7·5	8·9	50·6	26·8	9·9	11·6	43·0	60·0	16·5	20·2	33·6
English ..	41	27·5	17·9	21·7	79·0	16·7	7·2	10·0	60·1	30·8	11·2	14·9	48·4

In this Table the average thresholds, expressed in units of the instrument, are given in the columns headed by the names of the colours. The figures under the heading M. V. give the mean variations of the results of the individuals of each group from the average result of that group. Under σ are given the standard deviations[2] of the individual results from the average; under C.V. the coefficients of variation as worked out from the formula

$$\frac{\sigma \times 100}{\text{Average}}.$$

This table shows that the Todas have the highest thresholds for red and yellow obtained in any community hitherto tested. The

[1] *Bull. Madras Gov. Museum*, v. 3, 1903.

[2] *I.e.*, $\sqrt{\frac{\Sigma\delta^2}{n}}$, where Σδ is the sum of the squares of the individual differences $\delta_1, \delta_2, \ldots$, from the mean, and n is the number of individuals.

differences, however, between the Todas on the one hand and the Sholagas and Uralis and Egyptians on the other are very slight and within the limits of the probable error.

More important is the difference between the Todas and the Papuans of Torres Straits. There is no great difference between the thresholds for yellow of the two communities, but the thresholds for red differ greatly, the difference, 14·5, being considerably more than three times the probable error of the difference[1], which is 2·8.

This difference is probably connected with the fact that among the Papuans red-green blindness does not occur, while among the Todas it reaches the highest frequency recorded in any community. The difference seems to show that even in those Todas who were able to pass the tests for colour-blindness, there was some deficiency in the sensibility for red as compared with the Torres Straits islanders.

For blue the Todas have a very distinctly higher threshold than the English observers, though lower than the other savage or barbarous races tested. The difference between the figures for the English and the Toda observers is enormously greater than the probable error of the difference, which is only 2·8. The Todas confirm the conclusion previously reached by Rivers, that the defective nomenclature for blue which is so generally found among races of low culture is associated with a certain degree of defective sensibility for this colour.

Rivers made observations on the colour fields of the Papuans and the Todas. The former showed colour fields of considerable size, and differences in the limits for different colours were clearly demonstrated. The Todas had very small colour fields, so small that it was impossible to detect any difference in size. Only in one man did the field for blue seem larger than those for other colours. Since the Todas were more intelligent than the Murray Islanders it is probable that the small fields point to a definite sensory defect.

McDougall[2] suggests that the colour names of the Homeric Greeks and uncultured peoples may be explained by environment. The superior power of red to strike the attention may be due to the fact that red objects in nature are rare, while blue and green are constantly spread out in large tracts of sky and sea and foliage. Further, while many of the rare red objects (blood, fruits, animals, ironstone) are of practical importance, and while the abundant green objects are presented in

[1] *I.e.*, $\sqrt{\Sigma_x^2 + \Sigma_y^2}$ where Σ_x and Σ_y are the probable errors of the two figures to be compared.

[2] *Brit. Jl. of Psychol.* II. 349, 1908.

endless variety of tones, shades and shapes, many of which call for the exercise of discriminatory perception, the widespread blue surfaces of sky and sea are commonly of uniform tone, and in hardly any circumstances is the discrimination of blue tones of practical importance to men of the lower cultures.

The Egyptian peasants examined by Rivers were, however, well acquainted with blue objects and many were wearing blue garments. McDougall attaches much importance to the undoubted greater affective value of warm colours as compared with cold tones, and holds that this factor, rather than defective sensibility for blue and violet, explains the defects in nomenclature and in colour matching. He suggests the view that primitive vision corresponded to our sense of grey, that our senses for blue and yellow became differentiated as the affections produced by the light of the two ends of the spectrum, and that at a later period the senses of red and green became differentiated in a similar way from the sense of yellow. The facts of colour-blindness and the distribution of colour-sense in the periphery of the retina (as generally accepted) fit well with this scheme of development.

Myers[1] holds that "language affords no safe clue to sensibility. A colour name occurs when it is needful. Where it is needless, it will not be formed, be the sensibility to that colour ever so great. If we are to gauge the colour sense of a people by colour nomenclature, nearly every primitive people must be dubbed 'brown-blind' or 'brown-weak,' inasmuch as it is very rare to find a special word for brown.

"The 'red-blindness,' which occurs among the colour-blind, and in the intermediate zone of the normal retina, is strong evidence against the view that red is the first colour-sensation phylogenetically acquired. The one prominent fact, which stands out clearly in this discussion, is that both primitive peoples and infants are attracted most by red and next by yellow; this fact being manifest among the former in their nomenclature and among the latter by their readiness to grasp objects of these colours. I suggest that this superior attractiveness of red is a fundamental characteristic far too deeply and immutably ingrained to be attributable, as McDougall so ingeniously suggests, to the greater utility or rareness of red and yellow objects or to the relative unattractiveness of the broad surrounding expanse of uniformly blue sky, blue-green sea and green foliage. The excitatory action of red is manifest in organisms lower than man."

[1] *Brit. Jl. of Psychol.* II. 361, 1908.

CHAPTER IV

THE DEVELOPMENT OF COLOUR VISION IN THE CHILD

Darwin[1] first pointed out that the power of distinguishing colours is a very late accomplishment in childhood; he found that his children were unable to name colours correctly at an age when they knew the names of most common objects. Preyer[2] made many investigations on one child. Various methods were attempted without very encouraging results. Up to the third year it was found impossible to hold the attention of the child sufficiently long to obtain concordant results by such methods as sorting out coloured wools, cards, etc. or naming different colours. In 1897[3] Preyer drew attention to a more successful device for naming colours. Children of an early age show no facility for comprehending abstract terms. It was found, however, that interest could be awakened by association of different colours with concrete objects. Thus Mrs Stanley Hall's son[4] in the forty-sixth week of life called all black objects "Kitty," because a black cat was so named. The method does not seem to have been much used and could only be employed at a period when probably the colour sense is already fully developed.

Garbini[5] made observations on 600 children. Both Preyer and Garbini agree that the child is unable to distinguish colours until towards the end of the second year, and that red is distinguished and named correctly at an earlier age than blue. Garbini emphasises the fact that the power of distinguishing colours develops earlier than that of naming them, and these early experiments give evidence of little beyond that fact, for the methods were not suited to determining the earliest age of colour discrimination at all accurately.

Methods better adapted to this purpose have been employed by Baldwin[6], Marsden[7], Shinn[8], McDougall[9], Myers[10] and Valentine[11].

[1] *Kosmos*, I. 376, 1877.

[2] *Die Seele des Kindes*, Leipzig, 1881.

[3] *Ztsch. f. Psychol. u. Physiol. d. Sinnesorg.* XIV. 231, 1897.

[4] *The Child-Study Monthly*, II. 460, 1897.

[5] *Arch. per l'Antropologia e la Etnologia*, XXIV. 71, 193, 1894.

[6] *Mental Development in the Child and the Race*, Chap. III. 3rd ed. London, 1906.

[7] *Psychol. Rev.* X. 37, 1903.

[8] *The Development of the Senses in the First Three Years of Childhood*, 148.

[9] *Brit. Jl. of Psychol.* II. 338, 1908.

[10] *Ibid.* II. 353, 1908.

[11] *Ibid.* VI. 363, 1914.

Baldwin's method consisted in placing small squares of coloured blotting paper upon a rod within reach of the child, one at a time, and recording for each colour the ratio of the number of times the piece was seized to the total number of presentations of that colour. He found that "the colours range themselves in an order of attractiveness, *i.e.*, blue, red, white, green, and brown" and that pieces of newspaper were as attractive as any of the colours and even more so. The ratios of acceptances to presentations of the colours were: blue 0·766, red 0·714, white 0·636, green 0·6, brown 0·5. McDougall points out that the number of experiments with white was only eleven, and though the figures would perhaps suggest some colour appreciation if the experiments had been more numerous they hardly can be claimed, as they stand, as evidence in that direction.

Marsden employed Baldwin's method and obtained similar results. In 175 presentations the acceptances were: newspaper 130, yellow 127, red 122, blue 121, white 113, grey 114, black 114, brown 107. It is to be noted that as white, grey, and black were taken with almost the same frequency, brightness appears to have no influence; yet of the colours yellow was taken most often and brown least. McDougall considers that the results obtained by Baldwin and Marsden "cannot be held to show that colour vision was present, or to throw any light on the state or on development of the colour sense" in the subjects.

McDougall's method was a modification of Baldwin's. It consists essentially in presenting two similar objects of different colours simultaneously, and recording the number of acceptances of each. For the first child coloured flowers were used, and later balls of worsted 1 inch in diameter and pieces of crinkled paper of low and high saturation. With flowers the results during the twenty-first and twenty-second weeks were: during the first two days red was taken 19 times, white 9 times: later, red 82 to white 33; blue 17 to white 13. With worsted and paper between the twenty-third and twenty-ninth weeks the results were:

R—B	R—G	B—G	R—W	G—W	B—W	R—Grey	G—Gy	B—Gy	W—Gy
30—26	32—16	32—31	36—21	35—15	32—22	30—4	25—7	24—5	38—15

An improved method was used for another child. The objects presented in pairs to this child were balls about 1 inch in diameter, each consisting of a pill box containing a pea and embedded in a loose sheath of knitted wool. The woollen thread was prolonged to form a plaited cord about three inches in length. The balls were red, green, blue, yellow, white and grey, the grey being decidedly brighter than the colours. Pairs were dangled before the child. The results between the eighth and tenth months were:

R—B	R—G	B—G	R—W	Y—W	Y—R	Y—B
14—13	6—9	0—2	4—0	6—2	6—2	5—3

R—Gy	B—Gy	G—Gy	Y—Gy
22—12	27—11	6—3	19—5

The most favourable time for experimenting by this method occurs about the sixth month and lasts two months; at later periods both objects are often grasped simultaneously with the two hands. Probably good results might be obtained in precocious children in the fifth month.

The experiments indicate that the power of appreciating red is fully developed at the end of the fifth month; that red, green, and blue are appreciated during the sixth month, since they are decidedly preferred to white, and still more decidedly to grey of equal brightness with the colours. They also indicate that in the sixth month no one of these three colours is markedly preferred to the others; but there was a faint indication that during the fifth month blue is less appreciated than red.

Myers used wooden cubes ("bricks"), each measuring 33 × 20 × 15 mm., painted uniformly in a different shade of grey or colour. A pair of these bricks were placed before the child on a table covered with black velvet. Each time the child picked up a particular colour, *e.g.*, red, she was rewarded by being given a taste of honey, syrup, or sugar. Experiments between the twenty-fourth and twenty-sixth weeks of life failed to show the development of any association between colour and reward. In later experiments the reward was given if *either* brick was grasped, and from January (thirth-seventh week) to May a pair of grey bricks, one lighter than the other was used. Light grey was selected 101 times, dark grey 75. A vivid yellow and an intensely white brick were then used, yellow being selected 27 times, white 8. In May a saturated blue brick was chosen 8 times when presented with white; but later white was often chosen, so that in 78 times blue was selected 35 times, white 43. These results show the influence of *novelty* of colour. Yellow, however, was chosen with increased instead of diminished frequency at successive sittings.

Myers concludes that at a very early age, probably long before the sixth month, infants are susceptible to relatively small differences of brightness; that at this age reds and yellows are distinctly preferred to other colours and to colourless objects of far greater brightness;

and that novelty may play an important part in determining the infant's choice of colour. He is strongly of opinion that such experiments do not afford evidence of the course of the development of colour sense. He says, " It is true that the positive results of such experiments may be significant. When, for example, a child shows a distinct preference for yellow, presented with white, that is a clear indication that yellow has a different effect on him from white. And we are doubtless justified in assuming that this difference is not merely an affective and physiological one, producing greater pleasurable excitement in the infant and determining the choice of the brick which is grasped, but that it is also of sensational significance, that is to say, the visual sensation excited by yellow is different in the infant from that excited by white.

" I think it highly probable that the primary physiological basis of colour vision is completely installed before the infant has reached the stage when he can successfully differentiate from one another all the various colour sensations which such an apparatus permits him to receive; just as, in foetal life, he is provided with lungs before he can make use of them. If this be true, then it follows that the gradual differentiation of the colour sensations from one another is a process distinct from the developing constituents of the peripheral cerebro-retinal apparatus."

Valentine commenced his experiments on a child at the age of three months, before grasping was sufficiently developed to be of use. The method he adopted was to measure the time the child looked at either of two coloured wools held before him for two minutes at a time. The colours used were black, white, red, yellow, green, blue, violet, pink and brown. The following table gives all the scores (in seconds) of each colour, together with the scores against them.

	Yellow	White	Pink	Red	Brown	Black	Green	Blue	Violet	Totals A For	Totals A Agst.	Totals B For	Totals B Agst.	Percentage scores A	Percentage scores B
Yellow		76	17	106	31	88	133	50	24	525	137	282	48	79·3	85·4
White	42		48	70	104	53	153	22	188	680	246	487	108	73·4	81·8
Pink	4	96		46	79	19	77	102	53	476	186	280	68	72·2	80·9
Red	23	24	26		40	45	6	39	39	242	283	75	153	45·3	32·8
Brown	8	3	0	28		33	4	37	38	151	275	65	276	37·8	19·0
Black	0	38	39	10	18		3	37	4	149	263	152	109	35·7	58·2
Green	23	9	19	20	0	0		0	94	165	421	54	276	28·2	16·3
Blue	37	0	37	3	3	13	22		7	122	300	18	106	28·9	14·5
Violet	0	0	0	0	0	12	23	13		48	447	9	287	9·7	3·0
Totals	137	246	186	283	275	263	421	300	447						

In column A all scores of 3″ and over are reckoned. In column B only scores of 8″ and over are reckoned. That is, when the child only looked at a colour 7″ or less continuously, that particular score was ignored.

It would be unfair to draw up an order merely upon the total scores of each colour. For such conditions as the child's mood, or the light, may have been exceptionally favourable on those days when some particular colour, say pink, was used, and exceptionally unfavourable on the days when some other colour was used. Thus green in the table has 165 to its credit—about the same as brown (151). But far more seconds were scored *against* green (421) than against brown (275). We therefore get a fairer basis of comparison by adding the score of green (165) to the score against green (421), which gives us the total scored during the experiments in which green was used, viz., 586 seconds: and then finding what *percentage* of this total was scored by green. Such percentages are given in the above table.

From these results two kinds of inferences may be drawn,—as to colour preferences, and as to the development of the colour sense. We cannot of course infer from the *absence* of preference between two colours the absence of any difference of sensation: but from evidence showing that one colour is markedly preferred to another we can infer that the colours are sensed as different colours, unless the preference can be ascribed to differences in brightness.

Brightness certainly plays an important part, for the three first colours on the list are by far the brightest. That it is not the only factor is shown by the percentage scores for violet (9·7 %), red (45·3 %), and brown (37·8 %), which were of equal brightness: similarly for red (45·3 %), blue (28·9 %), and green (28·2 %), which were also of equal brightness. It is of course possible, but not probable, that the luminosity values for the infant are different from those for the adult. The experiments of Valentine confirm those of McDougall and Myers that novelty has a great attraction for the child.

When the child was seven months old Valentine commenced experiments by the grasping method, using the same wools except that brown was omitted and a grey of the same brightness as the red, blue, green and violet was introduced. In 36 experiments, involving 360 choices, yellow still held the first place, but red and pink were now almost bracketed second. The most striking difference apparent was the drop in the comparative attractiveness of brightness. White was now only on a level with violet, green, blue, and black, and at least not more attractive than a dull grey. Pink also scored only about the same as red. Valentine regards the grasping method as more open to objection than has been thought, owing to the eagerness to grasp anything and to the change which occurs in the favourite hand for grasping.

When the child was eight and a half months old the "grasp and reward" method, suggested by Myers, was tried, the reward being given only when a particular colour was chosen. There was some indication that an association of reward with blue was set up when it had to be discriminated from green, but less when it had to be discriminated from red, probably owing to the antagonistic effect of the greater attractiveness of red.

Valentine's results are summarised thus :

1. There is good evidence that at the age of three months an infant may experience the sensations of red, yellow, brown, green and blue.

2. In the case of the child investigated the order of preference of the colours used was as follows :

$$\text{yellow} \left\{\begin{matrix}\text{white}\\ \text{pink}\end{matrix}\right\} \text{red} \left\{\begin{matrix}\text{brown}\\ \text{black}\end{matrix}\right\} \left\{\begin{matrix}\text{blue}\\ \text{green}\end{matrix}\right\} \text{violet}$$

3. The order of preference seems to be partly determined by brightness, but cannot be explained entirely by reference to brightness or to novelty.

4. The order of preference is partly determined by the relative powers of the various colours as stimuli to the organism.

5. At seven months the same infant still liked yellow best of all the colours used, and then red, and pink. By this time the comparative attractiveness of white had decreased, being no greater than that of violet or even grey.

6. There was perhaps a trace of association between the grasping of the blue wool and the idea of a reward, when blue and green wools were offered to the child. The lack of more definite association can be ascribed to the difficulty of establishing any association of such a nature at this age, and need not be attributed to failure to discriminate blue and green.

PART II

THE CHIEF FACTS OF COLOUR BLINDNESS

CHAPTER I

INTRODUCTION: COLOUR NAMES

It has long been known that certain persons show peculiarities of colour vision distinguishing them from the normal[1]. The colour blindness of the chemist, John Dalton[2], first led the attention of scientists to the analysis of the sensations of the colour-blind. In 1807 that remarkable genius ("bewundernswürdiger Forscher," v. Helmholtz), Thomas Young, discussed Dalton's case in his *Lectures on Natural Philosophy*. So great was the stir produced by Dalton's defect that colour blindness was long known as Daltonism. In 1810, the great poet Goethe referred to these abnormalities of colour vision in his book on the *Theory of Colours*[3]. An enormous literature on the subject sprang up during the nineteenth century[4].

During this period two types of colour blindness were fairly clearly distinguished. They had this in common that in them the whole gamut of colour sensations could be referred to a function of two variables. Since normal colour vision is a function of three variables and these types of colour blindness display colour systems which are functions of two variables the normal are conveniently classed as *trichromats*, these types of the abnormal as *dichromats*.

As already mentioned the dichromats can be divided into two groups, and to these a rare third group has since been added. The names given to the groups varied according to the theoretical predilections of the writer. Thus, v. Helmholtz called them red-blind, green-blind, and

[1] Turberville, *Phil. Trans. Roy. Soc. Lond.* 1684; Huddart, *op. cit.* LXVII. 1, 14, 1777; Whisson, *op. cit.* LXVIII. 2, 611, 1778; and others.

[2] *Lit. and Phil. Soc. of Manchester*, 1794; *Edin. J. of Sc.* IX. 97, 1798—reprinted in *Edin. J. of Sc.* V. 188, 1831.

[3] *Zur Farbenlehre*; translated by Eastlake, London (Murray), 1840.

[4] v. Helmholtz, 2nd ed. Bibliography, pp. 1176–1198, complete to the end of 1894.

blue-blind, and this terminology has generally been adopted by physicists. Hering, on the other hand, regarded the first two groups as variants of a common class, the red-green-blind, the third group being due to abnormality of the mechanism subserving blue-yellow sensations. v. Kries introduced terms for the three groups which were merely descriptive and were prejudiced by no theory. I shall adopt his terms, viz., *protanopes*, *deuteranopes*, and *tritanopes*, corresponding respectively with v. Helmholtz' red-, green-, and blue-blind.

In 1881 Lord Rayleigh[1] made an important discovery. He found that many people with apparently normal colour vision require different amounts of red or green in their colour mixtures from the majority. His observations were confirmed by Donders[2] and have since been verified. As the colour system of these people is, like that of normal people, a function of three variables, they may be conveniently termed *anomalous trichromats*.

Later researches tend to show that these do not constitute the only type of abnormality of the trichromatic system.

All the varieties hitherto mentioned are abnormal from birth. The defect is congenital and incurable. The statistics are very unreliable. In its grosser forms (dichromats) amongst civilised races it is said to affect about 4 per cent. of the male population, and 0·4 per cent. of the female; but the tests from which these statistics are derived were often crude. There is good evidence to show that colour blindness is hereditary and that generally it is transmitted through the female, who is herself not usually affected[3]. An unaffected male never carries colour blindness, but an affected male sometimes transmits to his son; consanguinity of parents—by intermarriage of cousins—is rare[4]. Transmission through several branches of a family is not uncommon, and several siblings, usually of course male, of a childship are often affected. Nettleship has published pedigrees of colour-blind families in which females were affected[5]. Statistics are not available for any precise estimate of the slighter defects of colour vision (anomalous trichromats), but they are probably widespread and certainly occur in colour-blind childships.

Differing from all these groups there are people who apparently see all parts of the spectrum of one hue, the parts differing only in luminosity. These are the *total colour-blind* or *monochromats*.

[1] *Nature*, XXV. 64, 1882.
[2] *Arch. f. Anat.* 518, 1884.

[3] Cf. pedigree in Nettleship, *Trans. Ophth. Soc.* XXVIII. 248, 1908; also bibliography in Parsons, *Pathology of the Eye*, IV. 1413, 1908.

[4] Nettleship, *Trans. Ophth. Soc.* XXIX. p. lx, 1909.

[5] *Ibid.* XXVI. 251, 1906.

Colour vision is often affected in disease of the eyes or brain[1]. I do not propose to discuss acquired colour blindness, though some few references to it may be necessary.

The outstanding characteristic of all known abnormalities of colour sensations is that the abnormal people see *fewer* hues than the normal. The great difficulty in arriving at a true conception of the relationship of any abnormal colour system to the normal is psychological. No individual can judge with certainty the sensations of any other individual. We in general assume that another person has the same sensations as ourselves until, either by accident or research, we discover *differences* between their judgments of external stimuli and our own. Investigation of the sensations produced by various stimuli, through the mediation of afferent nervous impulses, is similarly extremely difficult in lower animals. We have to judge for the most part by motor responses which may or may not be directly contingent to the afferent impulses, and which are in any case particularly liable to misinterpretation. The investigation is rendered easier in man owing to the faculty of speech. Amongst the majority of mankind, however, multitudinous nuances of sensation, perception, and conception are often conveyed by the same word. The higher the intellectual status the greater is the discrimination of these shades of feeling and thought and the more elaborate is the terminology employed to express them. Education is, or should be, largely concerned with the equipment of the individual with a sufficiently comprehensive and finely discriminating vocabulary.

So far as these considerations apply to colour vision the majority of people are equipped with a vocabulary of colour names, such as white, black, red, yellow, green, blue, violet, purple, which are in common use and are used by most people in such a manner that no glaring discrepancy is noticed between the sensations of the various individuals as thus expressed. The more minutely trained observers have added to this vocabulary subsidiary terms which express the finer nuances of colour perceptions, such as orange, indigo, mauve, puce, drab, and so on. Unfortunately increased complexity of nomenclature has not been accompanied *pari passu* with accurately defined discrimination of meaning. Consequently many such terms are used in a loose and ill-defined manner, and it would be quite unreasonable from the use made of the terms to deduce differences of perception which may or may not exist amongst the various individuals.

[1] Köllner, *Die Störungen des Farbensinnes*, Berlin, 1912.

A fortiori such deductions are most untrustworthy amongst those whose colour vision is defective. Just as a person whose stereoscopic vision is defective may learn to estimate distances and judge solid shapes by accessory aids, such as apparent size, distinctness, shadows, the correlation of tactile sensations, and so on, and may even be wholly unconscious of his defect and of the greater endowment of the majority of his fellow-creatures, so too the colour-blind. His vocabulary of colour terms is often as full and comprehensive as that of his fellows in a similar walk of life. Experience teaches him that these terms are applied with a general consistency to the various objects of every-day life. These objects are generally well-defined to his senses by other criteria than colour, such as shape, size, and general relationship to other objects. He may therefore pass through life without being conscious of any inferiority of perception as compared with his fellows, and he may also fail to make any glaring mistakes, such as would convey to others a suggestion of his deficiency. Hence if we wish to analyse his sensations and to arrive at some idea of their divergence from ours we must take care to remove those accessory aids upon which he unconsciously or consciously relies. Because he calls a cherry red it does not follow that his sensation of red agrees with ours. We know indeed that in many cases the hue of the cherry is very little different to him from that of the cherry leaves ; yet he never calls a cherry green. If we show him small spots of coloured light he may or may not give them the names which we regard as correct. The fact that he is often right proves that his accessory aids are more complex than those already mentioned. It is our main object to study these accessory aids so that we may eliminate them and place him *hors de combat*.

It will suffice for our present purpose if it is clearly understood that the names which the colour-blind use for various colour sensations must not be relied upon as accurate criteria of their sensations *as compared with the normal*. On the other hand, to the practised examiner these names are full of suggestion and will often indicate the lines which the examination should pursue. When we deal with practical tests for colour blindness, the main object of which is to determine whether the colour-defective are dangerous for certain occupations, the problem is quite different and the colour names used by the examinee are themselves indications of his fitness or unfitness.

With regard to what is commonly known as "colour ignorance" it is found that there are very few civilised people who do not know the fundamental terms for colours, whereas many people are ignorant of the terms for the nuances of colour, such as mauve, puce, and so on. The latter are, however, quite unnecessary for colour testing, and we may conclude that, with the exception of the monochromats, the great majority of people know that the terms red, yellow, green, blue, violet, and purple are applied to different colour sensations. Amongst the uneducated, and even amongst those otherwise well educated but unpractised in describing differences of colour, there are many individuals in civilised races who from inaccuracy or carelessness apply generic colour terms erroneously—thus, it is quite common for blue-greens to be described as blue *or* green, violets and blue-purples as blue, deep orange as red and so on. This is still more common amongst primitive races, who, however, often have the excuse of an actual paucity of colour terms in their vocabularies. It is important that defective terminology shall not be interpreted as the expression of defective colour perception without adequate confirmatory evidence.

We must conclude then that we can have no accurate idea of the actual physiological sensations or of their psychological counterparts in the colour-blind. We soon discover, however, that he often misnames colours, and that if we compare the effects of two stimuli they are often dissimilar to him when they match to us, and *vice versa*. Thus, with many colour-blind we can find a certain intensity of monochromatic blue-green light which exactly matches for him a certain intensity of monochromatic yellow; they are obviously quite dissimilar to the normal. We shall therefore commence by investigating the laws of colour mixture for the colour-blind.

CHAPTER II

DICHROMATIC VISION

The Mixture of Pure-Colour Stimuli. We have seen that within a certain range which includes all ordinary conditions of colour vision and subject to certain limitations of stimuli before referred to, every conceivable light or light mixture gives rise to a sensation which can be accurately matched by the sensation produced by a suitable mixture of only three lights (p. 38). The vision of dichromats can similarly be expressed in terms of *two* lights. Thus, two monochromatic lights can be found, such that, by mixing them in various proportions, the mixtures will match every part of the spectrum as it appears to the dichromat, and also the unanalysed white light. It is found that there are two groups of dichromats, as was first pointed out by Seebeck[1], agreeing amongst themselves but differing from each other in the proportions of the two mixed lights required for the matches. These are the protanopes and deuteranopes, of whom the latter are more common (23 : 11, Nagel).

Now, since white light can be matched by the dichromat with a suitable mixture of two monochromatic lights, and since all spectral colours can be matched by mixing the same two colours in various proportions, it follows that there is some spectral colour which will match white. This point is called the *neutral point* of the dichromatic spectrum.

König[2] first made systematic examinations of the colour-mixtures of the colour-blind with spectral colours. He was followed by v. Kries and Abney[3].

The principle of the method adopted by König had been previously applied on a less extensive scale by Donders and van der Weyde[4]. König and Dieterici divide the dichromatic spectrum into three regions as compared with the five regions of the trichromatic spectrum. If L_1 and L_3 are two spectral lights from the end regions, and L_2 is any spectral light from the middle region then

$$L_2 = aL_1 + bL_3$$

where a and b are two coefficients determined experimentally. In other words any spectral colour can be matched by the mixture of appropriate quantities (a and b) of two colours selected from the end regions of the spectrum. If for L_1 a red (645 $\mu\mu$) is chosen, and for L_3 a blue (460 $\mu\mu$ or 435 $\mu\mu$), then König and Dieterici found that for protanopes no blue is necessary to match any colour from about 550 $\mu\mu$ to the end of the spectrum on the red side, hence $b = 0$. Similarly no red is needed to match any colour from about 460 $\mu\mu$ to the violet end, and $a = 0$.

A more complicated method, ensuring greater accuracy, was to divide up the spectrum into fractions, determining the matches for

[1] *Ann. d. Physik*, XLII. 177, 1837.

[2] König and Dieterici, *Sitz. d. Akad. d. Wiss.* Berlin, 805, 1886; *Ztsch. f. Psychol. u. Physiol. d. Sinnesorg.* IV. 241, 1892; König, *Brit. Assoc.* 1886.

[3] Much of Abney's work covers the same ground as that of v. Kries. Since, however, it is expressed throughout in terms of the Young-Helmholtz theory and was inspired by that theory detailed consideration of it will be left until Part III

[4] *Arch. f. Ophth.* XXVIII. 1, 1, 1882.

each part and correlating the results mathematically. The principle is the same.

The average of the results, which did not differ materially *inter se*, is shown in Fig. 44, where the abscissae are wave-lengths of the matched spectral colours and the ordinates are arbitrary units of intensity. W_1 is the deuteranopic red or "warm" curve, W_2 the protanopic red curve, and K the blue or "cold" curve common to both. H is the monochromatic curve of which more will be said later.

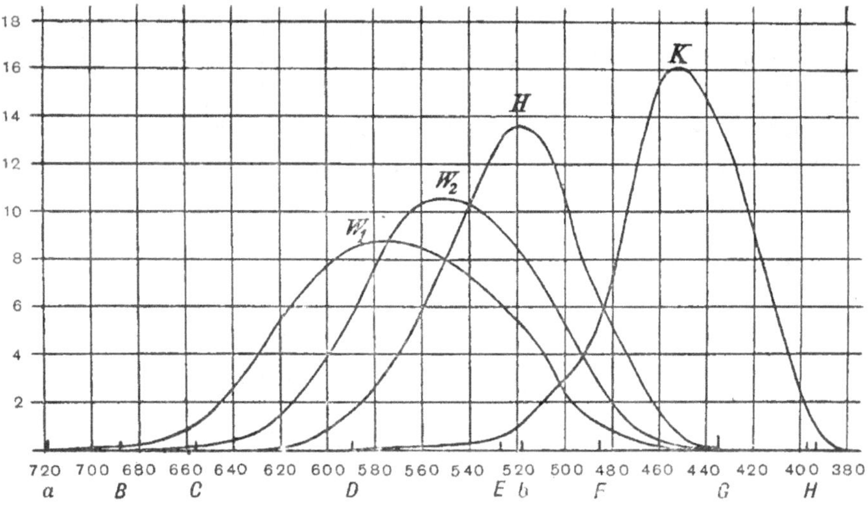

Fig. 44. Equal-area gauging curves for dichromats and monochromats (H). W_1, deuteranopic "warm" curve; W_2, protanopic "warm" curve; K, "cold" curve common to both types of dichromats. Abscissae, wave-lengths of the interference spectrum of sunlight; ordinates, arbitrary scale. (König.)

It is to be noted that the curves are so drawn that the areas enclosed between each curve and the axis of abscissae are all equal. They therefore represent the relative magnitudes of the stimulus values of the given elements—red or blue—in the unanalysed light from which the spectrum is derived (*v.* Part III, Section III, Chap. II). They do not establish any quantitative relationship between the stimulus values for different individuals, since these are qualitatively of a different order.

v. Kries[1] used as his gauging lights a red (589·2 $\mu\mu$ for protanopes, 645 $\mu\mu$ for deuteranopes) and a blue (460·8 $\mu\mu$), and determined the relative amount of each which must be mixed in order to match exactly the spectral colours.

[1] v. Kries and Nagel, *Ztsch. f. Psychol. u. Physiol. d. Sinnesorg.* XII. 1, 1896; v. Kries *op. cit.* XIII. 241, 1897.

The method of procedure was as follows. v. Helmholtz' spectrophotometer was used, one half of the field being illuminated with the homogeneous light, the other half with the mixture. In this apparatus the lights are derived from two sources. The mixture is obtained from one source by forming two spectra with the aid of a doubly refracting prism, so that these spectra are polarised at right angles to each other. The intensities of the lights in both halves of the field are altered by varying the widths of the slits transmitting the lights and by means of Nicol prisms.

Suppose that a deuteranope is being examined and that the mixing lights are 645 $\mu\mu$ and 460·8 $\mu\mu$. One half of the field is illuminated with a homogeneous red, say 670·8 $\mu\mu$. With this light a perfect match, both in colour and brightness, can be made with 645 $\mu\mu$ merely by altering the intensity and without adding any of the 460·8 $\mu\mu$ light. The red or warm (W-) value of 670·8 $\mu\mu$ is expressed in arbitrary units, which depend upon the width of the slit, which transmits this light from the second source of light, when the two exactly match. Let us suppose that it equals 33 under the given conditions.

A second wave-length is then chosen, *e.g.* 656 $\mu\mu$, the width of the slit which transmits this light from the first source of light being kept unchanged. We now find that the 645 $\mu\mu$ slit must be opened more in order to establish a perfect match, say to 48. For each succeeding wave-length this slit must be opened wider until about 600 $\mu\mu$ is reached. Beyond this point the slit-widths must be reduced.

At about 540 $\mu\mu$ it is found that no perfect match can be made with the 645 $\mu\mu$ light alone. For example, 536 $\mu\mu$ appears to the deuteranope less saturated than 645 $\mu\mu$. It is necessary to add a small quantity of light of shorter wave-length. On adding the appropriate amount of 460·8 $\mu\mu$ light a perfect match, both in colour and brightness, is obtained. This light, 536 $\mu\mu$, therefore possesses both a red or W-value and a blue or cold (K-) value, and these are recorded, viz., W-value 41, K-value 6·3.

The readings are not quite so simple as would appear from this description. For example, it is found necessary to alter the width of the slit which transmits the homogeneous light, otherwise the second slit has to be opened so wide that the two spectra derived from it are impure. Moreover the relative amounts of 645 $\mu\mu$ and 460·8 $\mu\mu$ lights mixed, as well as the brightness of the resultant mixture, are altered by rotation of the Nicol prism, and corrections have to be applied according to the angle of rotation.

If however the apparatus is kept as constant as possible and the same procedure is adopted in each series of observations concordant results are obtained from the same individual and comparable results from different individuals. v. Kries and Nagel compare directly the results obtained from deuteranopes, using the mixtures of 645 $\mu\mu$ and 460·8 $\mu\mu$ lights, with those obtained from protanopes, using mixtures

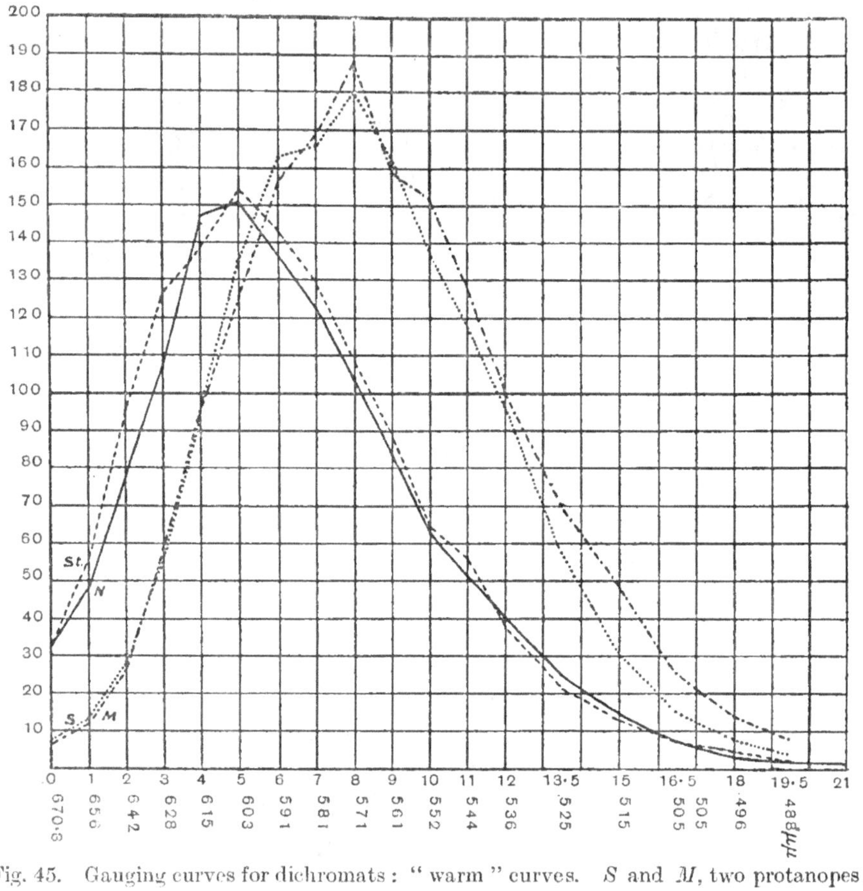

Fig. 45. Gauging curves for dichromats : "warm" curves. *S* and *M*, two protanopes *N* and *St*, two deuteranopes. Abscissae, arbitrary scale of prismatic spectrum of gaslight, indicating certain wave-lengths ; ordinates, arbitrary scale. (v. Kries.)

of 589·2 $\mu\mu$ and 460·8 $\mu\mu$ lights. While it is legitimate to choose two mixing lights of any wave-length so long as one is chosen from each of the two end regions of the spectrum, the curves in all such cases having the same characteristic form, the units are referred to different standards and it is a somewhat doubtful assumption to suppose that the results are directly comparable.

The red gauging values for two protanopes (*S* and *M*) and for two deuteranopes (*St* and *N*) are shown in Fig. 45. The corresponding blue values are shown in Fig. 46. The abscissae are the monochromatic colours of the spectrum, the ordinates the intensities in arbitrary units.

It will be noticed that König's blue curve extends red-wards as far as 600 $\mu\mu$, whereas v. Kries and Nagel's extends only to 536 $\mu\mu$. The difference shows the great importance to be attached to adaptation. Every care was taken in v. Kries' experiments to make the matches with good light adaptation; no such minute precautions were taken

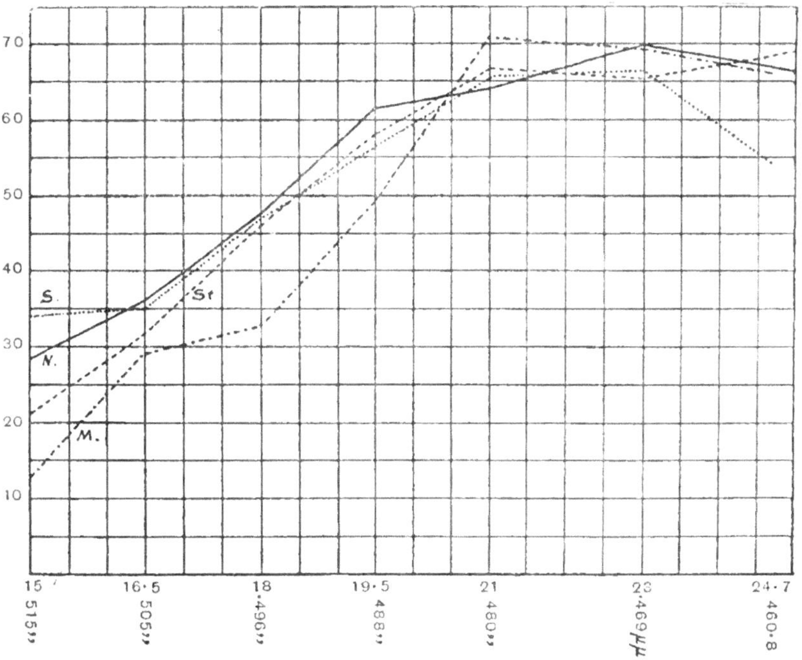

Fig. 46. Gauging curves for dichromats: "cold" curves. Same observers as in Fig. 45. (v. Kries.)

by König and his subjects. The latter are indeed chromatic scotopic curves, in which there is some dark adaptation combined with a large residual photopic condition. Another factor, however, is the much greater luminosity value of red compared with that of blue (*vide infra*). Hence the arbitrary units adopted by v. Kries do not signify equal stimulus values of red and blue for the same unit-number. In their gaslight dispersion spectrum one part of lithium red has about the same luminosity as 8—12 parts of blue (480 $\mu\mu$) for the deuteranope. In v. Kries' units one part of red is equivalent in luminosity to about

20 parts of blue. Hence 6 or 10 parts of blue will have relatively little stimulus value when mixed with 30 to 35 parts of red, whilst a trace of red will manifest itself by definitely increasing the brightness when mixed with 60 parts of blue.

The red curves show distinctly the difference in the two groups of dichromats. No blue is necessary for the match until beyond 530 $\mu\mu$. The red protanopic maximum is at 571 $\mu\mu$; the sharp fall towards the red end shows the relatively low stimulus value for the long-wave light. The deuteranopic maximum is at 603 $\mu\mu$, and the curve does not fall to so low a value at the red end. Rivers[1] has therefore introduced the terms *scoterythrous* and *photerythrous* for protanopes and deuteranopes respectively. The advantage of these terms is that they are purely descriptive of observed facts and are quite independent of any theory. Unfortunately they have not been generally adopted, and it has been thought best in this book to use v. Kries' terminology. The protanopes are relatively more sensitive to the short-wave light, the deuteranopes to the long-wave. In order that a yellow and a red may look equally bright a protanope will require a much more intense red than a deuteranope. This fact cannot be explained on physical grounds, such as macular pigmentation, since these rays are not appreciably absorbed by the yellow pigment.

Further to prove that the fact is true of the two groups v. Kries made thirteen equality of brightness observations on 9 deuteranopes and eleven on 11 protanopes, using the red lithium line (670·5 $\mu\mu$) with the yellow sodium (*D*) line (589·2 $\mu\mu$). The protanopes required the following quantities of red: 214, 213, 211, 205, 196, 198, 210, 200, 210, 203, 235: the deuteranopes required: 36·5, 36·3, 36·3, 36·5, 38·4, 37·3, 37·0, 37·0, 37·8, 37·0, 36·9, 38, 40. The protanopes therefore require on an average five times as much red as the deuteranopes in order that the red may appear as bright as the standard yellow. These observations confirm earlier results obtained by Donders[2].

The low stimulus value of red for the protanopes accounts for the so-called "shortening of the red end of the spectrum" in this class of dichromats. The limit of visibility of the red end, however, varies with normal people, and depends upon the intensity of the light, whether the whole spectrum or only the isolated colour is observed, and so on. Too much stress has often been put upon this point.

The blue curves show a general agreement, but more individual

[1] Schäfer's *Text Book of Physiology*, 1091, 1900.

[2] *Arch. f. Anat. u. Physiol.* 528, 1884.

variation, which is to be explained on physical grounds. This is the part of the spectrum where macular pigmentation makes itself most felt. Moreover, here too adaptation is most likely to introduce complexity. It is probable that there is no crucial difference between the blue stimulus values of the two groups.

Macular pigmentation also probably accounts for the difference between the two red curves (Fig. 45) beyond 552 $\mu\mu$. The ratios of the red of one observer to that of the other throughout the spectrum agree well with the determination of the absorption of the yellow pigment by Sachs. Similarly the ratio of blue to red in two persons gave the same value (0·3) as for the normal (v. Kries). The estimation of macular absorption is much easier in dichromats than in normal trichromats.

Macular pigmentation is a serious complication in the accurate determination of the neutral point. This point, where the monochromatic colour appears colourless or white to the dichromat, should be situated where the W- and K-curves intersect, and hence it should be situated rather nearer the violet end in protanopes than in deuteranopes. If, however, there is much macular absorption the light will look yellower and the neutral point will be displaced slightly towards the red end. Indeed, the neutral point of a protanope with densely pigmented macula may be nearer the red end than that of a deuteranope with slightly pigmented macula. v. Kries has made the following estimates, specially directed to elucidate this matter.

Nature of light	Wave length of homogeneous match: Deuteranope	Two protanopes	
Daylight—reflected from magnesium oxide coated surface	499 $\mu\mu$	498 $\mu\mu$	490 $\mu\mu$
Light reflected from clouds—weakened by ground glass	499 ,,	497 ,,	489 ,,
,, ,, ,, ,, weakened by smoked glass	495 ,,	494 ,,	486 ,,

These estimates were made with a comparison white light.

The existence of a neutral point shows that dichromats receive the same sensory impression from what normal colour-sighted individuals call white, and also from a certain homogeneous spectral light and from the mixture of red and blue which to them matches that homogeneous light. The homogeneous light appears to the normal a highly saturated bluish-green; the red-blue match appears a red-purple. If we suppress nuances it may therefore be said that one of the chief characteristics of both groups of dichromats is that they confuse red and green. But this is a very imperfect expression of the facts, for owing to the very low stimulus value of red for the protanope he requires much more red in his red-blue match of a blue-green homogeneous hue than does the deuteranope for the same amount of blue. Hence a protanope confuses a slightly bluish red (in the physical sense) with a dark green, *e.g.*, scarlet with olive green, whereas a deuteranope matches a much bluer red with a green which is of about equal brightness to the normal. "The red which appears to match a given green differs markedly both in colour-tone and intensity in protanopes and deuteranopes" (v. Kries).

We have considered the conspicuous difference in dichromatic vision from trichromatic vision. Its conspicuous similarity in an important respect was pointed out by Seebeck in 1837, viz., that all colour mixtures which appear equal to the normal eye, also appear equal to the colour-blind. This statement is too general, and the following is more accurate, *all colour equations valid for normal vision are also valid for dichromatic vision*, or colour matches which are valid for the trichromatic are also valid for the dichromatic eye. If this statement can be fully substantiated it follows that the dichromat possesses no variable which the trichromat lacks, but lacks a variable which the trichromat possesses. In other words, dichromatic vision is a *reduction form* (v. Kries) of normal vision, and not a fundamentally different kind of vision.

v. Kries[1] has made a very extensive series of observations of the equivalence of trichromatic and dichromatic matches, and they strongly support the validity of the law. Especially is this the case for the red end of the spectrum, where macular pigmentation is least disturbing and where the typical differences in the two groups of dichromats are most obvious. Monochromatic yellow is matched by a red (670·8 $\mu\mu$) and yellow-green (550 $\mu\mu$) mixture. As the ratio of red to green is altered a suitable intensity of yellow can always be found which will match the mixture. The match for the protanope, however, is not valid usually for the deuteranope. For the former a very red mixture matches a dark yellow and a very green mixture a bright yellow. The deuteranope finds the mixture too bright in the first case and too dark in the second. When the mixture is such that it exactly matches the yellow for both dichromats it also matches for trichromats, and that with extraordinary exactitude. In fact when we succeed in finding matches with which both protanopes and

[1] *Ztsch. f. Psychol. u. Physiol. d. Sinnesorg.* XIII. 274, 1897.

deuteranopes agree trichromats will also agree with them. The following table (v. Kries) bears out this statement.

Wave-length of homogeneous light	Ratios of red (670·8 $\mu\mu$) to yellow-green (550 $\mu\mu$) in mixtures which match the homogeneous light are for deuteranopes too dark	for protanopes too light	for trichromats valid
639 $\mu\mu$	0·012	0·026	0·016
625 ,,	0·038	0·062	0·044
613 ,,	0·07	0·12	0·09
589 ,,	0·22	0·49	0·33
569 ,,	1·00	3·00	1·34

The stimulus values of the red and green can indeed be calculated from the matches for the normal. The latter are given on p. 34 and are repeated in the next table. We see that the normal requires 88·5 units of standard red to match, both in colour and brightness, 670·8 $\mu\mu$, and 71 units of standard green to match 550 $\mu\mu$. A certain deuteranope required 33 and 64 units respectively for the same matches. Now for the normal trichromat,

$$Q_\lambda = Q_r + Q_g$$

where Q_λ is the quantity of homogeneous light, Q_r the quantity of red (670·8 $\mu\mu$), and Q_g the quantity of green (552 $\mu\mu$) to make a perfect match.

But in the method used, *i.e.*, with the spectrophotometer, Q_λ belongs to one spectrum, and Q_r and Q_g belong to two spectra derived from another source of light. By making $r = \lambda$, we obtain the value of Q_r in terms of the Q_λ spectrum, and similarly for $g = \lambda$.

Now, if observations under identical conditions by different observers are directly comparable,

$Q_r = 88{\cdot}5$; $Q_g = 71$......for the normal trichromat.

$Q_r = 33$; $Q_g = 64$......for the deuteranope.

Therefore, in the intensity scale of the deuteranope

$$Q_\lambda = Q'_r + Q'_g$$

where $$Q'_r = \frac{33Q_r}{88{\cdot}5}, \text{ and } Q'_g = \frac{64Q_g}{71}.$$

For example, the normal trichromat requires 202 units of red and 67 units of green to match 591 $\mu\mu$, or

$$Q_{591} = 202Q_r + 67Q_g.$$

We shall expect the intensity value of 591 $\mu\mu$ for the deuteranope to be

$$\frac{202 \times 33}{88{\cdot}5} + \frac{67 \times 64}{71} = 135.$$

v. Kries found the observed value to be 137, and so on, as in the following table.

Wave-length of homogeneous light	Quantities of 670·8 $\mu\mu$ and 552 $\mu\mu$ in normal match		Stimulus value for deuteranope		Stimulus value for protanope	
	670·8 $\mu\mu$	552 $\mu\mu$	Calculated	Observed	Calculated	Observed
670·8	88·5	—	33	33	4·9	4·9
628	251	10	106	107	28·8	38·5
615	276	27	126	147	54·2	63
603	270	49	145	151	86	84
591	202	67	135	137	108	105
581	123	76	114	124	117	113
571	73	91	110	103	137	126
561	21	80	76	82	111	106
552	—	71	64	64	101	101

From this table we also see that the stimulus value of the yellow-green (552 $\mu\mu$) is to that of the red (670·8 $\mu\mu$) as 101 : 4·9 or about 5 : 1 for the protanope, whereas for the deuteranope it is only as 64 : 33 or about 2 : 1.

The luminosity of the spectrum. The luminosity curves of dichromats were investigated by Hillebrand (1889)[1], who found the protanopic maximum at 560—658 $\mu\mu$, and by König and Ritter (1891)[2]. The following table gives the values for two trichromats and three dichromats at the intensity value *H*.

	Trichromats		Dichromats		
			Deuteranope	Protanopes	
Wave-length	König	Köttgen	Brodhun	Ritter	X
670	0·855	1·120	0·540	0·0518	0·071
650	2·381	2·137	1·368	0·155	0·183
625	3·460	3·413	2·630	0·493	0·517
605	3·650	3·247	3·003	0·996	0·976
590	3·030	2·645	2·539	1·389	1·370
575	2·358	1·923	2·183	1·615	1·477
555	1·695	1·389	1·661	1·412	1·339
535	1·	1·	1·	1·	1·
520	0·554	0·553	0·576	0·606	0·700
505	0·224	0·250	0·225	0·314	0·492
490	0·0994	0·092	0·0846	0·152	0·250

Figs. 47 and 48 show the curves.

Ritter's protanopic curve for the lowest intensity *A* is almost identical with König's. König thus early demonstrated the identity of the protanopic achromatic scotopic and the normal achromatic

[1] *Sitz. d. Wiener Akad.* XCVIII. 3, 70, 1889. [2] König, p. 144.

scotopic luminosity curves. As the intensity increases the divergence increases. At the highest intensity the protanopic maximum is at about 560 $\mu\mu$ as compared with the normal 615 $\mu\mu$. Brodhun's deuteranopic maximum is almost identical with the normal. The deuteranopic achromatic scotopic curve is also nearly identical with both the normal and the protanopic, having a maximum at 535 $\mu\mu$.

König emphasises the fact that nothing as to heterochromatic luminosity values can be deduced from the equivalence of colour matches of two individuals, as of course follows directly from the validity of such matches for both normal and dichromatic vision (*v.* p. 170).

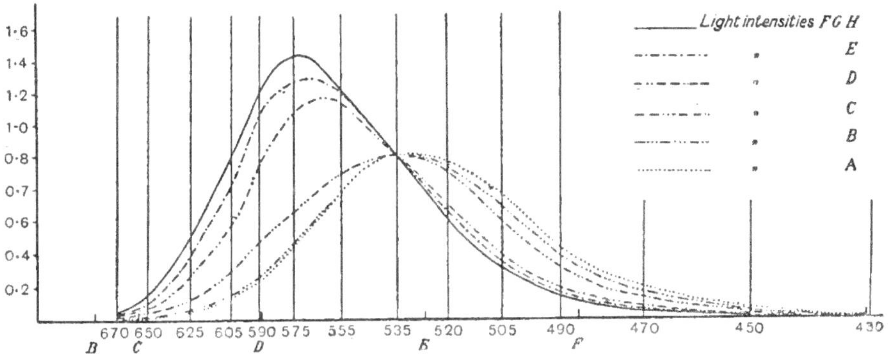

Fig. 47. Protanopic luminosity curves for different intensities of light, *A* being the lowest, *H* the highest. Abscissae, wave-lengths of the prismatic spectrum of gas-light; ordinates, arbitrary scale. (König.)

König's curves agree well with Abney's[1] (Fig. 49). His normal maximum is 585 $\mu\mu$, protanopic 559·6 $\mu\mu$, and deuteranopic 599·6 $\mu\mu$.

Polimanti[2] obtained similar results with the flicker method (Figs. 50 and 51). The curves show the general resemblance of the flicker periphery luminosity values. The normal maximum is 589 $\mu\mu$, the protanopic 565 $\mu\mu$, and the deuteranopic 606 $\mu\mu$. It is noteworthy, that though Polimanti found his flicker and periphery values appreciably different from Nagel's (deuteranope), v. Kries found no appreciable difference between his own and Nagel's periphery values. However this may be explained it is certain that the divergence of the deuteranopic luminosity curve from the normal is less than that of the protanopic.

Watson[3] has also published a series of observations by the flicker

[1] Abney, p. 279; *Proc. Roy. Soc. Lond.* A, LXXXIII. 1910.

[2] *Ztsch. f. Psychol. u. Physiol. d. Sinnesorg.* XIX. 263, 1899.

[3] *Proc. Roy. Soc. Lond.* A, LXXXVIII. 404, 1913.

method, which agree with those already mentioned. We may more conveniently discuss his results at a later stage (Part III).

The spectrum as seen by the dark-adapted eye. Tschermak[1] has stated that the process of adaptation varies according to the type of

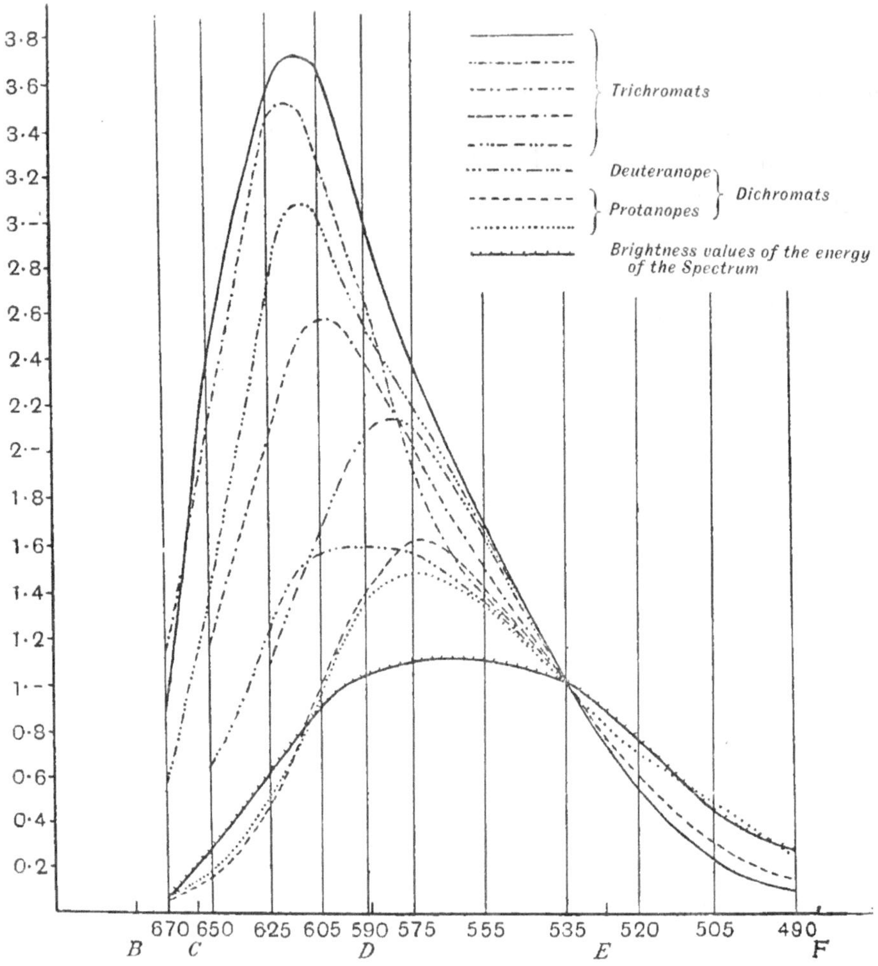

Fig. 48. Photopic luminosity curves (intensity *H*) of trichromats and dichromats. Abscissae, wave-lengths of the prismatic spectrum of gaslight; ordinates, arbitrary scale. (König.)

colour blindness, being normal in deuteranopes and much below normal in protanopes. Nagel and v. Kries, however, are fully convinced that

[1] *Arch. f. d. ges. Physiol.* LXX. 297, 1898; *Ueber physiol. u. path. Anpassung des Auges*, Leipzig, 1900; *Ergeb. d. Physiol.* I. 2, 700, 1902.

adaptation occurs exactly as in the normal in all types of colour blindness.

It has already been mentioned that the achromatic scotopic luminosity curve is identical with the normal in all cases of colour blindness.

With regard to Purkinje's phenomenon, owing to the relatively far greater ratio of the achromatic scotopic values of the yellow-green region of the spectrum to the red as compared with normal vision all

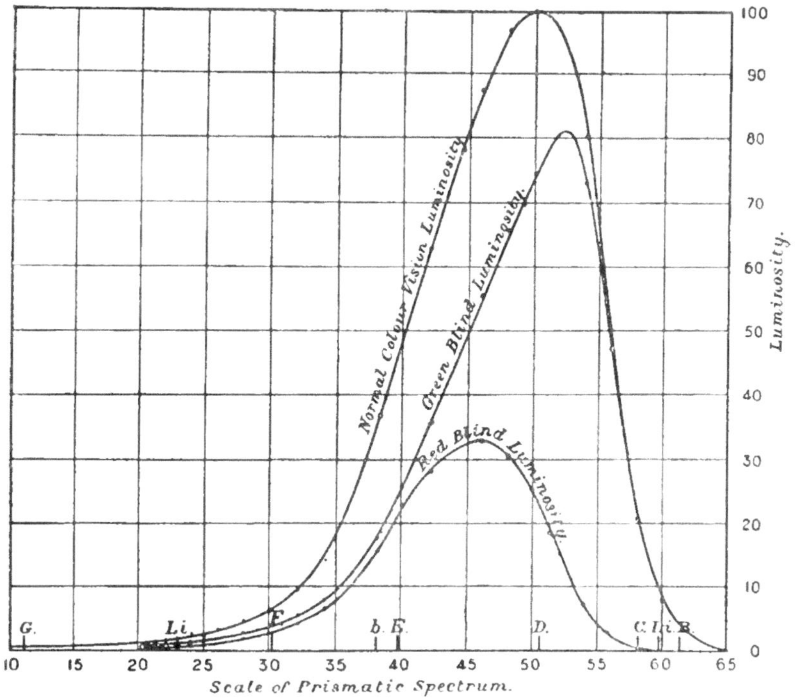

Fig. 49. Photopic luminosity curves of trichromats and dichromats. (Abney.)

the effects are accentuated. This fact was early brought out by Preyer[1] and van der Weyde[2] and more conclusively by König[3]. Thus König found a change of maximum brightness from 605 $\mu\mu$ to 535 $\mu\mu$ for the deuteranope Brodhun and from 575 $\mu\mu$ to 535 $\mu\mu$ for the protanope Ritter on diminution of the intensity of the light, associated of course with increasing dark adaptation. König and Tonn made a

[1] *Arch. f. d. ges. Physiol.* xxv. 31, 1881. [2] *Arch. f. Ophth.* xxviii. 2, 1, 1882.

[3] König and Brodhun, *Sitz. d. Akad. d. Wiss.* Berlin, 311, 1887; Brodhun, *Ztsch. f. Psychol. u. Physiol. d. Sinnesorg.* v. 323, 1893; Tonn, *op. cit.* vii. 279, 1894.

number of matches between a mixture of two spectral lights and monochromatic light of an intermediate wave-length, and observed the effect of diminishing the intensity of the light. v. Kries and Nagel[1] took greater precautions as to the condition of adaptation and found that a scotopic colourless homogeneous blue-green possesses a six or seven times higher scotopic value than the photopic equivalent red-blue mixture. The greatest difference is shown between homogeneous reds and yellow-greens. The latter, from 544 $\mu\mu$ violetwards, give with red

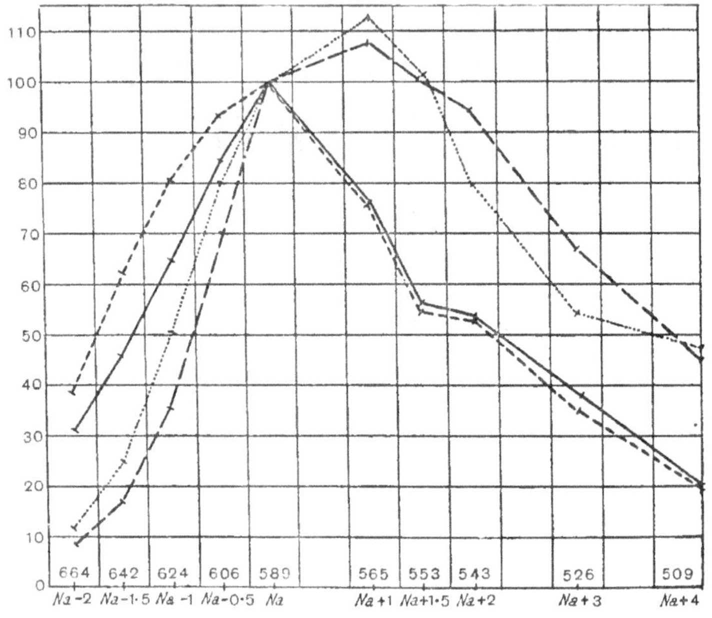

Fig. 50. .... Photopic luminosity curve of a protanope (flicker method).
— — — Periphery luminosity curve of the same protanope.
- - - - - - Photopic luminosity curve of a trichromat (flicker method).
——— Periphery luminosity curve of the same trichromat. (Polimanti.)

exactly equivalent photopic values, whereas the achromatic scotopic value of the yellow-green is more than 100 times that of the photopic equivalent red (642 $\mu\mu$). These remarks apply to the deuteranope and are illustrated in Fig. 52. Similar though less marked differences occur in protanopes.

The differences to which reference has already been made (Part I, Section IV, Chap. I) between the photopic and scotopic periphery values of the trichromat are accentuated in the dichromat. Colours

[1] *Ztsch. f. Psychol. u. Physiol. d. Sinnesorg.* XII. 1, 1896.

which, when viewed by peripheral parts of the retina, accurately match under light adaptation and with high intensities of light, may possess very unequal achromatic scotopic values, and the inequality is much greater with dichromatic than with trichromatic vision.

Regional effects. As might be expected the dichromat, like the trichromat, sees colours best with foveal stimulation. For certain conditions, indeed, his powers of discrimination with central vision

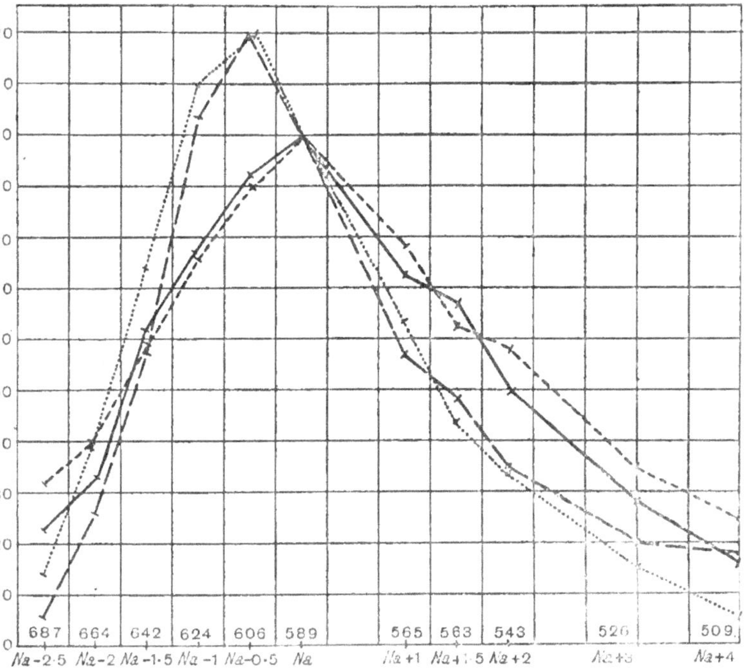

Fig. 51. .... Photopic luminosity curve of a deuteranope (flicker method).
— — — Periphery luminosity curve of the same deuteranope.
- - - - - - Photopic luminosity curve of the same trichromat as in Fig. 50 (flicker method).
———— Periphery luminosity curve of the same trichromat. (Polimanti.)

are markedly superior to those of the normal. Thus, in the protanope a yellow-green light (545 $\mu\mu$) possesses at least 100 times the achromatic scotopic value of its photopic red (670 $\mu\mu$ or higher) match, whereas in the normal the maximum ratio is 6 : 1. He is, therefore, in a peculiarly advantageous condition for determining whether the fovea is sensitive to changes of adaptation. Nagel[1], a deuteranope, was

[1] v. Kries and Nagel, *op. cit.* XXIII. 161, 1900.

unable to discover any difference produced by dark adaptation in colour matches with small central fields. A greenish yellow spot on a red background appeared to match the background both for the light-adapted and dark-adapted eye so long as it was fixated exactly. On

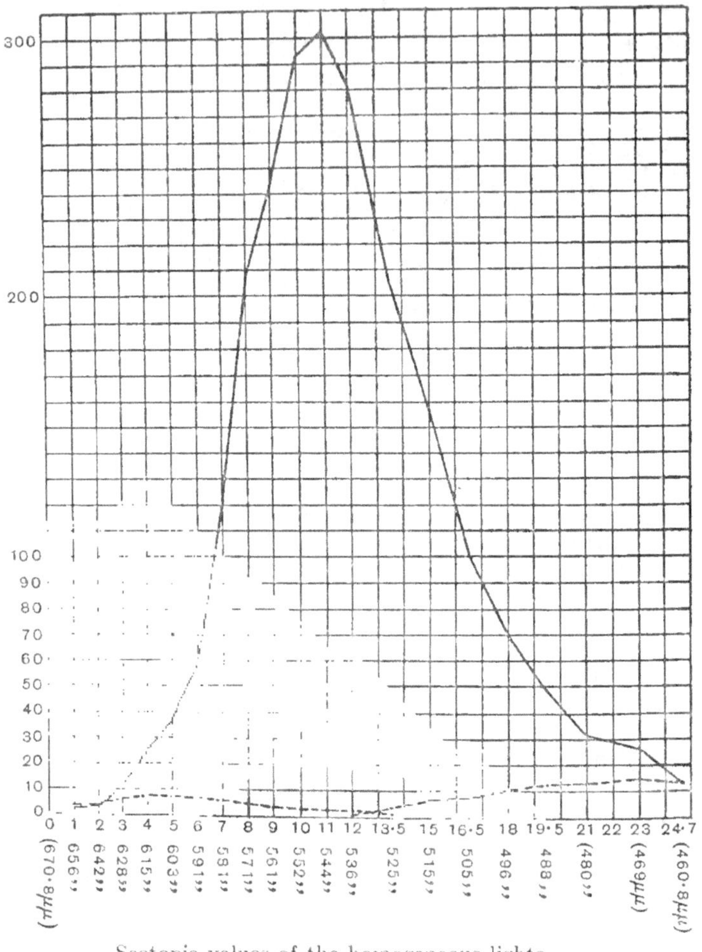

Fig. 52. ——— Scotopic values of the homogeneous lights. .... Scotopic values of the photopic equivalent red (642 $\mu\mu$)—blue (460·8 $\mu\mu$) mixture. Abscissae, wave-lengths of the prismatic spectrum of gaslight; ordinates, arbitrary scale. (v. Kries and Nagel.)

slight deviation (1° to 2°) of the dark-adapted eye the spot appeared much brighter than the background. The scotanopic foveal area subtends a visual angle of about 1·5° (Nagel), but its exact dimensions are difficult to measure.

With regard to the periphery of the retina v. Kries[1] compared a long series of normal colour matches with those of dichromats. His results have been confirmed by van der Weyde[2]. He found that whilst the deuteranopic matches agreed well with the normal, the protanopic matches were very different. The difference can be shown by the different brightness of various coloured lights without any comparison light (Levy[3], Schenck[4]). The divergence is most marked for colourless red-blue mixtures. Such a mixture which matches a grey background for the normal also matches for the deuteranope within the somewhat wide range of experimental error for such observations. For the protanope such a mixture looks distinctly blue and much too dark; his match contains less blue and much more red.

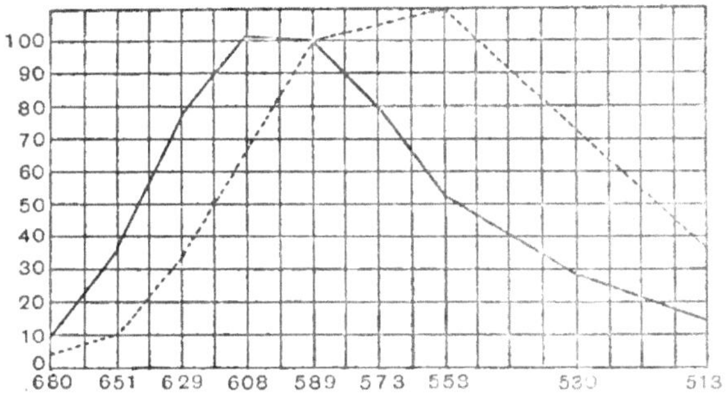

Fig. 53. Photopic peripheral luminosity curves for the normal trichromat (————) and for the protanope (......). Abscissae, wave-lengths of the prismatic spectrum of gaslight; ordinates, arbitrary scale. (v. Kries.)

Dichromats have a monochromatic peripheral zone as have trichromats. The normal and protanopic periphery values for this zone are shown in the curves in Fig. 53. The diminished sensitiveness for light of long wave-length and relatively increased sensitiveness for light of short wave-length in protanopes is clearly shown.

The deuteranopic periphery values indicate that the summit of the curve is rather red-wards of the normal. Angier[5] claims to have proved more marked differences from the normal in this group of dichromats, but as Frl. v. Maltzew[6] has shown considerable individual variations in normal trichromats the question must be left open.

[1] *Ztsch. f. Psychol. u. Physiol. d. Sinnesorg.* xv. 266, 1897
[2] *Onderzoekingen*, Utrecht, iv. 3, 2, 1882.
[3] *Ztsch. f. Psychol. u. Physiol. d. Sinnesorg.* xxxvi. 74, 1904.
[4] *Arch. f. d. ges. Physiol.* cxviii. 174, 1907.
[5] *Ztsch. f. Psychol. u. Physiol. d. Sinnesorg.* xxxvii. 401, 1905.
[6] *Ztsch. f. Sinnesphysiol.* xliii. 76, 1908.

Areal Effects. Nagel[1], who was a deuteranope, found that he was only completely dichromatic for small fields. With larger fields, involving the extra-foveal regions, he became partially trichromatic. By fatiguing his eyes with red and orange lights he became completely dichromatic. His perception of red was much better than that of green, possibly due to red not causing strong contrast effect. Good dark adaptation had the same effect as fatiguing with red. He found a similar condition in 30 other dichromats. Stilling[2] regards Nagel's observations as erroneous.

The Colour Sensations of Protanopes and Deuteranopes. Abney has given illustrations of the names applied by dichromats to the various parts of the spectrum. Since they have only two true colour sensations the distinctions are based chiefly upon variations in luminosity, and are therefore often contradictory. Most observers think that the two sensations experienced correspond most closely to normal yellow and blue[3]. Uncomplicated cases of unilateral congenital colour blindness would afford valuable evidence, but most such cases recorded are of doubtful value. One case for example was regarded by Holmgren[4] as a typical protanope with shortening of the red end of the spectrum, but v. Hippel[5] found that he could see the rubidium line y. Both agree that his colour sensations were yellow (D line) and blue (indium or caesium line). Holmgren recorded a second case and Becker[6] a third. Hayes[7] has recorded a case of a woman with partial protanopia in one eye and normal vision in the other. So far as I am aware no other congenital cases have been recorded, and pathological cases are valueless for the purpose under consideration.

TRITANOPIA. Cases of tritanopia or so-called blue-blindness are rare and mostly due to disease. Since the defect causes little risk of confusion of red and green lights it is not of much practical importance. It is, however, of considerable theoretical importance, and a bibliography of the literature on the subject is appended. Goethe[8] referred to the condition as "akyanoblepsia[9]." König[10] investigated five pathological

[1] *Arch. f. Anat. u. Physiol.* 543, 1907; *Ztsch. f. Sinnesphysiol.* XLIV. 5, 1909.
[2] *Ztsch. f. Sinnesphysiol.* XLIV. 371, 1909.
[3] Pole, *Phil. Trans. Roy. Soc. Lond.* CXLIX. 322, 1859.
[4] *Centralbl. f. d. med. Wiss* 898, 913, 1880.
[5] *Arch. f. Ophth.* XXV. 2, 205, 1879; XXVI. 2, 176, 1880; XXVII. 3, 47, 1881.
[6] *Centralbl. f. Augenhlk.* 353, 1888.
[7] *Amer. J. of Psychol.* XXII. 369, 1912.
[8] *Zur Farbenlehre*, 1798.
[9] König, p. 4.
[10] p. 396; *Sitz. d. Akad. d. Wiss.* Berlin, 718, 1897.

cases. The subjects match yellow (566—570 $\mu\mu$) with unsaturated complementary blue. They confuse blue-green with blue, greenish yellow with grey and rose-purple, yellowish green with bluish violet, orange with reddish purple. They appear to be a reduction form of trichromatic vision. Tritanopes call the red end of the spectrum red, the violet end green or blue. Vintschgau and Hering's case was congenital, but showed changes in the red and green, thus approximating to total colour blindness. There was a neutral band in the yellow (598—568 $\mu\mu$), but the violet end also appeared colourless, though of good luminosity and without marked shortening. Yellow and blue could be matched with grey, but a match could not be made between red and green. The most saturated green was at 532 $\mu\mu$, and the site of maximum brightness was between 558 $\mu\mu$ and 565 $\mu\mu$. In Donders' case the spectrum was shortened at each end and the neutral band in the yellow occupied one-third of the spectrum. Tritanopia appears to be commonest in cases of detachment of the retina. It is simulated in cases of jaundice and sclerosis of the crystalline lens, these being due to absorption by yellow pigment. The same ambiguity may arise in people with unusually dense macular pigmentation[1].

Bibliography of Cases of Tritanopia

Stilling. *Klin. Monatsbl. f. Augenhlk.* XIII. Suppl. 2, 41, 1875; XIV. Suppl. 3, 1, 1875.
Cohn. *Studien über angeb. Farbenblindheit,* 139, Breslau, 1879.
Donders. *Ann. d'ocul.* XXXIV. 212, 1880.
Holmgren. *Med. Zentralbl.* XVIII.; *Centralbl. f. Augenhlk.* V. 476, 1881.
Hermann. *Inaug. diss.* Dorpat, 1882.
Wundt. *Phil. Studien,* VIII. 173, 1892.
Vintschgau. *Arch. f. d. ges. Physiol.* XLVIII. 431; LVII. 191, 1894.
Hering. *Arch. f. d. ges. Physiol.* LVII. 308, 1894.
König. *Sitz. d. Akad. d. Wiss.* XXXIV. 718, 1897 (Pathological).
Piper. *Ztsch. f. Psychol. u. Physiol. d. Sinnesorg.* XXXVIII. 155, 1905 (Pathological).
Levy. *Arch. f. Ophth.* LXII. 464, 1906.
Collin and Nagel. *Ztsch. f. Sinnesphysiol.* XLI. 2, 74, 1906 (Pathological).
Schenck. *Arch. f. d. ges. Physiol.* CXVIII. 161, 1907.
Krienes. *Ztschr. f. Augenhlk.* XX. 392, 1908.
Köllner. *Die Störungen des Farbensinnes,* Berlin, 1912 (Bibliography).

[1] Cf. Abney, p. 343; *Proc. Roy. Soc. Lond.* XLIX. 1891; Hess, *Arch. f. Anat.* LXI. 29, 1908.

CHAPTER III

ANOMALOUS TRICHROMATIC VISION

Slight variations in the colour matches made by people with apparently normal colour vision are commonly met with, and variations occur in the same individual under as nearly as possible identical conditions at different times of examination. Setting aside physical causes, such as differences in macular pigmentation, pigmentation of the lens, etc., ample reasons for slight variations will be found in successive induction, fatigue, the psychological state, and so on. There yet remain, however, cases which cannot be explained on any such grounds. The majority on exhaustive examination show intermediate grades linking them with the normal on the one hand and the dichromats (protanopes and deuteranopes) on the other. König called this form of colour vision anomalous trichromatic vision. As Greenwood says[1], "It is not improbable that these abnormal trichromatics are extreme variants of a frequency system representing the whole range of visual types. The matter can only be settled when the quantitative mixing ratios for a definite match have been determined on a large number of persons taken at random; we may then find that the results are in accordance with some well-known frequency distribution, the normal equation representing the modal value."

We owe the discovery of probably the two largest classes of these anomalous trichromats to Lord Rayleigh[2]. They approximate to the protanopes and deuteranopes. Lord Rayleigh found that if homogeneous yellow (*D* line, 589 $\mu\mu$) is matched with a mixture of homogeneous red (*Li* line, 670·8 $\mu\mu$) and homogeneous green (*Th* line, 535 $\mu\mu$) some persons require much more red, others much more green than the normal. The latter are the more numerous class and may be called *partial deuteranopes* (*deuteranomal*, Nagel). Of them, Donders[3] found four cases amongst 60 people examined; König and Dieterici[4] 3 amongst 70. Many cases have been thoroughly investigated by Hering[5], Lotze[6], v. Kries[7], and Abney and Watson. Of the *partial*

[1] *Physiology of the Special Senses*, p. 137.
[2] *Nature*, XXV. 64, 1882; *Brit. Assoc. Rep.* 728, 1890.
[3] *Arch. f. Anat. u. Physiol.* 520, 1884.
[4] *Ztsch. f. Psychol. u. Physiol. d. Sinnesorg.* IV. 293, 1892.
[5] *Lotos*, VI. 1885.
[6] *Dissertation*, Freiburg, 1898.
[7] *Ztsch. f. Psychol. u. Physiol. d. Sinnesorg.* XIX. 64, 1899.

protanopes (*protanomal*, Nagel) Donders and König do not record any case, v. Kries one only[1], whereas Nagel[2], Guttmann[3], and Abney and Watson record a considerable number. The two last have exceptional opportunities as examiners for the Board of Trade. Their results, of which only a very small proportion have been published, will be discussed later (Part III).

v. Kries and his pupils made a series of investigations on the ratio of green to red in the matches with intermediate homogeneous lights for normal and anomalous trichromats. The quotients of long series of average ratios is given in the following table, I for v. Kries (normal) and Lotze (abnormal), II, for Halben (normal) and Lotze (abnormal), III, for Polimanti (normal) and Zehender (abnormal).

Homogeneous light	Quotients I	II	III	Homogeneous light	Quotients (Levy)
628 $\mu\mu$	4·51	4·35	4·82	625 $\mu\mu$	0·019
615 ,,	3·74	—	—	613 ,,	0·123
603 ,,	3·15	3·7	4·17	601 ,,	0·230
591 ,,	3·14	—	—	589 ,,	0·278
581 ,,	2·68	3·0	3·92	579 ,,	0·262
571 ,,	2·48	—	—	569 ,,	0·249
561 ,,	2·15	2·6	2·98	559 ,,	0·176
552 ,,	2·12	—	2·09	550 ,,	0·080

The table shows conclusively that the anomaly is the result of a physiological condition, not of physical conditions, such as macular pigmentation as suggested by Hering[4]. If it were due to the latter cause all the quotients of any series would be the same. On the contrary the quotients of partial deuteranopes diminish *pari passu* with the diminution in wave-length of the comparison homogeneous light.

The divergence is even more marked for the partial protanope (Levy); here the quotients also vary with the wave-length, increasing up to 589 $\mu\mu$ and then diminishing.

If the results are compared with Breuer's[5] for macular pigmentation we find that his ratio of green to red for central fixation (1° field) was 1·1 times that for paracentral fixation (3° field, 3°—6° paracentral). The difference therefore between normal and anomalous trichromats

[1] Levy, *Dissertation*, Freiburg, 1903.
[2] *Klin. Monatsbl. f. Augenhlk.* XLII. 356, 1904.
[3] *Ztsch. f. Sinnesphysiol.* XLII. 24, 250, 1907; XLIII. 146, 199, 255, 411, 1909.
[4] *Lotos*, VI. 142, 1885.
[5] *Ztsch. f. Psychol. u. Physiol. d. Sinnesorg.* XIII. 464, 1897.

equally manifests itself with paracentral fixation. There might, however, be more widespread dense macular pigmentation or pigmentation of the refractive media. This possible factor can be tested by comparison of the achromatic scotopic values of spectral lights for a normal and an anomalous trichromat with a fixed blue (460 $\mu\mu$) comparison light. The ratios of the quantities of blue to match the homogeneous lights for Halben (normal) and Lotze (partial deuteranope) were

Wave-lengths	591	581	571	561	552	544	536	529
Ratios	1·03	1·49	1·31	1·10	1·24 (0·99)	1·18	0·90	1·09

The difference is therefore not due to more extensive pigmentation.

As might be expected the luminosity curves of the anomalous trichromats show corresponding differences from the normal (Watson[1]). It has already been mentioned (*v.* p. 179) that v. Maltzew[2] found individual variations in trichromats, and these formed a complete series between the trichromats and complete deuteranopes by way of the partial deuteranopes. The protanopes and partial protanopes showed a quite different luminosity distribution. In red-green mixtures the red component is much more powerful than the green. She concludes that the differences in colour matches between the normal and the anomalous have a different cause from the individual variations of the normal. The latter correspond with the luminosity differences, whereas the former do not.

Guttmann[3] has made important contributions to the knowledge of anomalous trichromatic vision. He is himself a partial deuteranope. He finds that anomalous trichromats show seven chief differences from normal trichromats.

(1) For partial deuteranopes the discernible difference in hue is smaller in the yellow and greater in the green than for the normal. The difference in the green is not marked, but that in the yellow is very appreciable. Guttmann's mean error (*v.* p. 19) at 589 $\mu\mu$ was from 12 to 13 $\mu\mu$, whereas that for the normal under like conditions was 1 to 2 $\mu\mu$.

(2) The anomalous deuteranopes are more dependent on intensity.

[1] *Proc. Roy. Soc. Lond.* A, LXXXVIII. 1913 ; see Part III.

[2] *Ztsch. f. Sinnesphysiol.* XLIII. 76, 1908.

[3] *Neurol. Centbl.* 491, 1904 ; *Ztsch. f. Sinnesphysiol.* XLII. 24, 250, 1907 ; XLIII. 146, 199, 255, 1908–9 ; *Münch. med. Wochenschr.* 566, 1910 ; *Ztsch. f. Sinnesphysiol.* LVII. 271, 1910.

They can only distinguish colours at the optimum intensity, and their optimum is narrower than the normal and of greater intensity.

(3) They are more dependent on luminosity differences, which they are expert in translating into hue, thus showing a specially well developed capacity for distinguishing differences in brightness of coloured objects.

(4) They need a considerably larger area of stimulation or visual angle for the accurate perception of hue, a fact confirmed by Nagel[1]. Diminution in field causes a marked diminution in their capacity for distinguishing differences in hue.

(5) They need longer time for the correct perception of colours, a fact of great practical importance in certain occupations.

(6) Fatigue for colour, and with it defective discrimination, occurs more rapidly than in the normal.

(7) They have a very marked increase in simultaneous contrast effects as compared with the normal. Contrast depends to an exceptional extent upon the luminosities of the contrasting fields, and the anomalous trichromatic colour thresholds are largely dependent upon it. Nagel[2] also drew attention to the acuteness for contrast of the partial deuteranopes. He found that a red and a yellow light, side by side, of equal luminosity to the normal appeared different to them, and they often called the yellow greenish or green, whereas in the absence of the red light the yellow was correctly named.

Guttmann found his own periphery values agreed with the normal. Like Donders, he calls anomalous trichromatic vision a "weakness" of colour vision, a term to which Nagel objects. Guttmann found that the "extreme anomalous dichromats" nearly resemble complete dichromats, and show diminished differential sensibility for hue, rapid fatigue and increased perception of simultaneous contrast effects. He also found the after-images of anomalous dichromats agreed with those of the dichromats, but only with homogeneous lights. With pigments the after-images appeared to resemble those of the normal, and no accurate deductions could be drawn without comparison lights, since the naming of colours is very liable to lead to mistakes.

Koffka[3], himself a partial protanope, confirmed Guttmann's general conclusions for this group. They show the same greater sensitiveness

[1] *Ztsch. f. Psychol. u. Physiol. d. Sinnesorg.* XXXIX. 1905.
[2] *Klin. Monatsbl. f. Augenhlk.* XLII. 356, 1904.
[3] *Ztsch. f. Sinnesphysiol.* XLIII. 123, 1908.

to simultaneous contrast effects, but these are spread over the whole spectrum with the exception of yellow (compare the partial deuteranopes). The contrast-responding field is equal in luminosity to that of the contrast-exciting field. Contrast extends over a larger area and commences more rapidly than in the normal. It is strongest in the green, and is greatest for small fields except towards the violet end. Colour-fatigue sets in more quickly with them, as with the partial deuteranopes. The two groups are thus easily confused. The normal variations in the Rayleigh equation—matching *D* light with mixed thallium- and lithium-line lights—are more restricted in one group of partial deuteranopes than in the partial protanopes.

It has been found that the partial dichromats vary relatively little in their individual matches for the sodium line. If, however, they match a wave-length materially shorter than 589 $\mu\mu$ their matches become very indefinite and variable. Considerable quantities of red can be added without upsetting the match. On the other hand, for 536 $\mu\mu$ for example, the red can be reduced almost to zero without the fields ceasing to be at any rate nearly equal. These are extreme cases of partial deuteranopia, and they therefore show very defective sensibility for colour differences in the neighbourhood of 570—535 $\mu\mu$. Similarly there are extreme cases of partial protanopia in which pure yellow and especially lights of somewhat greater wave-length appear almost the same as the spectral red.

CHAPTER IV

MONOCHROMATIC VISION

There are certain persons who appear to have no perception of colour; their vision is monochromatic. The condition is congenital, and is known as *total colour blindness* or achromatopia. The subjects, apart from the colour defect, usually have very bad central vision (less than $\frac{6}{18}$), marked photophobia, and nystagmus. Several members of a family (11 groups) may be affected either with the same condition or less commonly with other forms of dyschromatopia. Consanguinity (five cases) and heredity appear to be factors in the incidence of the disease. Males are affected about twice as often as females. Nettleship[1] has published 10 pedigrees containing 34 cases affected: 18 males, 15 females, and 1 of unrecorded sex.

[1] *Trans. Ophth. Soc.* XXIX. cxci, 1909.

Grunert[1] has collected all the recorded cases up to the date of his paper, adding four others. Cases have since been recorded by Bjerrum[2], Rönne[3], Hessberg[4], Köllner[5], Juler[6], and Gertz[7].

The total of published cases is 84 (Nettleship, 1909). Refractive errors are common, generally moderate myopia; correction produces little improvement of vision. One case recorded by v. Hippel and Uhthoff[8] could see Röntgen rays, but this observation has not been confirmed and was negatived in Rönne's case. The only case with good central vision was Frau Prof. R., examined by Raehlmann[9], but this case is peculiar in other respects. Objective causes for defective central vision have been found occasionally:—macular changes[10], pallor of the discs[11], moderate albinism[12], and corneal nebulae[13]. In the majority of cases the ophthalmoscopic appearances are quite normal. In König's experiments[14] on the influence of intensity of illumination on visual acuity, as the intensity rises the curve shows a well-marked angle where the intensity changes from scotopic to photopic. In the wholly colour-blind König found that this angle was absent, the scotopic part of the curve being continued in the same direction without interruption until an intensity was reached which caused dazzling and diminished visual acuity. In monochromatic vision moreover the usual diminution in acuity in the parafoveal region is not noticed.

Photophobia and nystagmus are almost always present. The former increases with the intensity of the light and is absent with low illuminations. Bright light causes an unpleasant sensation of a luminous cloud before the eyes. Central vision is also slightly improved by

[1] *Arch. f. Ophth.* LVI. 1, 132, 1903. [2] *Hospitalstidende,* 1145, 1904.

[3] *Ibid.* 1230, 1906; *Klin. Monatsbl. f. Augenhlk.* XLIV. Beilageheft, 193, 1906.

[4] *Klin. Monatsbl. f. Augenhlk.* XLVII. 2, 129, 1909.

[5] *Ztsch. f. Sinnesphysiol.* XLIII. 409, 1909.

[6] *Ophthal. Rev.* 65, 1910. [7] *Arch. f. Augenhlk.* LXX. 202, 228, 1911.

[8] *Bericht. d. Ophth. Gesellschft.* Heidelberg, 150, 158, 1898.

[9] *Wochenschr. f. Therapie u. Hygiene d. Auges,* II. 165, 1899; *Ztsch. f. Augenhlk.* II. 315, 403, 1900.

[10] Nettleship, *St Thomas's Hosp. Rep.* X. 37, 1880; Uhthoff, *Ztsch. f. Psychol. u. Physiol. d. Sinnesorg.* XX. 326, 1899; Nagel, *Arch. f. Augenhlk.* XLIV. 153, 1901; Hess, *Ztsch. f. Psychol. u. Physiol. d. Sinnesorg.* XXIX. 99, 1902; and Grunert, *loc. cit.*

[11] Landolt, *Arch. d'Opht.* IV. 211, 1893 and Grunert, *loc. cit.*

[12] Uhthoff, *op. cit,* XXII. 1, 200 and König and Dieterici, the same case as Uhthoff's, *Sitz. d. Akad. d. Wiss.* 805, 1886.

[13] Raehlmann, *Arch. f. Ophth.* XXII. 29, 1879.

[14] *Sitz. d. Akad. d. Wiss.* Berlin, 559, 1897; see also Parsons, *Roy. Lond. Ophth. Hosp. Rep.* XIX. 2, 283, 1914.

lowered illumination. Uhthoff found the maximum at 12 metre-candles; the normal maximum is 30 metre-candles or over. The scotopic visual acuity resembles the normal, and the light sense of the totally colour-blind, whenever it has been tested, has been found good. No objective cause can be found for the photophobia. The unpleasant sensation experienced in a bright light is due rather to the interference with vision than to any painful sensation. Thus Nagel and May's patient[1] could look at an Auer burner without discomfort; she was, however, practically blind for several minutes after doing so. Similarly, examination with Thorner's ophthalmoscope and dilated pupil caused no discomfort, but great diminution of vision followed for a quarter of an hour.

The nystagmus is not found quite so often as the amblyopia and photophobia. Amongst Grunert's last 23 cases it is not mentioned by Fukala[2], nor in two cases recorded by Hess. In Nagel's case it was absent in one eye. In v. Hippel's first case it was present, but had disappeared four years later when examined by Hess and Hering[3]. Grunert noticed diminution in one case in the course of eleven years. These were all elderly people, whereas most of the recorded cases were children. The nystagmus, sometimes rather slow in the condition of rest, becomes very rapid, with short excursions, on fixation. There is a striking resemblance between the nystagmus and that met with in miners[4]. Many cases showed divergent strabismus, and when absent it could be elicited by eliminating the tendency to binocular vision, as on shutting the eyes or going to sleep. The defect of foveal vision renders binocular fixation difficult and the eyes readily take up a position of rest, which is usually one of divergence.

The field of vision is generally normal, though Grunert found ring scotomata in one of his cases. Of greater theoretical interest is the frequency of an absolute central scotoma. Owing largely to the accompanying nystagmus its presence is very difficult to demonstrate, and certainly undue importance has been attached to it since Mrs Ladd-Franklin (1892) and König (1894) hypothecated it on theoretical grounds. Nearly 30 cases have been carefully examined as to this point. Central scotoma was absent in 14 cases, published by v. Hippel (1), Pflüger (1), v. Kries (1), Hess (5), Grunert (2), Juler (3),

[1] *Ztsch. f. Sinnesphysiol.* XLII. 69, 1907.
[2] *Klin. Monatsbl. f. Augenhlk.* XXXVI. 175, 1898.
[3] *Arch. f. d. ges. Physiol.* LXXI. 105, 1898.
[4] Llewellyn, *Miners' Nystagmus*, London, 1912.

and Gertz (1). Gertz used a special method and was convinced that if there were a central scotoma it was less than 50′. There was a central scotoma in nine cases: König (1), Nagel (1), Uhthoff (3), Grunert (3), and Hessberg (1). Bjerrum and Rönne were unable to decide with certainty; in Bjerrum's case the blind spot could not be demonstrated. The positive cases include those with macular changes and albinism, but several had quite normal fundi. Whether all cases have an absolute central scotoma or not, it is certain that foveal vision is very defective even as compared with parafoveal, as is admitted by Hess.

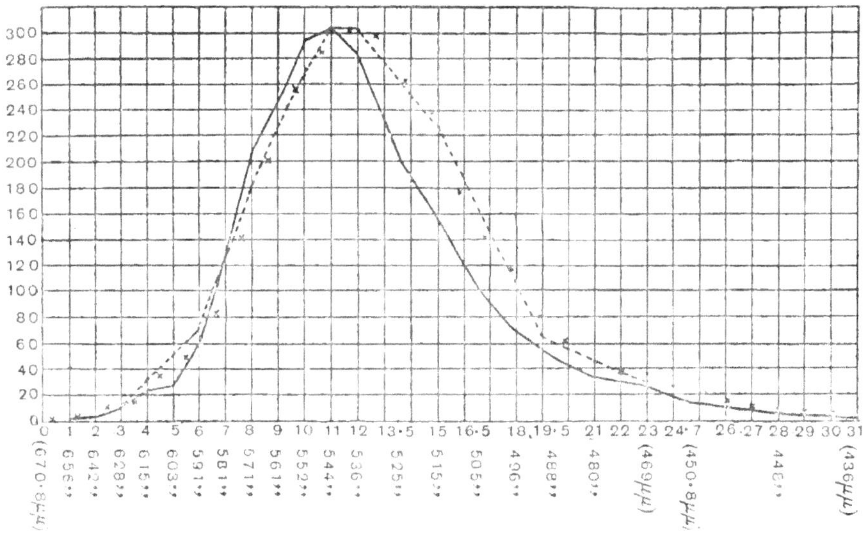

Fig. 51. ——————— Achromatic scotopic luminosity curve of a deuteranope. .... Luminosity curve of a monochromat. Abscissae, wave-lengths of the prismatic spectrum of gaslight; ordinates, arbitrary scale. (v. Kries.)

The spectrum appears to the totally colour-blind as a monochromatic strip, which is usually described as grey. No colour distinctions are made, but the luminosity varies in different parts. The part which appears to them brightest is what the normal call green, and when the luminosity curve is worked out it is found to agree in a very remarkable manner with the normal achromatic scotopic luminosity curve. This fact was first discovered by Hering and Hillebrand[1] and has received conclusive confirmation, notably in the researches of König and

[1] *Sitz. d. Wiener Akad.* XCVIII 70, 1889.

Dieterici[1] and König and Ritter[2], Hering[3], v. Kries[4], Nagel and May[5], and Abney and Watson. The maximum luminosity with the gaslight spectrum is about 536 $\mu\mu$, with sunlight about 527 $\mu\mu$. The red end is shortened, but not the violet (Figs. 54 and 55).

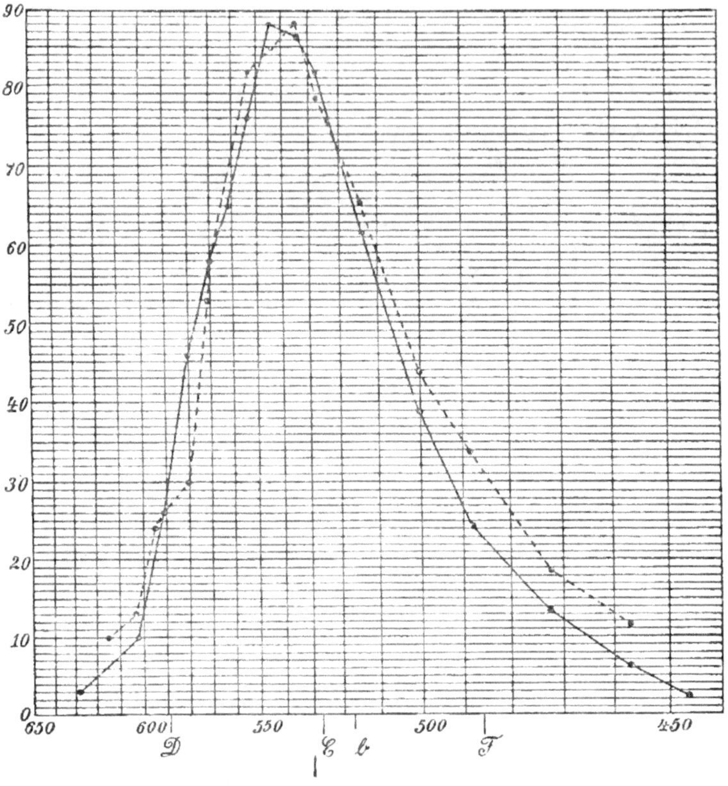

Fig. 55. ———— Achromatic scotopic luminosity curve of a deuteranope. .... Luminosity curve of a monochromat. Abscissae, wave-lengths of the prismatic spectrum of the Nernst light; ordinates, arbitrary scale. (Nagel and May.)

Whereas, however, increasing the intensity of the light shifts the maximum for the normal towards the yellow (see Section III, Chap. II), it merely increases the luminosity for monochromatic vision. The curve is also independent of adaptation. We have already drawn

[1] *Sitz. d. Akad. d. Wiss.* Berlin, 805, 1886; *Ztsch. f. Psychol. u. Physiol. d. Sinnesorg.* IV. 241, 1892.

[2] König, p. 144.

[3] *Arch. f. d. ges. Physiol.* XLIX. 598, 601, 1891.

[4] *Ztsch. f. Psychol. u. Physiol. d. Sinnesorg.* XIII. 239, 1897.

[5] *Ztsch. f. Sinnesphysiol.* XLII. 69, 1907.

attention to the similarity of the scotopic luminosity curve and the curve of bleaching values for different monochromatic lights for the visual purple (p. 55).

T. C. Porter's and Schaternikoff's experiments, especially the latter, (p. 95), have shown that the rate of change of fusion frequency of intermittent stimulation of the retina is lower for achromatic scotopic than for photopic vision. Uhthoff[1] examined one of his cases and found that the totally colour-blind reacts like the normal with achromatic scotopic vision. A rotating disc with black and white sectors ceases to flicker with an intensity of light even above the normal photopic threshold whilst it is still flickering to the normal eye. Nagel has confirmed this observation.

The facts of monochromatic vision are inconsistent with the view that it is a simple reduction form of trichromatic vision, though some cases have been regarded as of this nature. The theoretical explanation will be discussed in Part III, Section I.

Bibliography of Cases of Monochromatic Vision

Huddart. *Phil. Trans. Roy. Soc. Lond.* LXVII. 260, 1777.

Schopenhauer (1812). Griesebachsche Ausgabe, VI. 81, 1875.

Rosier. *Obs. sur la physique, etc.* XIII. 87, 1779.

d'Hombres-Firmas. *C. r. acad. des sci.* II. 1849.

Rose. *Arch. f. Ophth.* XII. 2, 98, 1860.

Galezowski. *Du diagnostic des maladies des yeux par la chromatoscopie rétinienne*, Paris, 1868.

Donders. *Klin. Monatsbl. f. Augenhlk.* 470, 1871.

Rachlmann. *Arch. f. Ophth.* XXII. 29, 1879; *Ztsch. f. Augenhlk.* II. 315, 403, 1900.

Cohn. *Studien über angeb. Farbenblindheit*, Breslau, 1879.

Becker. *Arch. f. Ophth.* XXV. 2, 205, 1879.

Nettleship. *St Thomas's Hosp. Rep.* X. 37, 1880; *Roy. Lond. Hosp. Ophth. Rep.* XI. 373, 1887.

Magnus. *Centralbl. f. Augenhlk.* IV. 373, 1881.

Landolt. *Arch. d'Opht.* I. 114, 1881; XI. 202, 1891.

Schöler and Uhthoff. *Beiträge z. Path. d. Sehnerven*, Berlin, 1884.

Dor. *Rev. gén. d'Opht.* IV. 434, 1885.

König and Dieterici. *Sitz. d. Akad. d. Wiss.* Berlin, 805, 1886; Uhthoff, *Arch. f. Ophth.* XXXII. 1, 200, 1886: König, *Arch. f. Psychiat. und Nervenkr.* XXI. 284, 1889; in König, p. 206.

Kressig. *Mitt. a. d. ophth. Klinik zu Tübingen*, II. 332, 1890.

Querenghi. *Ann. di Ottal.* 35, 1891; *Ann. d'ocul.* CVI. 333, 1891.

Hering. *Arch. f. d. ges. Physiol.* XLIX. 563, 1891.

v. Kries. *Ztsch. f. Psychol. u. Physiol. d. Sinnesorg.* XIII. 241, 1897.

Colburn. *Amer. J. of Ophth.* XIV. 237, 1897.

[1] v. Kries, *Ztsch. f. Psychol. u. Physiol. d. Sinnesorg.* XXXII. 113, 1903.

A. v. Hippel. *Festschrift*, Halle, 1894: *Bericht. d. Ophth. Gesellschf.* Heidelberg, 150, 1898.

Hess and Hering. *Arch. f. d. ges. Physiol.* LXXI. 105, 1898.

Pflüger. *Bericht. d. Ophth. Gesellschf.* Heidelberg, 166, 1898; *Internat. Congress*, Moscow, 315, 1898.

Fukala. *Klin. Monatsbl. f. Augenhlk.* XXXVI. 175, 1898.

Uhthoff. *Bericht. d. Ophth. Gesellschf.* Heidelberg, 158, 1898; *Ztsch. f. Psychol. u. Physiol. d. Sinnesorg.* XX. 326, 1899; XXVII. 344, 1902.

Hess. *Arch. f. Ophth.* LI. 225, 1900; *Ztsch. f. Psychol. u. Physiol. d. Sinnesorg.* XXIX. 99, 1902.

Abney. *Proc. Roy. Soc. Lond.* LXVI. 179, 1900.

Nagel. *Arch. f. Ophth.* XLIV. 153, 1901.

Pergens. *Klin. Monatsbl. f. Augenhlk.* XL. 2, 46, 1902.

Grunert. *Arch. f. Ophth.* LVI. 1, 132, 1903.

Wehrli. In Nagel's *Jahresbericht f. Ophth.* XXXIV. 92, 1903.

Bjerrum. *Hospitalstidende.* 1145, 1904.

Piper. *Ztsch. f. Psychol. u. Physiol. d. Sinnesorg.* XXXVIII, 155, 1905.

Rönne. *Klin. Monatsbl. f. Augenhlk.* XLIV. Beilageheft, 193, 1906.

Nettleship and Holmes Spicer. *Trans. Ophth. Soc.* XXVIII. 83, 1908.

Nettleship. *Trans. Ophth. Soc.* XXIX. cxci, 1909.

Hessberg. *Klin. Monatsbl. f. Augenhlk.* XLVII. 2, 129, 1909.

Köllner. *Ztsch. f. Sinnesphysiol.* XLIII. 409, 1909.

Juler. *Ophth. Rev.* 65, 1910.

Gertz. *Arch. f. Augenhlk.* LXX. 202, 228, 1911.

PART III

THE CHIEF THEORIES OF COLOUR VISION

SECTION I

GENERAL REVIEW

CHAPTER I

INTRODUCTION

In the previous parts I have endeavoured to set forth the best-established facts of normal and abnormal colour vision. There are other equally well established facts, but they are so intimately associated with the theories which we have now to consider that it has been thought better to defer consideration of them. We have already, however, accumulated sufficient to warrant an attempt at this stage to classify them. Such as have been mentioned form the basis of the chief theories of colour vision and will enable the reader to obtain a grasp of the significance of these theories.

No theory has ever been propounded which suffices to explain all the facts of the department of science to which it refers. If it succeeds in offering a complete solution of all the problems it ceases to be a theory and merits at least as secure a position in the domain of knowledge as the facts themselves. As McDougall[1] says, "the most fruitful hypothesis ever developed is perhaps that of an ethereal medium to which an impossible and inconceivable combination of properties is assigned by physicists." Theories must be judged solely according to their efficacy as working hypotheses. In so far as they serve the purpose of sign-posts, pointing out the paths of future research, so far are they of value. "Sterile theories easily relinquish immortality. Fruitful theories hand down their immortal part to their children, while their ephemeral shell falls to pieces" (Hering)[2].

[1] *Brain*, XXIV. 611, 1901.

[2] *Lotos*, N. F. I. 15, 1880.

The task which we have set before us is that of discovering in the realm of vision "what psychical event a and what physical stimulus a are universally connected in the order of nature, and of finding the law by which a undergoes a definite change and becomes β, when a by a change equally definite (but definable only by a physical standard and not a psychical one) becomes b (Lotze[1])." In the accumulation of the facts already set forth we may discern two distinct methods which I will term the synthetic and the analytic. In every case there is a stimulus which excites and a sensation of which the individual is conscious. In most cases—one might say in all—both are complex. In the investigation two methods may be adopted. In the first the stimulus is reduced to its simplest form and the resulting sensation observed. The sensation is evoked by the simplest possible physical stimuli: hence the designation synthetic. In the second method the sensation is reduced to its simplest form and the varieties of stimuli which elicit this simple sensation are classified and analysed. This is the analytic method. *A priori* one is inclined to attach more significance to the results obtained by the synthetic method. It is the method which prevails in the exact sciences, chemistry, physics, and so on. Our sensations are notoriously liable to play us false. They are complex and they are modified by all the other sensations to which the individual is subject at the moment of observation. It is impossible to nullify all the conflicting sensations and it is easy to overlook those potent to mislead. On the other hand the problem itself deals with the sensation and its modifications, and it may therefore be reasonably urged that the analytic method of attack is of the essence of the problem. In the exact sciences the sensations involved are generally simple and well-defined and their modifications either complicate the observations little, or are so disturbing as to indicate their own corrective. They are one cause of "errors of observation," and the manner in which these are minimised in the exact sciences is familiar to all.

The two methods are not antagonistic but complementary, and as such should lead to identical results. That they do not is the fault of ignorance and is not due to any innate defects. If we had certain knowledge of all the effective factors in the physical stimuli and of all the effective factors in the resultant sensations and of all their quantitative and qualitative relations, we should arrive at consistent results. But that is a truism. It is the rôle of physiology to deal with complex relations of this nature, and especially the rôle of physiological

[1] *Metaphysik*; Bosanquet's translation, 295, 1894.

psychology. A more material analogy may be drawn from metabolism. Here we have more or less accurate information as to the nature and constitution of the food material supplied to an organ or to the body and as to the nature and constitution of the secreted or excreted material. The intermediate steps are full of gaps. In the domain of the special senses physiology is the realm of the intermediate steps, physics and psychology the termini. It is natural that the physicist should adopt the method characteristic of his branch of science, the psychologist that characteristic of his own. But if we survey the advance of psychology in recent years we cannot but be struck by the fact that it has been largely due to the adoption of the synthetic method. Experimental psychology and the elaboration of "psycho-physical laws" are results of this tendency[1].

It appears to me, therefore, that more credence is to be attached to the results of the synthetic method. They alone are submissible to approximately accurate quantitative estimates, and it is only by quantitative estimates that the facts can be conclusively correlated. We thus obtain a group of correlations which themselves attain the dignity of precise knowledge. Outside this aristocracy of facts is a vast multitude of undigested facts. Either they have not yet been submitted to accurate quantitative relationship or are as yet incapable of so being. In so far as they fall into line with precise correlations they are of confirmatory value. In so far as they are antagonistic they are impotent to destroy these correlations, but offer a well-stocked field for further research.

Not that they themselves are incapable of correlation, but it is qualitative in nature and therefore less precise. Always remembering their relative smaller value as coins of the realm these qualitative correlations are well worthy of extended study.

We have therefore in *quantitative* relations a criterion which can be applied to the grouping of the facts which we have already brought forward. If we rapidly survey the sections of Part I we shall find that the quantitative relationships are best established for luminosity and colour with the photopic fovea and for luminosity with the achromatic scotopic eye. When we consider peripheral vision, temporal, and areal effects, both for photopic and scotopic vision, the quantitative relations are far less well established. The same grouping applies to Part II.

Bearing in mind the relative precision of our knowledge of the various facts we can at once hypothecate certain relationships with

[1] Cf. Myers, *Experimental Psychology*, Chap. I, London, 1909.

greater or less accuracy. First, there is the divergence between photopic and achromatic scotopic vision, a divergence so striking as almost necessarily to hypothecate diverse mechanisms. Second, there is the outstanding triplex relationship between colour and colour-less sensations that three colour-components suffice to arouse almost the whole gamut of colour and colour-less sensations. Third,—and here the relative precision of our knowledge is less—there is a certain opposition evinced by certain colour sensations to each other, between black and white, and between the complementary colours. Observations by the analytic method particularly indicate that there are specially differentiated opponent activities between certain particular colour sensations, such as those of red and green, yellow and blue.

CHAPTER II

HISTORICAL REVIEW OF MODERN THEORIES OF COLOUR VISION

In 1866 Max Schultze[1], as the result of anatomical researches, human and comparative, came to the conclusion that the rods were the more primitive organ of vision and were concerned with the perception of light, but were incapable of initiating impulses leading to colour perception. The cones he regarded as more highly differentiated and capable of initiating impulses leading to both light and colour perceptions. The only arguments available to him were (1) the parallel diminution of visual acuity and colour sensations in indirect vision and of the cones in the periphery of the retina : (2) the absence of cones in certain animals of nocturnal habits (bat, hedge-hog, mole, eel, etc. ; relative paucity in the owl) and the paucity of rods in certain animals of diurnal habits (lizard, snake) (*v.* p. 10).

The discoveries of the visual purple by H. Müller (1851) and that it was bleached by the action of light by Boll (1876) were followed by the exhaustive researches of Kühne (1878). They led Kühne to the conclusion that we could not only perceive the spectrum by means of the rods and the visual purple, without the intervention of the cones, but that it would under these circumstances appear grey and colourless as it does to the totally colour-blind. He hypothecated the existence of other visual substances to account for the colour phenomena of vision

[1] *Arch f. mikr. Anat.* II. 1866 ; III. 371, 1867.

and thought that one such was the so-called visual yellow. Haab[1] elaborated similar suggestions on the basis of Schultze's theory and Hering's theory.

Charpentier (1877 *sqq.*) distinguished " perception lumineuse brute " or " vision diffuse " from " vision nette," the former with vague localisation, the latter with sharply defined. The " photaesthesic elements " initiate impulses which mutually modify each other as in the interference phenomena of light and thus the two apparatus, each capable of initiating only colourless perceptions alone, become capable of giving rise to colour-perceptions. He did not attempt to define the exact locality of the apparatus; it is supposed to be partly peripheral or retinal, partly central or in the nervous system. He conjectured that diffuse vision is initiated by the rods and visual purple, but only in achromatic scotopic vision, since the visual purple can itself be viewed entoptically[2].

Parinaud[3], in ignorance of Schultze's theory, elaborated much the same views with more extensive material. He attributed the disease known as night blindness (often badly termed hemeralopia) to defects in the rods and visual purple[4], and first demonstrated that central vision is intact in this complaint. He asserted the failure of adaptation at the fovea in 1884, having previously in 1881 pointed out that the photochromatic interval is absent here. These facts, confirmed by the night blindness of fowls and pigeons owing to absence of visual purple, led him to the conclusion that the cones, which are alone present in the fovea, are incapable of dark-adaptation, whereas achromatic scotopic vision is a purely extrafoveal phenomenon and is the function of the rods and visual purple. This is the " theory of two retinas." Colour-perception according to Parinaud is a purely cerebral function.

Similar views were expressed by Liesegang[5] and by Parinaud's pupil Weiss[6]. Berry[7] suggested that the pigment epithelium is the seat of colourless light sensations.

König[8] also regarded the visual purple as the excitant of the rods (Kühne) and with low intensities of light stimuli the basis of achromatic scotopic vision. He considered the visual yellow, the first product of

[1] *Correspondenzbl. f. Schweizer Aerzte*, IX. 1879.

[2] *C. r. soc. de biol.* 1890; *C. r. acad. des sci.* 1891.

[3] *C. r. acad. des sci.* 1881, 1884, 1885; *Ann. d'ocul.* LXXXV. 113, 1881; CXII. 228, 1894; *La Vision*, Paris, 1898.

[4] *Arch. gén. de méd.* 1881.

[5] *Photogr. Arch.* 1891.

[6] *Rev. gén. des sci.* 1895.

[7] *Ophth. Rev.* 1890.

[8] *Sitz. d. Akad. d. Wiss.* Berlin, 1894.

bleaching of visual purple with higher intensities, as the basis of the blue sensation, which is therefore also carried out by the rods and is absent from the fovea.

v. Kries[1], also independently of any knowledge of Schultze's paper and apparently of Parinaud's writings, elaborated a similar theory, the duplicity theory (*Duplizitätstheorie*), which has received wide acceptation. It will be considered in Section II.

The physical basis of colour vision, as exemplified in the wonderful researches of Sir Isaac Newton, opened up the ground for the modern theories. Newton himself compared the simple colour notes of the spectral scale to the tones of the musical scale. This idea was elaborated by Hartley, Young, Drobisch, and others, but was soon found wanting[2]. Attempts to explain the facts of colour-mixtures directly from the undulatory theory of light by Challis, Grailich, and later Charpentier have also proved inadequate[3].

More recently Hartridge[4] has attempted to give a purely physical explanation of the sensation of yellow. Yellow (650 $\mu\mu$—560 $\mu\mu$) is accurately matched by a suitable mixture of red (740 $\mu\mu$—690 $\mu\mu$) and green (550 $\mu\mu$—510 $\mu\mu$) if a small quantity of white light is added to the yellow. By drawing on mathematical paper two sine curves of equal amplitude, which have periods corresponding approximately to the mean wave-lengths of red and green components of this compound yellow, it will be found that their summation gives a curve which approximates closely to a sine curve of wave-length 620 $\mu\mu$. It shows beats at every 2000 $\mu\mu$; at the nodes the amplitude is almost zero whereas at the antinodes it is nearly double that of either of the curves of which it is compounded. By compounding a red and green wave motion one has obtained a yellow wave motion, the mean wave-length of which approximates closely with that found by experiment.

If this hypothesis were accurate the combination of the same red and green, polarised at right angles to each other, should fail to arouse the sensation of yellow; but such is not the case. Further, although the compound curve obtained by combining the sine curves corresponding to the red and green has between any two consecutive minima a period equal to that of the yellow light, yet at each minimum the curve has

[1] Especially in *Bericht d. naturf. Ges. zu Freiburg i. B.* IX. 2, 1894; *Arch. f. Ophth.* XLII. 3, 95, 1896; *Ztsch. f. Psychol. u. Physiol. d. Sinnesorg.* IX. 81, 1896.

[2] v. Helmholtz, 3rd ed. II. 97.

[3] *Ibid.* II. 129; Charpentier, *La Lumière et les Couleurs*, Chap. XII, Paris, 1888.

[4] *Proc. of the Physiol. Soc., J. of Physiol.* XLV. p. xxix, 1913.

an abrupt change of phase of half a period (Fig. 56). Hence if a disturbance of this character were to act on a system of which the natural period corresponds to that of the yellow light there would be little response, because the disturbance produced during the interval between two consecutive minima would be neutralised by the disturbance produced during the next interval. An illustration will make the point clear. If a succession of correctly timed small impulses be given to a heavy pendulum the pendulum will in time be set in violent motion. If, however, after giving, *e.g.* four of these timed impulses the timing is suddenly altered by half a period the new impulses will tend to check the motion already communicated, and after four impulses the pendulum will be brought to rest[1].

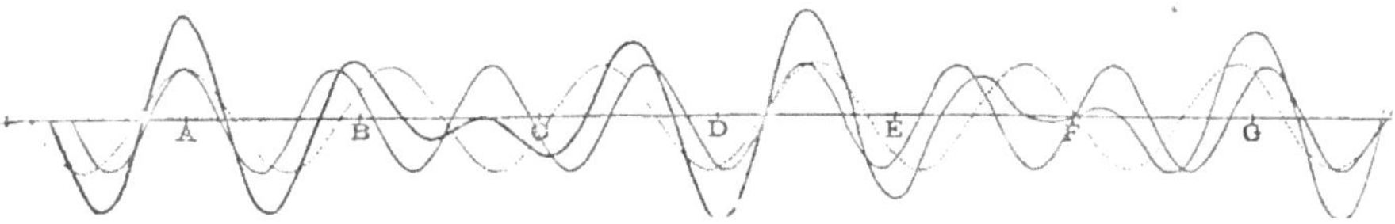

Fig. 56. Combination of two sine curves.

In 1801, in the Bakerian Lecture before the Royal Society, Thomas Young[2] propounded the theory which now commonly bears the name of the Young-Helmholtz Theory. His third hypothesis of "the theory of light and colours" was that the sensations of different colours depend upon the different frequencies of the vibrations of the light which falls upon the retina. Since it is well nigh inconceivable that each sensitive point of the retina possesses innumerable parts capable of responding to the individual vibrations, he concluded from Newton's researches that three parts would suffice to account for all the colour sensations, including white. He chose three chief colours, red, yellow, and blue, the wave-lengths of which were in the ratios 8 : 7 : 6. Each affected a corresponding part of the sensitive mechanism. In 1802, after Wollaston's description of the spectrum, he chose red, green, and violet, which he confirmed on experimental grounds in 1807. He considered that the simplest conception of the fundamental "parts" was three kinds of nerve fibre. Excitation of the first aroused the sensation of red, of the second green, and of the third violet. The first type of fibre was most excited by lights of long wave-length, the third by those of short wave-length, and the second by those of intermediate wave-length, but

[1] I am indebted to Prof. W. Watson, F.R.S., for this explanation.

[2] See *Roy. Lond. Ophth. Hosp. Rep.* XIX. I. 1, 1913.

light of all kinds excited all three kinds of fibres, though in varying degrees.

Young's hypothesis received scant acknowledgment, largely owing to his resuscitation of the undulatory theory of light, which was regarded as a grave heresy by the majority of scientists, who firmly adhered to Newton's corpuscular theory. It remained unheeded until the middle of the nineteenth century, when v. Helmholtz[1] and Clerk-Maxwell[2] adopted it as the explanation of their experiments on the mixture of colours. Grassmann[3] simultaneously enunciated the laws of colour mixture which bear his name.

An essential feature of the Young-Helmholtz theory is the *additive* process, especially as applied to colourless light sensations. Addition of physical stimuli entails additive physiological reactions resulting in compounded psychical end results. Goethe[4] approached the subject from the psychologist's point of view and quickly accumulated facts which were difficult to explain on the Newtonian basis. Such are particularly the phenomena of after-images and simultaneous contrast. The addition theory seemed incapable of supplying a satisfactory explanation[5]. The claims of *four* fundamental colours as opposed to three were emphasised by Aubert[6], and this psychological point of view became crystallised into the theory of opponent colours which bears the name of Hering[7].

The clash of the contending theories led to modifications of each. The psychophysical difficulties led Donders[8], Ad. Fick[9] and v. Kries to limit what the latter calls the components theory (the Young-Helmholtz theory) to the peripheral link in the visual path. v. Kries has elaborated this view in the *theory of zones*.

Hering, regarding the question from the psychological point of view, and endeavouring to bring the facts into a universal common relationship with other physiological processes, emphasised the complementary and opponent characters of certain fundamental colour sensations. From the psychological point of view black, white, red, green, yellow, and blue are fundamental sensations (Mach[10]). All other hues appear to

[1] Müller's *Arch. f. Anat.* 1852.
[2] *Trans. Roy. Soc. Edin.* XXI. 1855.
[3] *Ann. d. Physik* LXXXIX. 1853.
[4] *Zur Farbenlehre*, 1810.
[5] See, however, McDougall, *infra*.
[6] *Physiologie der Netzhaut*, Breslau, 1865; Graefe-Saemisch, *Handb. d. ges. Augenheilkunde*, 1st ed. II. 1876.
[7] *Sitz. d. Wiener Akad.* 1872–1874; *Zur Lehre vom Lichtsinne*, 1876.
[8] *Arch. f. Ophth.* XXVII. 2, 155, 1881; XXX. 1, 15, 1884.
[9] *Arch. f. d. ges. Physiol.* XVII. 152, 1878; XLIII. 441, 1888.
[10] *Sitz. d. Wiener Akad.* LII. 2, 320, 1865.

our consciousness as mixtures of these sensations. They may be divided into two groups, the tone-free or colourless (black and white) and the toned or coloured. The tone-free are simple sensations, neither contains any element of the other. The toned are also, *inter se*, simple sensations in the same meaning of the term. Both groups may be divided into three opponent pairs, black and white, red and green, yellow and blue. So much for the fundamental psychological conceptions.

From the physiological point of view these opponent sensations can be hypothetically brought into line with other physiological processes. We can imagine three substances of unstable chemical constitution: when white is seen the black-white substance undergoes dissimilation (*D*) or katabolic change, when black the same substance undergoes assimilation (*A*) or anabolic change. The sensation is dependent upon the ratio of $D : A$, not upon the absolute intensity of either. Similarly red is seen when the red-green substance undergoes the *D*-process, green when it undergoes the *A*-process; and yellow when the yellow-blue substance undergoes the *D*-process, blue when it undergoes the *A*-process.

Several difficulties are at once apparent. First, while we readily accept the proposition that katabolic changes arouse sensations it will not be so readily admitted that anabolic changes can produce opponent sensations, or indeed any sensations at all. Though this may affect the physiological analogies of the theory it is not of fundamental importance to the theory as a theory of colour vision. Opponent chemical processes on the analogy of oxidation and reduction, or electrical on the analogy of positive and negative electricity, and so on, would serve the purpose equally well and avoid the difficulty.

Second,—what must, however, be conceded as a great difficulty of all theories of colour vision,—black and white occupy a peculiar relationship as compared with the others. Black is on this theory the result of a physiological process excited by an internal stimulus and not the result of mere absence of stimulation. Moreover, whereas we can pass continuously from black to white, or *vice versa*, through innumerable gradations of grey, there is no such uniform passage from red to green or from yellow to blue. We can indeed pass by innumerable gradations from red to yellow, yellow to green, green to blue, and blue to red, respectively, but there are no intermediaries between red and green, and yellow and blue, corresponding to grey between black and white. Further, the fundamental toned colours differ in brightness and darkness, and this may be regarded as an inherent black-white element in the colours. Hering has therefore found it necessary to hypothecate a white valency for the toned colours, thereby introducing a complication which mars the symmetry of his design.

The peculiar position of black and white in the gamut of colour sensations early made itself felt. Woinow[1] distinguished between the white which is a mere sensation of light and is due to stimulation of the rods, the binary red-green and yellow-blue whites, and the quaternary white which is a combination of the two binaries. Preyer[2] also distinguished between the whites due to stimulation of the chromatogenous elements, the cones, and that due to the photogenous, the rods. König[3] distinguished between the simple white of rod stimulation and the trichromatic white of the cones. v. Kries expressly adopts this view and thinks that " it would perhaps be more correct not to say that the rods initiate colourless sensations, but that they initiate a sensation-effect which is variable in only one sense."[4] There is certainly a peculiarity, which may be described as a bluish greyness, about the scotopic colourless sensation which distinguishes it from photopic " white."

Evidence derived from the colour-blind led Young in his sole reference to the subject[5] to ascribe Dalton's defect to absence or paralysis of the fibres which were supposed to initiate the red sensation. König[6] adopted the explanation brought forward by Ad. Fick and Leber[7] that so-called partial colour-blindness (dichromatism) is due to coincidence of two of the elementary-sensation curves. v. Kries[8] adopted v. Helmholtz' reduction theory or congenital absence of one of the fundamental components. Both König and v. Kries accepted Liesegang's view[9] that total colour-blindness (monochromatism) is due to rod- or visual purple-vision. Hess and Hering[10] adduce against this view the complete analogy in the normal and totally colour-blind dark-adapted eyes of the low central and increasing peripheral threshold values.

Later years have brought forth a crop of theories, mostly modifications of those already mentioned. The more important will be briefly mentioned in the following pages.

[1] *Arch. f. Ophth.* XXI. 1, 223, 1875.
[2] *Arch. f. d. ges. Physiol.* XXV. 31, 1881.
[3] *Sitz. d. Akad. d. Wiss.* Berlin, 1894.
[4] *Ztsch. f. Psychol. u. Physiol. d. Sinnesorg.* IX. 87 note, 1896.
[5] *Lectures on Natural Philosophy*, II. 315, 1807.
[6] *Ztsch. f. Psychol. u. Physiol. d. Sinnesorg.* IV. 241, 1892.
[7] *Arch. f. Ophth.* XV. 3, 26, 1869.
[8] *Ztsch. f. Psychol. u. Physiol. d. Sinnesorg.* XIII. 241, 473, 1897.
[9] *Photogr. Arch.* 1891.
[10] *Arch. f. d. ges. Physiol.* LXXI. 105, 1898.

SECTION II

THE DUPLICITY THEORY

The duplicity theory (v. Kries) states that achromatic scotopic vision is carried out through the mediation of the rods alone, the cones being the organ of photopic vision. It is not definitely stated that rod activity is in abeyance in photopic vision, but there is some evidence in favour of this view and in any case the influence of rod vision in the light-adapted eye may be regarded as slight.

It has already been necessary for the sake of clearness to point out the great probability of two separate mechanisms being involved in these two very different types of vision (*v.* p. 57). Broadly speaking vision with the dark-adapted eye, *i.e.*, scotopic vision, is monochromatic or tone-free. Vision with the light-adapted eye, *i.e.*, photopic vision, is polychromatic or toned. In the former the threshold stimulus intensity is low; in the latter relatively high. We have hitherto stated the facts and attempted to regard them impartially. It will now be instructive to review them briefly in the light of the duplicity theory.

So far as anatomical considerations are concerned the distribution of rods and cones in the retina is of prime importance. Rods are absent from the fovea, an area subtending a visual angle of 50′—70′, and also over a surrounding zone, the whole subtending a maximum of 3°. At the same time it should be pointed out that the structural peculiarities of the rods and cones are not precisely differentiated. The macular cones are elongated and more rod-like than those found in peripheral parts of the retina[1]. This merging of structural peculiarities is even more marked in the retinae of lower animals[2], and while on the whole later researches have confirmed the observations of Max Schultze (*v.* p. 196), precise anatomical diversity of the two types of neuro-epithelium has been somewhat discounted. Moreover, if we regard the

[1] Cf. Greeff, in Graefe-Saemisch, 2nd ed. Bd. I. Abt. 2, Kap. V.

[2] Cf. Putter, in Graefe-Saemisch, Bd. II. Abt. 1, Kap. X; Franz, in Oppel's *Lehrbuch d. vergleich. mikr. Anat. d. Wirbeltiere*, VII. Jena, 1913.

rods as the more primitive type of visual neuroepithelium, as we are probably justified in doing, the persistence of recognisable rod attributes in the cones, even if modified, differentiated, and rendered more complex, might well be expected. Apart therefore from the difficulties of isolating the physiological results of excitation of the rods from those of excitation of the cones it may be anticipated that the latter cells will retain some measure of the functions which are in the highest degree characteristic of their prototypes. Hence, if it should ever be conclusively proved that the rod-like foveal cones of the human eye possess some trace of visual purple and are endowed with some slight degree of light-adaptation it would not be surprising; neither, on the other hand, would it militate seriously against the view that the rods and cones have become essentially diverse in function.

Beyond the rod-free central area the cones diminish continuously in number and the rods correspondingly augment in passing towards the periphery in all directions.

The chief characteristic of central vision in the photopic condition is its great acuity as compared with peripheral vision. This acuity is most marked in the form sense, and the rapid diminution in "visual acuity" in passing from the centre towards the periphery is strong evidence in favour of the view that the cones are the essential retinal end-organs concerned in the discrimination of form. A striking feature of the vision of lower animals not endowed with a specially differentiated fovea is the remarkable acuteness in the perception of the movement of objects. This feature is also prominent in human peripheral vision, though it is certainly equally, and perhaps more highly, developed in foveal vision. Thus Ruppert[1] found that while visual acuity and ability to perceive movements both diminish in passing from the centre towards the periphery the former diminishes more rapidly than the latter. On teleological grounds the perception of movement, a function specially associated with the light sense as opposed to the form sense, must be regarded as primitive; and we have here, if such be needed, an example of the persistence of this primitive attribute in the more highly differentiated cones.

When the field of vision of the photopic eye is further investigated it is found that the perception of colours requires an increasingly intense stimulus in passing from the point of fixation towards the periphery. The complicated details of peripheral colour vision have already been

[1] *Ztsch. f. Sinnesphysiol.* XLII. 409, 1908; cf. Basler, *Münch. med. Woch.* p. 1904, 1906.

discussed, and though in photopic vision they afford little incisive evidence in favour of the duplicity theory they cannot be regarded as seriously discounting it. It is certain that the almost, if not complete, colour blindness of the extreme periphery cannot be attributed to mere paucity of cones. The great difference in luminosity values with different lights, in spite of the tone-free perceptions to which they give rise, is against such a view. We must therefore conclude that the scanty cones of the periphery are incapable of arousing colour perceptions, or that there is some block in the conduction of such impulses from this region.

The duplicity theory depends therefore for its support chiefly upon the facts of achromatic scotopic in relation to those of photopic vision, and in this relationship the evidence is abundant and confirmatory.

On this theory the rods are the end-organ of achromatic scotopic, the cones of photopic vision. In other words, the rods possess a very high degree of adaptation, the cones little or none. The photopic apparatus is isolated in the fovea, but the scotopic apparatus is nowhere completely isolated. The threshold values for the cones, however, are considerably higher than for the rods, and hence in complete dark adaptation the rods become almost, if not wholly, isolated physiologically. In dark adaptation, with low intensities of light, vision is carried out through the rods alone (achromatic scotopia). As the intensities are increased the liminal stimulation values for the cones are exceeded and vision is carried out by both rods and cones (chromatic scotopia). At still higher intensities vision is carried out chiefly or wholly by the cones (photopia), but whether the rod effects are added to the cone effects or are abolished is as yet uncertain.

If the rods are the organ of achromatic scotopic vision, the visual purple, which so far as has yet been proved is present in them only, attains a new significance. The early researches of Kühne and Sewall[1] sufficed to show the slight effect of rays of long wave-length upon this substance, and they found that the maximum effect is in the green, not in the part of the spectrum which is brightest to the photopic eye.

Köttgen and Abelsdorff[2] in more recent researches showed that the curve of absorption values of the visual purple of mammals, birds and amphibia with the interference spectrum of the Auer light has its maximum at about 500 $\mu\mu$, of that of fishes at about 540 $\mu\mu$. These results do not agree fully with Kühne's, and further researches on human

[1] *Untersuchungen*, Heidelberg, III. 221, 1880.
[2] *Ztsch. f. Psychol. u. Physiol. d. Sinnesorg.* XII. 161, 1896.

visual purple are desirable. Judging by the position of the maximum it should approximate more nearly to the type found in fishes. It should be borne in mind that visual purple has not been isolated in a pure state, free from hæmoglobin.

Trendelenburg's curve for bleaching values of the frog's visual purple agrees more closely with the achromatic scotopic luminosity curve of the human eye (Fig. 1).

There can be no doubt that the visual purple is of fundamental importance in scotopic vision and that its accumulation is the basis of dark adaptation. It follows that the relation of the achromatic scotopic luminosity values of two lights, *e.g.* a green which is strongly absorbed and an orange which is weakly absorbed by the visual purple, should depend upon the concentration of visual purple in the rods, *i.e.*, it should vary with the degree of dark adaptation. Stegmann[1] has shown that such is the case. If a luminosity match is made between green and orange with intensities at which they appear colourless after 5–15 minutes' dark adaptation, and the lights are again compared after much more prolonged adaptation the orange appears much brighter and must be diminished to about three-quarters of its former intensity to restore the match. It is to be noted that the change is in the opposite direction to that of the Purkinje phenomenon.

Sachs[2] showed that the pupil-reactions vary with the luminosities of the lights, independently of their colour, both in the normal and colour-blind. Abelsdorff[3] confirmed these observations and showed further that maximum pupil-constriction occurs in nocturnal animals from green light, whereas in animals of diurnal habits the maximum is obtained from yellow light.

Similar, but more reliable and much more striking results, have been obtained from the electrical reactions, especially in day- and night-birds by Himstedt and Nagel[4] and Piper[5].

Vision of lights of low intensities with the dark-adapted eye is characterised by (1) the absence of colour sensations, (2) a greatly increased sensitiveness for lights of low intensity, (3) a relatively increased

[1] *Dissertation*, Freiburg, 1901.

[2] *Arch. f. d. ges. Physiol.* LII. 79, 1892; *Arch. f. Ophth.* XXXIX. 3, 108, 1893; *Ztsch. f. Psychol. u. Physiol. d. Sinnesorg.* XXII. 388, 1900.

[3] *Ztsch. f. Psychol. u. Physiol. d. Sinnesorg.* XXII. 81, 451, 1900; *Arch. f. Augenhlk.* XLI. 155, 1900; *Arch. f. Anat. u. Physiol.* 541, 1900.

[4] *Ber. d. naturf. Ges.* Freiburg, II. 1901; *Ann. d. Physik*, IV. 1901; in v. Helmholtz, 3rd ed. II. p. 328.

[5] *Arch. f. Anat. u. Physiol.* 543, 1904.

sensitiveness for rays of short wave-length as compared with those of long wave-length, red showing no appreciable increase. The third characteristic is the cause of the Purkinje phenomenon. The characteristics of rod vision will therefore be (1) total colour blindness, (2) maximum sensitiveness in the situation of the green of the photopic spectrum, and shortening of the red end, (3) a very high degree of adaptation.

The theory explains satisfactorily the apparent deviations from Newton's law of colour-mixtures described by the earlier investigators. Of these, Hering[1] and v. Kries and Brauneck[2] held that colour equations were independent of the intensity of the light. König and his pupils[3] disagreed with this conclusion, and v. Kries found it necessary later to modify his opinion[4]. The photopic values of the matches are essentially cone-values. At lower intensities rod- and cone-values are mixed, and at the lowest only rod-values persist. The results of König and his pupils are partly vitiated by lack of attention to adaptation, but more to wandering fixation and the use of objects whose retinal images surpass the rod-free limits. The striking examples brought forward by Ebbinghaus and Mrs Ladd-Franklin (*v.* p. 60) are easily explained by the duplicity theory, and indeed strongly support it. v. Kries[5] extended these observations and explained the anomalous results of other observers. He showed that it was theoretically possible to obtain a photopic "white" equivalent to a scotopic "white," *i.e.*, a "white" which would lose only in subjective intensity on diminution of the physical intensity. The difference in rod-values between a homogeneous scotopic white and a mixture-white are so slight in normal colour-vision that the results are ambiguous; they are much more conclusive in dichromats. The theory also accounts for the "wandering of the neutral point" in dichromats on altering the physical intensity of the light. In most of the observations referred to above macular pigmentation is a disturbing influence (cf. Hering). In general form it may be stated that matches valid for high intensities become invalid for low intensities and dark-adaptation in the sense that the mixture which possesses the greater rod-value exhibits the greater luminosity in tone-free scotopic vision (v. Kries). The regional peculiarities of scotopic as compared with photopic vision afford very strong evidence in favour of the

[1] *Lotos*, VII. 1886; *Arch. f. d. ges. Physiol.* LIV. 277, 1893.

[2] *Arch. f. Physiol.* 79, 1885.

[3] Brodhun, *Ztsch. f. Psychol. u. Physiol. d. Sinnesorg.* V. 323, 1893; Tonn, *op. cit.* VII. 279, 1894.

[4] v. Kries, *op cit.* IX. 81, 1896, etc

[5] *Ibid.* IX. 81, 1896

duplicity theory. The "night blindness" of the fovea, with its almost if not quite complete absence of dark adaptation, the absence of Purkinje's phenomenon on direct fixation with sufficiently small areas of stimulation, the almost if not quite complete absence of a photochromatic interval at the fovea, and so on have already been sufficiently discussed, but should be referred to again in the light of the theory.

The difference between the peripheral and the achromatic scotopic luminosity curves, the former having the same character as the foveal luminosity curve, shows, as has already been mentioned, that the duplicity theory cannot be held to account for the peripheral total colour blindness of the photopic eye.

Temporal effects, such as those of recurrent vision, are so complicated that the support they give to the theory is equivocal. MacDougall, as has been seen, brought forward evidence to show that the "ghost" is not necessarily, as was thought, a purely scotopic image, though it is so in its typical form. The change in the fusion frequency in passing from lights of low to lights of high intensity, as shown particularly in T. C. Porter's experiments (*v.* p. 95), and confirmed in those of Ives (*v.* p. 96), Dow, Schaternikoff[1] and v. Kries[2], demonstrate the change over from the scotopic to the photopic mechanism. Particularly noteworthy is the sudden change in value of the constant in Porter's logarithmic equation, which is exactly parallel to the change in the constant for König's logarithmic equation for visual acuity[3] and is attributed to the same cause. The agreement in the intensity, about 0·25 metre-candle, at which the sudden change in the curve takes place, is striking. There is also some evidence to show that the latent period of excitation of the scotopic apparatus is appreciably longer than that of the photopic apparatus.

The experiments of Piper, Loeser, and Henius and Fujita (*v.* p. 123) show that in the areal effects of the periphery as compared with the fovea at low intensities summation of stimuli plays a much greater rôle in the scotopic than in the photopic apparatus.

Certain cases of abnormal vision afford valuable evidence in support of the duplicity theory. Of these, total colour blindness or monochromatic vision may be explained as due to functional abeyance of the cones, and night blindness to functional abeyance of the rods.

[1] *Ztsch. f. Psychol. u. Physiol. d. Sinnesorg.* XXIX. 242, 1902.

[2] *Ibid.* XXXII. 113, 1903.

[3] König, p. 378; see Parsons, *Roy. Lond. Ophth. Hosp. Rep.* XIX. 2, 283, 1914; Cf. Bloom and Garten, *Arch. f. d. ges. Physiol.* LXXII. 372, 1898.

Total colour blindness, as we have seen, is characterised by luminosity values which correspond with those of the normal achromatic scotopic eye. Comparison of the curves (Figs. 54, 55) shows their almost complete identity. Whereas, however, the normal achromatic scotopic curve is valid only for low intensities of objective lights the achromatopic curve is valid for all intensities, though with the higher intensities photophobia occurs. The process of dark adaptation pursues the normal course in the totally colour-blind. Exposure to bright light causes prolonged diminution of vision, and recovery follows the course which would be expected if it were dependent upon restoration of the visual purple.

All totally colour-blind people have marked diminution of central visual acuity, and in many cases there is undoubtedly a central scotoma. The curve of visual acuity with gradually increasing light-intensities shows no sudden bend, as in normal-sighted people, but continues in the same direction as for lower intensities until photophobia sets in (König). The reduction in central vision tends to absence of binocular fixation and divergence of the optic axes. We may conclude that the foveal neuroepithelium, if it retains its function at all, approximates in character to that of the normal rods.

Uhthoff and v. Kries[1] have shown that the flicker phenomenon in the totally colour-blind follows the same laws as in normal achromatic scotopia.

Nagel[2] has tested a monochromat with matches between orange-yellow (600 $\mu\mu$) and greenish-blue (490 $\mu\mu$) (*vide supra*). A monochromat can make such a luminosity match at ordinary intensities of light, whereas a trichromat must be dark-adapted and the intensities must be very low. With the photopic eye the intensity (*i.e.*, slit-width of the spectrophotometer in millimetres) was 0·44. After one hour's dark adaptation it was 0·8. Compared with the achromatic scotopic trichromatic, the achromatopic photopic retina contains less visual purple: hence the trichromatic achromatic scotopic value for greenish-blue light is lowered by absorption relatively to the achromatopic.

Night-blindness is found in several diseases of the eye, most commonly in retinitis pigmentosa and allied conditions, least adulterated by other pathological symptoms and signs in congenital night blindness. The last-named is congenital and hereditary[3].

[1] v. Kries, *Ztsch. f. Psychol. u. Physiol. d Sinnesorg.* XXXII. 113, 1903.

[2] v. Helmholtz, 3rd. ed. II. p. 328.

[3] Nettleship, *Trans. Ophth. Soc.* XXVII. 1907; Parsons, *Pathology of the Eye*, IV. 1400, 1908.

Parinaud[1] regarded night blindness as strongly supporting the views which he propounded and which have since become incorporated in the duplicity theory. Night blindness may be looked upon as the obverse of total colour blindness. In the latter rod-vision is isolated, in the former rod-vision is seriously disturbed or in abeyance.

In night blindness dark adaptation may be almost abolished or much slower than normal; in high degrees it is both slowed, and diminished quantitatively, *i.e.*, the higher degrees of sensitiveness of the retina are never reached and the highest possible are reached only after prolonged exclusion of light from the eye[2]. In low degrees central vision is normal in the light-adapted condition, and may be so in high degrees of the disease, *e.g.* in retinitis pigmentosa. Colour vision is normal with the exception of occasional diminution of sensibility for blue lights. In retinitis pigmentosa the field of vision is diminished, often almost down to the fixation point, and dark adaptation may be completely absent.

Purkinje's phenomenon is much less marked in the night-blind. If a red and a green are chosen, which are equal in luminosity for the normal and night-blind in light adaptation, and the room is then darkened the green becomes much brighter than the red in the course of a few minutes for the normal, but only after a long time, if at all, for the night-blind. Quantitative experiments show that for lights of short wave-length the increase in luminosity after half-an-hour's dark adaptation is 10 to 100 times as great for the normal as for the night-blind. With stimulation areas exceeding the foveal limits the sensibility for mixed white lights increases much more rapidly for the normal than for the night-blind on dark adaptation, but if both are tested with red lights there is very little difference. This is further proof of the diminution in the appreciation of Purkinje's phenomenon by the night-blind.

The temporal effects in the night-blind have not been investigated as thoroughly as could be wished, and the results are not concordant.

The condition is often, in fact generally, partial. It is not surprising therefore that cases occur in which Purkinje's phenomenon occurs and which show some degree of dark adaptation, colourless interval for red pigments and so on. Hess[3] has laid great stress upon

[1] *Arch. gén. de méd.* 1881; *C. r. acad. des sci.* 1881; *La Vision*, Paris, 1898.

[2] Heinrichsdorff, *Arch. f. Ophth.* LX. 405, 1905; Messmer, *Ztsch. f. Sinnesphysiol.* XLII. 83, 1907; Lohmann, *Arch. f. Ophth.* LXV. 3, 1907; Stargardt, *op. cit.* LXXIII. 1, 77, 1909; Behr, *op. cit.* LXXV. 201, 1910; Wölfflin, *op. cit.* LXXVI. 464, 1910.

[3] *Arch. f. Augenhlk.* LXII. 50, 1908; LXIX. 205, 1911.

these cases and regards them as seriously opposed to the duplicity theory. Taken alone the phenomena associated with night blindness are by no means unadulterated evidence in favour of the theory, but viewed in conjunction with the other facts already discussed they are on the whole confirmatory and highly suggestive. Moreover it is by no means certain that in diseases accompanied by night blindness the cones remain unaffected. Except in congenital night blindness it is almost certain that they do not.

The pathology of retinitis pigmentosa[1] shows that the condition is primarily due to vascular degeneration in the choroid, whereby the chorio-capillaris is destroyed. The pigment epithelium and the outer layers of the retina are dependent for their nutrition upon the integrity of the chorio-capillaris. From its proximity the pigment epithelium must suffer first. The production of visual purple in the rods is undoubtedly bound up in the integrity of the pigmented epithelial cells, so that primary disorder of the functions of the rods might be confidently anticipated on pathological-anatomical grounds. It is the rule in most nutritional disorders for the most highly differentiated and complex structures to suffer first. That there is good evidence of a survival of the cone-functions after destruction of rod-functions is evidence of an intermediary process such as that described.

It must be admitted that the researches of Hess on the comparative physiology of vision show that little support to the duplicity theory can be derived from lower animals. He found (*v.* p. 132) that all classes of vertebrates possess good powers of dark adaptation, including even tortoises, which possess neither rods nor visual purple.

The arguments against the duplicity theory have been collected by Sivén[2]. He lays stress upon the peculiarity of the achromatic scotopic "white" or grey, which he calls blue or violet. He thinks that the rods are chiefly concerned in the perception of lights of short wavelength. He finds the strongest support of his view in the colour-fields, which are admittedly difficult to reconcile with the duplicity theory. He admits the absence of Purkinje's phenomenon at the fovea, and says that when colour is no longer perceived centrally it can still be elicited from the periphery, presumably however only by lights of short wavelength. His experiments in conjunction with Wendt on the effects of santonin poisoning and the yellow vision of jaundice afford him additional

[1] Parsons, *Pathology of the Eye*, II. 602, 1905.

[2] Sivén and Wendt, *Skand. Arch. f. Physiol.* XIV. 196, 1903; Sivén, *op. cit.* XVII. 306, 1905; XIX. 1907; *Ztsch. f. Sinnesphysiol.* XLII. 224, 1907; *Arch. of Ophth.* XLII. 2, 1913.

arguments, and he regards Hess's observations on birds[1] as also confirmatory.

Bauer[2] has brought forward arguments to show that the rôle of the visual purple is not limited to the condition of dark adaptation. Since Kühne's researches it has been known that it is difficult to bleach the visual purple completely so long as the retina is in contact with the pigment epithelium. Bauer found that though frog's visual purple was rapidly bleached when exposed to bright sunlight, the retina again became red after several hours in spite of continuous exposure. He concluded that increased destruction of the substance is associated under physiological conditions of exposure to bright light by correspondingly increased production, and that therefore the visual purple plays an important part in photopic as well as in scotopic vision.

The clear explanation which the duplicity theory affords of the chief differences between human photopic and achromatic scotopic vision and of the peculiarities of the intermediate stage, scotopia with only moderate dark adaptation (chromatic scotopia), tempts one to carry the theoretical considerations farther than is perhaps warranted. Dark adaptation appears to be directly associated with the visual purple. On teleological grounds extreme sensitiveness to light and shade are most needed in the dusk, and while the loss of visual acuity for form is a serious disadvantage the gain in concentration is a counterbalancing merit. The rods are more intimately connected with each other by nervous paths than the cones (Ramón y Cajal), so that relatively widespread impulses become summated in the resultant psychological impressions. An even less complete insulation of the rods may be brought about by dark adaptation, possibly through the retraction of pigment in the retinal pigment cells. On the other hand the photopic position of the pigment tends to protect the more sensitive rods with their contained visual purple and to isolate the less sensitive cones. The rôle of the pigment cells in dark adaptation has already been the subject of conjecture[3], but it must be remembered that the wandering of the pigment has not been conclusively proved to occur in warm-blooded animals.

[1] *Arch. f. Augenhlk.* LVII. 298, 317, 1907; LIX. 143, 1908.

[2] *Arch. f. d. ges. Physiol.* CXLI. 479, 1911.

[3] Exner, *Sitz. d. Wiener Akad.* XCVIII. 3, 1889; Nagel, in v. Helmholtz, 3rd ed. II. 331.

SECTION III

THE THREE-COMPONENTS THEORY (YOUNG-HELMHOLTZ)

CHAPTER I

STATEMENT OF THE THEORY

The Young-Helmholtz theory of colour sensations is based upon the facts of the mixture of pure-colour stimuli (see Part I, Sec. II, Chap. III). We found that within a certain range, which includes all ordinary conditions of colour-vision, and with certain well-defined exceptions (*v.* p. 36), every conceivable light or light-mixture gives rise to a sensation which can be accurately matched by the sensation produced by a suitable mixture of only three lights. If we choose three actual wave-lengths, R, G, and V, on the colour-diagram and join them by straight lines, we find that part of the curve is outside the triangle thus obtained. This means that there are certain spectral colours which cannot be obtained in their full spectral saturation by the mixture of R, G, and V. If we choose a point on the curve outside the triangle, *e.g.*, GBl, we can by experiment obtain an equation of the following form :

$$aR + \beta GBl = \gamma G + \epsilon V.$$

We thus find an expression for GBl

$$\beta GBl = \gamma G + \epsilon V - aR$$

which represents the unmixable colour in terms of R, G, and V.

In order to avoid negative quantities we must *assume* the existence of colour-sensations which lie outside the colour-diagram. The fact that, by previously stimulating the eye with the complementary colour, we can obtain a colour-sensation which in saturation far exceeds that obtained by viewing the spectral colour without such previous excitation (*v.* p. 109), affords some evidence that this assumption is not unwarranted.

The assumption is minimised by describing a triangle around the diagram which will only just succeed in including every part of the diagram. Such a triangle is seen in Figs. 8 and 9 (pp. 39, 40). We can then obtain a universal equation for any spectral colour, F, viz.

$$F = x\mathrm{R} + y\mathrm{G} + z\mathrm{V}$$

in terms of the three theoretical sensations, R, G, and V, in which x, y, z are all real positive quantities.

The objective quantities of light in this equation come into consideration here only as sensation-stimuli, and as such have a physically measurable value. If we make a further assumption, viz., that the physiological processes which accompany sensations have a definite quantitative relationship to the physical stimuli, we may say that x, y, and z are respectively the red, green, and violet values of the light F in terms of the fundamental colours R, G, and V [1].

It also follows that in the sensory process there must be three corresponding kinds of activity, which coexist side by side without interfering with each other, and upon which every variety of colour sensation depends.

Let us suppose that there is some method whereby we can determine three measurable quantities, ϕ, χ, ψ representing three physiological processes, which taken together completely define the character of the visual sensation. We should then be able in every case to find by observation the relationship between ϕ, χ, ψ and the values x, y, z of the incident light. We should then have ϕ, χ, ψ represented as three functions of x, y, z and conversely x, y, z as three functions of ϕ, χ, ψ. That is,

$$\phi = f_1(x, y, z), \quad \chi = f_2(x, y, z), \quad \psi = f_3(x, y, z) \text{ and}$$
$$x = f_1'(\phi, \chi, \psi), \quad y = f_2'(\phi, \chi, \psi), \quad z = f_3'(\phi, \chi, \psi).$$

Since no two different groups of values for x, y, z give the same sensation, *i.e.*, the same values of ϕ, χ, ψ, therefore x, y, z can be expressed solely by ϕ, χ, ψ. These values of the x, y, z functions of ϕ, χ, ψ (*i.e.*, f_1', f_2', f_3') are therefore quantities which depend only upon the character of the sensation, and moreover possess a certain individuality, since each can be aroused, exist and again disappear in the nervous apparatus independently of the other two and unaffected by them. This independent existence is, however, exactly what we are in search of when we speak of elements, ingredients, or components of the sensation. If we therefore

[1] See v. Helmholtz, 2nd ed. p. 341.

denote the function of ϕ, χ, ψ which represents x by R, and the corresponding other two functions by G and V, then these quantities, R, G, V, are to be denoted as components of the colour sensation, and similarly any linear function of them (aR + bG + cV) may also be thus denoted.

From the mathematical elaboration of these assumptions v. Helmholtz stated the Young-theory in the following form :

"(1) In some part of the conducting nerve substance, under the influence of coloured light, three different, independent, and mutually unopposed elementary activities arise ; we will them call the elementary stimulations. Their amount is directly proportional to the corresponding colour-values, x, y, z of the objective light ; they correspond to the R, G, V of the above description.

"(2) All activities passing further towards the brain, as well as the sensations actually entering into consciousness under the given conditions of the reacting brain, are only actions of the three elementary stimulations, R, G, V, and in amount are functions, ϕ, χ, ψ, of those elementary stimulations.

"(3) Either the elementary stimulations themselves or three mutually unopposed actions dependent upon them are conducted independently to the central organ."

Putting these conclusions in simpler language and in their most general form, R, G, V, are any three points so situated that, when joined, the triangle thus constructed completely encloses the colour-diagram of the given spectrum. In this manner positive values are ensured. From observations on colour-mixtures with the given spectrum we can construct valency curves which represent the stimulation values of any spectral light for each of the three components, R, G, V, of the resultant sensation. Thus

$$F = xR + yG + zV$$

means that the light F is matched by a mixture of x parts of R light, y parts of G light, and z parts of V light, R, G, V being the physical stimuli in the mixture. If these physical stimuli act respectively upon the physiological counterparts or elements of sensation, R, G, V, then xR, yG, zV clearly represent the strengths with which the light F acts upon the R, G, V elements, *i.e.*, they are its R, G, V valencies or values.

The valency curves are therefore nothing more than the gauging curves of the spectrum to which reference has already been made (*v.* p. 39). But it has been shown that every gauging value belonging to one such group of curves must always be a linear function of the three gauging values belonging to any other group of curves. In any given spectrum, therefore, the R, G, V values must be some linear function of the three empirically observed gauging values (*R*, *G*, *V*). The three gauging curves therefore represent the *relative* values of the three sensations for each light throughout the given spectrum.

The simplest concrete conception of the bases of the three sensation elements or ingredients is that there are three components which are counterparts of the physical stimuli. We shall at present use the term component in the broadest sense: it may represent a chemical, an electrical or some other process acting upon different substances or nerve-fibres and giving rise to nervous activity, but the general statement of the theory necessitates no such concrete conception.

In this, its most generalised form, the Young-Helmholtz theory explains satisfactorily the sensations resulting from colour-mixtures in the normal visual system, since it is indeed founded upon them.

It also explains satisfactorily the gross divergences from the normal system. Thus dichromatic vision is due to absence of one of the theoretical components; in the protanopes this is the R component, in the deuteranopes the G component, and in the tritanopes the V component. Indeed, the determination of the absent component follows mathematically from the correlation of the facts of colour-mixtures in dichromats. In their colour-diagram all the colours which appear to them to match must lie upon a straight line, since the line joining any two points representing homogeneous colours contains all the points representing the colours which can be mixed from those homogeneous colours. Similarly the mixtures of any of these colours with any other colours lies on a series of straight lines. v. Helmholtz has shown that all these lines either meet in a point or are parallel[1]. The point of intersection corresponds to a colour which has no stimulus value for the dichromatic eye. It is generally called the Null-point (*Fehlpunkt*) of the system.

Conversely, the normal colour diagram can be constructed from the combined protanopic and deuteranopic observations (Fig. 57). It cannot be expected to coincide precisely with that of a single individual on account of differences in macular pigmentation, variations in the spectra used, and so on, but it shows a remarkable similarity[2].

Anomalous trichromatic vision may be regarded in various ways on this theory. The simplest explanation is that it is a reduction system

[1] v. Helmholtz, 3rd ed. p. 123; Greenwood, *Physiology of the Special Senses*, p. 153.

[2] Greenwood, *loc. cit.* p. 150; v. Kries, in Nagel's *Handb. d. Physiol. d. Menschen*, III. p. 161.

in which the stimulus values for any light of *one* of the components is uniformly less than normal. Partial protanopia is then a diminution of sensitiveness of the R component, partial deuteranopia of the G component. Other modifications are theoretically possible and are included in the general form that if in the normal system $\phi = f_1(x, y, z)$ and so on, then in the anomalous trichromatic system $\phi' = f_1'(x, y, z)$ and so on. This generalisation is, however, too vague to be of much practical value, and there are other possibilities arising directly out of

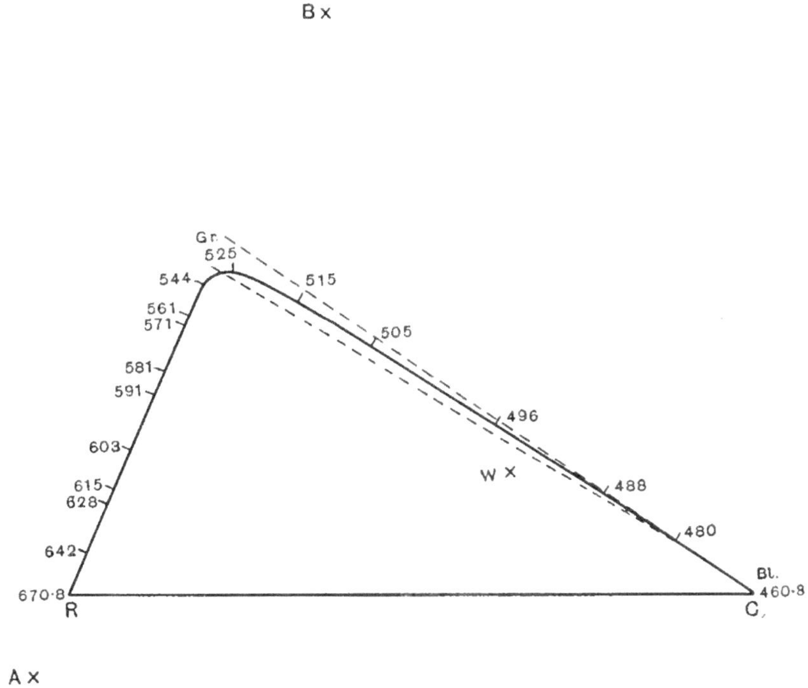

Fig. 57. Normal trichromatic colour diagram constructed from combined protanopic and deuteranopic observations. *A*, null-point of protanopes; *B*, null-point of deuteranopes. (v. Kries.)

the Young-Helmholtz theory, such as a shift of one of the curves (*vide infra*), which account for at least one group of the anomalous trichromats.

Monochromatic vision may be explained on the Young-Helmholtz theory by the identity of all three components. In this case

$$\phi = f_1(x, y, z) = \chi = f_2(x, y, z) = \psi = f_3(x, y, z).$$

The facts do not support this view, and are much more satisfactorily explained by the duplicity theory. At the same time there are some observers, *e.g.*, Schenck, who regard monochromatic vision as divided into various types, some of which are due to modifications in the cones and must therefore be correlated in some such manner as that suggested with the three-components theory.

Difficulty is experienced when the attempt is made to explain the phenomena of peripheral vision and of induction by the theory. It is at once clear that neither can be explained as evidence of any reduction system. Fick[1] suggested that the reaction-values of the components were not the same in all parts of the retina. The suggestion is inadequate; on the one hand because it implies a simple reduction system and this fails to account for the phenomena, or on the other hand because it is too general to be of practical value. Schenck's attempt to correlate the facts with a modification of the trichromatic theory will be described later. The relationship of normal and deuteranopic peripheral colour vision to central colour vision approximates more closely to a reduction system than the corresponding relationship in the protanopic system. In all, however, the modifications produced by areal effects negative so simple an explanation and afford some evidence in favour of v. Kries' theory of zones.

The greatest difficulty, however, is experienced in explaining the facts of induction. In general terms it is not difficult to conceive a diminution in response of the components in one direction, associated with an increase in another, after previous stimulation. We might thus account for the increased response to the complementary after stimulation with a given light. Indeed, such a view falls in well with other physiological findings, so admirably elaborated in Sherrington's work. If all spectral lights act upon all three components, then the increased response to the complementary after previous stimulation with a colour can be explained, and this was the view adopted by v. Helmholtz. It lands us, however, on the horns of a dilemma, for the facts of dichromatic vision—and the same is true of trichromatic (*vide infra*, Chap. II)—show that lights of greater wave-length than about 550 $\mu\mu$ do not act at all upon the V component, since no standard blue has to be mixed with the standard red in order to match colours in this part of the spectrum. Yet the saturation of yellow (589 $\mu\mu$) is undoubtedly increased by previous stimulation with the complementary blue. v. Kries has shown that this effect is not to be explained by any alteration of the intrinsic light of the eye, but is caused by a quantitative change in the response to the secondary light. If yellow light acts only on the red and green

[1] *Arch. f. d. ges. Physiol.* XLVII. 274, 1890.

components we cannot explain on the theory the increase in saturation which follows previous activity in the blue components. Hess refuses to admit that the facts can be brought into line with the theory. We must therefore accept the theory as explaining satisfactorily *either* the phenomena of after-images *or* those of dichromatic vision, but not both. The large mass of accurate evidence which has now accumulated, chiefly from the observations of Abney and v. Kries and their fellow-workers, showing that all spectral lights do not act upon all the components makes it impossible to accept the explanation as it stands for successive induction. Moreover, successive induction is a complex condition allied to simultaneous induction, and it must be admitted that the facts of simultaneous contrast cannot be explained directly by the trichromatic theory alone.

With regard to spatial induction v. Helmholtz made no serious attempt to correlate the facts with the theory. In his opinion the phenomena of simultaneous contrast are purely psychical and are explained as "illusions of judgment." The arguments which can be advanced in favour of this view do not concern the three-components theory, and it is only by modifications of the theory, which will be dealt with at a later stage, that any more purely physiological explanation, on the three-components' basis, of spatial induction can be advanced.

Finally, it may well be asked whether there is any direct positive evidence of the existence of independent visual components answering to the theoretical components. It is in this respect that the electrical researches of Gotch, Himstedt and Nagel, and others, and the fatigue experiments of Burch are so valuable. They offer no crucial proof, but they are suggestively concordant with the view that such components exist. It has already been mentioned that Burch is inclined to predicate four. Theoretically this is of no importance, though it complicates matters and is unnecessary for the explanation of the facts of colour-mixtures, etc. It does not in any way detract from the support which Burch's experiments afford of an additive theory dependent upon processes occurring in certain components.

As is usually the case, the three-components' theory becomes less plausible the more concrete the form it takes. We have seen that Young suggested three different types of nerve-fibre, others have suggested three substances which undergo chemical change, others again have suggested electrical changes. Each such hypothetical fibre or substance, etc., leads inevitably to further hypothetical conceptions of the details of the processes. These become the subject of controversy and the whole theory is thrown into disrepute, the cardinal fact being overlooked that they are in no integral sense germane to the theory.

It may, however, be interesting to record some of the suggestions which have been made.

As regards the three fundamental component sensations König's experiments led him to regard them as a red just outside the spectrum and rather more purple than the spectral colour, and a blue at 470 $\mu\mu$ slightly more saturated than the spectral blue. v. Helmholtz, on the basis of König and Brodhun's observations on the sensitiveness for discrimination of hues in the spectrum (*v.* p. 30), chose a carmine-red, bluer than spectral red, a yellowish-green between 540 $\mu\mu$ and 560 $\mu\mu$, and an ultramarine blue, all much more saturated than the spectral colours.

As regards the retinal bases for the theory, König as already mentioned regarded the visual purple as the basis of colourless scotopic vision. With greater stimulus intensities the visual purple is transformed into visual yellow, which forms the basis of the fundamental blue sensation. He placed the substrata of the red and green sensations in the pigment epithelium. If this were true, foveal vision should be monochromatic in protanopes and deuteranopes. He regarded the cones as a purely dioptric mechanism.

CHAPTER II

RESEARCHES BASED UPON THE THEORY

I. Normal Colour Vision

The first researches based on Young's theory were made by v. Helmholtz (1852–3)[1]. From them he elaborated the three-components or Young-Helmholtz theory. He was followed by Clerk-Maxwell (1855–6)[2].

Clerk-Maxwell placed three slits in the spectrum of daylight at the following places: (1) in the red (R) between the Fraunhofer lines C and D, twice as far from the latter as from the former; (2) in the green (G) near E; (3) in the blue (B) between F and G, twice as far from the latter as from the former. Lights from these slits were mixed in the proportions to match a comparison white (W) derived

[1] References in v. Helmholtz, 3rd ed., II. p. 137.

[2] *Scientific Papers*, Cambridge, 1890.

from the same source of light. From the slit-widths he thus obtained a standard equation :

$$18{\cdot}6\,R + 31{\cdot}4\,G + 30{\cdot}5\,B = W.$$

He then obtained 14 other equations for W, in each case mixing three lights from different parts of the spectrum in suitable proportions. By eliminating W from each of these equations he obtained the sensation-values of 14 positions in the spectrum in terms of the sensation-values of the three standard colours, R, G, B. Fig. 58 shows the curves plotted from these values. It will be noticed that the R and B curves pass below the base line. His standard colours were therefore not chosen so as to eliminate negative values.

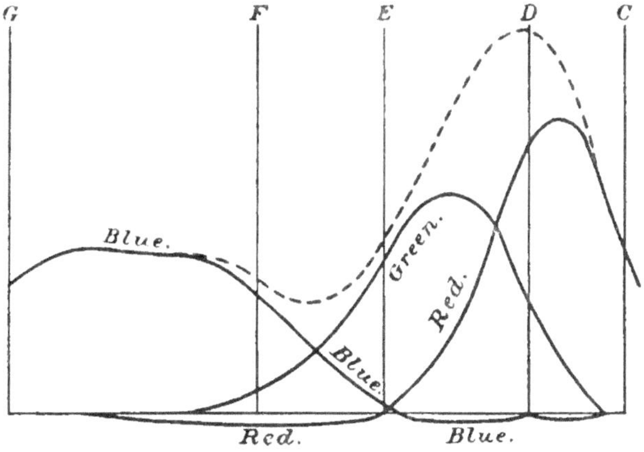

Fig. 58. Clerk-Maxwell's sensation curves. The dotted line is the algebraical sum of the ordinates at each point; it is not a true luminosity curve. Abscissae, wave-lengths of the prismatic spectrum of sunlight; ordinates, arbitrary scale. (Clerk-Maxwell.)

Papers followed by J. J. Müller[1], Preyer[2] and Donders[3], but no other researches on the three "sensation curves" were made until König embarked upon his observations in 1883, continuing them until his death in 1901. Almost simultaneously, Abney commenced the work which he has recorded in a series of papers, culminating in his *Researches in Colour Vision* (London, 1913), and which is happily still in progress. Certain points on the sensation curves have also been worked out independently by F. Exner[4].

[1] *Arch. f. Ophth.* xv. 2, 208, 1869. [2] *Arch. f. d. ges. Physiol.* i. 299, 1869.

[3] *Arch. f. Ophth.* xxiii. 4, 282, 1877; xxvii. 1, 155, 1881; xxx. 1, 15, 1884; *Onderzoek. i. Lab. Utrecht.* 1882.

[4] *Sitz. d. Wiener Akad.* cxi. i; *a*, 1902.

König's experiments on normal colour vision were carried out in conjunction with Dieterici[1] and an abstract was communicated to the British Association in Birmingham in 1886. The curves were calculated from a vast number of matches made with Helmholtz' spectrophotometer. An objection to this instrument is that the variations in intensity are made by a polarisation method and account is not always taken of the appreciable polarisation of the light by the prism of the spectroscope itself. The observations and calculations were of the same kind as those made for dichromatic systems (*v.* p. 163), but were necessarily of a more complicated nature. Fig. 59 shows the curves

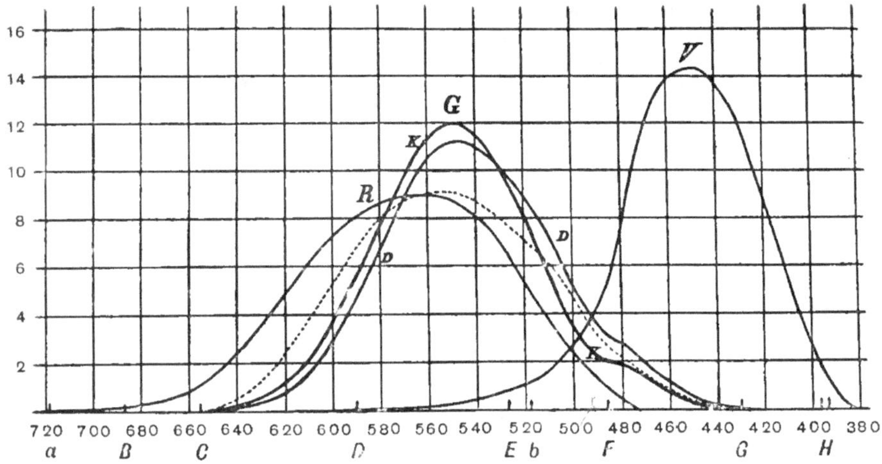

Fig. 59. *R*, *G*, and *V*, sensation curves. *K*, König's *G*-curve; *D*, Dieterici's *G*-curve; ..... *G*-curve of an anomalous trichromat. Abscissae, wave-lengths of the interference spectrum of sunlight; ordinates, arbitrary scale. (König and Dieterici.)

referred to the interference spectrum of sunlight. König's and Dieterici's *R* and *V* curves coincide; the *G* curves are slightly different. The distortion of the *G* and *V* curves between 535 $\mu\mu$ and 475 $\mu\mu$ is due to absorption by the macular pigment.

By far the most exhaustive experiments have been made by Abney, and they will be discussed in greater detail. He has adopted another method of determining the three sensation curves, dependent upon the luminosities of the colours. His results confirm and correct in detail the curves obtained by König. The principle of the experiments is as follows[2].

[1] König and Dieterici, *Sitz. d. Akad. d. Wiss.* Berlin, 1886; *Ztsch. f. Psychol. u. Physiol. d. Sinnesorg.* IV. 241, 1892; in König, pp. 60, 214.

[2] Watson, *Proc. Roy. Soc. Lond.* A, LXXXVIII. 404, 1913.

We have already described the methods of obtaining the luminosity curve of the spectrum. In it the abscissae are wave-lengths of the spectrum, the ordinates luminosities in arbitrary units, the maximum brightness being 100.

Suppose that when making a set of observations we start with the movable slit at the extreme end of the spectrum and determine the intensity w_1 of the white which appears of the same brightness as the colour and then move the slit towards the blue through a distance equal to its width and again determine the intensity w_2 of the white, and so on throughout the spectrum. We should in this way determine piece by piece the brightness of the whole spectrum, and the sum $w_1 + w_2 + w_3 +$, etc., could be taken to represent the total brightness of the whole

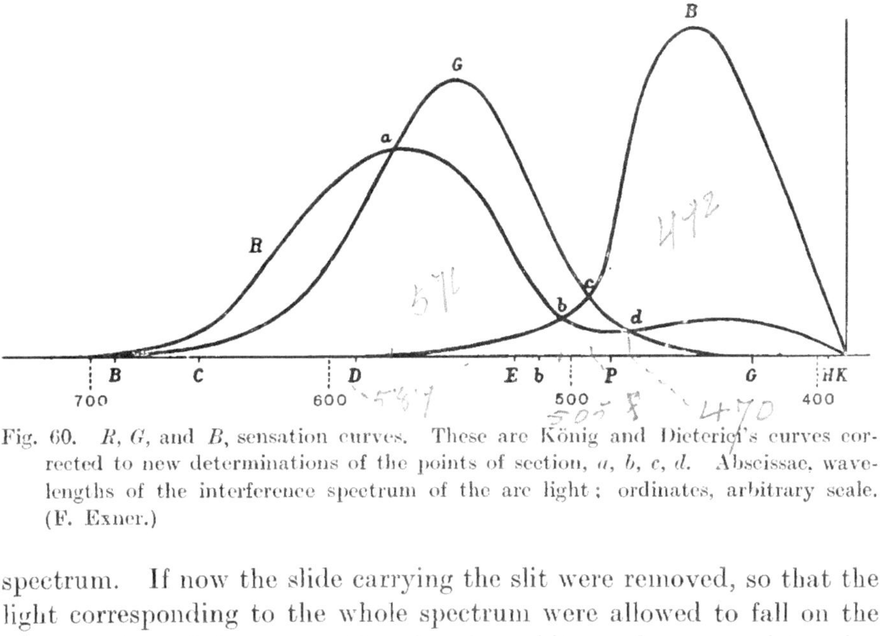

Fig. 60. *R*, *G*, and *B*, sensation curves. These are König and Dieterici's curves corrected to new determinations of the points of section, *a*, *b*, *c*, *d*. Abscissae, wave-lengths of the interference spectrum of the arc light; ordinates, arbitrary scale. (F. Exner.)

spectrum. If now the slide carrying the slit were removed, so that the light corresponding to the whole spectrum were allowed to fall on the same portion of the screen, thus forming white, and we now determine the intensity W of the comparison white which is equal in brightness to this recombined spectrum, then it has been shown by Abney, Tufts, Ives and others that

$$W = w_1 + w_2 + w_3 + \text{, etc.}$$

That is, the luminosity of the recombined spectrum is equal to the sum of the luminosities of its parts.

Now the sum $w_1 + w_2 + w_3 +$, etc., is proportional to the area enclosed by the luminosity curve. Hence the area of the luminosity curve represents the total brightness of the light which is formed into the spectrum and is, therefore, a constant whatever the condition of the vision of the person who makes the observation. This is at once apparent if we remember that if the brightness of the whole recombined spectrum is compared with the comparison white, since these whites are derived from the same source and must, therefore, have exactly the same composition, a setting which appears correct to one person must also appear correct to any other, whatever the differences which may exist between their vision.

On the Young-Helmholtz theory the sensation produced by light of any colour is the sum of the sensations due to stimulation of the three component mechanisms. König and others obtained their curves for the three components by matching light of one wave-length with a mixture of lights of two other wave-lengths. Abney, using a similar method, adopted the principle that the sum of the ordinates of the luminosity-values of each component for any given wave-length is equal to the ordinate of the luminosity curve of the spectrum for that wave-length. He then proceeded thus[1]:

The red sensation can be perceived in purity at one end of the spectrum. From the darkest red to a point near the *C* line, a little above the red lithium line, the colour is the same, though, of course the brightness varies, but the brighter red colour can be reduced so as to form an exact match with the dark red, and no mixture of any colours will give a red of the description we find at the end of the spectrum.

At the violet end of the spectrum we also find that the colour is the same throughout, from the extreme visible limit to a point not far removed from *G*, but it is not for this reason to be accepted that the colour is due to only one sensation. It might be due to two or three sensations if they were stimulated in the same proportions along that region, and if the identical colour could be produced by the combination of other colours. Experiment shows that a combination of two colours will under certain conditions make violet, and that instead of a simple sensation of violet we have in this region a blue sensation combined with a large proportion of red sensation. If we know the percentage composition of the violet mixture we may provisionally use this part of the spectrum as if it excited but one sensation, and subsequently convert the results obtained with it into the true sensations. Thus in calculating the percentage of red in any colour, that existing in

[1] Abney, *Phil. Trans. Roy. Soc. Lond.* CXCIII. 259, 1899; CCV. 333, 1905.

the provisional violet sensation would have to be added to it, and the same amount be abstracted from the violet to arrive at the true blue sensation. The green sensation would remain unaltered.

Having at one end of the spectrum a pure red sensation, and at the other mixed sensations, due to the stimulation of the red and a blue sensation, it remains to isolate the green sensation. Owing to the overlapping of the curves in the green of the spectrum, due to the fact that this region stimulates all three of the sensations, the effect of the pure green sensation is never experienced by a normal eye. In any colour where the stimulation of all three sensations occurs there must be always an admixture of white light, and we have to search for that point in the spectrum where white alone is added to the green sensation.

The following diagram, Fig. 61, will show some variations in composition of a colour that may be met with. The provisional use of a

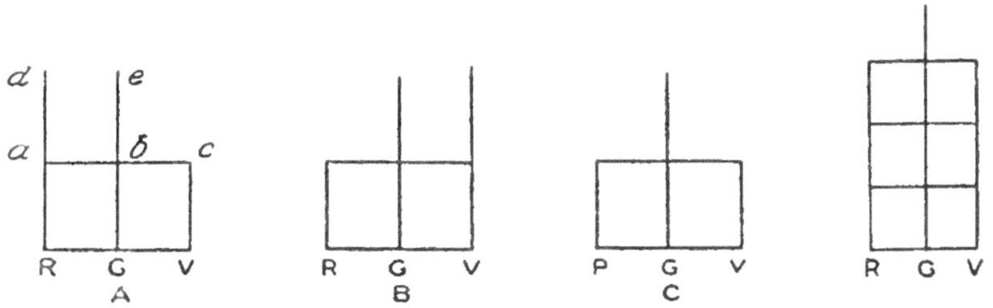

Fig. 61. Diagrams illustrating Abney's method of determining the normal sensation curves.

violet sensation will not alter the argument, since, as before said, we may replace it by blue and red sensations. The different figures are purely diagrammatic. They are constructed on the supposition that equal heights of line above the base line show the stimulation necessary to give the effect of white light. The scale applicable to each of the three lines is necessarily quite different in the scale of luminosity; that of the violet in particular is very greatly exaggerated.

A, *B*, and *C* represent colours each containing a sensation of white. Let the stimulation of the sensations be represented by vertical lines. In *A* we have the red and green sensations of equal heights, but *V* is less. Drawing a horizontal line through *c*, *aR*, *bG*, and *cV*, represent equal stimulations, which make white, leaving *da* and *eb* equal. We thus have a colour which is made up of a mixture of *R* and *G* sensations (*RS*, and *GS*), together with white. Now equal stimulations of *RS* and

GS, we shall see later, give the sensation of yellow. If we place a slit in the violet and move another slit along the less refrangible part of the spectrum, we shall find a place where this colour and violet together make a white, the slits being opened or closed to make the match. This position, then, is that in which the red and green sensations are equally stimulated, and answers to *A*. In *B* we have a green and violet with equal ordinates and a deficiency of red. If we place a slit in the red and move another about in the green, we shall find a colour which with the red makes white. This position, then, will have an equal stimulation of green and violet. This gives another fixed point. The next point to determine is shown diagrammatically by *C*, which illustrates the green we have to look for, mixed only with white. This is more difficult to find, as it would require a purple to be added to make a match with the white, and this does not exist in the spectrum. Suppose we mix *A* with *B*, we get a diagram of the kind shown in the fourth diagram. There are equal reds and violets stimulated, but a larger stimulation of green sensation. This gives a colour paler than the spectrum colour, but still a green which can be matched. There are also other plans, dependent on trial and error, for fixing this point.

When the observations for obtaining the fixed points have been made it will be found that the complementary of the violet is at scale number (*SSN*) 48·7 (577·2 $\mu\mu$), that of the red at *SSN* 34·6 (500 $\mu\mu$), and that where green is mixed only with white is at *SSN* 37·5 (515 $\mu\mu$). These are therefore the points of intersection of the three sensation curves (Fig. 64).

It is next necessary to ascertain the amount of white in the green at *SSN* 37·5. One slit is placed in this situation and another at *SSN* 59·8, the position of the red lithium line. The luminosities of these colours, with equally wide slits, are taken by comparison with another light, such as yellow or white. They are found to be 39·2 and 9·4 respectively. A patch of yellow light from a second spectrum, derived from the same source of light, is placed beside the mixture of red and green. In order to obtain a *colour* match it is necessary to add white to the homogeneous yellow. From the slit widths and the luminosity of the added white an equation in terms of luminosity is obtained :

$$a \text{ (yellow)} + b \text{ (white)} = c \text{ (red)} + d \text{ (green)}$$

or

$$a \text{ (yellow)} = c \text{ (red)} + d \text{ (green)} - b \text{ (white)}.$$

Since the red contains no white the percentage of white in the green is $\frac{b}{d} \times 100$. It was found to be 69 per cent. The percentage of green sensation is $\frac{(d-b)}{d} \times 100$.

Having obtained the percentage of white in the green the percentage sensation composition of other colours in terms of luminosity can be readily found[1]. Fig. 62 shows the percentage sensation curves.

From the data obtained by these experiments the analysis of the sensation-values can be carried further by calculation. Having determined the luminosity values of the different parts of the spectrum by heterochromatic photometry (585 $\mu\mu$ = 100) the luminosity-values of

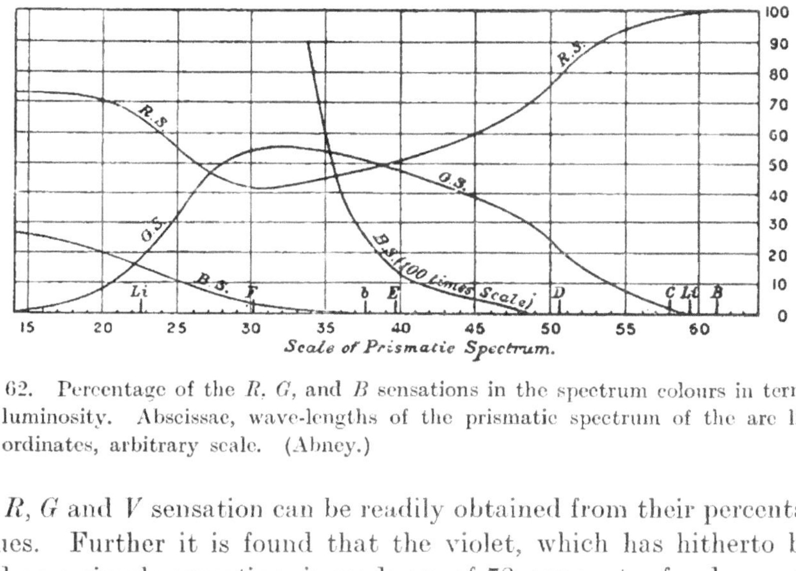

Fig. 62. Percentage of the R, G, and B sensations in the spectrum colours in terms of luminosity. Abscissae, wave-lengths of the prismatic spectrum of the arc light ordinates, arbitrary scale. (Abney.)

the R, G and V sensation can be readily obtained from their percentage-values. Further it is found that the violet, which has hitherto been used as a simple sensation, is made up of 72 per cent. of red sensation and 28 per cent. of blue sensation. The R, G, and V values can therefore be transformed into fundamental R, G, and B sensation-values, B being the fundamental blue sensation. We thus obtain the R, G, and B percentage-values, and from them, by calculation, their luminosity-values.

The luminosity curves of the spectrum and of the three components are shown in Fig. 63. For any wave-length the sum of the ordinates of the three sensation curves is equal to the ordinate of the total luminosity curve at that point. When white light, *i.e.*, light of all wave-lengths, enters the eye the effect produced on the three components will be

[1] Abney, p. 235.

proportional to the areas of the three sensation curves. The relative areas of these curves for the electric arc are *RS* 579, *GS* 248, *BS* 3·26.

When considering the matches made between different lights it is often convenient to adopt a different scale, viz., one in which the areas of the three sensation curves are equal to each other. With this scale equal ordinates of the three sensation curves correspond to a mixture which will appear white to the normal eye. If we multiply the ordinates of the green sensation curve by 579/248 = 2·21, and those of the blue sensation curve by 579/3·26 = 117, the green and blue sensation curves will have the same area as the red sensation curve.

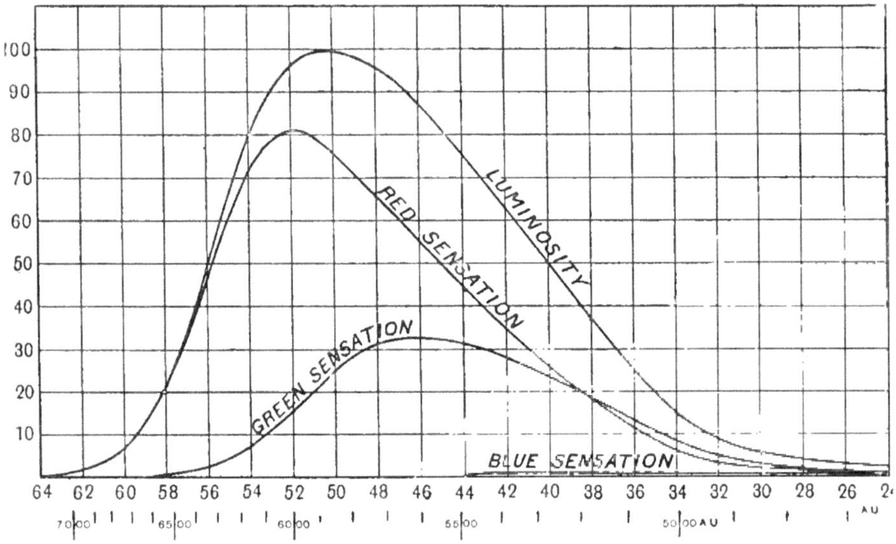

Fig. 63. Abney's *R*, *G*, and *B* sensation curves in terms of luminosity. The sums of the ordinates at any point are equal to the ordinate of the photopic luminosity curve. (Watson.)

In the curves in Fig. 63 the source of light was the crater of the arc light with a horizontal positive pole. The source of light in Abney's original investigations was the crater of the arc light with sloping carbons, and the corresponding factors are 2·3 and 190.

The luminosity curves are therefore brought to equal areas by multiplying the *GS* and *BS* luminosity-values by 2·3 and 190 respectively, thus giving the curves shown in Fig. 64, where equal stimulation of all three components, *i.e.*, equal ordinates, give the sensation of white. Sir William Abney was the first to work out the colour sensations of the normal trichromat exhaustively in this manner.

These results afford an explanation of the change in hue which occurs when white light is added to the spectral colours. When this is done the red becomes pinker, the scarlet orange, the orange yellow, the yellow green. At *SSN* 48·7 (577·2 $\mu\mu$) in the yellowish-green, no change in hue occurs. Beyond this point, the green becomes yellowish, the blue shows little change, and the violet becomes nearly salmon-pink. Now *SSN* 48·7 is the point where the red and green sensation-values are equal to their sensation-values in the white light. It therefore seemed probable that the change in hue in lights of medium and long wave-length was due to the addition of the red and green sensation-values of the white light, the value of the blue sensation being so small

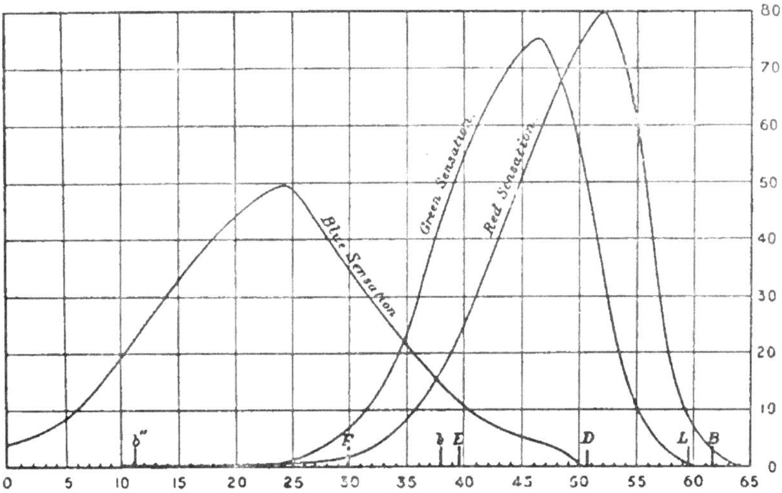

Fig. 64. Abney's *R*, *G*, and *B* equal-area sensation curves. The sums of equal ordinates of the three curves at any point represent the sensation of the unanalysed white light. (Abney.)

as to be negligible. This conjecture was fully borne out by experiment, the matches being identical with those calculated, within the range of experimental error. *SSN* 48·7 is easily found, since it is the complementary colour of the pure blue of the spectrum.

In the colour triangle (Fig. 9) a mixture of white with any spectral colour is represented by a point (a) on the line joining W with the given point on the curve, the position of a being determined by the relative amounts of the colour and white. The change in colour due to the admixture with white is found by joining the points B and a and producing Ba to meet the curve. The mixture will match the spectral colour which is represented by the point of intersection with the curve. That this should be the case shows that the blue element is practically in abeyance.

In experiments in matching white with mixtures of spectral rays it was found that about 2·8 per cent. of red or green could be added without being perceived.

If we examine the sensation curves shown in the previous diagrams we shall find that, besides the maxima of each sensation, there are important points where the curves intersect. We will call the point where the *R* and *G* curves intersect *a*, *R* and *B*, *b*, and *B* and *G*, *c*. These points have been determined by König, Abney, and Exner[1], and their values are as follows:

	a	*b*	*c*	*d*
König (sunlight)	573	503	496	450
Abney (arc light)	577·2	515	500	
Exner (arc light)	577	508	494	475

d is the complementary colour of *a*. From these data König and Exner deduced the fundamental colour sensations: *R*, a purplish red (complementary to 494 $\mu\mu$ (Exner); *G*, 505 $\mu\mu$ (König), 508 $\mu\mu$ (Exner); *B*, 470 $\mu\mu$ (König), 475 $\mu\mu$ (Exner); all, however, more saturated than the spectral colours.

We have here the explanation of the variations in the discrimination sensibility for hues in the spectrum (*v.* p. 30). In the equal area curves, *e.g.* Fig. 64, equal ordinates at any point make white. If we subtract the white in those parts of the spectrum in which all three sensations are stimulated, we can obtain the ratios of the ordinates of the sensation curves to each other throughout the spectrum. These ratios will vary in different parts. In regions where the variation occurs most rapidly we should expect the hues to change most rapidly. Calculations made by Steindler on this basis from Exner's values show that the positions of maximum change are at 500 $\mu\mu$, 570—590 $\mu\mu$, and 635 $\mu\mu$, of minimum change at 470 $\mu\mu$, 530 $\mu\mu$, and 625 $\mu\mu$. These calculations agree remarkably well with the results of direct observation, which show that the maxima of discrimination sensibility for hues were at II, 492 $\mu\mu$, III, 581 $\mu\mu$, and IV, 635·5 $\mu\mu$, the minima being at 458 $\mu\mu$, 533 $\mu\mu$, and 627 $\mu\mu$ (*v.* p. 31).

This very striking confirmation of the Young-Helmholtz theory was first pointed out by König[2].

The curves in Fig. 65 are derived by calculation from the same

[1] *Sitz. d. Wiener Akad.* cxi. ii*a*, 857 1902.

[2] König, p. 106.

numbers which gave the curves in Fig. 62[1]. They are useful for foretelling the results of fatiguing the eye for different colours. They are constructed on the basis that equal stimulations of all three components give rise to the sensation of white. If the eye is fatigued with white light the effect will be to tire each equally, and therefore the same white seen by such an eye will appear darker. If the eye is fatigued for *SSN* 48·6, *RS* and *GS* are equally fatigued. Suppose they are fatigued so that the ordinates of the curves are reduced to one-half, and then a colour, about *SSN* 42, of which the normal composition is 1*RS* to 2*GS*, is observed. The effect will be to make the new relationship $\frac{1}{2}$*RS* to 1*GS*. Since the proportion remains the same no change in hue

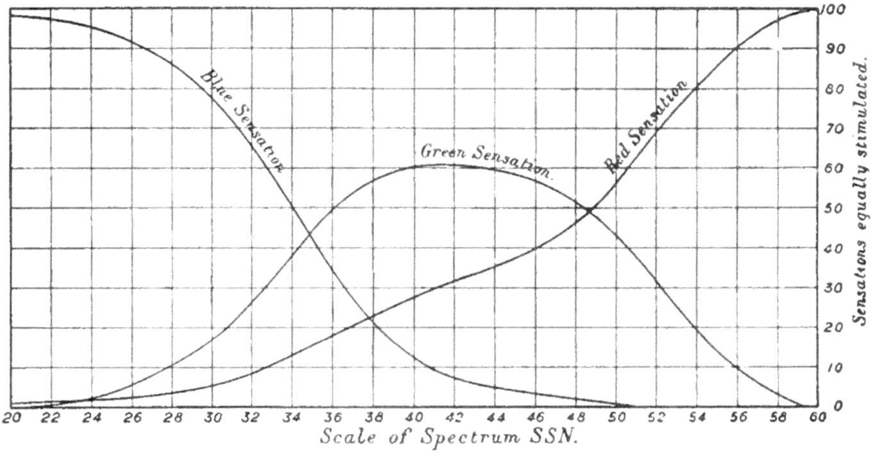

Fig. 65. Percentage of the *R*, *G*, and *B* sensations in the spectrum colours when equal stimulations of the three sensations give rise to the sensation of white. (Abney.)

will be observed. Suppose, however, a colour about *SSN* 60, where there is no *GS* is observed. The only effective fatigue will be for *RS*, and the red will merely appear darker.

One more example. Suppose the fatiguing colour is about 42, where the ordinate of *GS* is twice that of *RS*, and suppose the fatigue reduces the ordinates to one half. They are then *RS* = $\frac{1}{4}$ and *GS* = $\frac{1}{2}$. The eye then observes *SSN* 50, where *RS* is 54·5 and *GS* 42·5. As observed *RS* will be $\frac{54 \cdot 5}{4} = 13 \cdot 6$, and *GS* will be $\frac{42 \cdot 5}{2} = 21 \cdot 25$, *i.e.*, as 1 : 0·64. This is about the ratio found at *SSN* 44. Therefore the yellow at *SSN* 50 will appear to the fatigued eye as a green of *SSN* 44.

[1] Abney, p. 240.

Experiments made by Abney support these conclusions. He has shown how the factor of fatigue can be arrived at and how luminosity curves can be obtained for the fatigued eye. He did not employ the high intensities used by Burch.

II. Dichromatic Vision

Young himself[1] suggested that Dalton's colour blindness was due to absence of the red component. v. Helmholtz, Donders, König, and others found that this hypothesis accounted well for the facts, and further, that the second great type of colour blindness, now known as deuteranopia, could be attributed to absence of the green component. The rare cases of tritanopia were attributed to absence of the blue component.

If the red component is absent it will be seen from Fig. 64 that from *SSN* 65 to 60 there will be no sensation of colour, nor indeed of light. The red end of the spectrum will be shortened.

From *SSN* 60 to 50 the green component only is present. It will give rise to a sensation much exceeding in purity that of the normal unfatigued eye. The sensation will differ only in intensity, not in hue, just as in the red of the normal eye between *SSN* 65 and 60. As has already been pointed out we have no certain knowledge of the actual sensation which the protanope is conscious of, and there can be little doubt that it is very different from what we call "green," though he may call it green and often does; yet he often, too, calls it red.

At *SSN* 50 the third component is stimulated. At *SSN* 34·6 ($500\mu\mu$) the green and blue sensation curves intersect. As the ordinates are equal he will have a sensation similar to that of the trichromat when all three components are equally stimulated, *i.e.*, he will have a sensation of the same nature as that which he obtains from white light, and he will therefore probably call it white. At any rate he will match it with the white of the combined spectrum if the intensity is suitably arranged for him. In other words *SSN* 34·6 is his neutral point (*v.* p. 163). Between *SSN* 50 and 34·6, then, his colour-sensation, whatever it is, is becoming less saturated. Beyond *SSN* 34·6 his colour sensation becomes more and more saturated, until at *SSN* 16, where the green component ceases to be stimulated, it reaches its full spectral saturation, and remains the same, differing only in intensity, to the end of the spectrum.

[1] *Lectures*, II. 315, 1807.

If the green component is absent the visible spectrum will be the same length as to the trichromat. From *SSN* 65 to 50, and from *SSN* 16 to the end of the spectrum he will have isolated pure sensations, "red" and "blue" respectively. At *SSN* 37·5 (515 $\mu\mu$), where the two equal-area curves intersect, he will see "white": this is his neutral point, and we see that it is rather nearer the violet end than in the protanope.

In some parts of the spectrum it is easier for the dichromat to measure the luminosities of spectral lights than for the trichromat. In fact near the neutral points it is a simple matter of homo- as opposed to heterochromatic photometry. Theoretically, the protanopic plus the deuteranopic luminosity curves should equal the trichromatic plus one blue luminosity curve. The extra blue curve makes very little difference, as it is relatively very small compared with the other two (*v*. Fig. 63). Moreover, its effect is further diminished by macular absorption. As already mentioned, we have no means of making absolute measurements, but the relative values hold good.

We should expect the discrimination sensibility for hues in the spectrum to be very defective in dichromats. The first experiments of this nature were made by Brodhun[1], himself a deuteranope. His curve is given in Fig. 4. We see that he has only one maximum, at 500 $\mu\mu$, near the *F* line, but here the curve is very sharp and the value of $\delta\lambda$ is very low, so that his discrimination sensibility is very great at this point.

Steindler[2] examined three protanopes and five deuteranopes (Figs. 66, 67). She found that $\delta\lambda$ was much larger than for the normal in all cases. The deuteranopes showed only one maximum, the average being at 503 $\mu\mu$. The protanopes showed two maxima, at 500 $\mu\mu$ and 598 $\mu\mu$. On the same basis of calculation as for trichromats (*v*. p. 230) the maxima for deuteranopes should be at 500 $\mu\mu$ and 635 $\mu\mu$. The first position agrees well with that found experimentally; at 635 $\mu\mu$ the luminosity was too low for deuteranopes for accurate observations to be made. The calculated maxima for protanopes were 500 $\mu\mu$ and 600 $\mu\mu$ which agree excellently with the observations. Tritanopes are so rare that they could not be examined; their theoretical maxima are at 540 $\mu\mu$ and at 620 $\mu\mu$.

König[3] calculated that the number of hues which a deuteranope could discriminate in the spectrum was 140, as compared with the normal

[1] *Ztsch. f. Psychol. u. Physiol. d. Sinnesorg.* III. 89, 1892.
[2] *Sitz. d. Wiener Akad.* CXV. ii *a*. 115, 1906.
[3] König, p. 368.

160–165. The number seems high, especially when one considers that the integration interval is much less. It is explained by the fact that between the lines *E* and *F* deuteranopes possess a much greater discrimination sensibility than normal trichromats (*v.* Fig. 4). König thought that the number for protanopes was probably about the same as for deuteranopes.

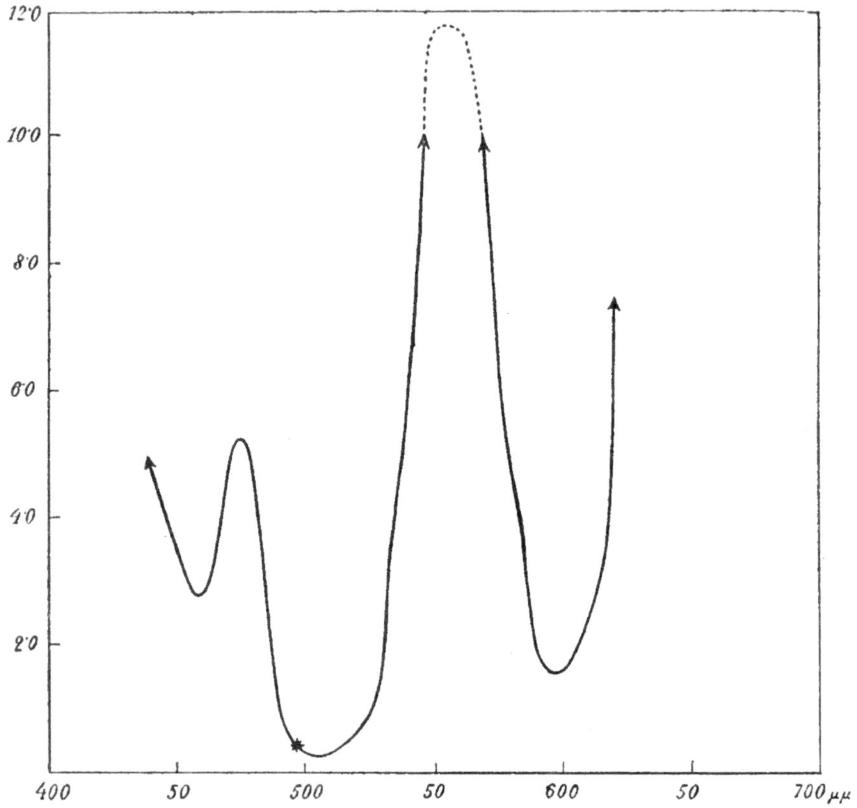

Fig. 66. Curve of discrimination sensibility for hues of the interference spectrum of the arc light for a protanope. ✻ Neutral point. Abscissae, wave-lengths; ordinates, differences of wave-length (δλ) capable of being discriminated. (Steindler.)

Liebermann and Marx[1] have compared the discriminative sensibility for hue of a protanope and trichromat by the method of mean error. They found that of the protanope much inferior. At 509·6 $\mu\mu$, near the neutral point, the mean of 50 observations gave $\delta\lambda = 3{\cdot}6\ \mu\mu$ for the normal, 16·2 $\mu\mu$ for the protanope.

[1] *Ztsch. f. Sinnesphysiol.* XLV. 103, 1911.

Brückner and Kirsch[1] found that the chromatic action time (*v.* p. 91) for deuteranopes, especially for red and green, is considerably greater than for normal trichromats. No experiments of this nature have been made upon protanopes.

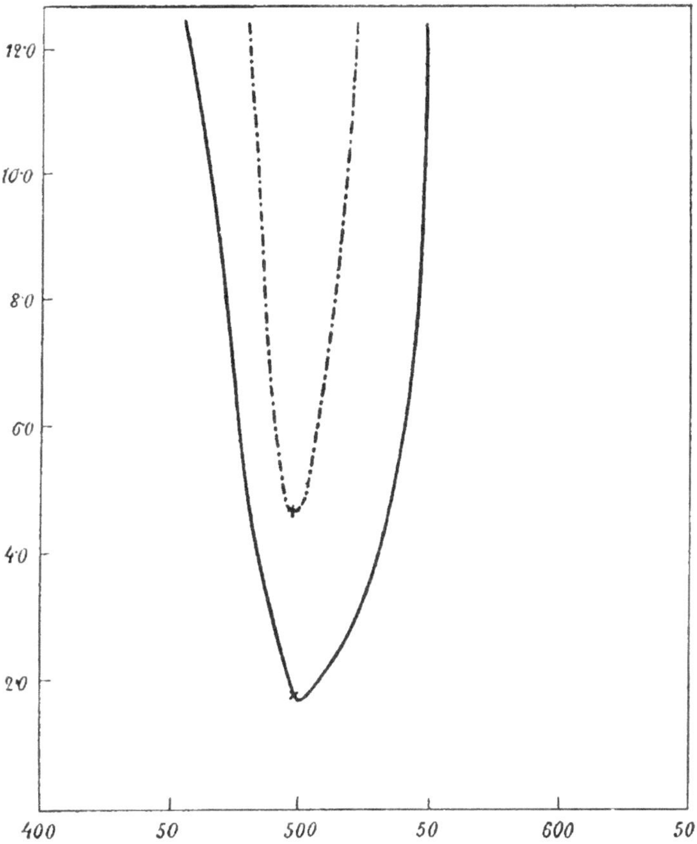

Fig. 67. Curves of discrimination sensibility for hues of the interference spectrum of the arc light for two deuteranopes. × Neutral point. (Steindler.)

III. Anomalous Trichromatic Vision

Approximate Dichromatism

When the anomalous trichromats were discovered by Lord Rayleigh the natural assumption was that the two groups correspond to the protanopes and deuteranopes, but that the defect is partial instead of

[1] *Ztsch. f. Sinnesphysiol.* XLVI. 229, 1911.

complete (*approximate dichromatism*). König and Abney worked on this theory and have brought forward much evidence in its favour. There is, however, another possibility, viz., that there is a displacement of the normal sensation curves. If, for example, the green sensation curve is of the same form and magnitude as in the normal, but is displaced towards the red end of the spectrum, the colour sensations of the individual will be abnormal. It is clear that it is possible to have a combination of the two characteristics, shift of one or more curves combined with reduction of one or more fundamental sensations. Of cases bearing out this conjecture we have at present no evidence, but there is good evidence that both reduction cases and cases in which one curve, otherwise normal, is shifted, actually occur. In this chapter we shall consider the cases of approximate dichromatism only.

If, for example, the red sensation is defective, the ordinate of the red sensation curve for any given wave-length will be less than the corresponding ordinate for the normal, *e.g.*, one-half. Then for all other wave-lengths the ordinates of the red sensation curve are also half those of the normal curve. Hence it follows that the area of the red sensation curve must be half the area of the corresponding normal curve.

We have no method of measuring in absolute units the sensation produced when light of a given intensity stimulates the retina. Consequently we are unable to determine whether the maximum ordinate of the sensation curves is the same for all persons. What is actually done is to compare the sensations produced by given amounts of light of different colours for each observer. Thus we take some one kind of light as a standard and compare the relative stimulation of the components produced by other kinds of light with that produced by this standard light. In determining a luminosity curve the standard is the white light of the recombined spectrum. In examining the colour-defective the complication arises that this standard white is not the same for the normal and colour-blind observers. The defect influences the sensation derived from stimulation with white light as well as the sensations derived from colours. Watson has so lucidly explained the bearing of this fact upon the deductions that I cannot do better than quote his remarks[1].

"As long as we confine our attention to the part of the spectrum between the extreme red and the blue, the effect of the blue sensation on the luminosity may in general be neglected as being too small to

[1] *Proc. Roy. Soc. Lond.* A. LXXXVIII., p. 410, 1913.

produce any appreciable effect; hence, in what follows, the effect of the red and green sensations on the luminosity will alone be considered.

"The easiest way to show the manner in which the luminosity curve of a colour-deficient person is obtained will be to consider a particular case, say, one where the red sensation is deficient to such an extent that all the ordinates of the red sensation curve are only half the normal. Such a person may be said to possess half-normal red sensation and will be indicated by the symbol 0·5 *RS*. Since each of the ordinates of the red sensation curve is half the normal, the total area of that curve will also be half the normal. As in the light from the crater of the electric arc the areas of the red and green sensation curves are as 579 to 248, it follows that the areas for the 0·5 *RS* are as 290 to 248.

"Now suppose such a person determines the luminosity of a colour of which the wave-length is λ, and that λ_r and λ_g are the ordinates of the normal red and green sensation curves for this colour, the corresponding ordinates for the observer will be $\frac{1}{2}\lambda_r$, and λ_g. The total sensation produced by the colour will be the sum of the two sensations, that is, for the normal it will be $\lambda_r + \lambda_g$ and for the observer (0·5 *RS*) $\frac{1}{2}\lambda_r + \lambda_g$.

"The sensation produced by the comparison white in the luminosity measurement will be proportional to the sum of the areas of the red and green sensation curves. Hence, if we represent the areas of these curves for the normal by Σr and Σg respectively, the sensations produced by the white for the normal will be $\Sigma r + \Sigma g$, and for the colour-deficient will be $\frac{1}{2}\Sigma r + \Sigma g$.

"Thus the brightness of the coloured light is for the 0·5 *RS* observer reduced in the ratio $(\frac{1}{2}\lambda_r + \lambda_g)/(\lambda_r + \lambda_g)$, while that of the white is reduced in the ratio $(\frac{1}{2}\Sigma r + \Sigma g)/(\Sigma r + \Sigma g)$. Let w be the intensity of the white when the normal observer makes the luminosity setting and w' the intensity of the white when the colour-deficient observer makes the setting. Then we have

$$w = a\,(\lambda_r + \lambda_g) \ldots\ldots\ldots\ldots\ldots\ldots (1)$$

and

$$w'\,\frac{\frac{1}{2}\Sigma r + \Sigma g}{\Sigma r + \Sigma g} = a\,(\tfrac{1}{2}\lambda_r + \lambda_g) \ldots\ldots\ldots\ldots (2),$$

where a is a constant which depends on the unit used to measure the intensity of the white light.

"Thus the ratio of the colour-deficient observer's luminosity to that of the normal is given by

$$\frac{w'}{w} = \frac{\frac{1}{2}\lambda_r + \lambda_g}{\lambda_r + \lambda_g} \times \frac{\Sigma r + \Sigma g}{\frac{1}{2}\Sigma r + \Sigma g} \ldots\ldots\ldots\ldots\ldots (3).$$

Thus, knowing w, we can calculate what is the ordinate w' of the luminosity curve for the 0·5 *RS* observer corresponding to the colour λ.

"The following statement may make the above argument clearer. When a colour-deficient observer makes a luminosity setting he matches the brightness of the colour as it appears to him against the brightness of the white as this appears to him. Owing to his deficiency both the colour and the white appear less bright. If there were no reduction in the brightness of the white to him, his luminosity setting would be $(\frac{1}{2}\lambda_r + \lambda_g)/(\lambda_r + \lambda_g)$ of the normal setting. Owing, however, to the comparison white being also reduced in brightness the size of his white unit is reduced in the ratio of $\frac{1}{2}\Sigma r + \Sigma g$ to $\Sigma r + \Sigma g$; and hence, as the size of the unit has decreased, he requires more of these units to match the colour, that is, we must multiply the number given above by $(\Sigma r + \Sigma g)/(\frac{1}{2}\Sigma r + \Sigma g)$. This decrease in the value of the white unit is the reason why the luminosity curve for a red-blind observer is higher than the normal in the green, and that for a green-blind observer it is higher than the normal in the red. These high values do not indicate that a red-blind person receives a greater stimulus from a given green light, or a green-blind receives a greater stimulus from a red light, than does a normal, but simply that relatively to the stimulus received from a given white light the stimulus received is greater.

"Using equation (3) and the luminosity curves for a normal eye given by Abney, the luminosity curves for persons having the following red sensations in terms of the normal, 0 *RS*, 0·33 *RS*, 0·7 *RS*, and the following green sensations 0 *GS*, 0·33 *GS*, and 0·6 *GS*, have been calculated. The results together with the normal luminosity curve are shown in Fig. 68.

"It will be observed that all the luminosity curves intersect at one point, *P*, which corresponds to *SSN* 48·8 or a wave-length 5770 Å.U. The condition that the luminosity should be the same for the normal as for, say, the 0·5 *RS* observer is that [equations (1) and (2)]

$$(\tfrac{1}{2}\lambda_r + \lambda_g)\frac{\Sigma r + \Sigma g}{\frac{1}{2}\Sigma r + \Sigma g} = \lambda_r + \lambda_g,$$

or

$$\frac{\lambda_r \Sigma g}{2} = \frac{\lambda_g \Sigma r}{2} \text{ or } \frac{\lambda_r}{\lambda_g} = \frac{\Sigma r}{\Sigma g} \quad \ldots\ldots\ldots\ldots\ldots (4),$$

that is at a wave-length such that for both observers the ratio of the ordinates of their red and green sensation curves is the same as the ratio of the total areas of these curves[1]. Equation (4) shows that the wave-length of the light corresponding to the point of intersection is independent of the amount or kind of the deficiency in colour sensation of the observer.

" The curves given in Fig. 68 depend on :

" (1) The accuracy of Abney's sensation curves.

" (2) The correctness of Abney's theory that in the case of the ordinary types of total or partial red or green colour blindness the

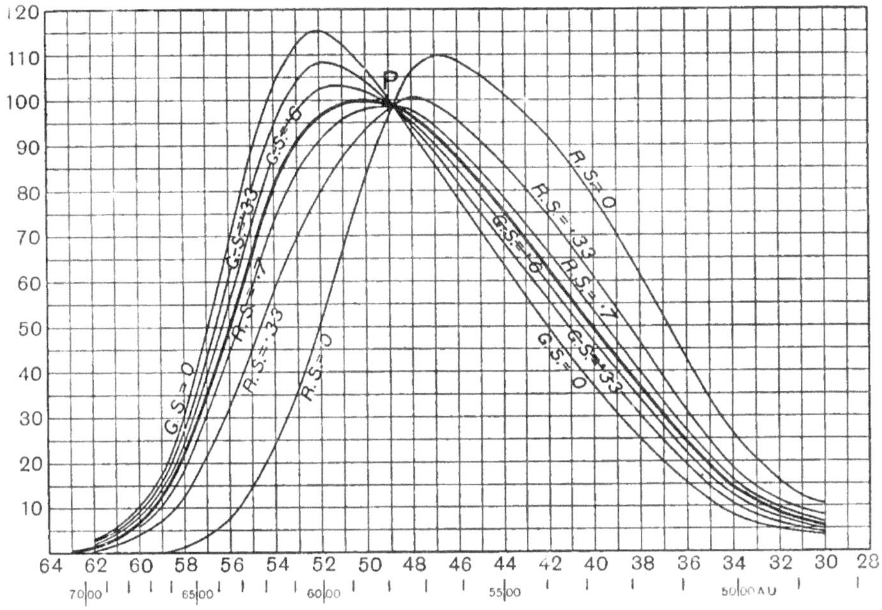

Fig. 68. Luminosity curves of persons having normal and reduced red and green sensations. Abscissae, wave-lengths of the prismatic spectrum of the arc light; ordinates arbitrary scale. (Watson.)

ordinates of one of the sensation curves are all reduced in the same proportion, and

" (3) The additive property which has been assumed and which involves the corollary that the areas of the luminosity curves obtained by normal and colour-deficient persons are the same. Thus, if it can be shown that the observed luminosity curves of persons who are colour-deficient agree with the calculated curves it is strong evidence in favour of the correctness of the above three assumptions."

[1] The wave-length at which all the curves will intersect depends on the distribution of light in the spectrum employed in the experiments, *i.e.* on the source of light.

Watson has adduced conclusive evidence in this direction, partly from his own observations by the flicker method, and partly by calculation from Abney's published cases. Since the observations in Abney's cases were all published before the calculated curves were obtained, and some were indeed published before the sensation curves used in the calculations had been obtained, they comprise an overwhelming volume of evidence.

If therefore we have the normal luminosity curve we can calculate the luminosity curves for various grades of approximate dichromatism (Fig. 68). If these are plotted on a large scale they will afford a means

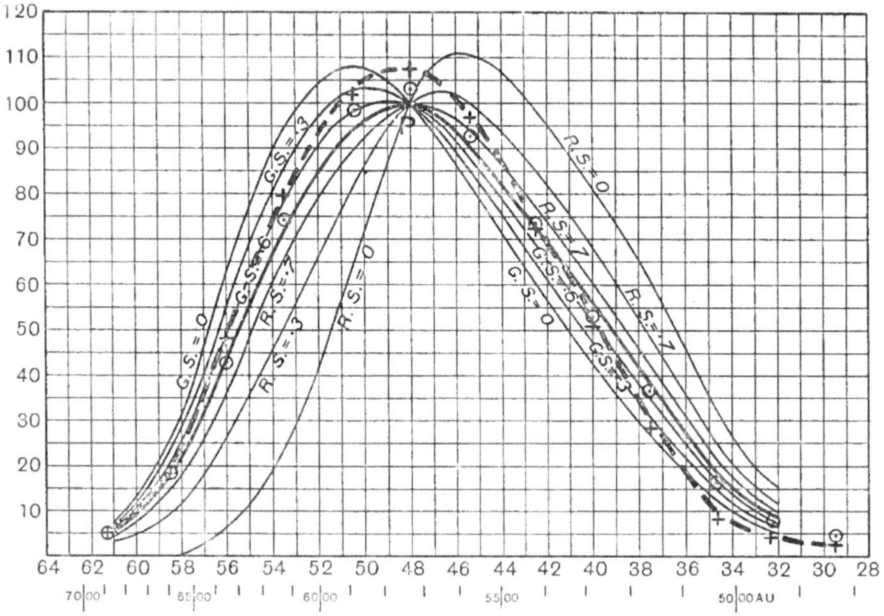

Fig. 69. Luminosity curves of a normal trichromat with excessive macular pigmentation. + + + foveal; ⊙ ⊙ ⊙ ⊙ parafoveal. (Watson.)

of measuring directly the amount of deficiency of red or green sensation in any protanope or deuteranope, whether partial or complete. All that is necessary is to obtain the examinee's flicker luminosity curve with the same source of light and under as nearly identical conditions as possible. The fact that all the curves intersect at a particular wave-length affords one means of deciding that the case belongs to the group of approximate dichromats. His average readings at this point should agree with the average readings of the normal trichromat, and in every case the normal readings should be taken at the same time. For purposes of diagnosis it is not necessary to take readings at all points of the curve. Readings at *SSN* 48·8 (5770 Å.U.), the point of intersection, and at *SSN* 42·8 (5410 Å.U.), in the green, and *SSN* 53·2 (6090 Å.U.), in the red, usually suffice.

We have now to consider some divergences from the calculated curves. In most cases these are slight and are limited to the green-blue, where differences may be expected, since the effect of the blue sensation has been neglected in the calculated curves; and further, slight differences in macular pigmentation begin to be important in this region. These divergences do not vitiate the method for purposes

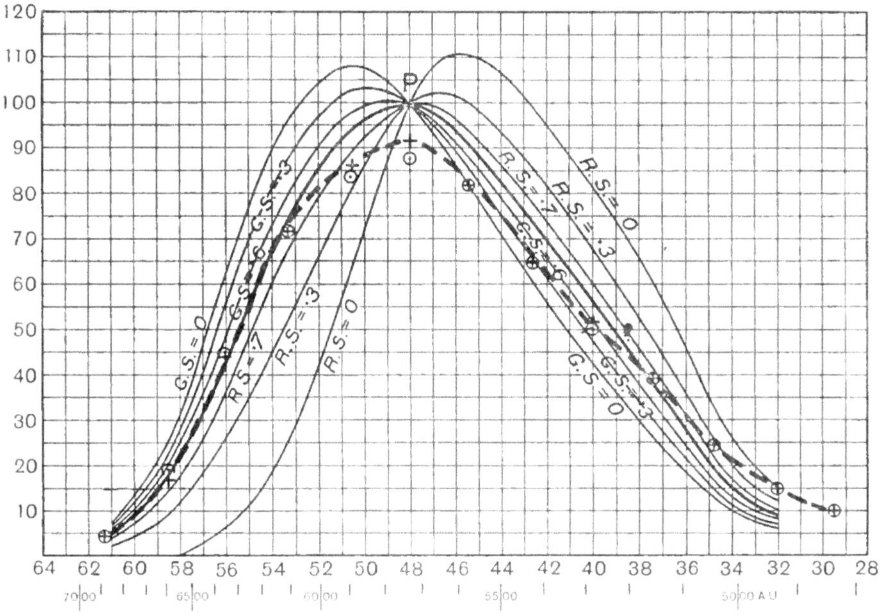

Fig. 70. Luminosity curves of a normal trichromat with subnormal macular pigmentation. + + + foveal; ⊙ ⊙ ⊙ parafoveal. (Watson.)

of diagnosis of protanopes and deuteranopes, since they occur in a part of the spectrum where their characteristic colour defects are least important from the practical point of view.

Cases, however, occur of marked excess or deficiency of macular pigmentation, and in these the luminosity curves show marked differences from the normal (Figs. 69, 70). Fig. 69 shows excess of pigmentation, Fig. 70 deficiency. By using a central fixation dot and a white ring, the inner and outer edges of which subtend visual angles of 3° 22′ and 5°, Watson was able to obtain luminosity curves of a parafoveal area. Fig. 71 shows his foveal and parafoveal curves. Unusual macular pigmentation may be combined with approximate dichromatism, as in Fig. 72, where partial deuteranopia coexists with excessive macular pigmentation.

Other methods can be employed for diagnosing approximate dichromatism. In addition to taking the ordinary equation, *i.e.*, matching the white of the source of light with a mixture of homogeneous red, green and violet, a pure colour may be matched with a mixture of two pure colours, as in the Rayleigh equation; or a mixed colour, such as that obtained by passing the white light of the re-combined spectrum

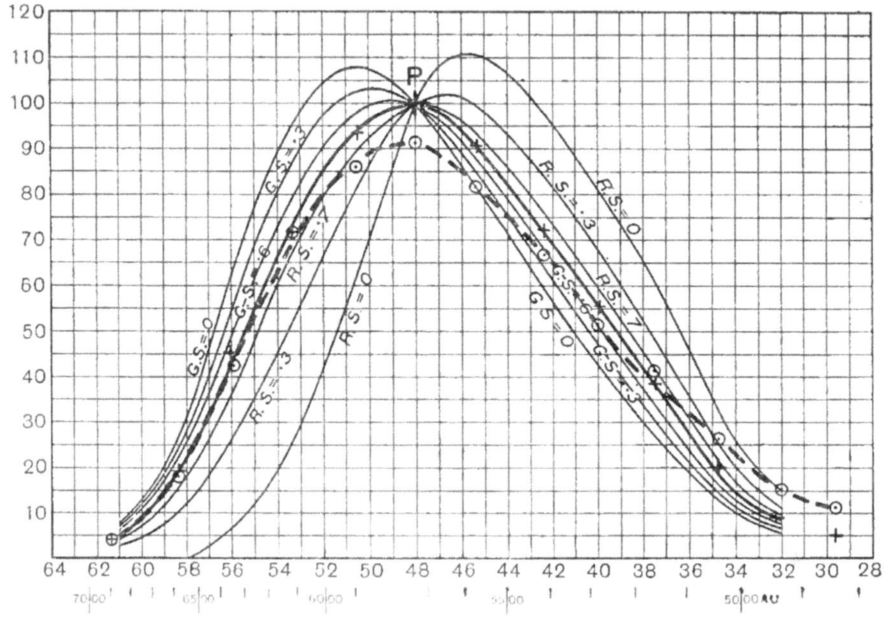

Fig. 71. Luminosity curves of a normal trichromat with average macular pigmentation. + + + foveal; ⊙ ⊙ ⊙ parafoveal. (Watson.)

through a saturated solution of potassium chromate, may be matched with a spectral colour.

A saturated solution of this salt, $\frac{3}{8}$ inch thick, will filter off nearly all the blue in the white light, so that the light appears yellow. Now, from about *SSN* 50 to the red end of the spectrum there is no measurable amount of blue sensation present. If a slit is caused to traverse the spectrum a position will be found where the light exactly matches that transmitted through the chromate. For the normal eye it is at *SSN* 49·6 (583 $\mu\mu$). If a partial deuteranope makes the match the slit must be moved towards the red, if a partial protanope towards the green.

There is a considerable band of the spectrum over which the slit may be moved without vitiating the approximate dichromat's match, but Watson[1] has pointed out that the match which satisfies the normal person is always one limit of the band, though the band lies sometimes on one side and sometimes on the other of this position. There is at present no explanation of this fact. We shall find that the

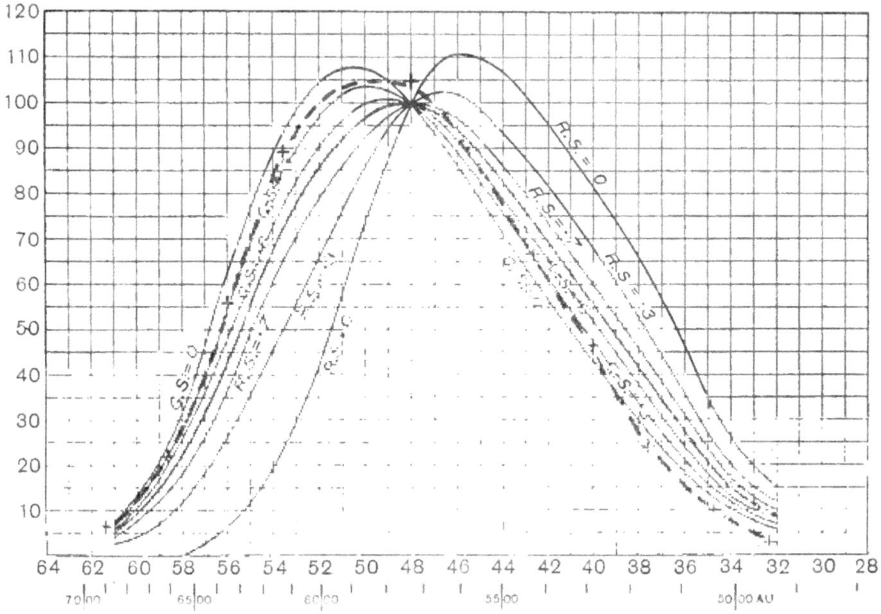

Fig. 72. Foveal luminosity curve of a deuteranope with excessive macular pigmentation. (Watson.)

anomalous trichromat whose peculiarity is due to a shift of one of the sensation curves makes a much more accurate setting by this method.

IV. Anomalous Trichromatic Vision

Shift of a Sensation Curve

Abney and Watson[2] have published an exhaustive account of a case of anomalous trichromatic vision in which the green sensation curve is of normal shape and size but is displaced towards the red end of the

[1] *Proc. Roy. Soc. Lond.* May 28, 1914.

[2] *Ibid.* A. LXXXIX, 232, 1913.

spectrum. There is good reason to think that cases of the same nature are not uncommon, but in the cases hitherto examined the shift has always affected the green sensation curve and in the same manner.

Figs. 73 and 74 show the normal sensation curves in terms of luminosity, Fig. 73 being the equal areas curve.

If an observer is an "approximate dichromat," *e.g.*, a partial

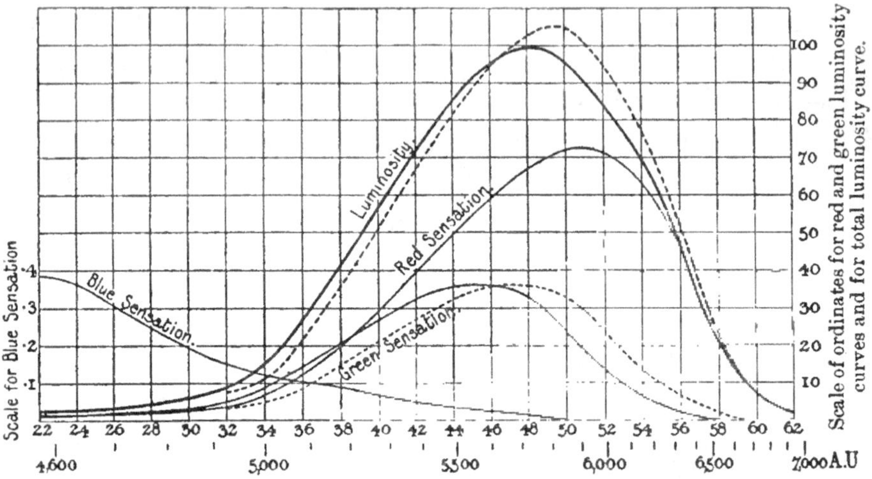

Fig. 73. Normal sensation curves in terms of luminosity. (Abney and Watson.)

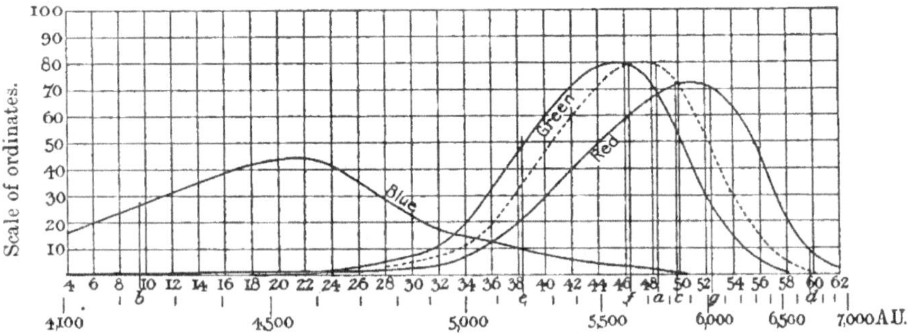

Fig. 74. Normal sensation curves on equal area scale. (Abney and Watson.)

deuteranope with half the normal green sensation, on the luminosity scale the ordinates of his green sensation curve will be half those of the normal curve. On the equal area scale, however, his green sensation curve will be the same as the normal, for since the area of the green sensation curve on the luminosity scale is now 124, to obtain the equal area scale we must multiply by 579/124 = 4·42 (cf. p. 228). Hence, since the multiplier is twice as great as for the normal, the resulting curve will be the same as for the normal.

"Now, if we take a yellow at *SSN* 18·4 (5760 Å.U.), *i.e.* at *a* (Fig. 74), and mix it with a violet at *SSN* 9·5 (4235 Å.U.), *i.e.* at *b* (Fig. 74), the width of the violet slit being 2·5 times that of the yellow, and read off the three sensations at these places from the full line curves given in Fig. 74, the values in the violet being multiplied by 2·5, we get the following numbers:

Position of slit	Sensations Red	Green	Blue
a	67·9	69·3	1·6
b	1·4	0	67·7
Sums....	69·3	69·3	69·3

Since the sums for the three sensations are the same it follows that the mixture will look white to the normal eye. Further, since the curves for the person who has half the green sensation are precisely similar, the sums will be equal for him also and hence he will match the mixed colour with his own white. Similarly for any other case of colour defect, where the defect is due to a deficiency of one of the sensations, the curves of the sensations on the equal area scale will be the same as those of the normal eye.

"Although the person who has the defect of one of the sensations will agree with the normal match, it will be found that when making the match the position of the yellow slit can be moved some little distance from the correct position for the normal without the match becoming defective to him." Watson has measured the range over which the match is valid by making himself artificially colour-blind by fatiguing his eye with a colour (*v.* p. 106).

"If the sensation curves are the same for a given observer as for the normal, except that one of them is shifted along the spectrum, quite a different result will be obtained. Thus suppose that the green sensation curve is shifted towards the red end of the spectrum by an amount equal to 2 *SSN* and occupies the position shown by the dotted curves in Figs. 73 and 74. The sensations at the points *a* and *b* for such a person are as follows:

Position of slit	Sensations Red	Green	Blue
a	67·9	79·2	1·6
b	1·4	0	67·7
Sums	69·3	79·2	69·3

"The sums of the blue and red sensations are still equal but the sum of the green sensation ordinates is greater, and hence the mixed colour will not match the white but will appear to such a person too green. If, however, the yellow slit is moved towards the red to *c*, Fig. 74 (*SSN* 49·8, 5860 Å.U.) and the width of the violet slit is made 2·72 times that of the yellow slit we get

Position of slit	Red	Sensations Green	Blue
a	71·8	73·5	0·5
b	1·7	0	73·0
Sums....	73·5	73·5	73·5

"The three sums are now equal and hence the mixed colour will match the white to such an observer, although it will appear orange to normal vision.

"Hence if an observer does not agree with the normal when violet and yellow are matched to form white, but requires that the yellow slit be moved towards the red to form a match, we conclude that his green sensation curve is displaced towards the red and vice versâ."

This explains the accuracy of the match which is made with the potassium chromate method when there is a shift as compared with cases where there is a reduction of one of the sensation curves (*v.* p. 243).

"In the case of a shift of the green sensation towards the red amounting to 2 *SSN* as indicated by the dotted curves in Figs. 73 and 74 we should expect the following effects to be produced :

"1. The part of the spectrum which to the normal appears yellow will appear greenish, for owing to the displacement the green sensation excited will be greater than in the normal. In the same way what appears orange to the normal will appear yellow, and so on.

"2. If we place three slits in the spectrum, one at the place of the red lithium line, *d*, Fig. 74, another at the *b* magnesium line *e*, Fig. 74, and the third in the violet at *b*, Fig. 74, and by varying the width of the three slits produce a mixture which to the normal appears to match the white, this match will not appear correct to the observer with the green shift (whom, for short, we may designate by *R*., the normal being indicated by *N*.). To *R*. the match will be imperfect, for the green sensation he receives from the light passing through the green slit at *e* will not be as great as it is to *N*. By opening the green slit, we can, however, obtain a match which is correct for *R*., but his match will appear green to *N.*, and he will never agree that the normal match is correct.

"If now we move the green slit to *f*, Fig. 74, where the normal green sensation curve cuts the displaced curve we shall find that a match which is correct for *N.* is also correct for *R.*, and that either can detect a small departure from this setting.

"3. The above is one arrangement of the three slits such that *R.* and *N.* make the same match. Another such position is obtained if the red slit is moved to *g*, Fig. 74 (*SSN* 52·4, 6000 Å.U.). The light which now comes through the red slit excites green sensation in the case of both *N.* and *R.*, but to a greater extent in the case of the latter. Since the red and blue sensations are the same for both it will be sufficient to consider the equality of the red and green in the two cases. If the width of the red slit is 0·62 times that of the green we get the following values of the sensations on the equal area scale:

	Sensations			
Position	*N.*		*R.*	
of slit	Red	Green	Red	Green
e	21·1	48·5	21·1	34·5
g	43·8	16·4	43·8	30·4
Sums..	64·9	64·9	64·9	64·9

where the sums are the same in the two cases and hence the mixture appears white to both *N.* and *R.* Thus if the green slit is kept in a constant position and the red slit is gradually moved up towards the green the matches made by *R.* appear to *N.* at first too green, but the excess of green gradually decreases till the red slit is at *SSN* 52·4. If the red slit is moved further towards the green the mixture which appears correct to *R.* will then appear too red to *N.*

"4. Owing to the displacement of the green sensation curve *R.*'s *luminosity* curve will be higher than the normal on the red side of the point where the normal and displaced green sensation luminosity curves cut and lower on the green side of this point, for the ordinates of the luminosity curve are the sums of the ordinates of the three luminosity sensation curves. The resulting luminosity curve for a displacement of 2 *SSN* towards the red is shown in Fig. 73 by the dotted curve, the corresponding normal curve being given by the thick continuous line."

The observer (*R.*), whom Abney and Watson examined, made a series of matches throughout the spectrum, and from these his sensation curves were deduced in the manner described on pp. 224, *sqq*.

"His red and practically his blue sensation curves are identical with those of the normal, but his green sensation curve is markedly different. It is similar in shape to the normal, but is displaced by about 2 *SSN* towards the red end of the spectrum. Thus to him the maximum for the electric arc light occurs at wave-length 5690 Å.U. in place of at 5575 Å.U., which is that of the normal.

"When white is matched by mixing light which passes through three slits placed at the points *d*, *e*, and *b*, Fig. 74 (6705, 5190, 4235 Å.U.), *R.* requires very much more green than the normal, as is shown by the first line in the next table. If, however, the red slit is moved towards the yellow, the green and violet slits remaining fixed in position, the excess of green required by *R.* got less and less, till finally

Position of "red" slit		Slit Widths					
			R.			*W.W.*	
SSN	Å.U.	Red	Green	Violet	Red	Green	Violet
59·8	6710	28·3	17·2	26·0	62·5	17·2	26·0
57·1	6450	8·5	17·2	26·0	16·5	17·2	26·0
54·5	6200	7·2	17·2	26·0	8·6	17·2	26·0
53·0	6080	9·2	17·2	33·0	9·2	17·2	33·0
52·5	6040	10·4	17·2	33·0	9·5	17·2	33·0
52·0	6000	14·8	17·2	45·0	10·0	17·2	45·0

Changes in slit-widths required to match white by *R.* and a normal trichromat (*W.W.*). The positions of the green and the violet slits were kept constant, as was also the width of the green slit, the match being obtained by varying the widths of the red and violet slits and the brightness of the comparison white. With the red slit at 52·5 the match made by either was correct for the other.

a position for the red slit was found where the mixture matched white both to *R.* and to the normal. If the red slit is moved further towards the yellow *R.* required less green than the normal, so that his mixture looked slightly red to the normal. The above changes indicated that in the case of *R.* we had to deal with a shift of the green sensation curve."

"When matching *D* light with a mixture of red and green light if the red is at the lithium line, *R.* required considerably more green than did the normal. If, however, the red slit were moved towards the yellow, just as in the case of the white matches, the excess of green gradually decreased, though, owing to the fact that the *D* light in the case of *R.* excites the green sensation more strongly than the normal we did not get the marked change in the appearance of *R.*'s match to the normal which has been referred to in the case of the white match" (*v.* p. 247). "For this reason the white match is preferable to the Rayleigh match for bringing out the characteristic changes when the position of the red slit is altered. Another advantage of the white match is that the yellow produced by mixing green and red to match the *D* light is less saturated than the *D* light itself, and this causes considerable difficulty with some observers when making the match.

"When matching white by a mixture of violet light (*SSN* 9·5, 4235 Å.U.) and yellow light the following results were obtained :

	W.W.
Position of yellow slit	*SSN* 48·9 or 5780 Å.U
	R.
	SSN 50·0 or 5860 Å.U.

showing that the complementary to the violet is in the case of *R.* displaced towards the red, as has been shown on p. 246 we should obtain if the green sensation curve was shifted towards the red end of the spectrum.

"Again it was found that if the red and violet slits were in the standard positions *d* and *b*, Fig. 74, a position for the green slit, *f*, Fig. 74, could be found such that the mixed light matched white both for *R.* and for *N.*

"The luminosity curve obtained by *R.*, using the equality of brightness method, agrees with what it ought to be if his green sensation curve is displaced towards the red by about 2 *SSN*, such a calculated curve being given in Fig. 73. Attention may be drawn to the fact that *R.*'s luminosity curve does not agree with the normal at *SSN* 48·6, as it would if *R.*'s abnormality were due to a deficiency of either the red or green sensations" (*v.* p. 238).

"It is of practical importance to consider what effect a shift of the green sensation curve such as that exhibited by *R.* will have on the power of discriminating colours, particularly those colours which are used as signals at sea and on railways. As has been mentioned, one effect of the displacement of the green sensation curve is that the part of the spectrum which to the normal appears yellow, to such persons appears green or greenish. Thus *R.* places the change from green to yellow in the spectrum at *SSN* 49·9 or 5810 Å.U. while to a normal (*W.W.*) this point appeared to be at *SSN* 48·8 or 5780 Å.U. One effect of this difference is that a light, such as that given by a paraffin lamp, which to the normal appears decidedly yellow appears to a person with the shift of a greenish hue and in fact *R.* often calls such a light green.

"Another effect of the displacement is that the perception of a green light when diluted with white light is very much more difficult than for the normal. The reason for this effect is at once apparent from a consideration of the sensation curves. Consider a green at *SSN* 36 (5090 Å.U.). At this point in the spectrum the red and blue sensation curves for *N*. on the equal area scale intersect. Hence we may regard the effect produced by light of this wave-length as an amount of green sensation (represented by the difference between the ordinate of the green sensation curve and the ordinate of either the red or the blue sensation curve) diluted by white light (this white light corresponding to the equal amounts of red, green, and blue sensation excited). It will be observed that the amount of the *diluting white* is the same for the normal and the person with the displaced green curve; but to *R*., the amount of *residual green* sensation is less than half that of the normal. In other words the green perceived by *R*. when light of this wave-length enters his eye is very much more diluted than it is to a person having normal colour vision. As a certain amount of dilution with white light will obliterate the perception of green in the coloured ray, it follows that the amount of white light which will obliterate it is considerably less for *R*. than it is for a normal vision."

"Further, the want of saturation of the green light makes the chromatic threshold for green much higher than normal, so that a green light must be made brighter for a person with a green shift before it can be distinguished from a white light than for the normal.

"The above results both as to the effect of dilution with white and as to the chromatic threshold are of great practical importance, for they both affect the power of an observer to identify green lights such as those used at sea. These lights are never pure spectral lights, though they are equivalent to spectral colours diluted with white. Thus the Board of Trade standard light-green light can be matched by a mixture of spectral green at *SSN* 37·4 or 5115 Å.U. with an equal amount of white (arc light). Further, if the size of the image of the coloured patch on the retina is diminished, it must be remembered that the amount of white required to extinguish a spectral colour is very much reduced."

SECTION IV

THE OPPONENT COLOURS THEORY (HERING)

CHAPTER I

STATEMENT OF THE THEORY

The three-components theory approaches the subject from what I have called the synthetic point of view. It provides a theory of colour sensations in terms of stimulus intensities. The opponent colours theory approaches the subject from the analytic point of view and provides a theory in terms of visual sensations.

Mach[1] had already pointed out in 1865 that the black-white series of sensations differed fundamentally from the chromatic series. On the principle of psychophysical parallelism the two series should have different physiological bases. Hering[2] adopted the psychological analysis of Goethe, Mach and others, that red, yellow, green, and blue were the only simple and unmixed colour-sensations, but advanced novel views about black. He adopted the view generally accepted by psychologists[3] that black is a sensation and is not the expression of the mere absence of stimulation[4]. The completely dark-adapted eye when sheltered from all external stimuli gives a sensation which is variously described as the light chaos, the intrinsic light of the retina, and so on. Hering called this sensation " mean grey." According to him " black " occurs only as the result of external stimulation, *i.e.*, under the influence of simultaneous or successive contrast. The " black " of a black patch seen on a white background, or of the after-image of a white patch, is blacker than the intrinsic light of the eye and is regarded by Hering as the true black sensation.

[1] *Sitz. d. Wiener Akad.* LII. 2. 320, 1865. [2] *Zur Lehre vom Lichtsinne,* 1876.

[3] Cf., however, Ward, *Brit. Jl. of Psychol.* I. 407, 1905.

[4] Contrast Leonardo da Vinci—" L' ombra è diminuzione di luce, tenebre è privazione di luce." *Trattato della Pittura,* ed. 1817, Rome, p. 274.

Hering thus arrived at six primary sensations, white, black, red, green, yellow and blue, from which all other visual sensations are derived. His theory consists essentially in the arrangement of these primaries into three pairs, the members of each pair being antagonistic to each other and dependent upon antagonistic physiological processes. The physiological processes are assumed to affect three different hypothetical visual substances, white-black, red-green and yellow-blue substances. These substances exist somewhere in the sub-cortical visual paths: their exact position is not defined, and it is indeed unnecessary to predicate three separate substances, except for the sake of clearness[1]. The opponent physiological processes are expressed in terms of antagonistic directions of metabolic change.

Hering[2] supposes that when a living substance is protected from external stimuli it undergoes spontaneous *autonomous* metabolic changes. Some molecules break down or undergo dissimilation (or katabolism), fresh ones are built up or undergo assimilation (or anabolism). When the two processes balance each other the substance is in a state of *autonomous equilibrium*. It is to be noted that autonomous equilibrium does not necessarily mean physiological inactivity. Fresh formative matter (Beale) may be brought from the blood in the exact quantity necessary to replace the formed matter which is poured out into the blood. If the substance is acted upon by an external stimulus *allonomous* metabolic changes are set up. They may be either anabolic or katabolic, but they induce a spontaneous tendency in the opposite direction so as to re-produce autonomous equilibrium, *i.e.*, allonomous katabolism, for example, induces autonomous anabolism. With constant stimulation the autonomous anabolism becomes equal to the allonomous katabolism, and a new condition of equilibrium at a lower potential is set up, which is called *allonomous equilibrium*. Upon removal of the stimulation autonomous anabolism will prevail for a time until autonomous equilibrium is again set up.

Hering's metabolic theory of the activities of living substances has been elaborated and put into more concrete form by Verworn[3]. It has had a considerable influence upon modern physiology. The fundamental principles have been adversely criticised by McDougall[4].

Applying Hering's hypotheses to the visual sensations[5], black, green

[1] Hering, *Sitz. d. Wiener Akad.* XCVIII. 3, 73, 1889.

[2] *Vorgänge der lebenden Materie*, Prag, 1888: translated in *Brain*, XX. 232, 1897

[3] *Allgemeine Physiologie*, Jena, 1901.

[4] *Brain*, XXVI. 153, 1903.

[5] Rivers, *Schäfer's Physiology*, p. 1112, 1900.

and blue excite assimilation, white, red and yellow dissimilation in the respective substances. Autonomous equilibrium in the black-white substance corresponds to "mean grey"; a descending change, or excess of dissimilation, causes a whiter sensation, an ascending change a blacker sensation. It is clearly a difficulty of the theory that autonomous equilibrium of the black-white substance causes a definite sensation.

In most kinds of stimulation of the retina all three substances are excited and the character of the sensation depends upon the relative amounts of action of each and their direction. All coloured lights, except the four primary colours, have three values or valencies, corresponding to their action on the three substances. The physiological value or "moment" of a light depends upon its physical value and also upon the condition of excitability of the visual mechanism.

Hering's explanation of the facts of adaptation and induction is lucidly summarised by Rivers[1] thus:

"The conditions of allonomous equilibrium are the basis of adaptation. When the black-white substance is completely adapted to the dark, it is in the condition of mean potential, corresponding to autonomous equilibrium. During the day the eye is always adapted to the surrounding illumination. The exact condition of adaptation must vary to some extent with the continual changes of external illumination to which one is normally exposed, but for practical purposes the condition of adaptation may be regarded as changing very slowly, and in any definite interval of time as corresponding to the mean illumination during that period. The white-black substance is then in a condition of allonomous equilibrium at a low potential. The brighter the illumination to which the eye is adapted, the lower is the potential at which equilibrium occurs. During the daytime the white-black substance is always to be regarded as in a condition of relatively low potential. The condition of allonomous equilibrium at a high potential is exceptional in the case of the black-white substance, owing to the fact that there is no external stimulus to anabolism. Black proper, according to Hering, only occurs under the influence of simultaneous or successive contrast; and the best example of allonomous equilibrium at relatively high potential, in the case of the black-white substance, occurs in Hering's simultaneous induction. If a black square on a white ground is fixed, the whole surface after a time is seen as a uniform grey. The black-white substance corresponding to the black square will have undergone

[1] *Loc. cit.* p. 1114.

an ascending change, that corresponding to the white a descending change, and the condition of uniform grey of the whole surface corresponds to equilibrium, which in the former case is at a high potential, and in the latter at a low potential. The potential of the former will only, however, be higher than that of the eye completely adapted to the dark, if the experiment is carried out with the eye adapted to the dark. In the case of the white-black substance it would seem as if allonomous equilibrium might in ordinary life take place at very different levels of potential, less than that of the autonomous condition; and that allonomous equilibrium, at a potential higher than that of the dark-adapted eye, only occurs under very exceptional conditions. This might be urged as an objection to the terminology adopted by Hering. It is due, however, to the absence of proper external stimuli to anabolism, and this difficulty does not occur in Hering's treatment of the chromatic substances.

"When the red-green and yellow-blue substances undergo the descending change, the corresponding sensations are red and yellow respectively. When they undergo the ascending change, they are green and blue respectively. The rapidity of the change (or the predominance of one process over the other) partly determines the weight of the particular element in question in the sensational complex, or, in other words, the purity or saturation of the colour; the other factor determining the purity being the degree of simultaneous stimulation of the other substances.

"The conditions of adaptation to coloured light may be readily referred to different conditions of allonomous equilibrium. When the chromatic substances are in a condition of equilibrium, they do not contribute to the quality of the sensational complex. They are equally in a condition of autonomous equilibrium, whether the eye has been wholly unstimulated or whether the stimulation has been exclusively by mixed colourless light. When the eye, after exposure to red light, no longer sees objects red, the red-green substance has become adapted to the light, and is in a condition of allonomous equilibrium, but at a low potential; on the other hand, in adaptation to green light, this substance is in allonomous equilibrium at high potential. With removal of the light to which the eye has become adapted, the complementary after-image colour is due to the autonomous change back to a condition of mean potential. After-images occupying limited portions of the visual field are due to local adaptation, and are explained on the same lines as general adaptation. The after-images seen with complete exclusion of light from the eye, which formed the great difficulty of the fatigue theory, are here referred to autonomous changes. Hering has formulated the nature of the active opposed change, which Plateau had previously suggested as the basis of after-image in distinction from the passive condition advocated by Fechner and Helmholtz.

"The absence of colour in all kinds of light at low intensity is, according to Hering, a function of the dark adaptation of the eye rather than of the low intensity of the stimulus, and is due to the fact that in the dark the white-black substance rises greatly in potential, while the chromatic substances remain in the condition of autonomous equilibrium. Consequently, the weight of the chromatic is very small compared with that of the colourless elements, and the former remain under the threshold."

Hering ascribes the positive after-image produced by closing the eyes after gazing at a bright object to exhaustion of assimilation during fixation. As a consequence all that remains is a feeble process of dissimilation due to internal stimulation. The fact that a positive after-image becomes negative if a surface, the brightness of which is greater than that of the positive after-image, is fixated, negatives this theory.

Simultaneous contrast is explained by Hering in the same manner as successive contrast. Allonomous katabolism in a retinal area acts as a stimulus to autonomous anabolism in that area, but the effect is not limited to the area. It extends to adjoining areas, being most marked at the junction of the reacting areas.

Hering attributes the bright halo, which under certain conditions surrounds complementary after-images (*v.* p. 101), to a process of successive induction. When, for example, a white square upon a black background has been for some time fixated, the assimilation process, which according to Hering has been especially active just beyond the contrasting edges of the white square, reaches such a height that finally a process of simultaneous induction is set up; assimilation gives way to dissimilation. When now the eyes are turned away from the white square, this dissimilation process continues. It is owing to this successive induction that a bright halo appears around the dark after-image of the white surface. And the dark after-image results from the contrasting assimilation process, which is evoked by the dissimilation process that produces the halo.

The dark halo, which under other conditions surrounds an

after-image, is attributed by Hering to the effect of simultaneous contrast. Thus, when a black square has been fixated upon a white background, the bright after-image of the former is produced by a subsequent process of assimilation which evokes a simultaneous dissimilation process in the adjoining retinal region.

Hering's theory thus gives a satisfactory explanation for the most important facts of temporal and spatial induction, and a less comprehensive explanation for the facts of adaptation. Hitherto the question of luminosity has been left out of account. In the earliest exposition of his theory (*Zur Lehre vom Lichtsinne*) Hering considered the luminosity of a visual sensation as wholly due to the black-white component. If this were true the four primary colours seen in a state of purity would be of equal brightness. This explanation of luminosity is untenable, and the "specific brightness of colours" has been substituted for it[1]. According to it the warm colours, red and yellow, which are due to dissimilation, increase the total brightness, whilst the cold colours, green and blue, which are due to assimilation, diminish it. Red and yellow therefore possess an inherent brightness (*Eigenhelligkeit*), green and blue an inherent darkness (*Eigendunkelheit*). "A toned colour may generally be regarded as made up of four fundamental components, two toned and two tone-free (white and black). It is only in colours of the tone of a primary that a single toned component is present. In any red-yellow colour, *e.g.* orange, we have therefore to distinguish three bright fundamental components (red, yellow, white) and one dark (black); in any green-blue on the other hand three dark (green, blue, black) and one bright (white). The red-blue and green-yellow colours would contain two bright and two dark fundamental components[2]." Hering deduces the following rules:

"If two colours of equal tone and equal purity differ in brightness it is due to the difference in their black-white components."

"Two colours of different tone may differ in brightness in spite of equal purity and equality of their black-white components."

"When the black-white components are equal, a yellow, red, or yellowish red colour is so much brighter, and a blue, green, or bluish green so much darker the more distinct the tone of the colour in comparison with the black-white components[3]."

The specific brightness of colours is held to explain the achromatic

[1] Hillebrand, *Sitz. d. Wiener Akad.* XCVIII. 3, 70, 1889.

[2] Hering, in *Graefe-Saemisch Handb. d. ges. Augenhlkde*, I. iii, xii, p. 61, 1905.

[3] *Loc. cit.*

scotopic luminosity of the spectrum. In dark adaptation the black-white substance is raised to a condition of high potential, while the chromatic substances are not appreciably affected. Hence with slight stimulation the coloured components remain below the threshold, and the curve of luminosity of the spectrum is that of the black-white substance. With increase of physical intensity the red and yellow add to the brightness, the green and blue detract from it, and consequently the point of maximum brightness shifts towards the red end of the spectrum.

This identification of the achromatic scotopic luminosity curve with the activity of the black-white substance has led many to the erroneous opinion that Hering regards the visual purple as being the black-white substance.

As Tschermak[1], a pupil of Hering, says: "The theory of the specific brightness of colours was propounded by Hering and Hillebrand to explain the unequal changes in brightness of different coloured lights in indirect vision and in dark adaptation (Purkinje's phenomenon), and therewith also to explain the different distribution of subjective brightness in the spectrum for the colour-seeing light-adapted eye as compared with the non-colour-seeing dark-adapted or totally colour-blind eye. The colour sensations, in general terms, may be said, according to Hering's theory, to be compounded of (*zusammengesetzt*) or analysable into (*zerlegbar*) a chromatic part and a non-chromatic grey part of different nature (brightness) determining the nuance, and of different relative magnitudes determining the saturation, so that so-called coloured lights bring about a double excitatory effect in the light-adapted eye, combining in addition to a colour valency also a white valency. The latter—in conjunction with the continuous processes which produce the intrinsic grey of the eye and with the contrast effects (increase of blackness) which are due to reciprocal action from the surrounding areas—determines the nature and relative magnitude of the non-chromatic sensation constituent, the grey components. The brightness of a colour sensation cannot be referred only to the brightness of its grey components, but must also depend upon the colour-components. Colour impressions, therefore, even with the greatest possible saturation, *i.e.*, with the greatest possible abstraction of the grey components, possess also 'brightness'—a quality which cannot be more closely defined and is only absent from absolute black."

The tone-free sensation derived from the mixture of two

[1] *Ergeb. d. Physiol.* I. 792, 1902.

complementary colours is due to the combined action on the black-white substance. With the correct intensities the anabolic effect of one colour neutralises the katabolic effect of the complementary on the chromatic substances, whilst their combined black and white valencies manifest themselves as white or grey.

The regional effects of stimulation of the retina are attributed to absence of response of one or of two of the substances. In the outermost zone only the black-white substance is stimulated; in the middle zone only the black-white and the blue-yellow substances are stimulated. Hess's experiments on the whole confirm this hypothesis (*v.* p. 70).

The fact, however, that the colour values diminish unequally with increasing excentricity, those red-wards of green (495 $\mu\mu$) most rapidly, those violet-wards most slowly, necessitates that the sensibility of the red-green substance diminishes more quickly than that of the yellow-blue. The total colour blindness of the extreme periphery affords another method of determining white valencies, but it gives totally different results from the values obtained with low intensities and dark adaptation. The latter can be explained as due to a different mechanism, the rods. If the normal peripheral values give the true white valencies then they must be different in the protanopic eye. But Hering considers both protanopia and deuteranopia as due to absence of the red-green substance (*vide infra*). This would be insufficient alone to account for the alteration in white valencies, which must depend upon change in the white-black substance.

As shown by Hess's experiments, confirmed by Baird and others, Hering's fundamental colours are those which, when passed from the periphery to the centre of the retina, develop sensations which undergo no change in hue. The red is a spectral red mixed with a small amount of blue. According to Hering spectral red has a not inconsiderable action on the yellow-blue substance. A mixture of spectral red and green produces the sensation of yellow because, although the red and green processes neutralise each other, the effect of the spectral red stimulus on the yellow-blue substance remains. It is noteworthy that the fundamental red and blue agree with those adopted by adherents of the Young-Helmholtz theory (p. 220).

Colour blindness is explained on the same principle. Thus, in total colour blindness only the black-white substance responds to stimulation by all lights. Hence the luminosity curve of the totally colour-blind should be the same as that of the achromatic scotopic eye, which is the case. On the other hand, the luminosity values of coloured lights should be the same for the totally colour-blind and for the extreme periphery of the retina, which is not the case (v. Kries) (*v.* p. 71). Dichromatic vision is attributed to insensitiveness or absence of the red-green substance, or of the yellow-blue substance (tritanopia).

The two classes of red-green blindness, protanopia and deuteranopia, offer serious objections to Hering's hypothesis, and these have not yet been overcome satisfactorily. His original explanation was that the differences were due to physical causes, especially macular pigmentation, and the same was applied by him to the variations in the Rayleigh match (anomalous trichromatic vision). Hering[1] very carefully examined Prof. Biedermann and Dr Singer, well-marked examples of individual variation in pigmentation. He regarded the former as relatively yellow-sighted, with little macular pigmentation, the latter as relatively blue-sighted, with greater pigmentation. He found Biedermann's matches agreed with deuteranopic matches, Singer's with protanopic. Experiments in which the subjects looked through the macular region of dried human retinae were held to give confirmatory results. His own extrafoveal matches compared with his foveal matches were of the same nature as the deuteranopic to the protanopic foveal matches. On the other hand Biedermann and Singer's peripheral matches did not agree, as should have been the case, but the differences were diminished in amount, and were attributed to absorption by the crystalline lenses.

v. Kries (*v.* p. 168), Abney and others have shown conclusively that the differences between protanopic and deuteranopic vision cannot be explained by any such physical causes.

Some of Hering's assumptions are difficult to accept. The absence of any direct evidence of anabolic processes acting as physiological stimuli has already been mentioned, but it is not a serious objection. The balance between assimilation and dissimilation is obviously comparable to the balance between excitation and inhibition[2], and analogies can be readily found in Sherrington's researches.

It is, however, a distinct objection that the theory demands twice as many variables as the results of colour-mixtures demand. Brunner[3] has attempted to eliminate this difficulty by ascribing to each substance a reversible photochemical process[4].

[1] *Lotos*, VI 142, 1885.

[2] Cf. Bernstein, *Naturwissenschaftliche Rundschau*, XXI. 497, 1906.

[3] *Arch. f. d. ges. Physiol.* CXXI. 370, 1908.

[4] See also Pauli, *Der kolloidale Zustand u. die Vorgänge in der lebendigen Substanz*, 1902. For examples of reversible photochemical processes, see Stobbe, *Ann. d. Chemie*, CCCLIX. 1, 1908.

Further, whilst red-green and yellow-blue show a null-point or absence of sensation, black-white shows no such null-point. Moreover the autonomous and allonomous equilibrium of the black-white are very different greys. In the light of the duplicity theory Hering's mean grey must be referred to a different mechanisn from the chromatic mechanism. Whilst long fixation of a toned light certainly tends to produce a tone-less sensation, the behaviour of black and white is quite different. Yet on no theory can the chromatic mechanism be deprived of its capacity to produce a tone-less sensation.

We have already stated that a given colour can be defined by its hue, its luminosity and its degree of saturation. Hering hypothecates three ratios: white to black, red to green, and yellow to blue. The question arises how the hue, the luminosity and the saturation are determined by these three ratios. Hering's early hypothesis that the luminosity was determined by the white to black ratio proved untenable and gave place to the specific brightness of colours. Similarly, the hue cannot be determined simply by the two chromatic ratios, since we have seen that the hue changes for most colours on admixture with white. These are serious difficulties attending acceptance of the theory, but it must be admitted that the relationship of luminosity to hue and saturation is not satisfactorily explained either by the three components or any other theory.

Hering's theory starts from the choice of psychologically pure colour sensations. If, however, spectral red and green are chosen and mixed they prove not to be complementary colours[1]. The colour adopted by Hering and his followers as fundamental red is a distinctly carmine or bluish-red (*v.* p. 258). Psychological analysis, however, does not afford a very secure foundation for the determination of the purity or simplicity of a colour sensation[2]. Most people would say that green is not a simple sensation, doubtless owing to experience derived from the mixture of pigments. On the other hand, most people would agree that yellow is a simple sensation, and this assumption is a necessary part of Hering's theory. Yet there are many arguments, apart from those derived from colour mixtures and fatigue already discussed, against such a view. McDougall[3] brings forward the following. (1) If patches of red and green light be thrown upon one area of one retina, they may under suitable conditions show the phenomenon of struggle as well as of fusion, *i.e.*, at one moment they may appear as yellow, at another

[1] Ladd-Franklin, *Psychol. Rev.* VIII.

[2] See Section I. Chap. III.

[3] *Mind*, X. N.S. 380. 1901.

the red or the green may alone affect consciousness, thus proving that the actions of the red and green rays on the retina are not mentally antagonistic or destructive, but that they proceed side by side in the one area of the retina. (2) On fixation of a bright yellow light it becomes after a few seconds a bright pure red or a bright pure green or shows struggle of red and green. (3) In the after-image of very bright light, whether white, or yellow, or of other colour, yellow never appears except as an incident in the struggle between red and green, just as purple occurs as an incident in the struggle of red and blue: it never appears as do red, green, and blue, forming one of the phases of constant colour of the recurring cycle, red, green, blue, red, green, blue (*v.* p. 111). (4) On diminishing the illumination of a patch of yellow after fixating it for 30 secs. or more, it usually becomes red unless the period of fixation has been considerably prolonged, when it usually becomes blue. (5) The after-image of bright yellow light may be yellow in the first phase, but this yellow always resolves itself into green struggling upon red as in the case of an initial yellow phase following bright white light. In the after-image of less bright yellow light blue usually appears, but red and green usually predominate. In fact "it is impossible to determine from the character of a sensation that the physiological process underlying it is simple and that the sensation is not the result of psychical fusion of the effects on consciousness of two or more separate physiological processes."

Although the theory of opponent colours offers an easily comprehensible explanation of the most prominent facts of induction, both successive and simultaneous, it is incapable of accounting for many other facts of the same nature. McDougall[1] brings forward the following formidable list.

(1) The occurrence of the sense of absolute darkness or blackness in the absence of any stimulation of white light which could produce it by simultaneous or successive contrast. If a dull or moderately bright patch of white or coloured light on a dark ground is fixated very steadily it will suddenly disappear. If the patch be upon a background not quite dark, but feebly illuminated, it happens not infrequently that the whole field of vision disappears, leaving a sense of complete and extreme darkness which is more complete than is experienced on excluding all light from the eyes. This "complete fading" occurs more readily if accommodation is relaxed.

[1] *Loc. cit.*

(2) Simultaneously induced light appearing:

(*a*) on a ground that has shown no previous contrast effect;

(*b*) almost or quite as bright as the inducing light;

(*c*) failing to appear on a ground on which a marked contrast is produced.

(3) Binocular contrast, whether of white or coloured light.

(4) Binocular fusion of complementary colours to give a white sensation.

(3) and (4) are only to be reconciled to the theory of opponent colours on the assumption, in the face of strong evidence to the contrary, that the cerebral areas for the two eyes are identical.

(5) Certain features of uniocular contrast:

(*a*) the total inhibition of a patch of colour by bright white light falling on an area of the retina at some distance from that affected by the coloured light;

(*b*) the inhibition of colour of low saturation by a white ground;

(*c*) the fact that contrast only appears as a modification of an existing sensation.

(6) Positive after-images in general:

(*a*) the phenomena of fading of after-images, especially of white light, with its recurring cycle of phases of pure and highly saturated red, green, and blue (*v.* p. 111);

(*b*) the fact that fixation of white light is invariably followed by an after-image brighter than the ground, if the conditions that lead to the production of a relatively bright halo are avoided;

(*c*) The same-coloured initial phase of the after-image of all very bright coloured lights (*v.* p. 102);

(*d*) the frequent appearance of a same-coloured phase in the after-image of less bright coloured lights (*v.* p. 102).

(7) The variety of colours that may appear in the after-image of any light save the dullest that will give any after-image, *e.g.*, pure blue phases in the after-image of red light.

(8) The array of facts indicating that the yellow sensation is due to psychical fusion of red and green (*v.* p. 260).

(9) The reversal of the colour of a fixated patch by addition of white light.

(10). The reversal of the colour of a patch of light during simple prolonged fixation.

(11) The appearance of colours of fair saturation during simple fixation of bright white light.

(12) The uniocular struggle of complementary colours during which they fuse at moments to give white and at other moments appear separately in consciousness.

(13) The fact that a white image, produced by uniocular fusion of two complementary colours, may be followed by an after-image, the character of which proves that the rays of each colour have produced throughout the appropriate retino-cerebral colour-systems their specific effects, and that therefore there has been no mutual destruction or interference of their physiological effects. (See McDougall's Theory in Section V.)

CHAPTER II

RESEARCHES BASED UPON THE THEORY

We have already, in Part I, discussed many of the researches which were inspired by Hering and his theory. Of these the most noteworthy are those referred to under the names of Hering, Hess, and Tschermak. They deal chiefly with the equivalence of colour equations under different conditions,—adaptation, area and region of retina stimulated, etc.—and with the facts of temporal and spatial induction. Those devoted to colour mixtures have been largely polemical and directed to controvert the statements of adherents of the duplicity theory or of the Young-Helmholtz theory.

Hering's theory affords an explanation of the general facts of successive contrast. If for example, the eye is stimulated with blue light, allonomous anabolism is set up in the yellow-blue substance, and a large amount of the substance is formed. If now yellow light stimulates the retina katabolism is set up in this much increased material and the resulting sensation is much greater than without previous stimulation. The abnormal saturation of the complementary to the stimulating colour is thus explained. A positive after-image is explained by a continuation for a certain period of the anabolic or katabolic process after the stimulus has been withdrawn.

v. Kries, however, pointed out that the theory fails to explain certain details adequately. Thus, since stimulation with colourless light does not act upon the chromatic substances it was to be expected that after previous stimulation with white light the same quantities of coloured light would be required on both the stimulated and resting areas to produce a colour-match. He found that it was not the case. Hering[1] made many objections to v. Kries's experiments and explained away his results (*v.* p. 108). He appears to hold that whilst previous stimulation with white does not affect colour valency, chromatic stimulation markedly affects white valency. As Greenwood points out[2], Hering's hypothesis becomes unsatisfactory by multiplying its detailed sub-hypotheses.

On simultaneous contrast Hering himself has done much work and has been the means of initiating more. The researches of Hess and Pretori have already been discussed. Those of Pretori and Sachs[3] on colour contrast are scarcely comprehensible except in terms of the theory and may now be mentioned. These authors endeavoured to discover the quantitative relations underlying colour contrast. According to Hering toned lights possess both colour and white valencies. In addition to these exogenous valencies there is an endogenous black valency dependent upon autonomous processes and manifesting itself in the intrinsic grey of the resting eye. There exists therefore between a coloured "contrast-exciting" (*kontrasterregend*) and a colourless "contrast-responding" (*kontrasterleidend*) field besides the colour contrast also a colourless brightness contrast so long as the white valency of the contrast-responding field is not exactly equal to the black induction due to the white valency of the contrast-exciting field. The saturation of the contrast colour depends therefore upon the relationship of the colour contrast to the simultaneous colourless contrast. Hering[4] has demonstrated the disturbing influence of simultaneous brightness contrast on colour contrast by special experiments.

Pretori and Sachs used a rotating disc with variable sectors. Three sets of circular papers were mounted concentrically on the disc. The diameters of the three sets were : upper 8 cm., middle 11·4 cm., lower 19·6 cm. ; so that the middle set formed a ring 17 mm. in breadth and

[1] *Arch. f. d. ges. Physiol.* XCIV. 533, 1903.
[2] *Physiology of the Special Senses*, p. 200.
[3] *Arch. f. d. ges. Physiol.* LX. 71, 1895.
[4] *Loc. cit.* XLI. 27, 1887.

constituted the contrast-responding field. The inner circle (upper set) and outer ring (lower set) always had the same sectors and together constituted the contrast-exciting field. If the exciting field was red, for example, and the responding ring black, the black appeared reddish[1]. If a white sector was introduced into the responding field the red disappeared, and if the white sector was increased in size the grey ring became tinged with the contrast colour, green. By further adding a suitable red sector to the responding field the contrast green could be counteracted. The size of the red sector afforded a measure of the contrast effect. If the red sector in the responding field was increased by 10° each time from zero to 120°, the white and black sectors being altered suitably to eliminate the contrast colour, it was found that with a constant coloured exciting field the grey responding field remained grey when its red and white valencies increased proportionately.

The contrast-exciting field was then varied in three ways: (1) the colour valency was changed while the white valency was kept constant; (2) the white valency was changed while the colour valency was kept constant; (3) both colour and white valencies were changed, but the ratio between them was kept constant.

(1) In the contrast-exciting field there were a coloured sector and sectors of white and black such that the grey produced by rotation looked exactly like the colour when seen by achromatic scotopic vision. In the contrast-responding field a definite grey made up of black and white sectors was used and a coloured sector was introduced until the initial contrast colour was eliminated. In the experiments the coloured sector in the exciting field was gradually increased; that in the responding field was kept constant; the contrast colour was eliminated by gradually increasing the white sector from zero. It was found that with constant white valency of the contrast-exciting field (and therefore constant black induction due to it), combined with increase of colour valency, the same amount of colour contrast is caused by a simply proportional diminution of white valency in the contrast-responding field. If therefore the white valency of the responding field is kept constant the contrast effect increases proportionally to the increase in colour valency. If the exciting light is kept constant and the white valency of the responding field increased from zero the saturation of the contrast colour increases up to a certain optimum value.

(2) In the contrast-exciting field the coloured sector was kept constant and the black-white sectors varied. In the contrast-responding

[1] Cf. v. Helmholtz, 1st ed. p. 400.

field the coloured sector for eliminating initial contrast was kept constant and the white gradually increased from zero until the contrast colour was eliminated. It was found that with constant colour valency of the exciting field, combined with increase in the white valency (and therefore increase of black induction due to it), the same amount of colour contrast is caused by a simply proportional increase of white valency in the responding field. Increase of colourless contrast therefore proportionally diminishes the colour contrast.

(3) In the contrast-exciting field the coloured sector and the white sector were increased in such a manner that the colour valency and the white valency increased in the same proportions. In the colour-responding field the coloured sector for eliminating initial contrast was kept constant and the white sector gradually increased from zero until the contrast colour was eliminated. It was found that with proportional increase of colour valency and white valency in the exciting field there was generally no increase in contrast, but in some experiments the contrast effect increased nearly proportionally to the intensity of the contrast-exciting mixture up to a certain optimum value.

With regard to colour blindness Hering[1] in 1885 examined a series of cases of anomalous trichromats as to their colour mixtures with rotating discs. He found that they could be divided into two groups, one group making the luminosity match of spectral red (660 $\mu\mu$) to spectral blue (447 $\mu\mu$) as 1·15 : 1, the other as 7 : 1. From his observations he called the first group, *i.e.* partial deuteranopes, relatively yellow-sighted; the second group, *i.e.* partial protanopes, relatively blue-sighted. Since colour equations are purely relative no exception can be taken to this nomenclature. He found the position of his fundamental green in the spectrum to differ in the two classes, for the first a relatively longer wave-length, for the seond a relatively shorter. For colourless mixtures of spectral red and blue-green, or yellow-green and violet, or to a less extent yellow and blue, the relatively yellow-sighted required a larger amount of the short wave-length component. Similarly they required more green for a match of spectral yellow with a red and yellow-green mixture, or of greenish-yellow with an orange and yellow-green mixture. He found the results inconclusive with the blue-sighted owing to too great differences of saturation. There was no typical difference in the matches of blue with a green and violet mixture. Similar, though less marked, differences of the same nature were found in peripheral matches by Biedermann (yellow-sighted) and Singer (blue-sighted). The

[1] *Lotos*, N. F. VI. 1885.

relatively yellow-sighted saw farther to the red end of the spectrum than the blue-sighted, and the violet end was less saturated to them. The yellow-sighted appeared to have more sensitive chromatic substances than the blue-sighted.

Hering compared the sensations of the two types of "red-green" blindness, *i.e.*, protanopes and deuteranopes, with those of the anomalous cases. He showed that the red-green blind with unshortened spectrum (deuteranopes) were analogous to the yellow-sighted in their grey matches. Similarly the red-green blind with shortened spectrum (protanopes) were analogous to the blue-sighted[1]. The colourless green of the neutral point, matched with a red-violet mixture, required a greater intensity of the green in the so-called green-blind than in the so-called red-blind. Hering specially recommends this match for statistical purposes, but unfortunately it is much vitiated by pigmentary absorption. Another typical difference was the greater luminosity of the red end of the spectrum for the so-called green-blind, the red-blind requiring a much darker grey luminosity-match. These and other effects were attributed to a weaker blue sensation in comparison with the white sensation in the red-blind as compared with the green-blind. Similar differences were found in peripheral vision. It will be noticed that Hering's researches confirmed those of König and other observers, but his interpretations are different.

Hering's researches on the totally colour-blind[2] first proved the identity of their luminosity curve with that of the normal dark-adapted eye for low intensities. He regarded this fact as strong confirmation of his estimates of the white valencies of lights for the dark-adapted eye. He also found that the sensitiveness of the totally colour-blind eye for slight differences of luminosity was the same as that of the normal achromatic scotopic eye. Hess and Hering[3] and their followers have strenuously opposed the view that the totally colour-blind have a central scotoma, but as we have seen, too much stress has been laid upon the negative evidence.

We have seen (*v.* p. 256) that Hering has attempted to explain the differences of the photopic and achromatic scotopic luminosity curves by the theory of the specific brightness of colours. Tschermak[4] does

[1] Cf. Rose, *Arch f. Ophth.* VII. 2, 72. 1861.

[2] Hering and Hillebrand, *Sitz. d. Wiener Akad.* XCVIII. 70, 1889; Hering, *Arch. f. d. ges. Physiol.* XLIX. 563, 1891.

[3] *Arch. f. d. ges. Physiol.* LXXI. 105, 1898.

[4] *Ibid.* LXX. 297, 1898; LXXXII. 559, 1900.

not think that this theory applies to the differences of luminosity observed in various colourless mixtures in passing from parafoveal to peripheral vision or on changing the condition of adaptation of the eye. He regards these changes as functions of the physical stimuli or wave-lengths of the light, not of their physiological valencies. He found that in the normal photopic eye the white valencies of different lights change unequally in passing from the centre to the periphery, as well as at the same site with dark adaptation. He therefore concludes that the white valencies of all lights change under different conditions. They increase for the normal and the colour-blind eye in passing from light to dark adaptation. In the normal this change is unequal, in that the white valencies of the long wave-length lights increase relatively less than those of the short wave-length lights. With relative yellow-sightedness this adaptative change of the white valencies is more pronounced than with relative blue-sightedness. The two types of red-green blind persons show analogous changes. In typical totally colour-blind people there is a change in the absolute white valencies, but none in their relative values.

These and the regional changes Tschermak attributes to changes "in the photo-chemical stimulus-intermediaries in the absorption apparatus of the visual organ." One of the photo-chemical white substances may be the visual purple and its accumulation during protection of the eye from light may underlie the increased excitability of peripheral parts of the retina. Thus, change in concentration of an elective absorbing substance alters the absorption equivalents, and might be expected to act in the opposite sense to the Purkinje phenomenon, a view which has been adopted by v. Kries[1] (*v.* p. 206).

Tschermak[2] indeed considers the theory of the specific brightness of colours insecurely founded (*nicht hinlänglich begrundet*), chiefly on the grounds of the supposed unequal summation of luminosities in mixtures. Thus Hering[3] mixed the lights from a red and a green glass of the same subjective brightness, and found that half the quantity of the mixed light was darker than either of the components alone. Similar results were obtained with complementary colours, thus agreeing with Ewald and Kühne's results[4]. Donders[5] obtained similar results with

[1] *Ztsch. f. Psychol. u. Physiol. d. Sinnesorg.* XXIX. 81, 1902.
[2] *Ergeb. d. Physiol.* I. 2, 797, 1902.
[3] *Lotos*, N. F. II. 31, 1882; VI. 57, 1885.
[4] *Untersuch. a. d. physiol. Inst. zu Heidelberg*, I. 153, 208, 1878.
[5] *Arch f. Ophth.* XXX. 1, 15, 1884.

the Rayleigh mixture. These experiments, however, require confirmation by more trustworthy methods of heterochromatic photometry.

Whilst the researches of Hering and his school have contributed many facts of value to our knowledge of colour vision, especially in the domain of induction, one cannot help being struck by the fact that they have led to far-reaching modifications and increased complexity in the theory itself.

SECTION V

OTHER THEORIES

I. Donders' Theory

Donders[1] accepted the principle of three "fundamental" colours, derived from Young and v. Helmholtz, and later elaborated by König and others. He also accepted four "simple" colour-sensations on psychological grounds,—red, yellow, green and blue. He further accepted the absolute correspondence of psychical and physical elements in Fechner's sense, that they may be compared to the concave and convex sides of the same curve. He was thus led, with Mach and Hering, to postulate four corresponding specific processes, the sensations of white and black excluded.

Donders placed the seat of these processes in the brain. The peripheral or retinal processes are trichromatic, the stimuli acting upon the three mechanisms of the "fundamental" sensations. Here each process acts upon a single form-element. In the cerebral centres more than one process can act upon the same element. From the combined action of two colours a third, containing none of the characteristics of either, can arise, *e.g.*, yellow from red and green, so that from two processes a third, *sui generis*, is evolved.

The processes may be regarded as chemical dissociations. Complete dissociation of the molecules gives rise to the sensation of white. It must be complete because the sensation continues unchanged and does not dispose to secondary sensations; this is the case with white only. Restoration and dissociation occur somewhat as described in Hering's theory.

The sensations of the "simple" colours are attributed to partial dissociation of the same molecules. In opposition to white they call

[1] *Arch. f. Ophth.* XXVII. 1, 155, 1881.

forth the complementaries, which process once begun increases in strength; hence the loss of saturation of colours on prolonged fixation. The primary, partial dissociation leaves a residuum of molecules which undergo secondary dissociation, giving rise to the complementary sensation. The residual molecules gradually dissociate spontaneously, without adequate stimulation, and this process increases more and more until there is equilibrium of direct and indirect dissociation, giving rise to the neutral sensation. If the eye is then stimulated with white light, the complementaries become more pronounced until, with the destruction of the residual molecules, equilibrium is re-established.

Donders thus introduced the ideas of chemical dissociation and separation of the peripheral and central processes, both of which have been further elaborated by later theorists.

II. Ladd-Franklin's Theory

Mrs Ladd-Franklin[1] propounded the following theory.

In the earliest stage of its development the visual sense consisted only in the sensation of grey. The term "grey" is used to express the whole series of black-white sensations. This sensation of grey was brought about by the action upon the retinal nerve-endings of a chemical substance set free by means of the decomposition of a certain kind of molecule, the grey molecule. This molecule is composed of an outer range of atoms, somewhat loosely attached to a firmer inner core, and having various different periods of vibration. The decomposition of this molecule consists in the tearing off of its outer portion, which then becomes the exciter of the nerve-endings and the immediate cause of the sensation of grey. The tearing off is brought about by the ether vibrations of the entire visible part of the spectrum, but in the greatest amount by those near the middle part, as is shown by the sensations of the totally colour-blind.

In the course of the development of the colour-sense some of the grey molecules become differentiated into colour-molecules in the following manner. The atoms of the outer range segregate themselves into three groups or pairs of groups at right angles to each other and having three different average velocities. The adaptation between the present structure of the retina (as regards colour) and the constitution of physical light consists in the fact that the mean vibration periods of

[1] *Ztsch. f. Psychol. u. Physiol. d. Sinnesorg.* IV. 211, 1893; *Mind*, N. S. II. 473, 1893.

the atoms of each group are synchronous with, and probably submultiples of certain vibration periods of the ether, *i.e.*, the vibration periods of the three fundamental colour-tones. Hence, when light of a fundamental colour-tone, *e.g.*, green, falls on the retina it will have the effect of tearing off from a large number of molecules those atom-groups whose periodicity is such as to render them particularly exposed to its shocks, and hence that special substance will be set free which is the exciter of the sensation of green.

When the wave-length of the light which falls on the retina is anywhere between the wave-lengths of two fundamental colour-tones—for example, blue and green—then a certain number of molecules lose their blue constituents and a certain number their green constituents, and the resulting sensation is a mixture of green and blue. This fact explains why we are unable to distinguish between a single intermediate wave-length and the appropriate mixture of two out-lying wave-lengths.

There will be certain mixtures of objective light which will set free all three kinds of nerve-exciting substances in equal amounts. These three substances, however, are the chemical constituents of the exciter of the grey sensation. Hence, when they are present in the right amount they recombine to form that substance and the sensation produced is exactly the same as that caused by the decomposition of the grey molecules.

There are five instances in which we are incapable of receiving any sensation but that of grey. In all, the grey molecule is alone decomposed. Thus in the peripheral totally colour-blind zone of the retina the differentiation of the grey molecule into colour-molecules has not taken place. Similarly, total colour blindness is an example of atavism, the grey molecules remaining undifferentiated. When such small areas of the retina are stimulated, or areas are stimulated with light of such weak intensity, that no colour-sensation is aroused it is to be concluded that the colour-molecules are not decomposed in sufficient quantity. When the stimulus is so intense that the colour-sensation is blotted out, it is to be supposed that the colour-molecules have become exhausted sooner than the grey, or that a strong energy of ether vibrations affects all the colour constituents equally without reference to their periodicity. In all these cases the important feature is the capacity of the substance which excites the sensation of grey for independent existence.

Mrs Ladd-Franklin holds that the theory explains not only the facts of colour-mixture, but also after-images and simultaneous contrast. Thus, in her own words: " When a red light, say, has fallen for some time upon the retina a large number of molecules have lost their red constituents—they have become partly mutilated molecules. But in this condition they are extremely unstable; they gradually go to pieces completely, and the setting free of their remaining constituents, the blue and the green producing parts of the molecules, causes a sensation of blue-green. The red sensation, therefore, in the case of careful fixation, becomes paler and paler; if the objective illumination is weakened, it may even be overpowered by the blue-green sensation; and if the eyes are closed, the blue-green sensation alone remains after a few seconds and continues until the injured molecules have all become completely destroyed. Since, as is well-known, the circulation of the retina is extremely rapid, the half mutilated molecules are in large numbers dragged across the border of the original image and there their complete destruction causes the phenomenon of simultaneous contrast."

The facts of scotopic vision are explained by the theory on the view that the grey substance is present in the rods, which subserve vision at low intensities, whilst the differentiated material is present in the cones, which subserve colour-vision and vision at higher intensities. A novel suggestion is that the grey substance in the rods is responsible for the change in the luminosity curve at higher intensities, its decomposition undergoing change as the intensity increases.

The theory is held to offer a satisfactory explanation of the relative saturation of colours in the spectrum. The number of molecules decomposed by a given light depends on the closeness of the coincidence of the vibration periods. For wave-lengths half-way between those of two fundamental colour-tones this coincidence will be very slight, and hence the number of molecules decomposed will be small, so that the resulting colour-tone is very little saturated. Green is less saturated than red and blue because the grey substance is most decomposed by lights of this region of the spectrum.

It also explains the relative sensitiveness of the eye to change of colour per change of wave-length, which is greater in the yellow and blue-green than anywhere else (Part I, Section II, Chap. II). Where the number of colour-molecules decomposed by a light of given wave-length is relatively small a given amount of change of wave-length is necessarily more effective in changing the quality of the sensation.

Mrs Ladd-Franklin severely criticises both the Young-Helmholtz and Hering theories, yet it must be admitted that her theory is a legitimate offspring of the three-components theory. It perhaps owes more than she would readily admit to Donders' theory.

v. Kries[1] raises the fundamental objection that the complete decomposition of the differentiated molecule gives rise to the same sensation as the undifferentiated. This objection may be surmounted by supposing that the differentiated molecule still retains a core or substratum of undifferentiated atoms, which are in a more stable condition than the rest of the differentiated molecule.

Whilst the explanation of after-images may pass muster, that of simultaneous contrast is unsatisfactory. We know of no "retinal circulation" which is so rapid as to account for the phenomena. It would have to be almost instantaneous and it is impossible on physical grounds to conceive of a mechanism so potent as to transfer molecules so instantaneously through a finite distance. The reciprocal action of retinal areas must be explained on some more plausible grounds.

The suggestion that both the scotopic and photopic luminosities are to be attributed to the rods and their contained grey substance is attractive, but the fact that the luminosity curve of the totally colour-blind remains the same as the normal achromatic scotopic curve even when the intensities of the incident light are raised far above the scotopic level is against the conjecture.

III. McDougall's Theory

McDougall[2] strongly supports the three-components theory of colour vision. He prefers to term it Young's theory rather than the Young-Helmholtz theory, because he considers that v. Helmholtz did it scant service by his far-fetched psychological explanations of the facts of induction.

McDougall's views of colour vision are part of a general theory of psycho-physical processes[3]. He defines a psychological process as that part of the total process of physiological excitation within the nervous system which stands in a relation of immediate interaction with psychical process or consciousness. He thus rejects the hypothesis of psycho-physical parallelism held by Fechner, G. E. Müller and others. He adduces strong evidence derived from anatomy, physiology and psychology in favour of the view that the seat of the psycho-physical process is in the synapses or arborisations at the sites of contact of nerve cells or neurones. Many of his arguments on this part of his theory receive

[1] In Nagel's *Handb. d. Physiol. d. Menschen*, p. 277.
[2] *Mind*, x. N.S. 52, 210, 347, 1901.
[3] *Brain*. xxiv. 577, 1901: xxvi. 153, 1903.

considerable support from Sherrington's researches[1]. Reflex action as compared with the conduction of an impulse along a nerve, is characterised by "lost time" or appreciable delay. Sherrington has brought forward abundant evidence to show that the delay is due to resistance to the passage of the impulses and that the resistance probably has its seat in the synapses. It is further probable that in the lower levels of the nervous system, *e.g.*, in the spinal cord, where the reflex paths are paths of high degree of constancy of function, the synapses are very thoroughly organised, *i.e.*, their degree of resistance has been reduced to a minimum by frequent repetition of the particular reflex action in the individual and in the race, while in the higher parts of the nervous system the resistance, and therefore the loss of time, occasioned by the synapses is greater in the inverse order of their degree of organisation.

Repeated stimulation causes fatigue, which also probably is due to changes occurring in the synapses. This is the explanation of the "complete fading" of retinal images under certain conditions (*v.* p. 261). Complete fading may be brought about with greater ease by the simultaneous effect of a second stimulus. Thus, if a small white patch *a* is fixated for 15 secs. or more, and then a second similar patch *b* is suddenly exposed, so that the image of *b* falls on another part of the same retina or on a non-corresponding part of the other retina, *a* will usually disappear from consciousness at once, remain absent several seconds, and then return suddenly, appearing equally bright with *b*. McDougall has described numerous instances of these "mutual inhibitions" of visual images, amongst which those of binocular and uniocular struggle are the most striking. Thus, if a bright white surface is fixated with a red glass before one eye and a blue glass before the other, the surface usually appears alternately red and blue. If the white surface is less bright there is greater tendency for the colour impressions to fuse[2]. This alternation is most easily explained by supposing that one excitation ceases to pass through the neurones of the visual cortex, and that the factor which determines the regular alternation of the two images is the rapidly oncoming and rapidly disappearing fatigue of the synapses of the cortex.

In support of this view we have the following facts: (1) A very similar alternation in consciousness, *i.e.*, alternate predominance of an image and inhibition of it by another image, may occur in the case of two after-images formed on adjacent areas of one retina; (2) if, when a red

[1] See *The Integrative Action of the Nervous System*, London, 1906.

[2] Cf. Rivers, *Camb. Phil. Soc.* VIII.

field is presented to one eye and a blue field to the corresponding area of the other eye, one eye be closed or covered for a brief period—one second will suffice—the colour presented to that eye always predominates over and inhibits the colour presented to the other eye as soon as the eye is uncovered, *i.e.*, the rested tract predominates over the relatively fatigued tract, even if the period of rest be not more than one second; (3) if by any one of several devices, as, for example, slight movements of objects in the field (the drawing of a hair across the field a little before the eye will suffice), the predominance of one field, say the red field, be prolonged, the blue field of the other eye tends more and more strongly to assert itself until, no matter how vigorous the movements in the red field, the blue predominates and the red field disappears from consciousness; all such devices merely direct attention to the one field, *i.e.*, they cause the excitation of the one cortical conduction-path to be reinforced by the activity of higher levels, and we see that as the excitation continues to pass through this path the resistance of the path increases until, in spite of such reinforcement, it yields to the inhibitory influence of the other rested tract; (4) if, accommodation being relaxed, a white field be presented to the right eye and a much less bright white or grey field to the corresponding area of the left eye, and if the left eye be covered over for some ten to fifteen seconds, while the right eye continues to fixate the brighter field, then on uncovering the left eye the bright image of the right eye yields to the much less bright image of the left eye, and disappears from consciousness for some seconds. McDougall gives many examples of uniocular struggle[1].

So far as colour vision is concerned McDougall supplements the original Young theory by the addition of an independent white mechanism, the end organ of which is the rods. In other words he adopts the duplicity theory. It is a difficulty, even of these combined theories, that there is no place in them for a special black-exciting process. McDougall boldly accepts the view that such a process is unnecessary to explain the facts, and adduces cogent arguments in its favour[2]. The sensation of black, according to him, is experienced when "complete fading" occurs. The visual cortex is then at complete rest, as opposed to the condition of normal tone which manifests itself as the intrinsic light (*Eigenlicht*).

This combined theory therefore assumes a separate retino-cerebral apparatus or system for each of the primary or simple colour-affections, red, green, blue, and (scotopic) white. The next point of importance

[1] *Mind*, x. N.S. Sec. V. [2] Cf. also Ward, *Brit. Jl. of Psychol.* I. 407, 1905.

is the necessity for assuming that the cortical areas of the two eyes are separate, *i.e.*, that each retina contains the peripheral endings of the retino-cerebral nerve-fibres of its own set of four colour systems, and these are distinct from the four systems of the other retina. The view that the central connections of corresponding points of the two retinae are anatomically identical is untenable. It was rejected by v. Helmholtz[1] chiefly from a consideration of the influence of voluntary attention in effecting the predominance of one or other of two struggling fields. As already mentioned McDougall has shown that momentary stimulation of the retina by dim equally diffused light will bring back to consciousness after-images which have completely faded. This must be due to the second stimulus raising the excitability of the visual cortex, so that the feeble impulses coming from the retina are enabled to break down the resistance in these highest levels. Now, if the cortical areas of the two retinae were identical, when the after-image is formed on one retina only, the admission of dim light to either eye should be equally effective in reviving the faded after-image. But it is found that though it has a perceptible effect of this sort in both cases, that effect is very much slighter in degree, and ceases to be effective much more rapidly in the case of the eye in which there is no after-image. The slight effect of stimulating this eye shows that there is some close and sympathetic connection between the cortical areas of the two retinae, although they are not identical. McDougall represents the retino-cerebral systems demanded by the theory diagrammatically in Fig. 75.

It is to be noted that Hering's theory requires the same explanation of the cortical areas of the two eyes, with the greater complication of three pairs of colour-systems for each eye. If, however, the opponent metabolic processes are peripheral the theory then fails to explain the facts of binocular struggle with red and green lights and so on; and wherever the processes occur requires much modification to meet the case[2].

McDougall's experiments on the fading of after-images, already mentioned (*v.* p. 111), demonstrate the recurrence of colour-sensations attributable to four primary colour-systems. They further exhibit instances of uniocular struggle between the primary or simple colours. *Per contra*, experiments devised to exhibit uniocular struggle afford confirmatory examples of the spontaneous development of pure primary

[1] § 771, 3rd Ed. III. p. 407.
[2] Cf. G. E. Müller, *Ztsch. f. Psychol. u. Physiol. d. Sinnesorg.* XIV. § 32, 1897

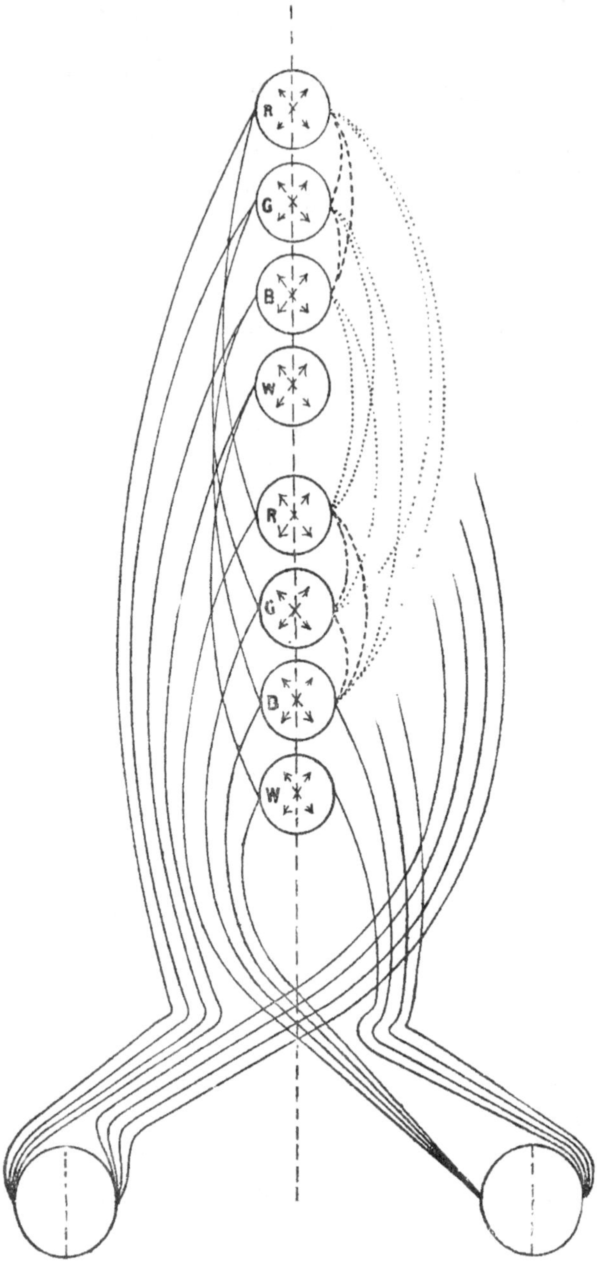

Fig. 75. Diagram representing the two retinae and the cortical centres connected with them. The upper four circles represent the cortical levels of the red, green, blue, and white systems connected with the left retina, the lower four those connected with the right retina. The broken line bisecting all the circles represents the purely anatomical separation of each centre into two halves lying in opposite cerebral hemispheres. The continuous lines on the left side represent the sympathetic relation between corresponding points of the two systems of similar function connected with the right and left retinae respectively. The dotted lines represent the antagonism between any point of any one colour-system of the one eye and the corresponding points of the other two colour-systems of the other eye. The broken lines represent the feebler antagonism between any point of any one colour-system of one eye and the corresponding points of the other two colour-systems of the same eye. The arrows radiating from the centre of each circle represent the antagonism between any point of the cortical level of any one of the systems and every other point of the same. (McDougall.)

colour sensations. These facts are strikingly in favour of the three-components theory.

Perhaps the greatest service which McDougall has done to the theory is to show that it can be made to give a reasonable explanation of the facts of induction. His theory of contrast was adumbrated by Rollet in 1867[1].

The darkening contrast effect exerted by a white area on adjoining grey areas may be attributed, as shown above, to the inhibitory effect of the more vigorous cortical processes excited by the white area on the feebler cortical processes excited by the grey areas. If the explanation be true, then by the theory it must also hold for colour-contrast. For (photopic) white being the resultant of simultaneous activity of the red, green, and blue colour-systems, inhibition of white by white must be expected to involve inhibition of red by red, green by green, and blue by blue. In the cortical level of each colour system the activity of any one part tends to inhibit the activity of all other parts, and when any one part is more intensely excited than the rest its activity does partially or completely inhibit that of all other parts of the cortical area of the same colour system (see Fig. 75). Suppose then that all parts of all three colour-systems are equally excited to a moderate degree, except that one small part of one system, *e.g.*, the red, is more highly excited. Then the activity of this more highly excited part of the red cortical area depresses that of the rest of the red cortical area, more especially that of the immediately surrounding parts, with the result that in the parts of the field surrounding the red patch the activity of the blue and green systems predominates over that of the red, and the grey ground appears blue-green. When the balance of the activities of the three cortical levels has once been turned in this way in favour of the blue and green systems, the predominance of the blue and green systems must be still further increased by the antagonism between the corresponding parts of the cortical areas of the three colour-systems, *i.e.*, the activity of the red cortical area must be still further depressed or inhibited by that of the blue and green areas. In favour of these views are the facts that coloured light on one retinal area can be inhibited by white light on another area and one of the constituents of the sensation of white can be inhibited by a patch of bright coloured light.

Simultaneous induction, in Hering's sense of the term (*v.* p. 125), is the appearance of the same colour around a patch of any colour when it has been steadily fixated for some time, generally 10 secs. or

[1] *Berichte d. Wiener Akad.* LV. 344, 424, 741, 1867.

more. It may appear on a surrounding grey ground in the absence of or as a sudden reversal of the contrast-colour. It is most readily induced on an intensely black background, a fact which militates strongly against Hering's explanation of it (*v.* p. 255). The longer fixation is continued the brighter the induced light becomes and the further it spreads away from the inducing patch of light over the ground. McDougall attributes simultaneous induction to retinal changes. The light rays decompose certain retinal mother substances. Thus red light sets free more of the red substance than of the blue and green substances. The substances diffuse into adjoining areas of the retina, and as the red substance is in excess its excitatory effect upon the nerve-endings of the red system manifests itself beyond that of the green and blue substances upon their respective systems. It is to be noted that in the phenomenon of simultaneous induction (in Hering's meaning of the term) there is time for such diffusion to occur[1]. The effects of these peripheral stimuli, which are regarded as the basis of simultaneous induction, may of course be abolished or altered by inhibitory effects in accordance with the principles suggested above as the basis of contrast.

The explanation of after-images, founded on the same principles, is as might be expected much more complicated. All after-images are primarily due to the persistence in the retina of substances set free in it by the action of the light rays on stored-up mother substances. These specific substances continue to act upon the retinal nerve-endings and thereby to be used up gradually. In the dark the relative intensity of the action of any one of the different specific substances is chiefly a function of the quantity of that substance present in unit area of the retina. The frequently recurring changes in the brightness and colour effects of after-images are, with the exception of the gradual diminution of intensity due to the using up of the substances, all determined by changes in the cortex and not by changes in the retina.

There are two stages in the chemical changes, (*a*) the setting free of the specific substances (red, green, blue, and (scotopic) white substances), (*b*) the excitation of the nerve-endings by the substances. Red light, for example, may be conceived to cause the activity of the red system to predominate in three ways: (1) by setting free the red substance in larger quantity than the blue and green substances while reinforcing the exciting action of all three equally; (2) by setting free the three substances in equal amounts while reinforcing the action of the red more than that of the blue and green substances; (3) by exerting a more

[1] Contrast Ladd-Franklin, p. 274; Edridge-Green, p. 297.

vigorous effect upon the red substance in both stages. Reasons are given for deciding in favour of the third possibility. That the red substance is set free in excess in the first stage is shown by the phenomenon of simultaneous induction. That red light exerts a greater action on the red substance in the second stage is shown by the predominance of red sensation over green and blue in spite of facts which show that the free green and blue substances become at least equal in quantity to the free red substance. These facts are: (1) the induced light, at first red, on prolonged fixation loses in saturation as it gains in brightness until it becomes white or slightly tinged with green; (2) the phenomenon of reversal of red light to green-blue or green during continued fixation, either on diminishing its brightness or on adding white light to it, or on simple prolonged fixation; (3) the predominance, sometimes complete, of the green and blue systems in the after-image of red light of medium brightness.

This gradual increase in the green and blue substance cannot be attributed to fatigue of the process of setting free the red substance, but if the red light is more selective on the retinal processes in the second stage, that of excitation of the nerve-fibres, it follows as a corollary. For, if, for example, the red, green, and blue substances are set free in the proportion 3 : 2 : 2 and are used up in the proportion 4 : 2 : 2, the green and blue substances must accumulate more rapidly. This purely hypothetical assumption explains complementary after-images and the various cases of the reversal of colour.

Though there is no fatigue in the retinal processes of the first stage, it occurs in the second stage. It accounts for the rapid fall in intensity of the sensation during the first few seconds when a patch of bright white light is fixated, and also for the fact that the after-image of white light is more vivid the shorter the period of fixation, but declines in brightness more rapidly. The more intense the light the more the first retinal process exceeds the second in activity. The preponderance of the retinal excitement of the red system over the excitement of the blue and green systems is probably slight, even when a sensation of red of good saturation is experienced. For owing to the mutual antagonism between corresponding areas of the cortex any predominance of the excitement of one system in the retina is greatly exaggerated in the cortex.

McDougall has shown that these principles can be made to explain all the phenomena of after-images without undue straining. He emphasises the importance of the part played by the cortex by the following facts: (1) the tendency for well-defined and homogeneous parts of a complex image, whether a direct image or an after-image, to undergo "complete fading" and to be revived in consciousness as independent wholes; (2) the fact that when two images are fixated successively and so as to fall partially upon the same area of one retina each forms an after-image distinct and separate from that of the other, so that the two after-images may appear simultaneously or alternately in consciousness; (3) when an after-image is projected upon a not too bright surface it is not always modified at once by the effects of the light from this surface, but may maintain itself in consciousness unaltered for a certain length of time. Fixation of a patch of light therefore throws the cortical areas affected into a state of preparedness to function again or to continue to function in the same way as during the action of the light. This tendency may override and obscure changes initiated in the retina.

Hence, it is not proper to say that an after-image has its seat either in the retina or in the brain; both retain an impress from the original stimulation, and though the persistence of the exciting substances in the retina is perhaps the more important element, yet the cortical impress plays a large part in determining the exact form in which the after-image shall appear.

McDougall's views on the evolution of the colour-sense are shown in the following extract[1].

"It will be generally admitted that if we try to form a conception of the course of development of the colour-processes we must begin by assuming the vision of the lower animals, in which vision is but little developed, to be monochromatic, *i.e.*, we must assume the visual sensations to be of one kind only, varying only in intensity or brightness; and we must suppose one kind of light sensation to be similar to our white or grey sensation or at least to stand to it in the relation of a direct ancestor. If we then seek the probable first step in the development of the colour-processes from this stage of simple grey-vision, we must, I think, assume that it consisted in a differentiation of the effects of the light of the warm and the cold ends of the spectrum; the rays of the cold end would begin to set free, in addition to a white-exciting substance, a substance that by the excitement of a concurrently differentiated retino-cerebral apparatus would add the sensation of blue to that of white; and in just the same way the rays of the warm end would begin to set free an additional substance that

[1] *Mind*, N.S. x. pp. 212–214, 1901.

by the excitement of a second concurrently differentiated retino-cerebral apparatus would add the sensation of yellow to that of white. If we then consider the state of a species in which the visual apparatus has achieved this degree of development we shall see that it would obviously be an advantageous arrangement that, when the retina was stimulated by white light, *i.e.*, by light containing rays of all wave-lengths, the two new colour-systems, the yellow and the blue, both being excited in addition to the white system, should have the sensation-elements determined by them fused in consciousness to white. This compound white sensation-element would then add itself to and so reinforce the sensation of white due to the excitement of the older white apparatus. For suppose that the yellow and blue sensations neutralised each other when the yellow and blue systems were excited together, this would leave a sensation of white but would involve a waste of the energy that, under the other arrangement, would go to reinforce the white sensation. Or suppose the third possibility, namely, that yellow and blue when excited together fused to give a new kind of sensation. Then stimulation by mixed light would result in a sensation compounded of white and this new yellow-blue sensation; the ancient and primitive sensation of pure white or grey would have been lost, it could never again be experienced, and in place of the three perfectly distinct kinds of sensation yellow and blue and white yielded by the first arrangement, there would be possible only two, yellow and blue, and a mixture, bluish-yellow. To illustrate this by an example—it is obvious that a species or a variety endowed with the sensations of red and blue and white, would in this respect have an advantage over one endowed with red and blue and purple only.

"Further, it is obvious that the original white apparatus would not be likely to undergo much further development if the yellow and blue systems developed in importance and in the intensity of the impression produced by them in consciousness, for they would yield when excited together a white sensation of correspondingly developed intensity.

"It seems not unnatural to suppose that the developing differentiation of the colour-sensibility of the retina should have proceeded outwards from the centre, the region of acutest vision, and the one that is most used. In the peripheral zone of the human retina we have then the perpetuation of the primitive monochromatic stage of development of the eye, while the very rarely occurring monochromatic eyes are cases of reversion to, or arrested development in, this remote ancestral condition. In the same way the zone of the human retina, stimulation of which causes the sensations of yellow and blue and white only, remains in that stage of development in which only the first step of differentiation has been effected and the frequent cases of bichromatic vision, in which yellow and blue and white seem to be the only sensations that can be aroused by stimulation of the retina, are cases of reversion to or arrested development in this more recent ancestral condition.

"If we try to picture the further evolution of the colour-sense, the process that would seem to be likely to give the best results, and therefore the one most likely to be effected by the factors that have controlled the origin and development of species, is a repetition of the process of differentiation such as gave rise to the blue and yellow systems, but occurring within either the blue or the yellow system. For reasons, which we can hardly hope to determine, this differentiation has proceeded in the yellow system. The light of the two ends of the warm half of the spectrum must be supposed to have begun to set free, within the retinal elements of the yellow apparatus, two different substances in addition to the yellow substance, and with these two new substances, the red and the green, we must assume the concurrent differentiation of the red and green retino-cerebral systems. Then just as it was obviously advantageous that yellow and blue sensation-elements, when excited together, should fuse to give white, so obviously it would have been advantageous that red and green sensations when excited together should fuse to give yellow, else the primitive white and the original yellow sensation would again be lost. As these two new colour-systems became developed in the retina from the fovea centralis outwards, the primitive yellow apparatus would lose its importance and would probably undergo atrophy in this central region of most highly developed colour sensibility, just as the primitive white apparatus has become lost in the very centre, the fovea centralis itself. That the primitive white apparatus remains functional throughout the rest of these parts of the retina in which the colour-systems are developed is probably due to its having assumed the special function of vision under dim illumination, while no analogous functioning has justified the continued existence of the primitive yellow system in the area of red and green sensibility."

IV. Schenck's Theory

Schenck's theory[1] is founded upon the Young-Helmholtz theory. From the psychological point of view each simple or pure light-sensation is held to depend upon an independent physiological process. The simple light-sensations are white, red, green, yellow and blue. Since all sensations can be synthesised out of red, green and blue, but not out of white or yellow and two other simple sensations, red, green and blue are the three fundamental sensations. Their physiological counterparts are three "visual substances."

The difficulty that white and yellow have no simple physiological counterparts is explained developmentally. In an earlier phase of development the photopic apparatus, the cones, contained only one visual substance, the stimulation of which gave the sensation white, and which was nearly allied to the scotopic visual substance of the rods.

The white substance first underwent a "panchromatising" change whereby it became more sensitive to lights of long wave-length. It next became differentiated into two substances, a yellow substance, specially sensitive to rays of long wave-length, and a blue substance, specially sensitive to rays of short wave-length. These substances retain the peculiarity of the mother-substance that when they are simultaneously stimulated with strengths which correspond to the effect of ordinary daylight they give rise to the sensation white.

Analogously the yellow substance became differentiated into a red and a green substance, which when equally and simultaneously stimulated arouse the sensation yellow.

These changes may be represented diagrammatically thus:

Regional Effects. I. In the photopic normal eye: (*a*) the centre of the retina is trichromatic, (*b*) the middle peripheral zone is red-green-blind, (*c*) the outer peripheral zone is totally colour-blind.

II. The limit of the red-green-blind zone is only relative: it extends further peripherally with increase of size, intensity, and saturation of the observed object.

III. Colour matches valid for the centre are valid for the periphery.

IV. Luminosity matches valid for the centre are valid for the periphery.

[1] *Arch. f. d. ges. Physiol.* CXVIII. 129, 1907.

Arguments from Regional Effects. I. For the completely developed colour sense only three visual substances are necessary, the red, the green, and the blue. For the red-green-blindness of the middle zone only two are necessary, the blue and the yellow. For the total colour blindness of the outermost zone only one is necessary, the white.

II. The three developmental phases of the visual substances increase from without towards the centre. W is maximal at the periphery and diminishes steadily towards the centre; B and Y are slight at the periphery, maximal in the middle zone and slight at the centre; R and G are minimal at the periphery and increase to a maximum at the centre.

III. The validity of colour matches for centre and periphery is associated with a reduction of sensation. Hence visual substances of the same nature are present throughout, though perhaps in smaller number in the periphery, *i.e.*, either (*a*) one or two of the visual substances are absent, or (*b*) all the visual substances are present but initiate a smaller number of sensations.

IV. The validity of luminosity matches for centre and periphery necessitates the presence of all the visual substances associated with a smaller number of sensations. If one visual substance were absent the spectral colour which specially stimulates it would appear darker in peripheral vision, which is not the case. In the middle zone, of the fundamental colour sensations only blue is present; red and green are replaced by yellow. Hence the red and green substances here give rise to a single sensation, yellow, and must be represented by the yellow substance. In the outer zone all three fundamental sensations are absent, and all three must be represented by the white substance. These deductions are legitimate because each pair of derivative substances together combine the peculiarities of the respective mother substances.

On this basis the theory may be extended. Each visual substance must be compounded of two functionally distinct parts, one for luminosity, the other for hue. The first part, which is first affected by the incident light, may be called the stimulus-receptor (*Reizempfänger*). The second part, which determines the nature and intensity of the aroused sensation, may be called the sensation-stimulator (*Empfindungserreger*). The amount of energy set free by the receptor determines the excitation of the stimulator and thus the luminosity of the resultant sensation.

In the fully developed colour-sense the receptor for long waves in the red substance is associated physiologically with the red stimulator only, the receptor for medium waves in the green substance with the green stimulator, and the receptor for short waves in the blue substance with the blue stimulator. That is, each receptor transfers its whole energy to the corresponding stimulator.

In the early developmental stages other associations are possible. In the totally colour-blind zone each receptor is associated with each stimulator, so that each receptor divides its stimulating energy between the three stimulators. Hence no matter what the stimulating light the resultant sensation is white. In the red-green-blind zone the short wave receptor is limited to the blue stimulator, whilst the two others are associated indiscriminately with the other two stimulators. Hence in this case the red and green stimulators always initiate the sensation of yellow.

It was suggested by Schaum that the receptors act as optical sensitisers, and by Richarz that they may be regarded as optical resonators.

Deuteranopia. This type of colour blindness shows the following characteristics:

I. It is a reduction-system from normal colour vision.

II. It agrees thus far with the red-green-blindness of the middle retinal zone that (1) affected people describe three sensations, white, yellow and blue, and (2) their sensations are the same in quality and nearly so in luminosity as the sensations of white, yellow, and blue in regional red-green-blindness.

III. It differs from regional red-green-blindness in that (1) it is also present on direct fixation, and (2) it is not relative, since increase of area, intensity, and saturation of the object never arouses the fully developed colour-sense.

Hence it is to be regarded as an arrested development, in which the second phase $\left(Y \begin{smallmatrix} \nearrow R \\ \searrow G \end{smallmatrix} \right)$ has not taken place.

The strongest arguments in favour of this view are the equivalence of colour matches for the normal and deuteranope (*v.* p. 170) and the almost complete identity of the normal and deuteranopic luminosity curves.

Protanopia is a reduction-system which differs from deuteranopia and normal colour vision in the difference of the luminosity curves. Lights of long wave-length have strikingly low stimulus values for the protanopes, whereas beyond 580 $\mu\mu$ violetwards the stimulus values are relatively higher than for deuteranopes and normals.

Hence protanopia is to be regarded as an arrested development in which a receptor is absent, and that receptor must be the one which is set in action by lights of long wave-length. Hence the receptor or resonator of the red substances is absent, whilst the stimulator is present.

Tritanopia offers difficulties to the theory, but is explained as due to the second developmental phase having reached a certain stage without the first having taken place.

Monochromatic Vision also offers special difficulties and is probably complex. Schenck distinguishes three types: (1) the peripheral total colour blindness of normals and deuteranopes; (2) the peripheral total colour blindness of protanopes; (3) scotopic total colour blindness. He concludes that (1) the white visual substance of the rods develops in such a manner as to become relatively more sensitive to rays of medium wave-length, thus producing the white substance of the protanopic cones; (2) from the protanopic cone white substance the normal peripheral cone white substance is developed by further differentiation, so that it becomes more sensitive to rays of long wave-length.

Complete monochromatic vision may be due to (1) pure rod-vision; (2) arrest of cone development at the rod stage (total colour blindness without central scotoma); (3) arrest of cone development at the protanopic peripheral cone stage (pathological cases); (4) arrest of cone development at the normal peripheral cone stage (the cases of Becker[1], Piper[2], Schöler and Uhthoff[3], Siemerling and König[4], and Pergens[5]).

Anomalous Trichromatic Systems. Partial deuteranopia is caused by the receptor for light of medium wave-length possessing an absolutely diminished sensitiveness, with relatively diminished sensitiveness for about 560 $\mu\mu$, and relatively increased sensitiveness for about 580 $\mu\mu$. Partial protanopia is caused by absence of the receptor for light of long wave-length and modification of the receptor for light of medium wave-length.

It will be noticed that this theory is essentially the Young-Helmholtz theory modified and elaborated so as to overcome certain difficulties.

[1] *Arch. f. Ophth.* XXV. 2. 205, 1879.

[2] *Ztsch. f. Psychol. u. Physiol. d. Sinnesorg.* XXXVIII. 155, 1905.

[3] *Beiträge z. Path. d. Sehnerven.* Berlin, 1884.

[4] *Arch. f. Psychiat. und Nervenkr.* XXI. 284, 1889; in König, p. 206.

[5] *Klin. Monatsbl. f. Augenhlk.* XL. 42, 46, 1902.

Its weakest feature is the failure common to the three-components theory and most of its variants to account satisfactorily for the facts of induction. These are presumably relegated to the central nervous organs as in the theory of zones. Schenck elaborates Ad. Fick's[1] views as to the peculiar position of yellow. He adopts Tschermak's division[2] of each visual substance into two parts, a stimulus-receptor or intermediary, and a sensation-stimulator.

The rod visual substance is the primitive visual substance: it possesses a receptor or resonator for light of short wave-length, and a slightly damped resonator for light of medium wave-length.

The development of the cone visual substance from the primitive rod substance is accompanied by increased damping of the resonator for light of medium wave-length, and also panchromatisation, *i.e.*, development of a resonator for light of long wave-length.

As regards the sensation stimulators there is a white stimulator in the rods, and there are red, green, and blue stimulators in the cones.

In the lowest developmental phase of the cones all the resonator and all the stimulator molecules are intermingled, so that they act as a physiological unit and are equivalent to a white substance.

In the next phase the resonator for short waves becomes limited to the blue stimulator and thus forms a blue substance, whilst the others remain intermingled and are equivalent to a yellow substance.

In the final phase each resonator is limited to its corresponding stimulator.

As has been seen the theory has to be strained to account for all the facts of the different varieties of colour blindness, and it may well be doubted whether the complications thus introduced make it more acceptable than the ordinary three-components theory.

V. Wundt's Photochemical Theory

Wundt[3], from the data available at the time, concluded that the facts of colour-mixtures and so on did not necessitate a multiplicity of specifically different stimulation elements or substances. His theory is as follows.

Two different stimulation processes are set in action by every retinal excitation, a chromatic and an achromatic. The chromatic excitation is a function of the wave-length of the light; the achromatic,

[1] *Arch. f. d. ges. Physiol.* XLVII. 275, 1890. [2] *Ibid.* LXXXII. 589, 1900
[3] *Grundzüge d. physiol. Psychologie*, I. 535, 1893.

so far as its relative intensity is concerned, is also dependent upon the wave-length, and reaches its maximum in the yellow. Both stimulations follow different laws with increasing stimulus intensities. At low intensities the achromatic surpasses the chromatic; at moderate intensities the chromatic is the relatively stronger; at the highest intensities the achromatic regains superiority.

The achromatic stimulation consists in a uniform photochemical process, the intensity of which is partly dependent upon the objective light intensity and partly upon the wave-length, since it reaches its maximum in the yellow and falls off towards both ends of the spectrum.

The chromatic stimulation consists in a polyform photochemical process, which changes continuously with the wave-length. Thus extreme differences of wave-length produce effects which are of almost the same nature, whilst the effects of certain different intervening wave-lengths are related in such a manner that they completely compensate each other like opposed phases of one and the same movement.

Every photochemical process of stimulation outlasts the excitation for a certain period and exhausts the sensibility of the nerve-substance for the particular form of excitation. Positive and homochromatic after-images are to be explained by the persistence, negative and complementary after-images by the exhaustion of the sensibility. The phenomena of contrast are to be explained by the general principle that all impressions of light and colour are experienced in relation to each other, *i.e.*, by the general law of relativity.

VI. G. E. Müller's Theory

G. E. Müller's theory[1] is a modification of Hering's theory in the light of psychophysical principles. It is set forth at great length and would already require further qualification to account for the facts which have been discovered since its promulgation. It is based on the fundamental psychophysical hypothesis, which he wrongly terms an axiom, that "an equality, similarity, or difference in the condition of sensations corresponds to an equality, similarity, or difference in the condition of the psychophysical processes."

Müller's essential disagreement with Hering is that the antagonistic action of white and black, red and green, yellow and blue, would be different from what it is if Hering's assumption were true that the

[1] *Ztsch. f. Psychol. u. Physiol. d. Sinnesorg.* x. 1 and 321, 1896; xiv. 1 and 161, 1897

sensations depend solely upon the relationship of the three underlying metabolic processes. He considers that the light does not act directly upon the achromatic and chromatic substances. There are materials present in the retina—white, red, green, etc. materials—which are chemically altered by the action of the light. The chemical action is reversible under different conditions, thus resembling Hering's *A* and *D* changes. It is the modifications in these peripheral substances that are transmitted to the cerebral substrata of the actual sensations.

In addition to four chromatic retinal processes, red, yellow, green, blue, at the periphery, there are six central "values," the red process exciting the red, yellow, and white values, the green exciting the green, blue, and black values, and the blue exciting the blue, red and black values. A yellow stimulus excites the red and yellow processes, thereby exciting the red, yellow, green, and white central values, of which the red and green neutralise one another. By adding another link in the psychophysical chain many more possible explanations are available for the phenomena of colour vision. Thus, the red material has a yellow valency, and the total yellow valency is made up of two parts, a direct and an indirect, and so on.

The reasoning throughout is very involved, but one feature stands out clearly, viz., the division of the psychophysical processes into two parts, a peripheral and a central.

VII. Edridge-Green's Theory

Edridge-Green's theory is thus summarised in his own words.

"A ray of light impinging on the retina liberates the visual purple from the rods and a photograph is formed. The rods are concerned only with the formation and distribution of the visual purple, not with the conveyance of light impulses to the brain. There are cases in which the visual purple is differently constituted and is not sensitive to certain rays at one or both ends of the spectrum. The decomposition of the visual purple by light chemically stimulates the ends of the cones (very probably through the electricity which is produced), and a visual impulse is set up which is conveyed through the optic nerve fibres to the brain. If it were possible, in a case in which the spectrum appeared of similar length and brightness to both, for a normal-sighted person and a colour-blind one to exchange eyes, the normal-sighted would still see colours properly and the colour-blind would still be colour-blind. The character of the impulse set up differs according to the wave-length of the light causing it. Therefore in the impulse itself we have the physiological basis of light, and in the quality of the impulse the physiological basis of colour. The impulse being conveyed along the optic nerve to the brain, stimulates the visual centre, causing a sensation of light, and then passing on to the colour-perceiving centre, causes a sensation of colour. But though the impulses vary in character according to the wave-length of the light causing them, the colour-perceiving centre is not able to discriminate between the character of adjacent impulses, the nerve cells not being sufficiently developed for the purpose. At most seven distinct colours are seen, whilst others see in proportion to the development of their colour-perceiving centres, only six, five, four, three, two, or one. This causes colour blindness, the person seeing only two or three colours instead of the normal six, putting colours together as alike which are seen by the normal-sighted to be different. In the degree of colour blindness just preceding total, only the colours at the extremes of the spectrum are recognised as different, the remainder of the spectrum appearing grey[1]."

"It will be noticed that the theory really consists of two parts, one concerned with the retina and the other with the whole retino-cerebral apparatus[2]."

Edridge-Green holds that the visual purple is the sole visual substance and the essential feature in the retina which enables it to transform light into visual impulses. He admits that visual purple is found only in the rods and not in the cones, but he believes that it is liberated from the rods and stimulates the cones. From entoptic observations he considers that he has proved the inflow of visual purple to the fovea, chiefly by way of four canals which radiate from the fovea and branch[3]. He claims to have proved microscopically the presence of visual purple between the cones of the fovea in the dark-adapted eyes of two monkeys[4]. Edridge-Green thus supports the theory of the transference of the visual purple which was first suggested by Mrs Ladd-Franklin (*v.* p. 273).

It follows from this theory that "the Purkinje phenomenon, the variation in optical white equations by a state of light and dark adaptation, the colourless interval for spectral lights of increasing intensity, and the varying phases of the after-image" are present in the fovea.

"It is reasonable to suppose that the visual purple which is formed

[1] *Colour-Blindness and Colour-Perception*, p. 318, 1909.

[2] *Hunterian Lectures*, p. 11, 1911.

[3] *J. of Physiol.* XLI. 274, 1910.

[4] *Trans. Ophth. Soc.* XXII. 300, 1902.

by the pigment cells under the influence of a bright light would be somewhat different in character from that which is formed in darkness." This supposition affords the basis of an explanation of the photopic and scotopic luminosity curves, of the Purkinje phenomenon, of erythropsia or red-vision, and of green-vision.

The disappearance of lights falling upon the fovea is attributed to temporary absence of visual purple from the fovea.

"It is very probable that light acting upon the visual purple is, according to its wave-length, absorbed by particular atoms or molecules, the amplitude of their vibrations being increased. These vibrations may cause corresponding vibrations in certain discs of the outer segments of the cones, which seem especially constructed to take up vibrations. We know that when light falls on the retina it causes an electric current. We know how the telephone is able through electricity to convey waves of sound, and something similar may be present in the eye, the apparatus being especially constructed for vibrations of small wave-length. The current of electricity set up by light may cause the sensation of light, and the vibrations of the atoms or molecules the sensation of colour.

"In all vital processes there is a condition of katabolism or chemical change in the protoplasm, and an anabolic or building-up process, in which the protoplasm is restored to its normal state. We have therefore to consider two definite processes in the visual purple—namely, a breaking down of the visual purple photochemically by light and its restoration by the pigment cells and rods. Under ordinary conditions of light, and during the whole of the daytime, the visual purple is continually being bleached and re-formed. It is obvious, therefore, that when the eye has been kept in the dark and is then exposed to light, an observation taken immediately will not be comparable with one taken a few seconds afterwards, because in the first observation we have only to consider the katabolic change; whilst in the second observation the anabolic change has to be considered as well, as the visual purple has to be re-formed for subsequent seeing. There appears to be very little evidence in ordinary circumstances of this anabolic process; for instance, if we fatigue the eye with sodium light in a dark room, and then immediately examine a spectrum, we find that though all the yellow has disappeared there is no increase in the blue; in fact, the blue seems rather diminished than otherwise. Again, there is not the slightest diminution in either the red or green, showing conclusively that yellow cannot be a compound sensation made up by a combination of red and green[1]."

[1] *Hunterian Lectures*, p. 21, 1911.

The observations on fatigue are at variance with those of Burch, Abney and others.

The "cerebral" part of Edridge-Green's theory is founded on the principle of psychophysical units and series which dates from the time of Fechner. The reasoning upon which it is based will be found in the early chapters of his book on Colour-blindness and Colour-perception. According to the theory the colour-sense has been evolved in stages. First there was only a sensation of light. When colours were first recognised only red and violet—the two ends of the spectrum—were seen, and a spectrum seen by such an eye was red at one end, violet at the other, the colours merging in the centre. Such eyes are called "dichromic." In the next stage of evolution a third colour appeared between the other two, viz., green: these persons were "trichromic." In the next stage a fourth colour, yellow, appeared between the red and green ("tetrachromic"). In the next stage a fifth colour, blue, was seen between the green and violet ("pentachromic"). In the next stage a sixth colour, orange, was seen between the red and yellow. Persons having this type of vision are "hexachromic" and the majority of people to-day belong to this class. The highest development which has yet been reached is that of the "heptachromic," who in addition to the other colours distinguish a seventh colour between the blue and violet, viz. indigo.

Colour blindness is atavistic, and all stages are represented amongst the colour-blind. The "dichromics" correspond most clearly to what we have called dichromats for the sake of distinction from Edridge-Green's nomenclature. The anomalous trichromats, on this theory, include tri-, tetra-, and pentachromics.

In addition to these classes of the colour-blind there are others distinguished by shortening either of the red or the violet end of the spectrum. Such cases show a shift in the position of their psychophysical units towards the unshortened end.

Light perception and colour perception are therefore according to this theory quite distinct[1], and cases of colour blindness can be divided into two classes, according as the defect is one of light perception, or one of colour perception or differentiation without any defect in light perception: both defects may be present in the same individual.

Edridge-Green finds that the normal hexachromic, who describes six colours in the spectrum—red, orange, yellow, green, blue, violet,—will map out about 18 monochromatic patches. The supernormal

[1] *Proc. Roy. Soc. Lond.* B, LXXXII. 458, 1910.

heptachromics, who interpose indigo between blue and violet, usually map out 22—29 such patches. König, Lord Rayleigh, and all previous observers found a much greater discrimination sensibility (v. p. 30), and the very careful researches of Steindler confirm their results. There is a fundamental fallacy here which requires explanation. The discrepancy is borne out by the protocols of the author's investigations of 14 dichromics[1], in whom the number of monochromatic patches varies from 11 to 2. "There may be shortening of the red or the violet end of the spectrum; there may be defective perception for some of the other spectral rays; the luminosity curve may have its maximum at a different place from the normal; there may be defective perception when the image on the retina is diminished in size; and the size of the neutral region is very variable[2]." If so many varieties of one type of colour blindness occur it is difficult to imagine how they can be explained by any theory which is not a mere generalisation of facts, of little value for purposes of classification. Edridge-Green summarises his views of dichromics as follows: "(1) There are many degrees and varieties of dichromic vision. (2) There are not two well-defined varieties of dichromic vision, there are innumerable gradations connecting the two. (3) In many cases precisely the same errors are made both by those with and those without defective perception of red, when the rays for which there is defective perception are not involved. (4) All dichromics are not equally colour-blind, that is, one may have a much better hue perception than another. (5) Dichromic vision may be associated with defects of light perception which are also found in cases in which the vision is not dichromic. (6) Dichromics may have a perception of shade and a luminosity curve similar to the normal. (7) Many dichromics match very accurately, their colour perception being sufficient for the purpose when the colours are not too close in the spectrum. (8) The degree of colour blindness varies with the state of health. (9) Colour discrimination is diminished as a whole in dichromic vision. (10) Dichromic vision appears to be due to a defective power of colour differentiation probably corresponding to an earlier state in evolution of the colour sense. (11) The two colours seen are red and violet."

Edridge-Green's conclusions with regard to anomalous trichromatic vision are thus summarised by him[3]:

"(1) Trichromic vision is not synonymous with anomalous trichromatism. (2) Many persons with otherwise normal colour perception

[1] *Ophthalmoscope*, XII. 1914. [2] *Loc. cit.* p. 77.
[3] *Proc. Roy. Soc. Lond.* B, LXXXVI. 164 1913.

make an anomalous equation. (3) Many colour-blind persons (dichromics and trichromics) make an absolutely normal match with no greater mean deviation than the normal. (4) Colour weakness is not characteristic of anomalous trichromatism but of trichromic vision. (5) Anomalous trichromatism and colour weakness are not synonymous. (6) A large mean deviation indicates colour weakness. (7) Anomalous trichromatism appears to be due to an alteration in the normal relations of the response to the three colours (lights) used in the equation. If the eye be more or less sensitive to one of the components of the mixed colour whilst the other has its normal effect, an anomalous equation will result. An anomalous equation will also result when the yellow is more allied to green or red than is normal."

It is difficult to understand how any concordant classification of the colour-blind can be arrived at by Edridge-Green's methods. His classification is based upon the number of different colours distinguished in the spectrum, yet these may be subdivided into a variable number of monochromatic patches. He says: "They (the physicists) appear to take for granted that the perceptions of others are similar to those experienced by themselves[1]." Yet there can be no doubt that in practice he is much influenced by the names which the examinee applies to the various parts of the spectrum. "When it (the colour perception spectrometer) is used to test colour blindness, the examinee should first be shown some portion of the interior of the spectrum and then asked to name the various colours which he sees[2]." Indeed, he constantly lays stress upon the importance of colour names in testing for colour blindness. As has already been pointed out, the colour-blind subject uses a terminology for colours which is suited to describe the perceptions of normal-sighted people, and which is unsuited to describe his own, yet these colour names are apparently regarded by Edridge-Green as an accurate and reliable criterion of what the colour-blind person sees[3].

So far as the "retinal" part of Edridge-Green's theory is concerned I think that the evidence is strongly against it. It appears to me to be very improbable that the rods have no direct visual function. Anatomically and embryologically they must be regarded as the primitive visual neuroepithelium, the cones being a more highly differentiated

[1] *Colour-Blindness*, p. 14, 1909 [2] *Hunterian Lectures*, p. 75, 1911.

[3] To avoid any misconception on this important point I wish to emphasise the fact that these remarks apply to the determination of the *type of colour blindness* of the examinee. In practical testing the object aimed at is the determination of whether the examinee recognises red, green, and white lights as *red*, *green*, and *white* lights respectively, and it is obvious that the names which he applies are of great importance.

type. The arguments in favour of the duplicity theory are destructive of this part of Edridge-Green's theory. The presence of Purkinje's phenomenon, a photochromatic interval, and so on, at the fovea is admittedly disputed, and good observers are ranged on each side. The arguments in favour of the presence of visual purple in the fovea are of two kinds, direct observation and entoptic phenomena. So far as the former is concerned the observation has not been confirmed; if it should be it is most probable that the substance will be found there only in traces and will represent a vestige of the early ancestry of the cones (*v.* p. 204). In any case the evidence appears to be against the view that visual purple is the sole and indispensable factor in foveal vision. So far as entoptic phenomena, other than those due to opacities in the dioptric media, are concerned, they are open to the most various explanations. The "intrinsic light of the retina" is often described as a "light chaos," full of waves and currents; it is no safe foundation for any fundamental theory of vision. The rod-free area of retina subtends at least 1°—2° and therefore occupies a very definite finite space. That visual purple in solution should be transmitted to the centre of this area with the velocity necessary to account for the facts on the theory is very improbable, if not impossible on physical grounds. We are familiar with the theory of "sensitisers" and much may be said in support of them, but they are either bodies which travel in the circulation and show no such rapidity of action[1], or they are bodies produced by molecular change and act *in situ*. Those referred to in Schenck's theory, for example, belong to the latter category.

Much of the evidence in support of the "retinal" part of Edridge-Green's theory is founded upon after-images. As has been pointed out in Part I. Section VI. these phenomena belong to some of the most variable in the whole range of colour vision. They vary with the previous stimulation of the eye—and Burch has brought forward evidence to show that "fatigue" effects last much longer than has been thought—with a multiplicity of physical and physiological factors which may be easily overlooked or under-estimated, and above all with psychological factors which are almost uncontrollable. They can only be considered valid if they are repeatedly confirmed by different observers, and even then are usually open to a variety of explanations. This fact is well exemplified by McDougall's experiments. Such observations can be appraised only at the value which an uncertain method merits.

The "cerebral" part of Edridge-Green's theory offers a possible

[1] Cf. McDougall, p. 280.

explanation of the *psychological* evolution of colour perceptions. It must, however, be regarded as a pure hypothesis and must stand or fall by the accumulation of evidence for or against it. So far as the physiological processes underlying colour sensations are concerned it fails to afford any satisfactory explanation. In particular it does not account for the trichromatism of normal colour vision as revealed by the mixture of pure-colour stimuli. Edridge-Green says: "We must therefore explain in another way the apparent trichromatism of normal colour vision, which is so well known to every photographer, especially those who are concerned with colour photography. If my theory of the evolution of the colour sense be the correct one, and we have cases of colour blindness corresponding to every degree of the evolutionary process, we have an explanation of the facts. In past ages all saw the rainbow made up of only three colours—red, green, and violet. When a new colour (yellow) appeared between the red and green, it is obvious that a mixture of red and green would give rise, not to red-green, but to the colour which had replaced it—namely, yellow[1]." This is obviously at most a very partial explanation of the trichromatism of normal colour vision, which is a fact and not a theory.

It must be admitted that the evidence which has been collected from various sources on the evolution of the colour sense is of an uncertain character, but such as it is it affords no support to the theory. The discordant results and conclusions arrived at by different observers on the colour perceptions of lower animals are recorded in Part I, Section VII, Chap. II. If we consider only those arrived at by v. Hess, as being the most recent, most exhaustive, and in many respects the most accurate, we find that mammals have the same spectral limits as men; in birds and reptiles the spectrum is shortened at the violet end only; amphibia resemble mammals; and fishes are totally colour-blind. With regard to primitive races I agree with Myers that we have not sufficient evidence to show that the colour sense materially differs in different peoples, save that, as shown by Rivers's careful observations, their colour sense is defective for light of the violet end of the spectrum. On the recapitulation theory that the developing child passes rapidly through the stages of evolution of the race one might expect to obtain useful information from the development of colour perceptions in the infant. I do not think that the experiments recorded afford any evidence on this point, but only on the affective values of different colours for the

[1] *Hunterian Lectures*, p. 23 1911.

infant. If, however, this view is erroneous, the evidence is in favour of delayed development of perception of blue.

Further, if congenital colour blindness is atavistic, then such evidence, again uncertain and little trustworthy, as we have of the nature of the sensations experienced by gross cases of dichromatism—and most of these presumably belong to Edridge-Green's class of dichromics—is that the two colours they perceive resemble the blue and yellow of normal vision. "Anomalous trichromats" certainly perceive more than two colours, but we have adduced reasons for believing that this group includes different types, and it is by no means certain that any of these are due to atavism. If they are, the problem of discovering the nature of their colour sensations as compared with the normal is even more difficult than in the case of the dichromats, and certainly no dogmatic statements can be rightly made in the present state of knowledge.

INDEX OF SUBJECTS

(The numbers in heavy type indicate the principal references to the subjects.)

INDEX OF AUTHORS

CAMBRIDGE: PRINTED BY JOHN CLAY, M.A. AT THE UNIVERSITY PRESS

CPSIA information can be obtained
at www.ICGtesting.com
Printed in the USA
BVHW041321130619
550939BV00014B/1021/P

9 781314 694642